Teaching with
The Norton Anthology of
American Literature

FIFTH EDITION

A Guide for Instructors

THE EDITORS

Nina Baym
UNIVERSITY OF ILLINOIS AT URBANA-CHAMPAIGN

Wayne Franklin
NORTHEASTERN UNIVERSITY

Ronald Gottesman
UNIVERSITY OF SOUTHERN CALIFORNIA

Laurence B. Holland
LATE OF THE JOHNS HOPKINS UNIVERSITY

David Kalstone
LATE OF RUTGERS, THE STATE UNIVERSITY OF NEW JERSEY

Jerome Klinkowitz
UNIVERSITY OF NORTHERN IOWA

Arnold Krupat
SARAH LAWRENCE COLLEGE

Francis Murphy
SMITH COLLEGE

Hershel Parker
UNIVERSITY OF DELAWARE

William H. Pritchard
AMHERST COLLEGE

Patricia B. Wallace
VASSAR COLLEGE

Teaching with The Norton Anthology of American Literature

FIFTH EDITION

A Guide for Instructors

Bruce Michelson
UNIVERSITY OF ILLINOIS AT URBANA-CHAMPAIGN

Marjorie Pryse
STATE UNIVERSITY OF NEW YORK, ALBANY

W. W. NORTON & COMPANY
New York • London

The text of this book is composed in Fairfield Medium
with the display set in Bernhard Modern.
Composition by ComCom.
Manufacturing by Haddon Craftsmen.
Book and cover design by Antonina Krass.
Cover illustrations: FRONT: Detail from *Kindred Spirits,* 1849, by Asher Durand.
Oil on canvas. Reproduced by courtesy of the Collection of The New York Public
Library, Astor, Lenox, and Tilden Foundations.
BACK: Detail from *City Activities with Dance Hall,* from *America Today* (1930), by
Thomas Hart Benton. Distemper and egg tempera on gessoed linen with oil glaze;
92″ × 134 1/2″. Collection, The Equitable Life Assurance Society of the United
States. © The Equitable Life Assurance Society of the U.S.

ISBN 0-393-95875-2 (pbk.)

W. W. Norton & Company, Inc., 500 Fifth Avenue, New York, N.Y. 10110
http://www.wwnorton.com

W. W. Norton & Company Ltd., 10 Coptic Street, London WC1A 1PU

1 2 3 4 5 6 7 8 9 0

Contents

*For the convenience of teachers who wish to use The Declaration of Sentiments of the Seneca Falls Woman's Rights Convention in their classrooms, as occasionally suggested in this Guide, we have provided the text of that document—not readily available except in libraries—as an appendix. It may be photocopied and distributed to your students.

CHAPTER 1

Getting Started

Why Look at an Instructor's Guide?

It's no secret that, whatever their tastes, teachers of literature and culture tend to be independent people. It is also no secret that *The Norton Anthology of American Literature (NAAL)* is used on all continents and in many different instructional and cultural situations. With necessary skips and jumps, some people teach it stem to stern; others raid it for selections or even teach it backwards. It does service in history and American studies courses as well as in college and high school English classrooms.

When we try to teach a large swath of literary history, or the evolution of an idea or an important crisis, we may feel (rightly or not) a kind of dominion over it, like a tour guide hearing his or her voice boom around the Capitol Rotunda or at a tourist overlook above Hoover Dam. It's exhilarating—having a group of interested people trust you to explain The Whole Thing or to open big questions about The Whole Thing—and it may be instinctive and at some point professionally necessary *not* to want someone else's guiding hand on your sleeve while you try *your* hand at guiding others and experience the fun of finding your own way.

Finding your own way, after all, is at least eventually what The Whole Thing is about. Even in times of turmoil with regard to literary history—times like our own when there is so much controversy about defining American-ness and celebrating or debunking the Canonical Writers—some intentions remain steady in the classrooms. One of these is a hope that we and our students will someday achieve a reasonably informed, personal, whole-minded response not only to the authors in anthologies and

1

on syllabi but also to those larger, more disheveled questions that take shape over the course of an education:

What kind of relationship should a culture, and individuals within that culture, achieve with materials that constitute, or are said to constitute, its cultural inheritance?

What admixture of credence and robust skepticism should go into "literacy," of a sort that isn't archaic or a waste of time in an age of hypermedia and a blitz of sensory engagements?

What can imaginative works possibly offer, in terms of lasting value, in an age of quantum newness and change, when even the hot new computer on which you write your test questions and e-mail your students will soon be a relic?

As teachers and scholars, we want our undergraduate students and our advanced high school students to delight in a variety of literary styles and to speculate intelligently on the relationship between these styles and the historical moment in which they took shape. We want them to think pleasurably and effectively about the dialogue of some texts with other, earlier texts; we want them to be aware of the special lucidity and prophetic power of certain texts and of the element of the irrational, the touch of complacency, and the intellectual or moral blind spots that can turn up also in these same texts. No matter what celebration or indictment of the American past may flicker or burn in any classroom, the general process remains this: to "teach" intellectual independence, of a sort that even the Founding Fathers, and Fuller and Equiano and Occom and Du Bois (to name just a few others), might have approved—a lucid, patient, eloquent dominion of the self over the pressures of the culture, including the culture of the classroom, and of the printed word.

The Guide to *The Norton Anthology of American Literature*, Fifth Edition, can be part of this teaching process. Not only can it help you begin to figure out what you do and don't want to do in the classroom, but also it can assist on those occasions when you have to plan a whole course or class in a hurry.

Some Preliminary Considerations

Mistakes to Avoid When Planning a Survey Course

Individual personalities, enthusiasms, and circumstances have a great deal to do with success in teaching particular writers and themes, as does whether a course is one or two semesters long. Since survey courses in American literature have been around for about a hundred years, folk wisdom does circulate about how *not* to conceive of a survey or large-scale literary tour, if you want your students to stay with you and with the material for fifteen weeks or longer:

As an Inoculation

It can be tempting to think of an American literature historical tour as a kind of flu shot against barbarism. It would be wonderful if we could perfect a one-time downloading of all names, dates, and "-isms" so that our students wouldn't lack such reference points when they take more specialized courses and our nonmajors would have some basic facts and conventional interpretations clear in mind as they leave our courses, perhaps never to read such materials again. Such an education would be inert, however, if it conveyed no sense of the enthusiasm with which some of these texts have been read, argued over, and set apart as special in other times. Inciting some curiosity about the material seems essential to achieving any staying power in a student's mind; and though students may commonly lack inborn or conditioned zest for reading Paine's *The Crisis* or Bryant's *To a Waterfowl*, they can become very interested in why other well-intentioned people have found these works compelling and even wonderful. Without presenting these texts as musty or obsolete, we can open them as old sources of a certain (and increasingly scarce) kind of intensity and speculate on the transience and permanence of that spirit or cultural frame of mind. One way or another, a survey course needs to offer *reasons,* even if they are only speculations, for why this material should abide with your students.

As a Class without a Clear Subject and Compelling, Open-Ended Questions

Amid the theory controversies that have been with us for at least twenty-five years, courses can go forward without any direct address to the question of what "literature," in this case "American literature," is or has come to mean. Perhaps to avoid pedagogical chaos and outbreaks of back-row nihilism, perhaps out of sheer weariness, some instructors seem to affirm, or merely to concede, that literature is whatever is included in anthologies of literature or shelved under that heading in the nearest bookstore.

Good students will probably want to discuss these issues, and you may find it provident to open them frequently during the term. The matter is more awkward, and perhaps more interesting, with regard to the materials in Volume 1 of *NAAL*. Because these materials come from times before the system of commercial publishers, mass production of books, international copyrights, wide-circulation reviews and famous reviewers, and meddlesome college English departments took something like their modern shape, we can imagine a very different kind of relationship between a given author and his or her community of readers. *Uncle Tom's Cabin* may have been a runaway best-seller, but sales of *The Scarlet Letter* were meager by comparison; and works like Bradford's *Of Plymouth Plantation* and Taylor's *Poems* were not available in print until centuries after these writers had passed away. So whatever else we might be doing, we are not teaching the top hits of the last four hundred years or the works that made the biggest cultural splash in their own time. We face, then, a very interesting problem:

how some of these recovered texts, which did not shake the world in their own time, can be, or can become, important to our own.

AS AN ACT OF INDOCTRINATION

We need to remember that although our students may not be especially well read or culturally literate, they can be quick to perceive the difference between when a body of literature is being explored and when it is being pressed into some other service. If one objective of a college literature course is to help students improve as makers of distinctions and askers of strong *questions*, rather than to subject them to reductive answers, our students still need help achieving those skills that have been taught for generations in good humanities courses but that are hard to articulate as objectives in the undergraduate catalogs. Such objectives include acuity and sensitivity in the art of reading; practice in the arts of adult-level writing and conversation; and a heightened sense of what comes after what, and possibly *because* of what, in the onward flow or tumult of cultural history. All things may be political from some perspectives, but it is worth asking whether such perspectives are the best ones to work from in constructing a survey course for college undergraduates or high school students.

Teaching the survey as a large lecture or in small sections, many of us have changed strategy, and some fundamental assumptions, every time we have done the course. Most experienced instructors whom we have talked to have winced, in retrospect, over things they have said from the podium, Great Profundities that we eventually—too late!—recognize as ludicrous. Remorse of one kind or another isn't an unusual aftereffect for teachers trying this kind of grand tour. Some humility can help keep us honest. In reviewing your own assumptions as you begin planning a course, you might want to spend a few minutes thinking over the following questions, because students may raise them in one way or another and because they can underlie important decisions (conscious or otherwise) that can shape a syllabus and class presentation:

•*Do you intend to deal in answers or in questions?* We often tell students that a course can help them *begin* thinking about a vast, complex, and still-evolving arrangement of cultural experiences and that if their thinking continues (as it should) long beyond the end of the course, they should experience at some point the pleasure of some or all of what gets said in this classroom.

•*In a personal and academic quest for cultural literacy, do some perceptions naturally and helpfully come before others?* Everyday and professional realities, realities that students must be ready to face, seem to require a degree of familiarity with "major" and "canonical" authors. Familiarity doesn't have to mean reverence; literate, passionate antipathy can sometimes work just as well to bring the student into an independent, intense relationship with a challenging author, text, or literary period. As Richard Wilbur says, "All revolutions in art are palace revolutions," performed by people who know, with genuine expertise, exactly what they are rising up against. To dismiss the canonical and the major-author idea out of hand may be to risk denying students a fair chance to join in that conversation.

• *Has the question of an American cultural identity, discoverable in our literary heritage, been satisfactorily settled or laid aside?* If each generation of readers redefines the literary heritage and infuses it with its own values and imagination, then an appropriate survey course can be designed to open this issue and keep it alive, rather than close it down.

• *Is the survey course itself an interesting cultural practice?* There are more than three thousand four-year colleges in the United States, about two thousand community colleges, and tens of thousands of high schools. Most of the collegiate campuses have at least one, and sometimes several, historical courses in American literature; and many of these classes are large. It is a reasonable bet, therefore, that when you and your students open your anthology and start a discussion of Bradstreet or Douglass or Wharton, several thousand students and their instructors at that moment are doing pretty much the same thing. The survey course is a widespread American activity—possibly a kind of rite of passage—and not just an inquiry into cultural history but an actual part of its making, its transformation, and its continuance. When you point that out to students early in the term, you can provoke some interesting responses and a heightened interest in what you have begun to do together.

The Small Class: Special Considerations

If you review student questionnaires about humanities courses, you may see a strong correlation between how much high-quality discussion students experienced in a given class and how much they valued it and feel they learned from it. Your students are probably going to want to talk about a lot of things, including the course itself, as well as specific authors and readings. If you're doing a literary history and you want to take advantage of this willingness to participate, then you will have balances to think about—between getting the facts laid out sufficiently and helping your group to speculate, rearrange, play, and achieve some kind of personal and durable connection with the assigned material. Tromping through an anthology chronologically may strike some students as unimaginative, but the process can work well if you and the students pull back once in a while and try for some freewheeling talk about where you are and what kinds of questions and uncertainties they are harboring about specific literary and cultural moments or the worth of touring those moments.

The reading list and order probably have to be established right away, but certain decisions about strategy might wait until, say, the second week, when you have a better sense of the overall energy, commitment, and tone of your class. You might try to ascertain if there are any pockets of special interest in the room: interest in particular writers, periods, or major issues. You can sometimes get a sense of this by handing out index cards on the second day (when enrollment has stabilized a bit), and asking students to tell you something about other English courses that they have taken, the

best college course they have had so far (or high school class, if they are
first-term college freshmen), their plans (if any) for a major (a class of this
sort can attract a lot of nonmajors or undecided students), and some strong
personal interest or achievement that they feel comfortable mentioning,
academic or not. With a smaller class, you can pick up cues from their answers and develop a sense of who in your group might be attracted to a particular writer, cultural predicament, or large-scale issue.

If you do see a pattern of such interests, you might think about making
each student a resource person on a particular subject (or writer or literary
era), on a recurring and evolving question, or on some interesting topic parallel to literary concerns (architecture, race relations, the status of women,
religious minorities, book publishing and technical innovations). Students
need some room to choose, so you might want to hand out a list of available subjects, with one or two standard resources listed for them to consult
for a few hours sometime in the opening weeks of the term. Students may
not be ready or willing to chime in with deep-background information every
time a question comes up; but if you and they feel comfortable with their
offering insights once in a while, then you can hope for these benefits:
more voices participating in class discussion, better opportunity for some
students to connect the class to their own special interests, better preliminary thinking by students, and a bit more enthusiasm in regard to the design and writing of major papers.

If a plan like this seems incompatible with your students or your own design for this small class, then you might want to try some options that can
work well with groups of under thirty people:

TEACHING THE CRAFT OF THE QUESTION

Some students may tell you (in an office visit or, alas, when the course
is over) that they don't talk in class because they "don't have anything say."
Some students are just naturally quiet, of course; and their silence doesn't
signify boredom, hostility, stupidity, or lack of preparation. One major and
common problem, however, that can injure their efforts and morale and
your ability to keep the class moving is their belief that "anything to say"
means statements, broad opinions, and grandiose summaries rather than
measured, provocative *questions* about the material or ways of reading it.
Sometimes students may have been driven into unhappy silence by previous courses, where a human jukebox of semiuseless observations convinced
them that class participation amounted to a game of Trying to Have the Last
Word.

If you can convince these students that one or two well-aimed questions
per week can be wonderful contributions to a class, valued not only by the
instructor but by peers who were sitting there hoping that *somebody* would
ask that, then you will be doing them a great service. The craft of conversation is important to survival in most adult professions, and if some of your
students can grow comfortable with the notion that in many situations *asking* is wiser and more humane than *telling,* then this is a benefit that will

stay with them long after their textbooks have fallen apart or been sold back to the college bookstore.

TEACHING THE COURSE AS A PROCESS OF DISCOVERY

There may be some correspondence between the size of a given section and the percentage of students who will be puzzled by any variance from a march through time. But with a smaller group, some of the nonlinear arrangements, outlined elsewhere in this Guide, become easier as options.

Even with larger groups, instructors can successfully open a course with some unquestionably "big" work: major in terms of its sales, its mass-cultural impact, its staying power in the academic mind, and its durable appeal to a larger public. The *NAAL* excerpts from *Uncle Tom's Cabin* could be a good choice, if you wanted to open up large-scale questions which subsequent readings could help to answer. Where do the moral values which inform this book come from, and how is it that this novel found such a receptive audience? If a creed or a body of religious thought lies at the heart of it, shaping not only the major personages in the story but the narrative itself, what roots do these qualities have in the American literary experience? What are the sources of the novel's ideas of goodness, of evil, of salvation and damnation, of the well-lived life and the subtle ways in which well-intentioned people fall into terrible error? What kind of cultural landscape makes it possible for a novel, a tale about people who in a strict sense never existed and events that never took place, to figure centrally in an immense political and moral upheaval? In other words, you can work backwards from a book of this magnitude and lay the groundwork for reconsideration of Calvinism, the Enlightenment, Romanticism, Transcendentalism, and the evolving idea of the writer, the imaginative text, and the individual self—not as closed historical issues but as perceptions, crises, and questions that carry forward and shake the foundations of the country.

Huckleberry Finn, which is included as a complete work in Volume 2 of *NAAL*, could also work well, considering that this novel's status, as a required text in many school and college curricula, is still being hotly debated. How did this meandering tale of a river trip, a novel attacked as immoral at the end of the nineteenth century, achieve such high placement in official and popular lists of the "best" American novels? If the remarkable staying power of this mass-market adventure story suggests something about American culture (as it really is, or was, or as we want to imagine it is or was), then what are those qualities that it suggests, and where else in our literature might we see them in evidence?

The Lecture Course: Special Considerations

American literature survey courses flourish in undergraduate sections ranging from fifteen students up to several hundred. Thanks to new wireless microphones and other high-tech toys in our lecture halls and because many of us have taught the larger classes often enough to have memorized our orations, we can move around the big room, ask questions, work for some actual discussion, apply active-learning strategies, and generally try to make the gathering feel smaller and more human in scale than it really is. Technology and some cautious theatrics can help—up to a point. But a lecture is still a lecture, and when you try to lead a group through many authors and large complex issues in American cultural history, there are times when you may have to talk, and they have to listen, to avoid talk-show exchanges of enthusiastic ignorance.

In a small class, discussion can be freewheeling at times without creating anxiety among your students. But in the large lecture, the interesting sidelight, the digression, or the periodic discussion that engages some students can lose others and cause them to fear that the lecture is rambling or that all of this talk must be reverently remembered. To try to allay those worries, you might consider producing "lecture summaries" and making them available on-line and at the local copy shop. These summaries should not be transcripts of the lectures, and you would have to make clear that they are not a substitute for coming to class and taking good notes. Rather, the summaries can set down some of the core considerations, major dates, names, events, and questions, so that a student can put the pen down and actually think when an interesting question is posed, rather than sweat to catch up with what was being declaimed three minutes before. Such lecture notes can be easily drawn out of your own presentations, and local copy shops will be eager to accommodate you and your students—provided copyright laws are carefully respected.

Using "The Norton Websource to American Literature"

Designed as a springboard to help students extend their exploration of American literature and identify and frame topics for writing and research, this free Website supplements its own pedagogical materials with connections to authoritative resources on the Web. Included on the site are quick-reference timelines, historical-literary outlines, maps, and searchable "Exploration" sections that provide generative questions and projects that help students draw connections, close-read texts, and link texts to contexts for 120 of the anthology's authors. In addition, nearly every author in the anthology has a brief biography and annotated Weblinks. These materials can be used in countless ways—for example, an instructor might assign Explorations as writing assignments or students might use the site as a whole as a sort of "electronic workbook" and window onto current literary criticism on particular authors and subjects.

For instructors, we've created a password-protected "Instructors' Roundtable" that will include a gathering of syllabi and course notes and a conversation space for teachers. To obtain a password, simply contact your local Norton representative (a list of all representatives with their contact information is included on the Website).

CHAPTER 2

Planning a Historical Survey Course

NAAL is organized chronologically by authors' birth dates. Although as teachers we commonly write required reading lists that are roughly chronological, basically following the order in the anthology, mere chronology does not by itself produce historical perspective. The historical approach to teaching American literature makes room for students to ask questions about the writers' lives; about the ethnic, literary, geographical, and political environments within which they wrote; and about the prevailing beliefs that influenced their readers.

In teaching a historical survey, we can see ideas unfold and become powerful in our literary culture. From Volume 1, you can choose works connected to specific historical events; and the events themselves can inform the presentation of readings on the syllabus and give students a basis for asking questions in class or for selecting essay topics. Such an approach allows students to place literary works in the context of American history courses they may have taken, perhaps as part of their general education requirements. In Volume 2, in which American literature develops such a variety of voices, themes, and degrees of connection to actual events, you can both emphasize that diversity and teach individual writers and aesthetic movements.

You may need to make an educated guess about how much you are going to be teaching *literary* history and how much you need to teach *basic* history. Contrary to the horror stories about how little the typical college student knows of the major events in Western civilization, you may find that most of your students do have a reasonable familiarity with terms such as Puritanism, the Enlightenment, Romanticism, and Transcendentalism, although they may have problems with murkier formulations such as Realism and Modernism. They know the dates of the American Revolution and the Civil War; and they know about the settling of New England and the Spanish Southwest, about industrialism, the westward expansion, slavery, and the displacement and decimation of native peoples. What they lack, and what a historical survey can begin to give them, is voices to connect to these cultural moments.

Such an approach does not have to be a dry tour through antique "-isms." The period introductions in *NAAL* do a fine job of describing the various historical and cultural landscapes through which a literary history survey course must move; and your own presentations can, therefore, avoid the numbing idea that the only way to read each writer is as a mouthpiece for some supposedly dominant idea system or short list of aesthetic stipulations. The poorer essays that you will read this year and the most inert answers that you will receive on midterm tests and final examinations will probably reflect this unhappy assumption: describe to us the *zeitgeist* (in twenty-five words or so) and we will apply it forcibly to every writer whose career happens to fall within the defined dates of a defined literary period.

For these reasons, it seems important to present literary history as a lively interaction between the prevailing values (or prevailing moral conflicts) of a given time and individual minds and talents, with emphasis on *distinctions* among those minds and differences in the ways in which they engage with a historical moment. It's hard to imagine that any student or teacher really wants to read Bradstreet as the undifferentiated voice of New England Puritanism rather than as a many-sided sensibility living within and responding to that culture and creed. If the idea is only to find Romanticism or abolitionist ideology in Stowe, rather than seeing Stowe as an accomplished and individualized writer working *amid* the landscape of Romanticism and moral crisis, then there would really be no need to actually read Stowe after hearing a general description of American Romantic thought or a drab summary of mid-nineteenth-century politics and race relations. By that same token, there would be no need to read anything other than the author headnotes. On the contrary, to teach a historical survey now is to take on a compound responsibility: to offer students a background and context and to investigate authors as remarkable individuals *within* it. If we can accomplish this, we stand a chance of avoiding certain hypocrisies that students intuitively pick up on and quite rightly resent: the implicit notion that everyone (except, of course, some elite and very contemporary "us") has been a hopeless mental prisoner of some simplistically summarizable value system and that all we can properly do in reading back through American historical periods is hear that value system in the words of any given writer. You won't lose conscientious students if you can engage, at least now and then, with well-articulated paradox instead; with the contradictions that we seem to assume are essential to selfhood and modern literary identity; and with open-ended questions, instead of "answers."

If we begin planning a historical survey course from the idea that the American self is and has been commonly defined in terms of internal conflicts, ambivalence, and some sort of dialogue between reason and received ideas on the one hand and emotions and irrational urgencies on the other, then we can bring some of these texts to life as literature and discover in them lasting relevance and appeal. One key objective, then, can be to look for that humanizing, unhomogenized mix of motives, aspirations, and values.

If you have been teaching for a while, you know that no small number of your students haven't gotten used to the possibility that modern identity involves a measure of turmoil. Many of these students could be both comforted and inspired by the recognition that even in eras that seem saturated by dogmas and idea systems (e.g., Puritanism, Transcendentalism, literary Naturalism), something in the self may stand apart and that a text that offers access to that unreconciled presence within is a text worth reading and remembering and coming back to.

Accordingly, as you move from one literary era to the next and offer your own review of how historical and cultural situations have evolved around individual writers, you might want to talk about particular situations with regard to the act of writing itself and about what, at those times, it meant to read something. For instance, in talking about the religious and political tumult of seventeenth-century Europe and the conditions that propelled thousands of English puritans to try to establish a theocratic colony in the New England wilderness, you can lose many students in a footrace through historical events that, important though they may be, do not successfully open up the texts of that period. But the American students of this sometimes overwhelming "information age" can often gain imaginative entry into the seventeenth century if attention is paid to the printing and literacy revolutions that made the Reformation possible. These revolutions allowed, for the first time in history, a direct engagement between the ordinary citizen and the sacred text; consequently, a new theology developed and spread, one that placed immense importance on that encounter between citizen and text and on the responsibilities not only of reading but of reading *right*. In other words, the northeast coast of the United States was being settled at a time when, as never before, the printed word and its interpretation energized not only personal and community life but also the private encounter with belief and divine will.

Similarly, a discussion of the literary scene of mid-nineteenth-century America often benefits from attention to the technology and business of book publishing in those years: the sudden move to mass production and cheap, easy shipment deep into the American heartland, thanks to the Hoe rotary press, the reliable sheet feeder, and the web of railroads. Quite quickly, authorship in America offered an unprecedented chance for high profit, large-scale cultural impact, and real celebrity, not just in the United States but also elsewhere in the English-speaking world. A look at literary Modernism and Postmodernism will seem more plausible to students if it takes notice of the situation in which they themselves are reading: with the college and university as major presences in the establishment of literary value and taste and with film and television having a very great impact on what gets written, published, and noticed by the larger culture.

As suggested earlier, the historical survey course is also a good place for spending some time talking about what literary history *has been* in this century, in the thousands of survey classes taught on our campuses up to this moment. Reviewing this development need not mean condescending to it or congratulating ourselves for achieving some eleventh-hour wisdom that generations of benighted students and instructors had never glimpsed before. If the historical roots of the survey lie in an early-twentieth-century wish to acculturate an increasingly diverse population and stave off babel by requiring a kind of collective homage to a sequence of supposedly heroic (and mostly white male) American authors, then at the millennium's end one valid subject for us to discuss is the survey itself, and the cultural work that it can do, and the right of students to participate in reviewing and defining that mission. This need not be a posture: you may find that your students take the course much more seriously if they understand themselves to part of a collective process, rather than audience for an over-performed ritual.

The suggested readings listed below will promote the presentation of important historical situations, of the rise and transformation of literary eras and values, of the complex engagement between individual talents and their immediate contexts, and of a literary legacy. The teaching notes for individual authors included in this Guide are intended to help address these questions.

Suggested Readings

Volume 1

LITERATURE TO 1620

Literature of Colonial Expansion

Columbus: *Letter to Luis de Santangel; Letter to Ferdinand and Isabella*
Cortés: *First Letter from Mexico to the Spanish Crown*
Harriot: *A Brief and True Report of the New Found Land of Virginia*
White: *The Fifth Voyage*
Percy: *Observations Gathered out of a Discourse of . . . Virginia*
Smith: *The General History of Virginia*

Literature of Witness and Encounter

Casas: *The Very Brief Relation of the Devastation of the Indies*
Díaz del Castillo: *The True History of the Conquest of New Spain*
Cabeza de Vaca: *The Relation*
Barlowe: *The First Voyage Made to the Coasts of America*
Champlain: *The Voyages*

Native American Literature

The Iroquois Creation Story
Pima Stories of the Beginning of the World
Native American Trickster Tales

1620–1820

New England Puritan Writers

Bradford: *Of Plymouth Plantation* [The Mayflower Compact]
Winthrop: *A Model of Christian Charity*
Bradstreet: *The Prologue; A Dialogue Between Old England and New; Contemplations; The Flesh and the Spirit; The Author to Her Book; Here Follows Some Verses upon the Burning of Our House; As Weary Pilgrim*
Wigglesworth: *The Day of Doom*
Rowlandson: *A Narrative of the Captivity and Restoration*
Taylor: *Psalm Two;* the *Prologue* and *Preparatory Meditations; The Preface; The Joy of Church Fellowship Rightly Attended; Upon Wedlock, and Death of Children; Huswifery; A Fig for Thee, Oh! Death*
Sewall: *The Diary*
Mather: *The Wonders of the Invisible World; Galeacius Secundus: The Life of William Bradford; Nehemias Americanus: The Life of John Winthrop; Bonifacius*

Beyond Puritanism and the Bay Colony

Morton: *The New English Canaan*
Byrd: *The Secret Diary; History of the Dividing Line*
Woolman: *The Journal* ("Some Considerations on the Keeping of Negroes")

The New England Puritan Vision: Crisis, Revival, Metamorphosis

Edwards: *Personal Narrative; A Divine and Supernatural Light; Letter to Rev. Dr. Benjamin Colman; Sinners in the Hands of an Angry God*

Federalism, Deism, and the Enlightenment Spirit

Franklin: *The Way to Wealth; An Edict by the King of Prussia; Information to Those Who Would Remove to America; Remarks Concerning the Savages of North America; The Autobiography*
J. Adams and A. Adams: Letters
Paine: *Common Sense; The Crisis, No. 1; The Age of Reason*
Jefferson: *The Declaration of Independence; Notes on the State of Virginia; Letter to Peter Carr; Letter to Nathaniel Burwell*
Freneau: *On the Emigration to America and Peopling the Western Country; The Wild Honey Suckle; The Indian Burying Ground; On the Religion of Nature*

Slavery, Identity, and Personal Ethics

Byrd: *The Secret Diary*
Woolman: *The Journal*
Crèvecoeur: *Letter IX*
Jefferson: *The Declaration of Independence*

Equiano: *The Interesting Narrative*
Freneau: *To Sir Toby*
Wheatley: *On Being Brought from Africa to America; To the University of Cambridge, in New England; Thoughts on the Works of Providence; To S. M., a Young African Painter, on Seeing His Works*; Letters
S. Morton: *The African Chief*

Native Americans and the White Imagination

Bradford: *Of Plymouth Plantation*
R. Williams: *A Key into the Language of America*
Rowlandson: *A Narrative of the Captivity and Restoration*
Franklin: *Remarks Concerning the Savages of North America*
Occom: *A Short Narrative of My Life*
Freneau: *The Indian Burying Ground*

Colonial American Women and the Prevailing Ethos

Bradstreet: Poems
Rowlandson: *A Narrative of the Captivity and Restoration*
Mather: *The Trial of Martha Carrier; Bonifacius*
Knight: *The Private Journal of a Journey from Boston to New York*
Byrd: *The Secret Diary*
Edwards: [*Sarah Pierrepont*]
J. Adams and A. Adams: Letters
Jefferson: *Letter to Nathaniel Burwell*
Murray: *On the Equality of the Sexes*
S. Morton: Poems
Rowson: *Charlotte*

1820–1865

The New Americanness of American Literature

Irving: *Rip Van Winkle; The Legend of Sleepy Hollow; A Tour on the Prairies*
Cooper: *The Pioneers*
Sedgwick: *Cacoethes Scribendi; A Reminiscence of Federalism*
Bryant: *Thanatopsis; The Prairies*
Emerson: *The American Scholar; The Divinity School Address; Self-Reliance; The Poet*
Hawthorne: *Young Goodman Brown; The May-Pole of Merry Mount; The Minister's Black Veil; The Scarlet Letter*
Longfellow: *A Psalm of Life; Excelsior; The Jewish Cemetery at Newport; My Lost Youth*
Poe: *The Raven; Annabel Lee; Ligeia; The Fall of the House of Usher; The Philosophy of Composition*
Melville: *Hawthorne and His Mosses; Moby-Dick; Bartleby, the Scrivener; Billy Budd, Sailor*

American Transcendentalism

Emerson: *Nature*
Fuller: *The Great Lawsuit*
Thoreau: *Walden*
Alcott: *Transcendental Wild Oats*

Literature of a House Divided

Lincoln: *A House Divided; Address Delivered at the Dedication of the Cemetery at Gettysburg*
Stowe: *Uncle Tom's Cabin*
Thoreau: *Resistance to Civil Government; Slavery in Massachusetts*
Douglass: *Narrative of the Life*
Whitman: *Drum-Taps* poems
Melville: *The Paradise of Bachelors and The Tartarus of Maids; Battle-Pieces* poems
Dickinson: 49; 185; 199; 241; 258; 303; 305; 348; 435; 441; 510; 536; 547; 709; 732; 754; 824; 1099; 1129; 1138; 1545 (poems about being alienated)

Democratic Vistas

Lincoln: *Second Inaugural Address*
Whitman: *Preface to Leaves of Grass; Leaves of Grass [Song of Myself]; Letter to Ralph Waldo Emerson; From Pent-up Aching Rivers; Facing West from California's Shores; Scented Herbage of My Breast; Crossing Brooklyn Ferry; Out of the Cradle Endlessly Rocking; As I Ebb'd with the Ocean of Life; When Lilacs Last in the Dooryard Bloom'd; The Sleepers; A Noiseless Patient Spider; Democratic Vistas*
Dickinson: 67; 214; 249; 280; 303; 315; 328; 341; 448; 465; 501; 505; 528; 632; 712; 822; 1540; 1593; 1651; 1732 (poems about struggle, triumph, and vision)
Davis: *Life in the Iron-Mills*

Volume 2

1865–1914

Regionalism and Local-Color Writing

Harte: *The Outcasts of Poker Flat*
Harris: *The Wonderful Tar-Baby Story; Mr. Rabbit Grossly Deceives Mr. Fox*
Jewett: *A White Heron; The Foreigner*
Freeman: *A New England Nun; The Revolt of "Mother"*
Chesnutt: *The Goophered Grapevine; The Wife of His Youth*
Garland: *Under the Lion's Paw*
Austin: *The Walking Woman*
Bonnin: *Impressions of an Indian Childhood; The School Days of an Indian Girl; An Indian Teacher among Indians*

Realism

Clemens: *Adventures of Huckleberry Finn; Fenimore Cooper's Literary Offenses*
Howells: *Novel-Writing and Novel Reading; Editha*
Bierce: *Occurrence at Owl Creek Bridge*
James: *Daisy Miller; The Real Thing; The Beast in the Jungle; The Art of Fiction; The Jolly Corner*
Wharton: *Souls Belated; The Eyes*

Naturalism

Chopin: *The Awakening*
Washington: *Up From Slavery*
Gilman: *The Yellow Wall-paper*
Du Bois: *The Souls of Black Folk*
Norris: *A Plea for Romantic Fiction*
S. Crane: *The Open Boat; The Bride Comes to Yellow Sky; The Blue Hotel; An Episode of War*
Dreiser: *Old Rogaum and His Theresa*
London: *To Build a Fire*
H. Adams: *The Education*

1914–1945

Thematic Modernism

A. Lowell: Poems
Stein: *The Making of Americans*
Frost: *Mending Wall; The Death of the Hired Man; After Apple-Picking; An Old Man's Winter Night; The Oven Bird; Birches; "Out, Out—"; Nothing Gold Can Stay; Stopping by Woods on a Snowy Evening; Two Tramps in Mud Time; Desert Places; Design; Neither Out Far nor in Deep; The Gift Outright; Directive; The Figure a Poem Makes*
Anderson: *Winesburg, Ohio*
Stevens: *The Snow Man; A High-Toned Old Christian Woman; The Emperor of Ice-Cream; Disillusionment of Ten O'Clock; Sunday Morning; Anecdote of the Jar; Thirteen Ways of Looking at a Blackbird; The Idea of Order at Key West; Of Modern Poetry*
Yezierska: *The Lost "Beautifulness"*
W. C. Williams: *Portrait of a Lady; The Widow's Lament in Springtime; Spring and All; To Elsie; The Red Wheelbarrow; The Dead Baby; The Wind Increases; Death; This Is Just to Say; A Sort of a Song; The Dance; Lear; Landscape with the Fall of Icarus*
Jeffers: *Shine, Perishing Republic; Hurt Hawks; November Surf; Carmel Point*
Eliot: *The Love Song of J. Alfred Prufrock; Tradition and the Individual Talent; The Waste Land; The Hollow Men*
O'Neill: *Long Day's Journey into Night*

McKay: Poems
Porter: *Flowering Judas; Theft*
Cummings: *Buffalo Bill's; the Cambridge ladies who live in furnished souls; Poem, or Beauty Hurts Mr. Vinal; "next to of course god america i"; i sing of Olaf glad and big; anyone lived in a pretty how town; pity this busy monster,manunkind*
Toomer: *Cane*
Fitzgerald: *Babylon Revisited*
Faulkner: *As I Lay Dying*
Hemingway: *The Snows of Kilimanjaro*
Hughes: *The Negro Speaks of Rivers; Mother to Son*

Formal and Technical Aspects of Modernism

In an upper-division class or with a particularly motivated group, you could include—in addition to those listed just above—selections from the following list of works that illustrate formal and technical aspects of modernism.

Pound: *A Pact; In a Station of the Metro; Villanelle: The Psychological Hour; The Cantos*
H. D.: *Oread; Leda; At Baia; Fragment 113; Helen; The Walls Do Not Fall*
Moore: *Poetry; To a Snail; Bird-Witted; The Mind Is an Enchanting Thing*
Eliot: *Burnt Norton*
Dos Passos: *The Big Money*
H. Crane: *Chaplinesque; At Melville's Tomb; The Bridge*

Social and Political Writing

Robinson: *Richard Cory; Miniver Cheevy*
Yezierska: *The Lost "Beautifulness"*
Hurston: *The Eatonville Anthology; How It Feels to Be Colored Me*
Parker: *General Review of the Sex Situation*
Taggard: *Everyday Alchemy; With Child; A Middle-aged, Middle-class Woman at Midnight; At Last the Women Are Moving; O People Misshapen; Mill Town; To My Mother*
Brown: *Mister Samuel and Sam; He Was a Man; Master and Man; Break of Day; Bitter Fruit of the Tree*
Hughes: *I, Too; Refugee in America; Madam and Her Madam; Madam's Calling Cards; Silhouette; Visitors to the Black Belt; Democracy*
Rukeyser: *Effort at Speech Between Two People; Movie; Alloy; Suicide Blues; Who in One Lifetime; "Long Enough"; The Poem as Mask; Poem; Painters*

The "New Negro" Movement

Grimké
Hurston
Toomer
Brown

Hughes
Cullen
Wright

AMERICAN PROSE AND POETRY SINCE 1945

Rather than apply historical labels to contemporary writers, you might choose a few who suggest the various gatherings and traditions representative of later twentieth-century literature.

African American Writers

Ellison: *Invisible Man*
Baldwin: *Going to Meet the Man*
Morrison: *Recitatif*
Baraka: *Dutchman*
Major: *An Area in the Cerebral Hemisphere*
Reed: *The Last Days of Louisiana Red; Neo-HooDoo Manifesto*
Bambara: *Medley*
Walker: *Everyday Use*

Southern Writers

Welty: *Petrified Man*
O'Connor: *The Life You Save May Be Your Own; Good Country People*
Walker: *Everyday Use*

Jewish Writers

Malamud: *The Magic Barrel*
Bellow: *Looking for Mr. Green*
Paley: *A Conversation with My Father*
Ginsberg: *Howl*
Levine: Poems
Rich: Poems
Roth: *Defender of the Faith*
Dixon: *Time to Go*

Dramatists

T. Williams: *A Streetcar Named Desire*
Miller: *Death of a Salesman*
Baraka: *Dutchman*
Mamet: *Glengarry Glen Ross*

New Yorker Writers

Cheever: *The Swimmer*
Updike: *Separating*
Beattie: *Weekend*

Experimental or Postmodernist Writers

Le Guin: *Schrödinger's Cat*
Barthleme: *A Manual for Sons*
Major: *An Area in the Cerebral Hemisphere*
Pynchon: *Entropy*
Carver, *Cathedral*

Native American Writers

Momaday: *The Way to Rainy Mountain*
Gerald Vizenor: *Almost Browne*
Glancy: *Jack Wilson or Wovoka and Christ My Lord; Polar Breath*
Silko: *Lullaby*
Erdrich: *Fleur*

Latino/Latina Writers

Ortiz: Poems
Chávez: *The Last of the Menu Girls*
Ríos: Poems
Cervantes: Poems

Grouping Individual Poets

From the contemporary poets included in *NAAL,* here are a few who offer a variety of themes, techniques, and traditions:

Warren
Roethke
Bishop
Berryman
R. Lowell
Brooks
J. Wright
Rich
Plath

Presenting Individual Poems

Roethke: *My Papa's Waltz*
Bishop: *In the Waiting Room; The Moose; One Art*
Hayden: *Middle Passage*
Jarrell: *The Death of the Ball Turret Gunner; Well Water*
Berryman: *Dream Songs* (esp. 1, 14, 40)
R. Lowell: *Memories of West Street and Lepke; Skunk Hour; For the Union Dead*
Brooks: *kitchenette building; the mother; a song in the front yard*
Wilbur: *Love Calls Us to the Things of This World*
Ginsberg: *Howl*

J. Wright: *Autumn Begins in Martins Ferry, Ohio; A Blessing*
Sexton: *Sylvia's Death*
Rich: *A Valediction Forbidding Mourning; Diving into the Wreck*
Plath: *Lady Lazarus; Daddy*
Lorde: *The Woman Thing; Black Mother Woman*
Baraka: *An Agony. As Now.*
Dove: *Thomas and Beulah*

Poets Reflecting the Diversity of Contemporary American Life

Hayden
Brooks
Levertov
Merrill
Ginsberg
Rich
Lorde
Baraka
Harper
Dove
Ríos
Cervantes
Song
Lee

CHAPTER 3

A Course in American Literary Traditions

A literary traditions approach requires plurality, because the history of American literature is a history of the development of many important kinds of writing. If you decide to structure your course this way, you first need to decide which traditions you want to emphasize and which authors will represent them well to your students. Inevitably we end up privileging some kinds of writing over others; but if a little healthy self-consciousness is included in class discussions and presentations, students will understand what choices you have made, why you have made them, and how they might engage with such issues on their own.

NAAL offers familiar figures and representative selections from major works in each of several literary traditions: Euro-American, African American, Native American, and writers from various constituent cultures of New England and the South. The Fifth Edition features a stronger representation of women in all of these constituent cultures than did the last edition. Also included in *NAAL* are works that foster a discussion of twentieth-century immigrant and Jewish traditions. We can also read the anthology for the evolution of a populist voice and perspective and of a literature of working-class experience and protest.

Some general questions that might be raised early in the course:

To what extent is the concept of literary traditions useful in providing contexts for either writing or studying American literature?

What connections have students seen between artistic or literary traditions and popular culture or folk practices?

How does a "literary tradition" take shape? Does it typically begin in a large-scale cultural movement? Do we see traditions rising out of the creativity of a few individual artists?

Do writers and artists actually know when they are working as part of a tradition? Or do critics and classes like this one establish that continuity in retrospect? If an artist is self-consciously working within a tradition of some sort, can he or she be genuinely creative? Or merely derivative?

It is commonly suggested now that racial or ethnic origins and regional identity, gender, and class experience provide valid categories for grouping authors and works. Do some writers defy such classification, because of who they are (or were) or the themes and literary styles they work(ed) in? Do all writers in a given identity group reflect or express the same view of their experience as Americans, as writers, or as members of their group?

Teaching such a course may require a certain faith—that after hearing American literature as a chorus of different *kinds* of voices, different ideas of writing, of audience, of the cultural status and worth of the author, and of course of artistic kinship, the end result can be an enhanced ability to enjoy and investigate the combined literary legacy as a complex whole. The ultimate test of that faith, for many students, would be a discussion of contemporary American literature—and facing the question of whether such works resonate in this rich way. *NAAL* offers many contemporary authors and works that do this quite well.

The overall approach raises fundamental questions about universality. The implicit or explicit pluralism of your course may lead some students into dilemmas as to whether there is an "American" literature at all, as opposed to a kind of Babel on this continent. When that concern arises, you might want to point out that within the Euro-American male tradition, writers such as Hawthorne, Thoreau, Whitman, and Clemens show us that even in the nineteenth-century "American Renaissance" being a writer was a marginalized condition for an American white man. In America, anyone can feel like an outsider—this in mind, a collective sense of exclusion may provide a tradition that includes us all.

You might want to discuss the differences between, for example, Thoreau's choice to write from the isolation of Walden Pond and to flaunt himself, albeit playfully, as an eccentric, and Douglass's two different predicaments and his complex perspective: first as a slave and later as a highly visible and heroic fugitive. For Euro-American men, choosing marginality can help them achieve an individual voice. But they may begin with a sense of their own literary authority, a sense that minority writers may not share. Chesnutt and Hurston are central figures in a course about American literary traditions, for both of them, writing out of the perspective of black folk life, found a source for story-telling authority that was not only culturally accessible to them, but also powerful for addressing their own community and others beyond it. As the white local-colorist Joel Chandler

Harris recorded in the Uncle Remus tales of the 1880s and 1890s (included in *NAAL*), black people on the southern plantation well before emancipation were prolific oral storytellers and kept alive the traditions of African folklore. Chesnutt and Hurston brought that tradition to the printed page.

Engaging your students in comparative discussions of the sources of literary authority available to American writers can help them outgrow assumptions that only white males have had the authority to speak for the nation and its various cultures. It can also lead them to think in new ways about their own nascent authority, as thinkers, speakers, and writers in the classroom. The discussion that results when students consider the struggle for expression in others can ease the isolation and alienation white women and minority students often feel, and it can dissolve for all of your students their indifference to literary study. Students—whatever their gender or ethnic origin—learn to see cultural power as something they may not necessarily inherit, but may discover in themselves.

In the lists that follow, you will find writers and works that illustrate the development of several literary traditions. Within the tradition of literature by Euro-American males, you may want to discuss different choices of genre, perhaps even dividing the reading into subtraditions. Minority traditions and white women have written in full awareness of the literary standards established by Euro-American men; and one way to organize the course is to proceed chronologically, discussing literary traditions carefully as they emerge and speculating on the reasons for their emergence. This strategy allows you to compare writers from different traditions but working in the same historical context.

Another way to organize the syllabus is to group writers within these cultural contexts, so that students can observe prevailing literary values, along with individualized voices and acts of resistance. Anne Bradstreet, for example, can be introduced as (in some ways) a pious and conventional Calvinist who could admire a poem such as Wigglesworth's *The Day of Doom* but also as an independent voice, a woman with pride, and a questioner of prevailing conventions and habits of mind. You can also group polemicists together to intensify the contrasts among them: Edwards, Paine, and Jefferson; Emerson (including the March 7, 1854, antislavery speech), Fuller, Douglass, Washington, and Du Bois.

One grouping that can be used early on to set the tone of the course involves Frost's *The Gift Outright*, in which he speaks not only as a latter-day American bard but also as a male writer from a strongly European tradition. Students will notice the way that he feminizes the land and makes it the task of the writer both to "surrender" himself to her and to correct her "unstoried, artless, unenhanced" condition. The settlement is legitimized; the continent is de-barbarized; Galatea is brought to life. Contrast the theme and tone of this poem with that of Brooks's *kitchenette building,* in which she suggests that being poor in the fictional black neighborhood of Bronzeville makes it very hard indeed to "send up" a dream "through onion fumes" and "yesterday's garbage ripening in the hall."

Organizing Readings by Race and Gender

However you decide to present literary traditions—chronologically or by groupings—your students will benefit if they can imagine individual writers within their historical moment. What follows are lists of writers represented in *NAAL*, organized chronologically and also by race, nationality, and gender.

Volume 1

LITERATURE TO 1620

Northern European Men

Barlowe: *The First Voyage Made to the Coasts of America*
Champlain: *The Voyages*
Smith: *The General History of Virginia*

Native Americans

Stories of the Beginning of the World
Native American Trickster Tales

Hispanic and Southern European Men

Columbus: *Letter to Luis de Santangel; Letter to Ferdinand and Isabella*
Casas: *The Very Brief Relation of the Devastation of the Indies*
Cortés: *First Letter from Mexico to the Spanish Crown*
Díaz del Castillo: *The True History of the Conquest of New Spain*
Cabeza de Vaca: *The Relation*

1620–1820

Euro-American Men

Bradford: *Of Plymouth Plantation*
Morton: *The New English Canaan*
Winthrop: *A Model of Christian Charity*
R. Williams: *The Bloody Tenet of Persecution*
Taylor: *Psalm Two; Prologue; Meditations (8, 16, 38, 42); The Preface; Upon Wedlock, and Death of Children; Huswifery; A Fig for Thee, Oh! Death*
Edwards: *Personal Narrative;* [Sarah Pierrepont]; *A Divine and Supernatural Light; Letter to Rev. Dr. Benjamin Colman; Sinners in the Hands of an Angry God*
Franklin: *The Way to Wealth; Information to Those Who Would Remove to America; Remarks Concerning the Savages of North America; The Autobiography*
Crèvecoeur: *Letters from an American Farmer*
J. Adams: Letters

Jefferson: *The Declaration of Independence; Notes on the State of Virginia* (Query VI, Query XVII); *Letter to Peter Carr; Letter to Nathaniel Burwell*

Euro-American Women

Bradstreet: Poems
Rowlandson: *Narrative of the Captivity and Restoration*
Warren: *The Group*
A. Adams: Letters
Morton: Poems
Rowson: *Charlotte*

African American Men

Equiano: *The Interesting Narrative of the Life*

African American Women

Wheatley: Poems

Native American Men

Occom: *A Short Narrative of My Life*

1820–1865

Euro-American Men

Irving: *Rip Van Winkle*
Emerson: *The American Scholar; Self-Reliance; The Poet; Experience; Last of the Anti-Slavery Lectures*
Hawthorne: *Young Goodman Brown; The Minister's Black Veil; Rappaccini's Daughter; The Celestial Railroad; The Scarlet Letter*
Poe: Poems; Tales
Thoreau: *Resistance to Civil Government; Walden; Slavery in Massachusetts; Walking*
Whitman: *Preface to Leaves of Grass; Leaves of Grass* [*Song of Myself*], *Calamus* poems; *Out of the Cradle Endlessly Rocking; The Sleepers; Democratic Vistas*
Melville: *Moby-Dick; Bartleby, the Scrivener; Benito Cereno; Billy Budd, Sailor*

Euro-American Women

Sedgwick: *Cacoethes Scribendi; A Reminiscence of Federalism*
Kirkland: *A New Home*
Fuller: *The Great Lawsuit*
Stowe: *Uncle Tom's Cabin*
Dickinson: Poems, *Letters to Thomas Wentworth Higginson*

Davis: *Life in the Iron-Mills*
Alcott: *Transcendental Wild Oats*
Spoffard: *Circumstance*

African American Men

Douglass: *Narrative of the Life*

African American Women

Jacobs: *Incidents in the Life of a Slave Girl*

Native Americans

The Cherokee Memorials
Apess: *An Indian's Looking-Glass for the White Man*

Volume 2

1865–1914

Euro-American Men

Clemens: *Adventures of Huckleberry Finn; Fenimore Cooper's Literary Offenses*
Howells: *Novel-Writing and Novel-Reading*
Bierce: *Occurrence at Owl Creek Bridge*
James: *Daisy Miller; The Beast in the Jungle*
Norris: *A Plea for Romantic Fiction*
S. Crane: *The Open Boat; The Bride Comes to Yellow Sky*
London: *To Build a Fire*
Dreiser: *Old Rogaum and His Theresa*
H. Adams: *The Education*

Euro-American Women

Jewett: *A White Heron; The Foreigner*
Chopin: *The Awakening*
Freeman: *A New England Nun; The Revolt of "Mother"*
Gilman: *The Yellow Wall-paper*
Wharton: *Souls Belated; The Eyes*
Austin: *The Walking Woman*

African American Men

Washington: *Up From Slavery*
Chesnutt: *The Goophered Grapevine*
Du Bois: *The Souls of Black Folk*

Native American Men

Native American Oratory
Eastman: *From the Deep Woods to Civilization*
Oskison: *The Problem of Old Harjo*
Chants and Songs

Native American Women

Chants and Songs
Bonnin: *Impressions of an Indian Childhood; The School Days of an Indian Girl; An Indian Teacher among Indians*

1914–1945
Euro-American Men

Robinson: Poems
Frost: Poems
Stevens: *A High-Toned Old Christian Woman; Sunday Morning; Thirteen
Ways of Looking at a Blackbird; The Idea of Order at Key West; Of Mod-
ern Poetry*
Williams: *The Young Housewife; Portrait of a Lady; The Widow's Lament
in Springtime; Spring and All; To Elsie; The Dead Baby; This Is Just to
Say; A Sort of a Song*
O'Neill: *Long Day's Journey into Night*
Eliot: *The Love Song of J. Alfred Prufrock; The Waste Land; Burnt Norton*
Fitzgerald: *Babylon Revisited*
Faulkner: *As I Lay Dying*
H. Crane: *Chaplinesque; At Melville's Tomb*
Hemingway: *The Snows of Kilimanjaro*

Euro-American Women

Cather: *My Ántonia*
A. Lowell: Poems
Yezierska: *The Lost "Beautifulness"*
Moore: Poems
Porter: *Flowering Judas; Theft*
Millay: Poems
Taggard: Poems

African American Men

McKay: Poems
Toomer: *Cane*
Brown: Poems
Hughes: *The Negro Speaks of Rivers; Mother to Son; Mulatto; Song for a
Dark Girl*
Cullen: Poems
R. Wright: *The Man Who Was Almost a Man*

African American Women

Grimké: *The Closed Door*
Hurston: *The Eatonville Anthology; Their Eyes Were Watching God*

Native American Men

Black Elk: *Black Elk Speaks*

PROSE SINCE 1945

Euro-American Men

T. Williams: *A Streetcar Named Desire*
Malamud: *The Magic Barrel*
Bellow: *Looking for Mr. Green*
Miller: *Death of a Salesman*
Mamet: *Glengarry Glen Ross*

Euro-American Women

Welty: *Petrified Man*
O'Connor: *The Life You Save May Be Your Own; Good Country People*
Beattie: *Weekend*

African American Men

Ellison: *Invisible Man*
Baldwin: *Going to Meet the Man*
Baraka: *Dutchman*
Major: *An Area in the Cerebral Hemisphere*
Reed: *The Last Days of Louisiana Red; Neo-HooDoo Manifesto*

African American Women

Marshall: *Reena*
Morrison: *Recitatif*
Bambana: *Medley*
Walker: *Everyday Use*

Native American Men

Momaday: *The Way to Rainy Mountain*

Native American Women

Silko: *Lullaby*
Erdrich: *Fleur*

Latina

Chávez: *The Last of the Menu Girls*
Cisneros: selections from *Woman Hollering Creek*

American Poetry since 1945

Euro-American Men

Warren
Roethke
Jarrell
R. Lowell
Wilbur
Merrill
Ginsberg
Ashbery
Merwin
J. Wright
Levine

Euro-American Women

Bishop: *The Fish; The Bight; At the Fishhouses; Questions of Travel; The Armadillo; In the Waiting Room; One Art*
Levertov: *To the Snake; In Mind*
Sexton: *The Truth the Dead Know; Sylvia's Death; The Death of Fathers*
Rich: *Snapshots of a Daughter-in-Law; "I Am in Danger—Sir—"; A Valediction Forbidding Mourning; Diving into the Wreck*
Plath: *Morning Song; Lady Lazarus; Daddy*
Oliver: *Poppies; Hummingbird Pauses at the Trumpet Vine*
Glück: *The Drowned Children; Illuminations; Appearances; Vespers*

African American Men

Hayden: *Middle Passage; Homage to the Empress of the Blues; Elegies for Paradise Valley*
Harper: *American History; Martin's Blues; Tongue-Tied in Black and White*

African American Women

Brooks: *kitchenette building; a song in the front yard*
Lorde: *Coal; The Woman Thing; Black Mother Woman; Chain*
Dove: *Thomas and Beulah*

Native American Men

Ortiz: Poems

Native American Women

Harjo: Poems

Latino

Ríos: Poems

Latina

Cervantes: *For Virginia Chavez; Visions of Mexico While at a Writing Symposium in Port Townsend, Washington; Emplumada*

Asian American Men

Lee: *The Gift; Persimmons; Eating Alone; Eating Together*

Asian American Women

Song: *Beauty and Sadness; Lost Sister; Chinatown; Heaven*

The Southern Tradition

The southern tradition is represented in *NAAL* by the following authors.

Volume 1

Literature to 1820

Smith
Byrd
Jefferson

1820–1865

Thorpe
Douglass

Volume 2

1865–1914

Harris
Chopin
Washington

1914–1945

Porter
Hurston
Faulkner
Wolfe

American Prose and Poetry Since 1945

Warren
Welty
T. Williams
Dickey

O'Connor
Walker

The Protest Tradition

The tradition of protest literature begins early among the writers represented in *NAAL* and includes the following authors.

Volume 1

Casas
Cabeza de Vaca
Cherokee Memorials
Apess
Child
Fuller
Stowe
Jacobs
Thoreau
Douglass
Davis

Volume 2

Native American Oratory
Gilman
Du Bois
Oskison
Bonnin
Black Elk
Yezierska
Taggard
Brown
Vonnegut
Ginsberg
Reed

Marginality in the White American Male Tradition

The following lists present a few works illustrating relationships among social and political marginality, personal perspective, and literary voice.

Volume 1

1620–1820

R. Williams
Woolman

1820–1865

Irving: *Rip Van Winkle*
Hawthorne: *The Scarlet Letter*
Thoreau: *Walden*
Whitman: *Leaves of Grass* [*Song of Myself*]
Melville: *Bartleby, the Scrivener; Billy Budd, Sailor*

Volume 2

1865–1914

Clemens: *Adventures of Huckleberry Finn*
James: *The Beast in the Jungle*

PROSE AND POETRY SINCE 1914

Anderson: *Winesburg, Ohio*
Jeffers: *Shine, Perishing Republic*
O'Neill: *Long Day's Journey into Night*
Fitzgerald: *Babylon Revisited*
Faulkner: *As I Lay Dying; Barn Burning*
Berryman: *Dream Songs*
R. Lowell: *For the Union Dead*
Merrill: *An Urban Convalescence; The Broken Home; Lost in Translation*
Ginsberg: *Howl*
O'Hara: Poems
J. Wright: Poems

CHAPTER 4

A Course about Inclusion, Diversity, Minority Voices, and Current Controversies

The previous edition of this Guide reviewed the challenge of teaching a survey course with special focus on "the intersections of gender, race or ethnicity, class, region, and sexual orientation as they provide the social context within which writers create literature." Because the Fifth Edition of *NAAL* offers more resources for the exploration of these issues, the suggested readings in this chapter have been revised to take advantage of these new texts. You may determine, however, that you can raise these issues effectively within the chronological survey and in conjunction with other ways of reading. A multi-author, multi-era course, especially at the introductory level, can offer a variety that students will appreciate. More important, it can avoid segregating minority and contrarian voices or reducing the American literary experience to one dimension. It is no secret, however, that this issue is large, open, and evolving and that no one has the last word on how to ensure that the diversity of this culture is presented effectively to our students. For instructors interested in organizing a course or a major unit emphasizing these contexts, the following suggestions will be helpful.

Many instructors have been paying special attention to the intersections of gender, race or ethnicity, class, region, and sexual orientation in regard to the context within which writers live and work. An inclusion approach differs from a literary traditions approach by stressing these social, historical, political, and economic contexts and by holding that social and material conditions affect the text at least as much as does the personality of the author. Conversely, the inclusion approach also focuses on the ways that literary texts can themselves impact the social and cultural contexts from which they emerge. In effect, the inclusion approach surveys the ways in which gender, race, class, and region intersect in the literary work and how the literary text, in its representations of gender, race, class, and region, constructs and influences the perceptions of the reader.

The "Literature to 1620" section of *NAAL* develops the concept of encounter and displaces the term students are probably more familiar with—*discovery*—both as a reference to the early narratives preceding colonial American literature and as a description of the interaction of Europeans and indigenous peoples during exploration and colonization. To ask students to view colonization and conquest from the point of view of the colonized and conquered peoples, in keeping with some of the works in this section, is to ask them to question the paradigm from within which they, and generations of American students before them, have viewed the earliest experiences of Europeans in the New World. You might emphasize selections from Casas, Cabeza de Vaca, and Barlowe to provide evidence of the responses of the native peoples to the Europeans.

This concept of encounter opens an array of questions that can help organize a course about diversity and inclusivity. You are encouraging students to take a complex view of the literature they read: How does a given work represent material life at a particular time and in a certain cultural and political context? What ideologies underpin this representation? What interests might such a representation serve?

In such an approach to the American literature course, gender, race, class, and region can be looked at as categories by which society organizes hierarchies of status and value and by which literary texts either inscribe or critique. A question that seems almost universal in the survey course— "What is American about American literature?"—can, therefore, take a different shape: How do American literary texts reflect, construct, and critique social and cultural values that privilege Euro-Americans, the masculine gender, material wealth, and (up to 1890 at least) the perspective of northeastern white men?

In an inclusion approach, Native American writers and writers from other racial and ethnic U.S. minorities gain importance, along with women from various ethnic backgrounds and writers who focus on issues of class, region, and sexual orientation. Students can, therefore, explore ways in which cultural ideologies about gender, race, class, and region in the United States influence interpretation and the creation and transformation of literary canons.

If one basic objective, transcending any historical or thematic approach, is to make this material interesting and memorable, then teaching material from this perspective serves that purpose well. When a literature course confirms biases and paradigms that students bring to the opening sessions, then what cause do they have to remember and reconsider the experience that follows? If a course taught with special interest to inclusivity and diversity can challenge biases and paradigms, and encourage students to respond to those challenges, then what can result is refreshed and independent thinking.

Suggested Readings

Because this approach questions some conventional notions of cultural literacy and because students, to think effectively about such issues, have to know something about canonical works, you may want to consider mixing the orthodox and the heterodox. Please consult Chapter 5 of the Guide for reading lists organized by race and gender for each period and volume of *NAAL* and review the thematic lists in Chapter 6:

The Problem of American Identity
The Individual and the Community
The Problem of Literary Authority
The American Dream
The American Landscape
Immigration and Wandering
Family Relationships
Race, Segregation, and Slavery
Gender Issues: Women's Lives, Work, and Vision
Politics and War

The lists of suggested readings in the genre section may also be read dialogically. Most of the indigenous genres, for example, may be read as offering a critique, even as seeking to establish a literature that resists hierarchies of dominance. The following list identifies indigenous genres that offer a critique of American culture from the perspective of gender, race, class, region, and/or sexual orientation.

Volume 1

Early regionalism
Slave narrative

Volume 2

Folk literature
Feminist writing
Regionalism
Black fiction and poetry
Jewish fiction
Southern fiction
Regional fiction
Beat poetry
Feminist poetry
Protest and political poetry
Regional poetry

The "naturalist" writers of the 1865–1914 period also offer critiques, especially of gender and class.

Sexual Orientation as a Category of Analysis

If you are interested in examining representations of lesbian and gay experience, you will need to make this category more visible for students. The following list includes writers believed to be lesbian or gay, writers whose work raises questions concerning what Adrienne Rich has called "compulsory heterosexuality," and writers who have produced works of interest in the study of cultural representations of lesbian and gay experience.

Volume 1

LITERATURE TO 1620

Representations of La Malinche in Cortés and Pocahontas in Smith suggest that colonization follows the paradigm of heterosexual conquest.

1620–1820

Bradford: *Of Plymouth Plantation, Book II, Chapter XXXII,* establishes Bradford's concept of sexual deviance.

Sewall: *The Diary* offers a sometimes comic portrait of a thoughtful man trying to reconcile firm Calvinist beliefs, an elderly man's romantic inclinations (toward Mrs. Winthrop), and a wish for worldly comfort and prosperity.

Byrd: *The Secret Diary* represents marriage as an economic pact; a source of power and convenience, for men; and a source of (to Byrd) amusing rivalry and domestic skirmish, in which African Americans are the pawns and casualties.

Bradstreet (Poems) and J. Adams and A. Adams (Letters): These writings celebrate loving heterosexual relationships as the paradigm for the republic.

Rowson: *Charlotte* provides stern lessons about the dangers of sexuality and passion, mixed with celebrations of prudent middle-class love and marriage and of obedience to family elders.

1820–1865

Irving: *The Legend of Sleepy Hollow* presents the "masculine," ignorant Brom Bones versus an "effeminate" or asexual and scholastic Ichabod Crane; the real relationship in the story may not be Ichabod's heterosexual interest in Katrina Van Tassel but rather the rivalry between the men, ending in a caricature of erotic conquest.

Emerson: *The Poet,* which helped shape American aesthetics for generations, codifies a poetics of dominion over experience, of an agonistic relationship between the male "bard" and a vast and essentially female natural order.

Hawthorne: *The Scarlet Letter* contrasts the erotic and even sado-masochistic relationship between Dimmesdale and Chillingworth with the very different sort of passion between Dimmesdale and Hester Prynne.

Poe: *The Sleeper, The Raven, Annabel Lee,* and other elegiac poems seem to celebrate dead women as the ideal subject for the poet and the ideal consorts for the truly sensitive male lover; *Ligeia* seems to construct heterosexuality as a form of death.

Fuller: *The Great Lawsuit* critiques the reality of modern American bourgeois marriage.

Thoreau: How much does misogyny or unconventional sexuality figure into *Walden*, which, according to its opening chapter, offers essentially economic advice to "poor students" and supposedly genderless counsel on how to live "deliberately"?

Whitman: The *Calamus* poems contrast powerfully with the *Children of Adam* poems.

Melville: *Hawthorne and His Mosses* depicts the pervasive single-sex world of Melville's fiction. The *Moby-Dick* selections foster discussion of power structures and love relationships among this company of men, thousands of miles from women and standard family life.

Dickinson: 249, 520, and others suggest both homoerotic and heteroerotic themes. Her poems, which avoid a discourse of domination in regard to worldly experience, make up an eloquent rebellion against Emersonian poetics.

Volume 2

1865–1914

Clemens: Like the relationship between Dimmesdale and Chillingworth in Hawthorne's *The Scarlet Letter,* the relationships between Huck and Tom and Huck and Jim in *Adventures of Huckleberry Finn,* as Leslie Fielder observed many years ago, may exemplify a homoerotic bond that turns up frequently in American narratives by male writers: Hawkeye and Chingachgook, Ishmael and Queequeg, Jay Gatsby and Nick Carraway, Chief Bromden and Randall McMurphy.

James: *Daisy Miller* and *The Beast in the Jungle,* along with other James narratives, raise questions about male narcissism, the social and sexual predicament of upper-class, late-century women, and the fate of heterosexual and homosexual eroticism in the Gilded Age.

Jewett: Rejecting the requirement of "compulsory heterosexuality," Sylvy, in *A White Heron,* refuses to tell the heron's secret to the attractive male hunter.

Chopin: The enduring feminist novel *The Awakening* can be read as a critique not merely of an exhausted bourgeois existence but of all conventional descriptions and confinements of sexuality.

Freeman: In *A New England Nun,* Louisa Ellis rejects overwhelming social and economic pressures to marry.

1914–1945

A. Lowell; Stein; H. D.; and H. Crane: All offer poems with homoerotic themes and radical critiques of conventional (post-Emersonian) ways of seeing and dominating experience.

Parker: The poems and prose piece *The Waltz* offer razor-edged satire of twentieth-century bourgeois constructions of love and marriage.

AMERICAN PROSE SINCE 1945

T. Williams: *A Streetcar Named Desire* explores various forms of modern sexuality, socially sanctioned and otherwise.

Baldwin: *Going to Meet the Man* is a narrative of a white racist, his memory of a lynching, and a forbidden sexuality entwined with both the bigotry and the crime.

Vidal: *The Robin* is a narrative by an openly gay writer about entering, as a young man, into forbidden experience and about the long-lived guilt that came of that adventure.

AMERICAN POETRY SINCE 1945

Duncan; Merrill; Ginsberg; Rich; and Lorde: All bring gay perspectives to poems about contemporary life.

CHAPTER 5

A Course in Major American Authors

One heartening continuity: as a phrase, "major American authors" has almost never meant, to reasonably humble instructors in any season, an im-
mutable array of Greats. The academic, commercial, and public conversation about passing fads and durable quality dates only from around the end
of the nineteenth century, and a browse through old American literature
collections and college reading lists will provide plenty of evidence that
each generation changes the American Parnassus, lifting new writers and
pushing others down the hill. When Harriet Beecher Stowe died in 1896,
Uncle Tom's Cabin was widely regarded as America's *Les Misérables;* thirty
years later it was being condescended to as something misshapen, sentimentalist, and hopelessly mass-market; two generations later it was back
among the classics and available in half a dozen scholarly editions. At the
end of Henry James's life, he himself said that the best novelist then writing in the English language was Hugh Walpole. And Samuel Clemens spe-
cialists have seen the reputation of some of his works whipsaw up and
down like stocks on an over-the-counter exchange. Other examples of shifting valuations will occur to you, and the lesson that they teach is pretty
clear.

Such realities need not be grounds for debunking any given list of great
American texts, and a "Major Authors tour" with a little healthy skepticism
in it can be stronger and much more pleasurable for good students than either a solemn presentation of the unquestionably, timelessly sublime or a
prolonged and dreary exercise in iconoclasm. If we are having any luck in
the classroom, then these worries over majorness and greatness will take
care of themselves. Can we imagine that a sizable number of mature former

students would continue paying unexamined homage to works that, in a college class, they went through the motions of revering? Would we even want them to do so? For our own good as teachers, and for the continued worth of any discussion about American cultural history, we need participation from these students—and a survey course runs no risk of collapse if it welcomes that participation at the outset and sustains it throughout the term.

If that intention makes sense, you might consider opening the course with a discussion of how literary worth is determined and how modern Western culture has deliberated issues like the ones above. What are the forces at play, and how much should they matter? Mass appeal, as measured by sheer sales in a given year or over decades? Popularity among professors and literature departments? Regular mention in ponderous, official-looking histories of American letters? Big-budget Hollywood screen versions, with big stars? Students will have impressions to share—and if in sharing them, and in noting the strengths and limitations of these modes of selections, they see the whole process as a complex and open-ended one, then so much the better.

In a major-authors survey, as in a more general historical tour, you can present some writers as figures who *have been* regarded as important, by well-known writers who came after and imitated or quarreled with them, by influential critics and historians, or by a large and long-lasting reading public, as was true for Longfellow. In a semester-long course, you might open with some authors who have been recently rediscovered and talk about *why* they might have been rediscovered. You may also want to add some writers whose place on a major-authors list is still controversial. Again, the inclusion of a few such writers encourages students to think not just about literary meaning but also about the open-endedness of creating and re-creating an American canon and about the ways in which we use such texts to conduct a dialogue with ourselves about ourselves.

Presenting a course as a study of major authors makes it possible to read and discuss more of each writer's work. This approach does not have to eliminate the historical context or the literary history within which any given writer wrote, although such a course usually emphasizes the development of each writer's career, rather than broad historical and cultural contexts. If you require students to read the excellent *NAAL* period introductions, you can allocate class time to intensive discussion of writers and individual works.

The major-authors model works well in a multicourse curriculum in which first-year students take an "introduction to literature" course and upper-division students study literary periods in detail. The major-authors course can be an intensive reacquaintance with writers that students have read before, either in high school or elsewhere on your campus, and an incentive to read other writers who were contemporaries of these major figures or who owe them a literary debt.

As a start, you might find it useful to think through your own idea of *major*. Some of the words we might casually use to explain choices of cer-

tain writers over others—*great, universal, enduring,* and *major* itself—can
be evasive. Your students will have questions: How does an author become
major? Who decides? Is the question open to debate? Is there a "dictionary"
of major authors that establishes the criteria for inclusion, or does the inclusion of any particular author reflect the opinions of readers over time?
If so, which readers? Why do there appear to be so many major authors in
one period (e.g., 1820–65), and so few in others (such as 1620–1820)? If
the theaters were open and thriving in America during the Gilded Age, why
don't the anthologies include any of those plays? One way to open up questions about literary reputation is to allow students to choose a favorite author who is not on the syllabus and ask them to write about this author's literary value. Asking questions like these can help keep the conversation
refreshingly open-ended and encourage students to consider that this whole
issue of majorness and greatness is one in which they can participate as informed and thoughtful adults.

At one of the opening sessions, you might want to see if your class can
evolve its own tentative criteria. If you help them keep track by writing
their suggestions on the board, you may end up with a list like the following, regarding authors we could call major:

They still appeal to a variety of readers.
They wrote works that influenced more than one other major author.
They contributed an acknowledged "masterpiece" to American literature.
They sustained a literary career beyond a single *tour de force.*
They were pioneers or innovators in subject matter, literary tradition,
    technique, or genre.
They have been recognized as influential literary critics or historians.

Phrases like *major authors* and *major minor authors* add to students' confusion. We might need to distinguish between *major* meaning "significant"
in some way and *major* as "mainstream." One of the larger challenges in
teaching the major-authors course is helping some students reconsider assumptions that *major* always equals "Euro-American" or "male" and that
women, Native American, African American, and other minority writers—
because they take up fewer pages in *NAAL* and most other comprehensive
anthologies—are certified "minor" writers.

Suggested Readings

Volume 1

LITERATURE TO 1620

Díaz del Castillo
Cabeza de Vaca
Smith

1620–1820

Winthrop: *A Model of Christian Charity*
Bradstreet
Taylor
Edwards
Franklin: Including *The Autobiography*

1820–1865

Emerson: Including *Nature*
Hawthorne: Including *The Scarlet Letter*
Poe
Stowe
Thoreau: *Walden*
Douglass: *Narrative of the Life*
Whitman
Melville: Including *Billy Budd, Sailor*
Dickinson

Volume 2

1865–1914

Clemens: Including *Adventures of Huckleberry Finn*
James
Chopin
Wharton
Native American Chants and Songs

1914–1945

Cather
Frost
Stevens
O'Neill
Eliot
Hurston
Faulkner
Hughes

AMERICAN PROSE SINCE 1945

T. Williams
Malamud
Ellison
Bellow
Miller
O'Connor

Momaday
Walker
Beattie

AMERICAN POETRY SINCE 1945

Roethke
Bishop
R. Lowell
Brooks
Wilbur
J. Wright
Rich
Dove

A Broader American Canon

Volume 1

LITERATURE TO 1620

Stories of the Beginning of the World
Champlain

1620–1820

Bradford
Crèvecoeur
Jefferson

1820–1865

Irving
Fuller

Volume 2

1865–1914

Howells
Jewett
Freeman
Chesnutt
Eastman
S. Crane
Dreiser
H. Adams

1914–1945

Stein
Anderson
W. C. Williams
Pound
H. D.
Moore
Porter
Fitzgerald
H. Crane
Hemingway
R. Wright

AMERICAN PROSE SINCE 1945

Welty
Baraka

AMERICAN POETRY SINCE 1945

Olson
Hayden
Berryman
Levertov
Ammons
Merrill
Ashbery
Sexton
Plath
Lorde

Works by Noncanonical Writers Especially Suited for a Major-Authors Course

Volume 1

LITERATURE TO 1620

Barlowe: *The First Voyage Made to the Coasts of America*

1620–1820

Wigglesworth: *The Day of Doom*
Rowlandson: *A Narrative of the Captivity and Restoration*
Occom: *A Short Narrative of My Life*
Paine: *Common Sense; The Crisis, No. 1*
Wheatley: Poems

1820–1865

Bryant: *The Prairies*
Apess: *An Indian's Looking-Glass for the White Man*
Jacobs: *Incidents in the Life of a Slave Girl*
Davis: *Life in the Iron-Mills*

Volume 2

1865–1914

Harte: *The Outcasts of Poker Flat*
Harris: Tales
Washington: *Up From Slavery*
Garland: *Under the Lion's Paw*
Gilman: *The Yellow Wall-paper*
Du Bois: *The Souls of Black Folk*

1914–1945

Black Elk: *Black Elk Speaks*
Masters: Poems
Hurston: *The Eatonville Anthology; How It Feels to Be Colored Me; Their Eyes Were Watching God*
Parker: Essays
Cummings: Poems
Toomer: *Cane*
Wolfe: *The Lost Boy*

American Prose Since 1945

Cheever: *The Swimmer*
Baldwin: *Going to Meet the Man*
Updike: *Separating*
Roth: *Defender of the Faith*
Pynchon: *Entropy*
Erdrich: *Fleur*

American Poetry since 1945

Oppen
Jarrell
Wilbur
Creeley
Snyder
Harper

CHAPTER 6

A Course about Genres and American Literary Themes

This chapter offers reading lists for a survey course with special emphasis on the evolution of genres of American writing, including the personal and historical account, the poem, the fictional narrative, and the drama. A course of this kind can be organized to address questions such as the following:

1. How do the prevailing genres of a literary period reflect and converse with conventional thought and cultural values of that time?
2. How does a given literary work follow, resist, or reinvent the standard forms and rules of the genre?
3. In the American traditions, why are certain genres favored over others, at particular historical moments, for the exploration of important moral, political, philosophical, or spiritual themes?
4. In a literature with a proliferation of genres and a sizable inheritance from European literary traditions, what is originality or creativity?
5. Is it valid to talk about the evolution of certain American genres and about ways in which each new experiment grows out of the accumulated legacy? Or does the American cult of newness, and the nearly constant impact of innovations in England and Western Europe, hopelessly complicate or negate our wish to see each powerful new text as closely related to whatever came before it?

A course that pays special attention to the development of American genres will need to look carefully at the *literary* circumstances of each author, meaning his or her formal or informal cultural experience; the strength (in that historical moment) of indigenous and imported literary models and influences; the availability of other texts to the author; the supporting community and intended audience; and the clarity or uncertainty, at that time, of the function and responsibilities of authorship. Luckily, however, we can keep at least two different dialogues going in such a course: an investigation of literary history from this general perspective and a freer and (to some students at least) more pleasurable review of American genres from *our* viewpoint, whereby texts are read as engaged in a dialogue (author-intended or not) with a long sequence of other texts.

Suggested Readings: Genre

Volume 1

LITERATURE TO 1620

Historical narratives: Columbus, Casas, Cortés, Díaz del Castillo, Cabeza de Vaca, Barlowe, Harriot, White, Champlain, Percy, Smith
Indigenous forms: Stories of the Beginning of the World: Iroquois and Pima versions; Native American Trickster tales

1620–1820

Historical chronicles: Bradford, Morton, Rowlandson, Mather
Journals and letters: Winthrop, R. Williams, Sewall, Knight, Byrd, Franklin, Woolman, Crèvecoeur, the Adamses, Jefferson
Poetry: Bradstreet, Wigglesworth, Taylor, Freneau, Wheatley, S. Morton
Travel narratives: Knight; Byrd; *History of the Dividing Line*; Crèvecouer; Bartram; Dwight
Sermons: Winthrop; Taylor, *Sermon VI*; Mather, *Bonifacius*; Edwards
Personal narrative: Franklin, Occom, Equiano
Fiction: Rowson
American state papers and political nonfiction prose: Bradford, R. Williams, Franklin, Crèvecoeur, Paine, Jefferson, *The Federalist*, Murray
Drama: M. Warren

1820–1865

Fiction: Irving, Cooper, Sedgwick, Hawthorne, Poe, Stowe, Thorpe, Melville, Davis, Alcott, Spoffard
Journals and letters: Child, Whitman, Dickinson
Literary essays: Cooper, Emerson, Hawthorne, Poe, Whitman, Melville
Lyric poetry: Bryant, Emerson, Longfellow, Whittier, Poe, Whitman, Dickinson
Personal narrative: Kirkland, Jacobs, Douglass
Philosophical essays: Emerson, Thoreau
Southwest humor: Thorpe
Political nonfiction prose: Cherokee Memorials, Apess, Lincoln, Fuller, Fern, Thoreau, Douglass

Volume 2

1865–1914

Folk literature: Harris, Chesnutt
Humor: Clemens
Literary criticism: Clemens, Howells, James, Norris
Local color: Clemens, Harte, Harris, Garland, S. Crane
Lyric poetry: S. Crane
Naturalism: Bierce, Chopin, Gilman, Norris, S. Crane, Dreiser, London
Public/political writing: Native American Oratory, Washington, Du Bois
Realism: Clemens, Howells, James, Wharton
Regionalism: Jewett, Chopin, Freeman, Chesnutt, Austin, Oskison, Bonnin
Native American oral literature: Cochise, Charlot, The Navajo Night
    Chant, Chippewa songs, Ghost Dance songs, Wovoka
Personal narrative: Washington, Eastman, Gilman, Bonnin, H. Adams

1914–1945

African American fiction: Hurston, Toomer, Wright
Drama: O'Neill
Experimental prose: Stein, Faulkner
Humor: Parker, Thurber
African American lyric poetry: McKay, Brown, Hughes, Cullen
Populist and folk lyric poetry: Masters, Sandburg
Longer poems: W. C. Williams, Pound, H. D., Eliot, H. Crane
Modernist lyric poetry: Robinson, Frost, Stevens, W. C. Williams,
    A. Lowell, Pound, H. D., Jeffers, Moore, Eliot, Ransom, Millay, Cum-
    mings, Bogan, H. Crane
Political/feminist lyric poetry: Taggard, Rukeyser
Realistic fiction: Cather, Anderson, Yezierska, Porter, Hurston, Fitzgerald,
    Dos Passos, Faulkner, Hemingway, Steinbeck
Southern fiction: Porter, Faulkner, Wolfe
Native American autobiography: Black Elk

AMERICAN PROSE SINCE 1945

Drama: T. Williams, Miller, Mamet
Jewish fiction: Malamud, Bellow, Roth
Fiction from and about New York: Cheever, Malamud, Ellison, Bellow,
    Updike, Beattie
Southern fiction: Welty, O'Connor, Walker
African American fiction: Ellison, Baldwin, Marshall, Baraka, Morrison,
    Dixon, Major, Bambara, Walker, Reed
Native American fiction: Momaday, Vizenor, Glancy, Silko, Erdrich
Latino/Latina fiction: Chávez, Cisneros
Fantasy/science fiction: Le Guin, Pynchon, Russ
Asian American fiction: Kingston
Fiction in the realist mode: Malamud, Bellow, Cheever, Baldwin, Updike,
    Hannah, Walker

Metafiction and fiction in experimental modes and styles: Paley, Le Guin, Barthelme, Major, Pynchon, Russ, Bambara, Glancy, Beattie, Vollmann
Postmodern nonfiction prose: Vonnegut, Dillard

AMERICAN POETRY SINCE 1945

Asian American poetry: Song, Lee
Autobiographical and confessional poetry: Roethke, Bishop, Berryman, Lowell, Levertov, Merrill, Ginsberg, Sexton, Rich, Plath
The Beats: Ginsberg, Snyder
African American poetry: Hayden, Brooks, Lorde, Harper, Dove
Latino/Latina poetry: Ríos, Cervantes
Feminist poetry: Rich, Lorde, Harjo
Longer poems: Wilbur, Merrill, Ginsberg, Rich, Dove
Native American poetry: Ortiz, Harjo
Nature and landscape poetry: Niedecker, R. P. Warren, Roethke, Bishop, Wilbur, Ammons, Merrill, J. Wright, Snyder, Oliver
New York School: O'Hara, Ashbery
"Projective verse": Olson, Levertov
Protest and political poetry: R. Lowell, Levertov, Ginsberg, Rich
Short lyric poetry: Jarrell, Wilbur, Ammons, Merwin, J. Wright, Pinsky, Glück
Experimental poetry: Oppen, Creeley, Duncan

Suggested Readings: Theme

Any listing of major themes, and of American works in which those themes appear, will necessarily be reductive. The following listings refer to certain themes that are characteristic of, though not necessarily exclusive to, the American experience.

The Problem of American Identity

This theme so pervades American literature that it might serve as a basis for organizing an entire course, especially for students broadly interested in American history and culture. Following are lists of some of the works in *NAAL* grouped by the issues they raise.

Volume 1

LITERATURE TO 1620 AND 1620–1820

The New World and Its Nature

Casas: *The Coast of Pearls*
Harriot: *A Brief and True Report of the New Found Land of Virginia*
Smith: *A Description of New England*

Bradford: *Of Plymouth Plantation*
R. Williams: *A Key into the Language of America*
Rowlandson: *A Narrative of the Captivity and Restoration*
Crèvecoeur: *Letter X. On Snakes; and on the Humming Bird*
Equiano: *The Interesting Narrative of the Life*
Freneau: *On the Emigration to America and Peopling the Western Country; The Indian Burying Ground; On Mr. Paine's Rights of Man*
Wheatley: *On Being Brought from Africa to America*

Achieving a Personal Voice in the Bay Colony

Bradstreet: Poems
Taylor: Poems
Sewall: *The Diary*

Private Papers as a Way of Knowing

Díaz del Castillo: *The True History of the Conquest of New Spain*
Sewall: *The Diary*
Knight: *The Private Journal of a Journey from Boston to New York*
Byrd: *The Secret Diary*
J. Adams and A. Adams: Letters

The Self and Divine Revelation

Bradstreet: *Contemplations; To My Dear Children*
Wigglesworth: *The Day of Doom*
Taylor: Poems
Mather: *The Wonders of the Invisible World*
Edwards: *Personal Narrative; A Divine and Supernatural Light; Images or Shadows of Divine Things*
Woolman: *The Journal*
Wheatley: *Thoughts on the Works of Providence*

Inventing the Self in the Eighteenth Century

Franklin: *The Way to Wealth; The Autobiography*
Occom: *A Short Narrative of My Life*
Equiano: *The Interesting Narrative of the Life*

Public Discourse and the Formation of a National Character

Crèvecoeur: *Letters from an American Farmer*
Paine: *Common Sense; The Crisis, No. 1; The Age of Reason*
Jefferson: *The Declaration of Independence; Notes on the State of Virginia;* Letters
The Federalist
Murray: *On the Equality of the Sexes*
Rowson: *Charlotte*

1820–1865

Fiction, Poetry, and the Question of American Identity

Irving: *Rip Van Winkle; The Legend of Sleepy Hollow*
Cooper: *The Pioneers*
Bryant: *The Prairies*
Sedgwick: *Cacoethes Scribendi; A Reminiscence of Federalism*

Defining the American Intellect

Emerson: *The American Scholar; The Divinity School Address; Self-Reliance; The Poet; Fate*
Fuller: *The Great Lawsuit*

Problems of Self-Knowledge

Hawthorne: *Young Goodman Brown; The Minister's Black Veil; The Scarlet Letter*
Stowe: *Uncle Tom's Cabin* (Chapters III, IX, XX)

Fantasy, Dreams, and the Private Self

Poe: Poems; *Ligeia*

Slavery and the Achievement of Selfhood

Jacobs: *Incidents in the Life of a Slave Girl*
Douglass: *Narrative of the Life*

The Self as Triumphant

Emerson: *Self-Reliance*
Longfellow: *A Psalm of Life; Excelsior*
Thoreau: *Walden* ("Economy," "Where I Lived," "Spring," "Conclusion")
Whitman: *Leaves of Grass* (esp. *Song of Myself; Live Oak, with Moss*)
Melville: *Moby-Dick* (Chapters XXXVI, XCIV, CXXXII, CXXXV)
Dickinson: 214, 249, 303, 324, 435, 441, 632, 1072, 1125

The Self as Contingent, or Imperiled

Whitman: *Facing West from California's Shores; When Lilacs Last in the Dooryard Bloom'd*
Melville: *Moby-Dick* (Chapters I, X, XVI, XXVIII, XLII, Epilogue); *Bartleby, the Scrivener; Billy Budd, Sailor*
Dickinson: 185, 241, 258, 280, 305, 341, 348, 435, 448, 465, 505, 510, 520, 547, 664, 754, 822, 986, 1099, 1129, 1581, 1651, 1732
Davis: *Life in the Iron-Mills*
Spoffard: *Circumstance*

Volume 2

In the works by writers included in volume 2 of *NAAL*, the question of American identity joins with other compelling issues, and nearly every writer engages with it somehow. Here are some works useful for addressing issues of personal identity in the modern era.

1865–1914

Clemens: *Adventures of Huckleberry Finn*
James: *Daisy Miller; The Beast in the Jungle; The Jolly Corner*
Chopin: *The Awakening*
Freeman: *A New England Nun*
Washington: *Up From Slavery*
Chesnutt: *The Wife of His Youth*
Eastman: *From the Deep Woods to Civilization*
Wharton: *Souls Belated; The Eyes*
Du Bois: *The Souls of Black Folk*
Oskison: *The Problem of Old Harjo*
Chippewa Songs
Bonnin: *Impressions of an Indian Childhood; The School Days of an Indian Girl; An Indian Teacher among Indians*
H. Adams: *The Education*

1914–1945

Black Elk: *Black Elk Speaks*
Masters: Poems
Robinson: Poems
Frost: Poems (esp. *Once by the Pacific; The Gift Outright; Directive*)
Sandburg: *Chicago*
Yezierska: *The Lost "Beautifulness"*
Jeffers: *Shine, Perishing Republic*
McKay: Poems
Hurston: *How It Feels to Be Colored Me; Their Eyes Were Watching God*
Taggard: *O People Misshapen; Mill Town*
Thurber: *The Secret Life of Walter Mitty*
Cummings: *Buffalo Bill's; Poem, or Beauty Hurts Mr. Vinal; "next to of course god america i; i sing of Olaf glad and big*
Toomer: *Cane*
Fitzgerald: *Babylon Revisited*
Dos Passos: *U.S.A.*
H. Crane: *The Bridge*
Hemingway: *The Snows of Kilimanjaro*
Brown: *Mister Samuel and Sam; Master and Man*
Hughes: *Refugee in America; Madam and Her Madam; Madam's Calling Cards; Visitors to the Black Belt; Democracy*
Steinbeck: *The Leader of the People*

AMERICAN PROSE SINCE 1945

Ellison: *Invisible Man*
Bellow: *Looking for Mr. Green*
Miller: *Death of a Salesman*
Paley: *A Conversation with My Father*
Baldwin: *Going to Meet the Man*
Marshall: *Reena*
Momaday: *The Way to Rainy Mountain*
Major: *An Area in the Cerebral Hemisphere*
Reed: *The Last Days of Louisiana Red*
Kingston: *Tripmaster Monkey*
Chávez: *The Last of the Menu Girls*

AMERICAN POETRY SINCE 1945

R. P. Warren: *American Portrait: Old Style*
Bishop: *The Armadillo*
R. Lowell: *For the Union Dead; Skunk Hour*
Wilbur: *Love Calls Us to the Things of This World*
Ginsberg: *Howl; A Supermarket in California; Sunflower Sutra*
Rich: *Diving into the Wreck*

The Individual and the Community

Volume 1

Bradford: *Of Plymouth Plantation*
Mather: *The Wonders of the Invisible World*
Jefferson: *The Declaration of Independence*
Hawthorne: *Young Goodman Brown; The May-Pole of Merry Mount; The Minister's Black Veil; The Scarlet Letter*
Thoreau: *Resistance to Civil Government; Walden*
Douglass: *Narrative of the Life*
Whitman: *Leaves of Grass [Song of Myself]*
Melville: *Moby-Dick; Bartleby, the Scrivener; Billy Budd, Sailor*

Volume 2

Clemens: *Adventures of Huckleberry Finn*
James: *Daisy Miller; The Beast in the Jungle*
Jewett: *A White Heron; The Foreigner*
Chopin: *The Awakening*
Freeman: *A New England Nun; The Revolt of "Mother"*
S. Crane: *The Bride Comes to Yellow Sky; The Blue Hotel*
Oskison: *The Problem of Old Harjo*
Bonnin: *Impressions of an Indian Childhood; The School Days of an Indian Girl; An Indian Teacher among Indians*

H. Adams: *The Education* ("Editor's Preface," Chapters I, XIX)
Masters: *Poems*
Robinson: *Poems*
Cather: *My Ántonia*
Frost: *The Tuft of Flowers; Mending Wall; The Death of the Hired Man; Departmental; Neither out Far nor in Deep*
Anderson: *Winesburg, Ohio*
Eliot: *The Love Song of J. Alfred Prufrock; Tradition and the Individual Talent*
Cummings: *the Cambridge ladies who live in furnished souls; anyone lived in a pretty how town; pity this busy monster,manunkind*
Ellison: *Invisible Man*
Morrison: *Recitatif*

The Problem of Literary Authority

Volume 1

Bradstreet: *The Prologue; The Author to Her Book*
Taylor: *Prologue; Meditation 22; Upon a Wasp Chilled with Cold; Huswifery*
Edwards: *Personal Narrative; Sinners in the Hands of an Angry God*
Franklin: *The Way to Wealth*
Wheatley: *To Mæcenas; To the University of Cambridge, in New England; To S. M., a Young African Painter, on Seeing His Works*
Rowson: *Charlotte*
Irving: *The Legend of Sleepy Hollow*
Emerson: *The American Scholar; The Divinity School Address; Self-Reliance; The Poet*
Hawthorne: *The Scarlet Letter (The Custom-House)*
Poe: *The Philosophy of Composition*
Fuller: *The Great Lawsuit*
Thoreau: *Walden, or Life in the Woods*
Douglass: *Narrative of the Life*
Whitman: *Preface to Leaves of Grass; Leaves of Grass [Song of Myself]; Letter to Ralph Waldo Emerson; Trickle Drops; Here the Frailest Leaves of Me; As I Ebb'd with the Ocean of Life*
Melville: *Hawthorne and His Mosses; Moby-Dick*
Dickinson: 185, 441, 448, 505, 528, 754, 1129, 1545, 1651, *Letters to Thomas Wentworth Higginson*
Alcott: *Transcendental Wild Oats*

Volume 2

Clemens: *Adventures of Huckleberry Finn* (Chapter 1); *Fenimore Cooper's Literary Offenses*
Howells: *Novel-Writing and Novel-Reading*

Washington: *Up From Slavery*
Chesnutt: *The Goophered Grapevine*
Gilman: *The Yellow Wall-paper*
Du Bois: *The Souls of Black Folk*
H. Adams: *The Education* ("Editor's Preface," Chapter I)
Black Elk: *Black Elk Speaks*
Stein: *The Making of Americans*
Frost: *Directive; The Figure a Poem Makes*
Stevens: *A High-Toned Old Christian Woman; Thirteen Ways of Looking at a Blackbird; Of Modern Poetry*
W. C. Williams: *Portrait of a Lady; The Red Wheelbarrow; A Sort of a Song; The Dance* ("In Brueghel's great picture, The Kermess")
Moore: *Poetry; The Mind Is an Enchanting Thing*
Eliot: *The Love Song of J. Alfred Prufrock; Tradition and the Individual Talent*
McKay: *Outcast; If We Must Die; O Word I Love to Sing*
Ellison: *Invisible Man (Prologue)*
Paley: *A Conversation with My Father*
Pynchon: *Entropy*
Bambara: *Medley*
Hannah: *Midnight and I'm Not Famous Yet*

The American Dream

Volume 1

Columbus: Letters
Barlowe: *The First Voyage Made to the Coasts of America*
Smith: *A Description of New England; New England's Trials*
Native American Trickster Tales
T. Morton: *The New English Canaan*
Winthrop: *A Model of Christian Charity*
Franklin: *The Way to Wealth*
Equiano: *The Interesting Narrative of the Life*
Irving: *Rip Van Winkle*
Emerson: *Nature*
Hawthorne: *Young Goodman Brown*
Fuller: *The Great Lawsuit*
Thoreau: *Walden* (Chapters 1, 2)
Douglass: *Narrative of the Life*
Whitman: *Leaves of Grass [Song of Myself]; The Sleepers*
Davis: *Life in the Iron-Mills*

Volume 2

Clemens: *Adventures of Huckleberry Finn*
James: *The Jolly Corner*

Jewett: *A White Heron*
Chopin: *The Awakening*
Garland: *Under the Lion's Paw*
Masters: Poems
Cather: *My Ántonia*
Anderson: *Winesburg, Ohio*
Fitzgerald: *Babylon Revisited*
Dos Passos: *U.S.A.*
H. Crane: *The Bridge*
Steinbeck: *The Leader of the People*
Ellison: *Invisible Man* (Chapter I)
Miller: *Death of a Salesman*
Updike: *Separating*
Mamet: *Glengarry Glen Ross*

The American Landscape

Volume 1

Barlowe: *The First Voyage Made to the Coasts of America*
Bradford: *Of Plymouth Plantation* (Book I, Chapter IX; Chapter X)
T. Morton: *New English Canaan* (Chapter I)
Knight: *The Private Journal of a Journey from Boston to New York*
Byrd: *History of the Dividing Line*
Crèvecoeur: *Letters from an American Farmer*
Jefferson: *Notes on the State of Virginia*
Freneau: *On the Emigration to America and Peopling the Western Country*
Irving: *The Legend of Sleepy Hollow*
Cooper: *The Pioneers*
Bryant: *The Prairies*
Thoreau: *Walden*
Whitman: *Leaves of Grass* [*Song of Myself*] (section 33); *Crossing Brooklyn Ferry*

Volume 2

Clemens: *Adventures of Huckleberry Finn*
Jewett: *A White Heron*
Garland: *Under the Lion's Paw*
Austin: *The Walking Woman*
London: *To Build a Fire*
Cather: *My Ántonia*
Frost: *The Wood-Pile; Birches; "Out, Out—"; Design; Directive*
Sandburg: *Chicago; Prairie Waters by Night; Grass*
Jeffers: *November Surf; Carmel Point*
Momaday: *The Way to Rainy Mountain*
R. Lowell: *The Quaker Graveyard in Nantucket; Skunk Hour*

Warren, *Bearded Oaks*
Brooks: *A Street in Bronzeville*
Ginsberg, *Sunflower Sutra*
J. Wright: *A Blessing*
Snyder: *Milton by Firelight; August on Sourdough, A Visit from Dick Brewer; The Blue Sky*

Immigration and Wandering

Volume 1

White: *The Fifth Voyage*
Bradford: *Of Plymouth Plantation*
Franklin: *Information to Those Who Would Remove to America*
Crèvecoeur: *Letters from an American Farmer* (Letter III)
Equiano: *The Interesting Narrative of the Life*
Freneau: *On the Emigration to America and Peopling the Western Country*
Wheatley: *On Being Brought from Africa to America*
Irving: *A Tour on the Prairies*
Cherokee Memorials
Bryant: *The Prairies*
Thoreau: *Walking*
Whitman: *Leaves of Grass [Song of Myself]; Crossing Brooklyn Ferry*
Melville: *Moby-Dick* (Chapters I, X, XXVI, XXVII, CXI, CXXXII, CXXXV, *Epilogue*)
Davis: *Life in the Iron-Mills*

Volume 2

Clemens: *Adventures of Huckleberry Finn*
Native American Oratory: esp. Cochise
Jewett: *The Foreigner*
Eastman: *From the Deep Woods to Civilization*
Garland: *Under the Lion's Paw*
Austin: *The Walking Woman*
Dreiser: *Old Rogaum and His Theresa*
Oskison: *The Problem of Old Harjo*
Cather: *My Ántonia*
Yezierska: *The Lost "Beautifulness"*
Hurston: *Their Eyes Were Watching God*
Hughes: *Vagabonds; Refugee in America*
Malamud: *The Magic Barrel*
Marshall: *Reena*
Roth: *Defender of the Faith*
Kingston: *Tripmaster Monkey*
Ginsberg: *Howl; A Supermarket in California*

Family Relationships

Volume 1

Cabeza de Vaca: *The Relation* (esp. [*The Malhado Way of Life*], [*Our Life among the Avavares and Arbadaos*], [*Customs of That Region*])

Bradstreet: *To the Memory of My Dear and Ever Honored Father Thomas Dudley Esq.; To Her Father with Some Verses; Before the Birth of One of Her Children; To My Dear and Loving Husband; A Letter to Her Husband, Absent upon Public Employment; Another* [*Letter to Her Husband, Absent upon Public Employment*]; *In Reference to Her Children; In Memory of My Dear Grandchild Elizabeth Bradstreet; In Memory of My Dear Grandchild Anne Bradstreet; On My Dear Grandchild Simon Bradstreet; To My Dear Children*

Wigglesworth: *The Day of Doom*

Rowlandson: *Narrative of the Captivity and Restoration*

Taylor: *Upon Wedlock, and Death of Children*

Sewall: *The Diary*

Mather: *Bonifacius*

Byrd: *The Secret Diary*

J. Adams and A. Adams: Letters

Irving: *Rip Van Winkle*

Hawthorne: *Young Goodman Brown; Rappaccini's Daughter; The Scarlet Letter*

Fuller: *The Great Lawsuit*

Stowe: *Uncle Tom's Cabin*

Jacobs: *Incidents in the Life of a Slave Girl*

Douglass: *Narrative of the Life*

Volume 2

Clemens: *Adventures of Huckleberry Finn*

James: *Daisy Miller*

Jewett: *A White Heron; The Foreigner*

Chopin: *The Awakening*

Freeman: *The Revolt of "Mother"*

Gilman: *The Yellow Wall-paper*

Wharton: *Souls Belated*

Austin: *The Walking Woman*

Du Bois: *The Souls of Black Folk*

Dreiser: *Old Rogaum and His Theresa*

Bonnin: *Impressions of an Indian Childhood; The School Days of an Indian Girl*

H. Adams: *The Education* (Chapter I)

Masters: Poems

Cather: *My Ántonia*

Frost: *The Death of the Hired Man; Home Burial; Birches; "Out, Out—"*

Anderson: *Winesburg, Ohio* (esp. *Mother*); *The Egg*
O'Neill: *Long Day's Journey into Night*
Taggard: *With Child; At Last the Women Are Moving; To My Mother*
Thurber: *The Night the Bed Fell; The Secret Life of Walter Mitty*
Cummings: *if there are any heavens my mother will(all by herself)have; my
   father moved through dooms of love*
Faulkner: *As I Lay Dying*
Wolfe: *The Lost Boy*
Hughes: *Mother to Son*
Steinbeck: *The Leader of the People*
Welty: *Petrified Man*
Cheever: *The Swimmer*
O'Connor: *The Life You Save May Be Your Own; Good Country People*
Barthelme: *A Manual for Sons*
Updike: *Separating*
Walker: *Everyday Use*
Beattie: *Weekend*
Silko: *Lullaby*
Roethke: *My Papa's Waltz*
R. Lowell: *My Last Afternoon with Uncle Devereux Winslow*
Brooks: *a song in the front yard*
Levertov: Olga Poems
Ginsberg: *To Aunt Rose*
Sexton: *Little Girl; The Death of the Fathers*
Rich: *Snapshots of a Daughter-in-Law*
Plath: *Daddy*
Ríos: *Madre Sofía*
Cervantes: *Uncle's First Rabbit*
Song: *Lost Sister*

Race, Segregation, and Slavery

Volume 1

Casas: *The Very Brief Relation*
Cabeza de Vaca: *The Relation*
Smith: *The General History of Virginia*
Bradford: *Of Plymouth Plantation* (Book I, Chapter IX, Chapter X; Book
   II, Chapter XIX)
Williams: *A Key into the Language of America*
Rowlandson: *A Narrative of the Captivity and Restoration*
Byrd: *The Secret Diary*
Franklin: *Remarks Concerning the Savages of North America*
Woolman: *The Journal*
Occom: *A Short Narrative of My Life*
Crèvecoeur: *Letters from an American Farmer* (Letter IX)
Jefferson: *The Declaration of Independence*

Equiano: *The Interesting Narrative of the Life*
Freneau: *The Indian Burying Ground; To Sir Toby*
Wheatley: *On Being Brought from Africa to America; To S. M., a Young African Painter, on Seeing His Works;* Letters
Cherokee Memorials
Apess: *An Indian's Looking-Glass for the White Man*
Emerson: *Last of the Anti-Slavery Lectures*
Longfellow: *The Slave's Dream*
Lincoln: *A House Divided; Second Inaugural Address*
Stowe: *Uncle Tom's Cabin*
Jacobs: *Incidents in the Life of a Slave Girl*
Thoreau: *Resistance to Civil Government; Slavery in Massachusetts*
Douglass: *Narrative of the Life; The Meaning of July Fourth for the Negro*
Whitman: *Leaves of Grass [Song of Myself]; The Sleepers*
Melville: *Benito Cereno*

Volume 2

Clemens: *Adventures of Huckleberry Finn*
Native American Oratory
Harris: *The Wonderful Tar-Baby Story; Mr. Rabbit Grossly Deceives Mr. Fox*
Jewett: *The Foreigner*
Chopin: *The Awakening*
Washington: *Up From Slavery*
Chesnutt: *The Goophered Grapevine*
Eastman: *From the Deep Woods to Civilization*
Du Bois: *The Souls of Black Folk*
Oskison: *The Problem of Old Harjo*
Native American Chants and Songs
Bonnin: *Impressions of an Indian Childhood; The School Days of an Indian Girl; An Indian Teacher among Indians*
Black Elk: *Black Elk Speaks*
Hurston: *The Eatonville Anthology; How It Feels to Be Colored Me; Their Eyes Were Watching God*
Toomer: *Cane*
Brown: Poems
Hughes: Poems
Cullen: Poems
R. Wright: *The Man Who Was Almost a Man*
Ellison: *Invisible Man*
Baldwin: *Going to Meet the Man*
Walker: *Everyday Use*
Hayden: Poems
R. Lowell: *For the Union Dead*
Brooks: Poems
Lorde: Poems

Harper: Poems
Dove: *Thomas and Beulah*

Gender Issues: Women's Lives, Work, and Vision

Volume 1

Winthrop: *The Journal*
Bradstreet: *The Prologue; The Flesh and the Spirit; The Author to Her Book; Before the Birth of One of Her Children; To My Dear and Loving Husband; A Letter to Her Husband, Absent upon Public Employment; Here Follows Some Verses upon the Burning of Our House*
Rowlandson: *A Narrative of the Captivity and Restoration*
Sewall: *The Diary*
Mather: *The Trial of Martha Carrier*
Knight: *The Private Journal of a Journey from Boston to New York*
Byrd: *The Secret Diary*
J. Adams and A. Adams: Letters
Jefferson: *The Declaration of Independence; Letter to Nathaniel Burwell, Esq.*
Irving: *Rip Van Winkle*
Hawthorne: *Rappaccini's Daughter; The Scarlet Letter*
Poe: *The Sleeper; The Raven; To* ———. *Ulalume: A Ballad; Annabel Lee; Ligeia; Fall of the House of Usher; The Philosophy of Composition*
Fuller: *The Great Lawsuit*
Stowe: *Uncle Tom's Cabin*
Jacobs: *Incidents in the Life of a Slave Girl*
Whitman: *Preface to Leaves of Grass; Leaves of Grass [Song of Myself]; Letter to Ralph Waldo Emerson*
Melville: *The Paradise of Bachelors and The Tartarus of Maids*
Dickinson: 67, 214, 249, 303, 312, 348, 435, 441, 505, 510, 520, 528, 732, 754, 952, 1099, 1129, 1545
Davis: *Life in the Iron-Mills*

Volume 2

Clemens: *Adventures of Huckleberry Finn*
Harte: *The Outcasts of Poker Flat*
Howells: *Novel-Writing and Novel-Reading; Editha*
James: *Daisy Miller; The Real Thing; The Beast in the Jungle*
Jewett: *A White Heron; The Foreigner*
Chopin: *At the 'Cadian Ball; The Storm; The Awakening*
Freeman: *A New England Nun; The Revolt of "Mother"*
Gilman: *The Yellow Wall-paper; Why I Wrote The Yellow Wall-paper?*
Austin: *The Walking Woman*
S. Crane: *The Bride Comes to Yellow Sky*
Dreiser: *Old Rogaum and His Theresa*

Oskison: *The Problem of Old Harjo*

Native American Chants and Songs: *Chippewa Songs*

Bonnin: *Impressions of an Indian Childhood; The School Days of an Indian Girl; An Indian Teacher among Indians*

H. Adams: *The Education* (Chapter XXV)

Masters: *Serepta Mason; Margaret Fuller Slack; Lucinda Matlock*

Cather: *My Ántonia*

A. Lowell: *The Captured Goddess; Venus Transiens; Madonna of the Evening Flowers*

Frost: *The Death of the Hired Man; Home Burial*

Anderson: *Winesburg, Ohio*

Yezierska: *The Lost "Beautifulness"*

W. C. Williams: *The Young Housewife; The Widow's Lament in Springtime; To Elsie; The Dead Baby*

Pound: *The River-Merchant's Wife: A Letter*

H. D.: *Leda; At Baia; Helen; The Walls Do Not Fall*

O'Neill: *Long Day's Journey into Night*

Hurston: *Their Eyes Were Watching God*

Millay: Poems

Parker: *De Profundis; Résumé; General Review of the Sex Situation; The Waltz*

Taggard: *With Child; A Middle-aged, Middle-class Woman at Midnight; At Last the Women Are Moving; To My Mother*

Cummings: *the Cambridge ladies who live in furnished souls*

Toomer: *Cane (Fern)*

Dos Passos: *U.S.A. (Mary French)*

Faulkner: *As I Lay Dying*

Bogan: *Women; Cassandra*

Hughes: *Mother to Son; Song for a Dark Girl; Madam and Her Madam; Madam's Calling Cards*

Rukeyser: *Effort at Speech Between Two People*

Welty: *Petrified Man*

T. Williams: *A Streetcar Named Desire*

Malamud: *The Magic Barrel*

Ellison: *Invisible Man* (Chapter I)

O'Connor: *The Life You Save May Be Your Own; Good Country People*

Updike: *Separating*

Walker: *Everyday Use*

Beattie: *Weekend*

Silko: *Lullaby*

Chávez: *The Last of the Menu Girls*

Erdrich: *Fleur*

Niedecker: Poems

Roethke: *Frau Bauman, Frau Schmidt, and Frau Schwartze*

Bishop: *In the Waiting Room; The Moose; One Art*

Hayden: *Homage to the Empress of the Blues*

Brooks: Poems

Levertov: Poems (esp. Olga Poems)
Ginsberg: *To Aunt Rose*
Sexton: Poems
Rich: Poems
Plath: Poems
Lorde: Poems
Dove: *Thomas and Beulah*
Ríos: *Madre Sofía*
Cervantes: Poems
Song: Poems

Politics and War

Volume 1

Columbus: Letters
Casas: *The Very Brief Relation*
Díaz del Castillo: *The True History of the Conquest of New Spain*
Cabeza de Vaca: *The Relation*
Stories of the Beginning of the World: *The Story of the Flood*
Bradford: *Of Plymouth Plantation*
Rowlandson: *A Narrative of the Captivity and Restoration*
Franklin: *An Edict by the King of Prussia; The Sale of the Hessians; The Autobiography* (esp. [Part Three])
J. Adams and A. Adams: Letters
Paine: *Common Sense; The Crisis, No. 1; The Age of Reason*
Jefferson: *The Declaration of Independence*
The Federalist
Freneau: *On Mr. Paine's Rights of Man*
Wheatley: *To the Right Honorable William, Earl of Dartmouth; To His Excellency General Washington*
Irving: *Rip Van Winkle*
Cherokee Memorials
Hawthorne: *My Kinsman, Major Molineux*
Lincoln: *A House Divided; Address Delivered at the Dedication of the Cemetery at Gettysburg; Second Inaugural Address*
Thoreau: *Resistance to Civil Government*
Douglass: *The Meaning of July Fourth for the Negro*
Whitman: *Drum-Taps; When Lilacs Last in the Dooryard Bloom'd; Specimen Days*
Melville: *Battle-Pieces; Billy Budd, Sailor*

Volume 2

Bierce: *An Occurrence at Owl Creek Bridge*
Native American Oratory
Eastman: *From the Deep Woods to Civilization*

S. Crane: *An Episode of War*
Native American Chants and Songs
Black Elk: *Black Elk Speaks*
Taggard: *Mill Town*
Roth: *Defender of the Faith*
Hannah: *Midnight and I'm Not Famous Yet*
Jarrell: *The Death of the Ball Turret Gunner; Second Air Force*
R. Lowell: *For the Union Dead*
Brooks: *The White Troops Had Their Orders But the Negroes Looked Like Men; The Blackstone Rangers*

CHAPTER 7

Teaching Notes for Individual Periods, Authors, and Works

Because *NAAL* contains excellent period introductions, author headnotes, and bibliographies at the end of each volume, these teaching notes emphasize comparisons among individual authors and ways of relating their works to large-scale questions that may work for you as central issues in the course. The main purpose here is to suggest ways to *introduce* material to intelligent, reasonably mature readers who may not initially feel any bond with it or see any access into it. These notes, which are arranged chronologically following the *NAAL* table of contents, also suggest ways of encouraging students to think across periods and genres and to sense the development of literary traditions at given historical moments.

Volume 1

Literature to 1620

Over the past twenty years, in conversations largely among ourselves, scholars have grown accustomed to talking about "the literature of the Discovery" as a literature about cultural conflict. In bringing together these works from the century or so before the English colonies really began to take root, we have found a compelling drama about the opening encounters between a European and a Native American ethos, and about the momentous effect that each culture had on the other. Nonetheless, some of your students, who probably know little of that academic dialogue, will have questions like the following in mind—even if, at the outset of the course, they feel shy about voicing them.

1. How is this material "American literature" or even a significant precursor of American literature? Much of it was written by Europeans who never thought of themselves as belonging to anyplace other than their homeland; much of the rest wasn't really "written" in the strict sense at all but was spoken by members of cultures without written language—and in contexts that no quantity of headnotes or footnotes can make fully accessible to most of us. And all of this was set down, or overheard and translated and transcribed by outsiders, a very long time ago.

2. If so many of these works were never even published (in the modern sense) until very recently and were not written for any sort of publication, then what sort of reading are we engaged in here? Are we reading as any conventional kind of literary public, or as antiquarians, or as intruders?

3. Much of this material was not originally written in English and had no direct impact on writers who used English—and since this is (in all likelihood) an "English" class, labeled that way in the course catalog, why are we bothering with it, except perhaps to pay some kind of politically necessary homage before getting on with the real course?

Bewilderment of this kind can be a resource. It can help open up not just honest, lively access to this material from the early historical periods, but also core issues related to the creation, the teaching, and the learning of literary history.

This section can also help students reconsider the idea that the most interesting early writings from North America, writings in which the continent and its indigenous people had an impact on the consciousness of the European visitor, were all products of the English explorations and migrations. A drama begins here: a hubbub of voices in different languages, from different places, the verbal record of what Franklin later described as a "great mixing of peoples from the whole Atlantic basin" and as "a many-sided process of influence and exchange that ultimately produced the hybrid cultural universe of the Atlantic world." Indeed, as the Native American creation myths indicate, the continent was already "peopled" when the Europeans arrived, and the languages of the native inhabitants of the Americas would also contribute to this hybrid cultural universe. One good effect of including this section in your syllabus is that students can glimpse American experience as multicultural from the beginning, with an array of European peoples encountering a wide variety of nations already here.

To give students a sense that this many-voiced beginning of American literature is not a dead-end historical moment, you might briefly jump ahead to Lorna Dee Cervantes's poem *Visions of Mexico While at a Writing Symposium in Port Townsend, Washington,* from Volume 2. Here is a living Latina American writer who is writing in English as the dominant language of the United States yet who is reopening for herself the colonial experience and speculating on its connections to her own, and our own, identity. The "Literature to 1620" section invites students to encounter the possibility that American literature is more fluid than these boundaries; it invites students to cross them.

CHRISTOPHER COLUMBUS

Using Columbus to get the course started and open questions about the "literary" status of personal accounts and letters written centuries ago in languages other than English, and in immensely different cultural situations, can be ideal, because Columbus eventually became a huge figure in the mythology of the Americas. You can loosen the class up with a quick review of old and newer artifacts of that legend: the cities, rivers, and countries named after him, the countless statues in public parks and squares, the two handsome tombs (he is buried in grand style in Havana and also in Seville, and there is still no settlement to the dispute over which church has the real remains!), and the two big-budget films released in 1992 to mark the five hundredth anniversary of the San Salvador landing. The literary impact of Columbus shows up in the hagiographic biography by Washington Irving; the once-popular epic poem by Joel Barlow; and even the jokes in Samuel Clemens's *Innocents Abroad,* in which European guides expect American tourists to be floored by the sight of any object related to the Great Discoverer. All this can raise student interest in trying to hear the actual voice (more or less) of the actual human being who started the whole drama of European conquest and settlement.

To find an element of psychological familiarity in Columbus, these letters can be read as showing us a figure of deep and unresolved conflict. There is piety here, and covetousness, and self-righteousness, and pride, and political servility and manipulation; and these mingled inclinations and drives, even when seen through the thick distorting glass of so much intervening time, can make him seem eminently real. If one of your course objectives is to make these readings memorable and accessible, then attention to these very familiar contradictions can take the discussion in good directions

What happens if you read Columbus's 1493 letter with his 1503 *Letter to Ferdinand and Isabella Regarding the Fourth Voyage,* in which he complains bitterly of his own abandonment and betrayal and reveals his disillusionment with the experience of colonization? What do these letters suggest about the relative value of kings and great cities, the power of Spanish explorers, and the relative "importance" of the "people without number" who already inhabit the islands?

BARTOLOMÉ DE LAS CASAS

The selection from Casas's *Very Brief Relation* will open up interesting questions about assumptions held by Spanish explorers in their treatment of the Native Americans and challenge the notion that all these explorers were blind to the human worth of the people they encountered or mindless apologists for colonialism. Ask students to speculate on Casas's motives as a writer. Casas witnesses horrors in the Spanish treatment of native peoples, and the moral outrage expressed by this rough-and-tumble soldier-adventurer is based in Judeo-Christian teachings and ethics. This is the opening of a long and very important dialogue, as writers on the American continent try to reconcile political and social practice with religious values and to close the rift between professed creeds and actual practice. Equiano, Douglass, and Stowe are just three of the upcoming writers who will base their interventions on similar principles. A bit of foreshadowing can be effective here, in regard to the ways in which America will quarrel with itself.

HERNÁN CORTÉS

Cortés is a list maker, as were many of the explorer-writers who roamed the Americas and meticulously classified and cataloged what they saw. His *First Letter from Mexico to the Spanish Crown* contrasts dramatically in both content and style with Casas's inventories of atrocities and seems provocative in its suggestion that Mexico's greatest value lies in the material riches that can be received—or plundered—here. Students might be asked to speculate on the moral and psychological effects of inventory lists, of cultures and peoples reduced to items in a vast audit. Even though so much is lost in the move from the fifteenth century to the late twentieth, and from Renaissance Spanish to modern English, the impact of this way of seeing seems to come through unscathed. People seem to matter little in Cortés's account, and his strategy of conquest comes down to us, in this narrative, as an acquisition of riches.

BERNAL DÍAZ DEL CASTILLO

Like Casas, Díaz del Castillo writes a narrative of witness. Ask students to explore the differences between the imagined audiences for these narratives and those by Columbus and Cortés, who are writing official missives to the Spanish Crown. Does the difference in the implied reader make for differences in the kinds of observations Casas and Díaz del Castillo make and the images they choose? Does literature result in part from the choice to write for almost anyone other than the king and queen?

Díaz del Castillo's narrative *Gifts Presented to Cortés* provides more of the social context than does Cortés's list. Students can find evidence in this brief narrative that the meeting between Spaniards and Aztecs served as an encounter on both sides. The description of the physical resemblance between "our Cortés" and "the other Cortés," the Aztec chief Quintalbor, provides an emblem of the facing off between invaders and indigenous people. The first battle between Cortés and Montezuma is presented as a rhetorical one: whose insistence will allow the speaker to make the next move—Montezuma's that Cortés not try to travel to the Aztec capital to meet him or Cortés's that he must account to his own king and, therefore, must see Montezuma in person?

The instructor's role in this text, as in the following segment, *The Approach to Tenochtitlán,* is to help students locate the understated moments of tension between Cortés and his forces and Montezuma and the Aztecs.

Otherwise, the descriptions of violence and the quick shifts from apparent negotiations to killing and conquest, from gift giving to conflict, seem inexplicable. On Montezuma's side, Díaz del Castillo reports, the Aztecs call the Spaniards *teules,* or "gods," and this may explain why Montezuma does not simply crush Cortés, even though his own gods and priests (*papas*) urge him to do so. Yet such quick shifts perhaps convey the astonishment of Díaz del Castillo himself that such a marvelous place as Tenochtitlán should have been destroyed so quickly.

Another moment that also conveys both the tensions between Cortés and Montezuma and the volatility of their encounters occurs near the beginning of the *Cortés in Difficulties* segment. Díaz del Castillo writes, "On hearing Cortés say that he would have to come with us and visit the Emperor, Montezuma was even sadder than before." This "excited conversation" leads the soldiers to wonder "when the fighting would begin," but the shift from apparent diplomacy to anxiety continues to signal the understated conflict of the encounter between Cortés and Montezuma. The fact that Montezuma delays any attack and instead resorts to persuasion, expressing his annoyance that Cortés does not tell him about the arrival of Narvaez's ships and claiming to be "delighted" that "now you can all return to Spain without more discussion," suggests that Montezuma is simply not confident of victory over Cortés and Cortés's god.

Implicit in *The True History of the Conquest of New Spain* is the myth that has been perpetuated in Mexican history and culture that it was a native woman, Doña Marina—often called "La Malinche" to refer to the fact that she is believed to have been Cortés's mistress (Cortés in this text is referred to as Malinche)—who betrayed the Aztec Empire. She is visible in this text at the moment when Cortés first meets Montezuma, and she serves as his translator ("Cortés, speaking through Doña Marina, answered him"). Later, she seems to be in Cortés's power or employ and continues to serve as a translator. Discuss with students the effect of introducing a woman as the cultural translator. In attempting to translate, or to mediate, between two such oppositional interests as those of Cortés and Montezuma, Doña Marina is said to have betrayed her country. By implication, without her treachery, the Aztec Empire might not have fallen. Ask students to consider this rationally by focusing on the behavior of the Spaniards in this and in other narratives and to speculate on the reasons for the survival of the myth of La Malinche.

The narrator of *The True History of the Conquest* experiences the effects of colonial conquest in his own body. Ask students to locate the passages where this becomes clear and to speculate on his responses. Help students see the connection between the narrator's role in the conquest of Mexico and his inability to sleep "even when I go to the villages of my *encomienda.*" Does Díaz del Castillo find himself unable to rest because he ever after expects the descendants of the Aztecs to rise up and avenge the conquest?

Ask students to consider the Aztec practice of cutting out hearts from living persons. Viewed from the perspective of "encounter"—here between Aztec and Spanish forms of violence—discuss colonialism as one form of cutting out the heart from existing societies, and invite students to extend the metaphor in specific ways.

ÁLVAR NÚÑEZ CABEZA DE VACA

Cabeza de Vaca's *Relation* contrasts markedly with the narratives of Cortés and Díaz del Castillo; and although this text is written from a European point of view, it attempts to present the native peoples' way of life as much as possible from the inside. Thus the *Relation* serves as evidence that the colonial encounter did indeed have two sides and that the native peoples of the Americas did not view themselves as deficient before the arrival of the Europeans. Ask students to detail customs and manners of the various people Cabeza de Vaca describes. Notice that he is interested in aspects of their lives that bring women, children, and domestic life into view.

Students could trace his references to women's lives in particular and thereby bring women into focus. Cabeza de Vaca's interest in and concern for women (he writes in *The Long Swing-Around* that "among this people, women are better treated than in any part of the Indies we had come through") help compensate for the lack of attention most other narrators of texts in the "Literature to 1620" section give to women except as myths— such as the myth of Doña Marina in Díaz del Castillo's narrative or, later, the myth of Pocahontas in the writings of John Smith.

Cabeza de Vaca comes close to understanding and communicating with various American Indian groups. Locate with students those moments in his narrative when he seems to come closest to communicating—one may be his description of *Our Life among the Avavares and Arbadaos,* in which he describes dressing, eating, and dwelling in the way of his hosts. Cabeza de Vaca resembles a missionary or an anthropologist in his approach to the native peoples he encountered, expressing his great respect for them: "They are a substantial people with a capacity for unlimited development." Perhaps the most significant test of how the Native Americans themselves received Cabeza de Vaca's respect and understanding for their way of life emerges in *The Falling-Out with Our Countrymen,* when the American Indians refuse to believe that Cabeza de Vaca and his group were from the same race as the "Christian slavers." The passage near the end of the excerpt that begins "Conferring among themselves, they replied that the Christians lied" conveys the Indians' view of Cabeza de Vaca in imagery that comes close to giving them voice in this narrative.

In this beautiful work, students can deepen their understanding of "encounter" narratives. Cabeza de Vaca makes ample room in his work for readers to see the native people's view of their encounter with him as well as his encounter with them. In a further complication of the term, the *Relation* shows Europeans encountering their own internal contradictions. If resistance to the brutal practices of conquest and colonization was itself capable of transforming one group of Spaniards (Cabeza de Vaca and his group) into men the American Indians no longer recognized as "Christian slavers," then who are the true Europeans? Was it conquest and colonization that turned civilized men into monsters (so that Cabeza de Vaca may be viewed as someone who resists that transformation), or was it encounters with the native peoples themselves that turned Spaniards into potentially civilized men? In any event, the *Relation* offers an encounter between the elements of internal contradiction within European conquest itself.

STORIES OF THE BEGINNING OF THE WORLD

As Arnold Krupat writes in his introductory notes on these creation stories, both the Iroquois and the Pima narratives included here are in a Western chronological sense misplaced, since these versions date from the nineteenth and early twentieth centuries. However, including creation stories in the "Literature to 1620" section of *NAAL* is pedagogically appropriate. First, these written narratives are transcriptions or translations of oral stories whose origins long precede such transcription. Second, the Iroquois and Pima narratives present a worldview that contrasts markedly with the worldview the colonizers brought with them. Although these mythological narratives do not address the relatively more recent historical period of contact with the European invaders, they serve as representations of early Native American culture. Teaching them side by side with European narratives of invasion and colonization allows students to view their own reading as encounters of cultures as well as of historical persons.

Instructors who assign these materials in an American literature course will probably be coming to them from Western cultural perspectives—on mythological or cosmological origins and on narrative forms and elements. And students will probably be in the same situation. Is there a way for most of us to teach Native American materials in the American literature classroom without expertise in these cultures?

The answer has a great deal to do with what we, as teachers, assume that a survey course is about, on the most basic level. A survey, or an introduction, can mean a paying of ritualized or perfunctory attention or it can mean the opening of a much-longer acquaintance, deepening and broadening over the years, with many different texts that now belong, or that *might* belong, in a diverse culture's conversation with itself, about its very nature. If you have the latter intention in mind, then two mistakes to avoid in regard to these early Native American materials are probably obvious: a cursory glance that conveys, implicitly or otherwise, the sense that these texts are somehow beside the point and a presumptuous "analysis" or dramatized empathy, either of which can work the same kind of harm. As the century ends, we are still very much rethinking, as a culture, nearly everything having to do with our relationship to these recovered materials: how to read them, in what sort of context, and why. The best strategy, therefore, may be to keep such questions open with your class, assuring students that such issues are not to be dismissed quickly or lightly and that their participation is needed to help move our collective thinking forward. Good strategies for reading these Native American materials, in the very Euro-American context of a modern college or high school class-room, will take shape if literary culture and history can be presented as something changeful, alive, and available to all who read patiently and in good faith.

One excellent and influential essay on teaching Native American texts is Barre Toelken and Tacheeni Scott's "Poetic Retranslation and the 'Pretty Languages of Yellowman,'" in Toelken, ed., *Traditional Literatures of the American Indian: Texts and Interpretations* (1981), a volume with many strong suggestions and perspectives. Without discouraging readings by outsiders, Toelken draws our attention to the complications of approaching Native American texts, across the barrier of translation, and the enormous differences in cultural context and the historical moment. His encouragement to us, to try to proceed in spite of these obstacles and in full cognizance of them, is worth bearing in mind:

> I have encouraged—even forced—my students in recent years to go beyond mere reading of native literature and into the troublesome, frustrating, and often impossible task of recovering something of the original. "But what if we can't *speak* Tsimshian?" they ask: "How are we to presume we can reconstitute the original presentation properly?" My response is to suggest that—using the materials at hand—we can at least come *closer* to real presentation than is now provided for us in the awkwardly serviceable and often primitive-sounding prose translations of linguists who were not anyhow as involved in the study of live literature as in the recovery of almost moribund languages (p. 69).

Obviously there are limits to how much contextualizing material can be included in an anthology covering four hundred years and many different North American voices. Nonetheless, the headnotes and the helps in this section, and in other Native American materials in *NAAL,* can take us fairly far—at the very least into a recognition that other cultures were present, active, and imaginatively engaged on this continent at the time of European settlement. Students should understand that the American experience was being looked at passionately, and from many perspectives, as European and native cultures encountered one another.

Another good essay about the complications of reading these texts in English translations, and in the context of the American college campus, is Paula Gunn Allen's "Kochinnenako in Academe," in Robyn Warhol and Diane Price Herndl, eds., *Feminisms* (1991). Allen proposes a "feminist-tribal" approach to Native American narrative, allowing readers to understand the kinds of agency that Native American narratives give women. For Allen, these stories can be read as about balance rather than conflict, about agency rather than heroism, and about background rather than a possibly overvalued foreground. The art she speaks of, running counter to Western expectations, is about a "living web of definition and depth" with an "importance of balance among all elements." As Allen describes it, "tribal art functions something like a forest in which all elements coexist, where each is integral to the being of the others." See also Allen's *The Sacred Hoop: Recovering the Feminine in American Indian Traditions* (1986).

The Iroquois Creation Story

Because of the shifts in context and expectations required to engage with these works, it is important to devote some class time to close reading of these stories. But close reading, the way one closely reads Bradstreet or Eliot, will not take students where they want (or expect) to go—that is, to a full understanding of the human sensibility in these texts. That may have to wait, and you may need to reassure your students that patience and comfort with uncertainty are required of all mature readers who seek to move across time, landscape, and large cultural barriers. As you assign other Native American texts, these will create an intertextuality, and instructors will receive much help from the headnotes and introductory materials in *NAAL* in providing the historical and oral/literary contexts for Native American stories and storytellers.

For this first experience with Native American mythology, you might encourage your students to read comparatively, bearing in mind the creation stories that most of them already know and scrutinizing the differences between these Native American creation myths and accounts from other cultures. Two interesting differences to take note of right away: first, the Native American stories do not enforce a distinction that most students are used to—a distinction between the Creator and world created—and second, these stories do not talk about a world somewhere else—an Eden, a Mount Ararat, or some other landscape far away from the experience of the listener or reader. The world spoken of is a world that is right here, to be gazed on and known firsthand as the tale is told again and again.

These differences matter because, for most of your students, reading these stories will require a recognition of certain habits of mind, habits of imagining and telling, that are culturally contingent and yet rarely recognized by us as paradigms, as ways of organizing not just experience but our narratives to one another about experience. As an exercise to stimulate discussion and an awareness of such differences, construct with students a visual "map" or interpretive sketch of the events of the *Iroquois Creation Story*. You will probably develop a diagram with a vertical axis: the woman who conceived (note Krupat's reference to one version in which she conceives parthenogenetically) begins in the "upper world" but falls to the "dark world," where "monsters" collect enough earth to make a seat for her, on which she gives birth to the twins, the good mind and the bad mind. In *Native American Literature* (Boston: Twayne, 1985), Andrew Wiget provides a useful diagram that suggests connections between specific events in origin stories and genres of Native American oral narrative. The twins transform the earthen seat, the Great Island that the monsters have created for the woman who fell, into a world that begins to resemble a world of humans rather than of mythical people; indeed, the story ends with the twins retiring from the earth, as the creation has been accomplished. Wiget's diagram maps three "generations" of beings: the original parent (the woman who fell from the sky), the twins (one of whom, the good mind, creates the earth and, through deceiving the bad mind, sets in motion the "nature of the system" we know as the world), and the first people with souls (who come to inhabit the universe). Within these three levels, numerous narratives are possible; the *Iroquois Creation Story* students have before them is only one variant of a story whose main elements may be relatively fixed but that relies on communal and participatory retelling. Communal participation results from viewing creation as a process of descent rather than as a one-time construction in a single god's image.

Students may also read the creation account in the Book of Genesis and compare elements: descent in the Iroquois story suggests a *process* of creation rather than the completed act of a single creator; the woman who fell from the sky may have become parthenogenetically pregnant, thereby linking the origins of the world to women (or to an asexual being capable of parthenogenesis) rather than to a patriarchal god (note that the Iroquois were matrilineal); and the monsters in the "dark world" are benign compared with the devils that inhabit Western conceptions of hell, and these monsters actually help the falling woman give birth. The good twin creates "two images of the dust of the ground in his own likeness," unlike the single male image the Western God creates in Genesis, where the female image is later created from a rib of the male.

Another exercise that helps open up the *Iroquois Creation Story* for Western-oriented students involves making a list of the characters in the myth and trying to determine each one's particular contribution, without which the creation would not be complete. While a Western narrative might suggest that the woman who fell from the sky and the good twin are "central" characters, the Iroquois story highlights the importance of the other characters and the interdependence of all. The turtle, for example, who offers to endure the falling woman's weight and who enlarges to become an island of earth is essential to the origin of the world, as are the contrivances of the bad twin, without whom we would not have mountains, waterfalls, reptiles, and the idea that even the good twin's powers are limited (as are those of humans). This suggests that there is no human agency without help from a variety of participants and that all creative powers must know their limits. If possible, read Wiget's beautiful interpretation of the story of the woman who fell. He says, in part,

> The Earth-Diver is the story of the Fortunate Fall played out against a landscape more vast than Eden and yet on a personal scale equally as intimate. It is a story of losses, the loss of celestial status, the loss of life in the depths of the sea. But it is also the story of gifts, especially the gift of power over life, the gift of agriculture to sustain life, and the gift of the vision to understand man's place as somewhere between the abyss and the stars.

Pima Stories of the Beginning of the World

As Wiget's diagram of Native American oral narrative genres makes clear, there are two main story lines within various Native American creation myths: the stories that center around the "woman who fell from the sky," and those that depict the "emergence" of the world. The Pima *Story of the Creation* provides students with an example of the second kind, although students who wish to explore very different conceptions of emergence myths may want to read, or read about, Navajo or Pueblo myths. One of the images that distinguishes the emergence narrative, and here gives the Pima myth some elements of that genre, is the ability of Juhwertamahkai to poke a hole in the sky with his staff and to "emerge" through this hole into another dimension, where he begins his act of world creation anew. Some scholars have associated the emergence of a people through a hole in the ground or sky with the numerous migrations of Native American peoples. These myths may implicitly record those migrations.

In discussing this story, students can compare and contrast within Native American traditions—locating similarities and differences between Iroquois and Pima myths—as well as among other Native American and Western versions of "genesis." The point to make here is that even though some of the Native American creation stories follow two main story lines, the very concept of creation, or origins, itself seems to have inspired the creation of many variations on creation itself. Unlike the Judeo-Christian story told in Genesis, which identifies one and only one story of origin, Native American traditions offer many different creation stories, as if the fecundity of the creation process presupposed multiplicity rather than monotheism or the construction of a single dominant *mythos*. And this particular Pima story does not include many elements of other emergence narratives.

At first glance, the Pima *Story of the Creation* resembles the story of Genesis more closely than the Iroquois story. In the Pima, as in Genesis, the world begins "in the beginning" with a person who floated in the darkness; in Genesis, the spirit of God hovers over the darkness. Understanding the perils of the transcription of Native American legends is crucial to "reading" the opening of this story, because the language of the transcription itself echoes the language of Genesis. This leads to the question of whether this language truly characterizes the original Pima oral narrative or if it represents that oral story as viewed through the eyes of a translator who, despite his intentions to transcribe the stories of Thin Leather, still views creation through the lens of the Western Bible.

As the story progresses, it ceases to resemble Genesis. Indeed, Juhwertamahkai makes several mistakes in the process of creating the world. Unlike the Western god, whose destruction of the world by flood is blamed on human behavior, Juhwertamahkai takes a trial-and-error approach to creation, starting over or letting the sky fall each time the creative act sets in motion a process that will not sustain life. As the notes point out, he makes the world four times before he is satisfied with his creation, establishing the number four (corresponding to north, south, east, and west) as significant in Native American cosmology.

The Pima *Story of the Creation* includes the birth of Coyote, the trickster of many Native American legends, and the arrival of Seeurhuh, or the elder, who in this story seems to move the creation into a world of negotiation between powerful personages who "claimed to have been here first," perhaps suggesting the process of relating stories about the organization of the social world into native cultures. In the narrative that follows, the Pima *Story of the Flood,* Seeurhuh, or Ee-ee-toy, and Juhwertamahkai seem to engage in a struggle to determine, as the headnote points out, not creation but re-creation, "the reestablishment or rebirth of the divine, natural, and social orders." Ask students in reading the *Story of the Flood* to note images or details that indicate imbalance in this social order. For example, even though Juhwertamahkai has already created people, Ee-ee-toy makes a man of his own, arming him with bow and arrow. Then, when this man marries, word of him strikes fear in the marriageable daughter of the South Doctor (presumably a "doctor of the earth" or shaman with powers that resemble those of Juhwertamahkai and Ee-ee-toy). The arrival of the flood itself is an image of turmoil, as is the array of plans the doctors and other persons/animals make for escaping the flood. As the story unfolds, the arrival of the flood is linked to the birth of a child from the young man who turns into a pregnant woman; the birth produces springs that "would gush forth from under every tree and on every mountain."

The struggle between Ee-ee-toy and Juhwertamahkai may also be an attempt to achieve balance. One way of showing this is to ask students to trace and try to account for Juhwertamahkai's behavior during and after the flood. The two doctors, Juhwertamahkai and Ee-ee-toy, and the person/animal Toehahvs (Coyote) face directions that may imply territories or tribal lands, and they make new dolls, or persons, to replace those who have drowned. Juhwertamahkai deliberately makes dolls that will not survive, "because he remembered some of his people had escaped the flood thru a hole in the earth, and he intended to visit them and he did not want to make anything better than they were to take the place of them." But the defective dolls break to pieces, Juhwertamahkai turns into waste and excretion, and the original creator of the world in the Pima *Story of the Creation* brings sickness and death into that world. While the *Story of the Flood* may help listeners to understand death, and especially war, it may also associate such things with the work of the spirits; Juhwertamahkai's creation ultimately includes both birth and death, and this establishes order in the world.

ARTHUR BARLOWE AND THOMAS HARRIOT

As noted in the comments on Cabeza de Vaca, the encounters between the Spaniards and the American Indians revealed an internal contradiction within the Conquest. This internal contradiction may seem more muted to students in the earliest English narratives, but there are enough similarities between Spanish and English encounters to suggest patterns. Arthur Barlowe's account of Wingina and his people resembles that of Cabeza de Vaca; and like the Spaniard, Barlowe also is interested in the customs of the American Indians and in bringing women into focus: he describes their material lives in great detail. Barlowe's description of the people ranks with the respect Cabeza de Vaca showed; indeed, Barlowe's description creates a very different image of Native Americans from that of later English authors, especially when he writes, "We found the people most gentle, loving, and faithful, void of all guile and treason, and such as live after the manner of the golden age."

After reading Barlowe, students will find Harriot much less perceptive and more insensitive to the native peoples he meets. Ask students to locate evidence of Harriot's inability to move outside his own perspective: early in his *Brief and True Report,* he writes, "In respect of us, they are a poor people, and for want of skill and judgment in the knowledge and use of our things, do esteem our trifles before things of greater value." He also uses the American Indians' mythology to demonstrate their ignorance, thereby illustrating for students the limitations of his perspective.

One aspect of this mythology that contrasts markedly with Christianity concerns the Native American belief that "a woman was made first, who by the working of one of the gods, conceived and brought forth children." Harriot does not need to point out the absurdity of such a myth of origins, given the Bible's account of Adam; students in today's classroom will also notice the ideological link between religious belief and English attitudes toward women. Part of what Franklin terms Harriot's "propagandistic" purpose involves the conversion of the native peoples to "great doubts of their own [faith], and no small admiration of ours"; this reputed "conversion" lends credence to the English view of themselves as superior—in technology ("mathematical instruments" and "writing and reading"), in religion (God "so specially loved" the colonizers), and in ideology (any people who could make the error of believing they were descended from women must indeed be a "simple people"—they do conclude that the English are "not born of women").

SAMUEL DE CHAMPLAIN

Champlain's narrative suggests a different relationship with native peoples than some of the earlier Spanish and English explorers. His *Voyages* conveys a keener awareness of how to negotiate with people in an established, indigenous, and powerful culture. The story that Champlain tells recognizes the agency of the native peoples he meets, takes them seriously, and acknowledges the limitations of his own expedition and European power. At the end of Chapter VIII, he included the detail that his own musket "exploded in my hands and nearly killed me"; at the end of Chapter XIV, members of his force make a fatal miscalculation, disobey his orders, and leave themselves wide open to attack.

Encounter involves discovery on the part of each side that each is in effect being "discovered." The passage (and Champlain's entire account) contrasts markedly with the narratives of Columbus, Cortés, and Harriot, all of whom seemed to believe that they might observe and judge the Native American without in turn being seen.

JOHN WHITE AND GEORGE PERCY

The brief excerpts from John White and George Percy can be read together as accounts of the early results of the English encounter with colonization. White writes about the disappearance of the colony at Roanoke, and Percy writes about "the starving time" in the Virginia colonies. Of the two, Percy's is the more interesting formally, because it allows students to contrast his use of the catalog with earlier uses—the extensive lists of bounty in the early Spanish narratives, the inventories of features of landscape, the mappings of the Americas. The extensive list of deaths in Percy offers a commentary on the early harvest of exploration and colonization. The experience of the English colonists proved them to be less godlike than Harriot claimed. The measure of English greatness becomes not victory on the battlefield but survival, made possible by Indians.

JOHN SMITH

With Smith, many find themselves in more comfortable territory—not just because Smith, an Englishman, has become part of the American mythology but also because his narrative is different, and more familiar in shape and pace, than the others encountered thus far. Students may want to look at *The General History* as an American adventure story and observe ways in which it configures actual events and experiences to appeal to a London audience. The moment of encounter has passed, for Smith, and the shift to settlement and exploitation has begun. Indeed, Smith's job was to make the Americas safe for colonial growth; and as his *General History of Virginia* demonstrates, when "trade and courtesy" failed, he resorted to force.

Most scholars suggest that Smith's account of Pocahontas may be mostly fiction; and students may want to take note of another important instance of this archetypal story of the young woman who crosses boundaries and changes the world. If students want to talk about the Disney restyling of this story or other ways in which it has been reworked to reflect values of other times in our cultural history, why not encourage them? What we have here, after all, is a supremely literary moment—a moment that not only unfolds by the rules of old tales of love and adventure but also inspires a long succession of other American imaginative texts.

Pocahontas does not survive as a cultural myth in the United States in the way La Malinche does in Mexico. Ask students to speculate on why this is the case. In Mexico, the myth of a treacherous Doña Marina represents the betrayal of one culture to another, in a nation where native peoples and Europeans have commingled and where native strains remain strong but culturally subordinate. In the myth of La Malinche, she betrays Mexico itself. In the United States, Native American cultures did not become synonymous with American culture, and thus Pocahontas has not come down to us as a betrayer of American interests.

Smith's approach to women—Native American women in particular—also anticipated attitudes about women and racial differences that would become features of colonialism, surviving to the present time. In this way, reading the "Literature to 1620" section also becomes an encounter for our students with their own attitudes toward exploitation, toward racial differences, and toward the role of women in today's society.

NATIVE AMERICAN TRICKSTER TALES

The headnotes to this section will be invaluable for your students to read carefully, not just for their cautions and its suggestions about historical context but also as a basis for considering whether "literature" can have any stable definition or description across times and cultures and whether the transformations worked by the passage of time and the change of context and even language are inevitably a loss, a harm, or a gain. These matters, when brought out early in a course, can intensify the interest and participation of students who have been wondering (or grumbling) about the cultural worth or aesthetic appeal, to themselves and contemporary America, of most of what you have been reading thus far (private letters, eyewitness accounts by soldiers and explorers and other amateur or infelicitous writers, propaganda for colonization and exploitation).

One cautious generalization that we can begin with is that these stories are about change, about shape-shifting: change in physical form; change in relationships among natural and supernatural creatures (including human beings); changes of mind and intention. Furthermore, from a European perspective these narratives seem to shape-shift in terms of mood and mode: farce gets mixed up with the sacred; bawdiness and scatological humor break out in places where a white listener would least expect them. There are elements in these stories that can make them seem like caricatures of a creation story; there are also tales here that seem didactic or etiological—lessons in how to be careful and how the natural world came to be as it is.

How can we account for this? If you live in a subsistence culture in the midst of a vast natural environment and, therefore, see indications, every day, that creation is an ongoing process, rather than something that happened far away and long ago, what might be the effects on the way that stories are told? In other words, if you perceive the events and consequences of one of these trickster tales not as history or pseudo-history but as timeless, or as a process that not only continues but involves the participation of the teller and listener as the *story* happens as a literary and cultural event, how might those very different assumptions affect the shaping of a narrative?

Students could have a lot to say, therefore, about the way that the world is categorized and stabilized by certain basic structures in narratives constructed in the European tradition and the way that emotional and psychological experiences are blended in some of these Native American texts. Even so, to go from that generalization, or from any other, into conventional close reading or a hunt for parallels or universal themes and motives is to run into troubles that the headnotes caution us against. No amount of academic guidance, in the context of a broader and ongoing survey, can prepare us to read and understand a Chinook tale from a Chinook perspective, a

Navajo tale from a Navajo point of view, and so on, because the very ideas of telling, of listening, of fiction, of truth, and of belief can vary so much among Native American cultures.

So what else can we talk about of relevance to these tales and the anthology and survey course in which they are located? We can take guidance from that recurring emphasis on change, on shape-shifting, and talk about the shape-shifting of literary texts—Native American or otherwise—from the oral to the written, from one culture to another, from the popular world to the solemnity and supposed high seriousness of academe, from the notepad or the popular edition to the footnoted portable Hall of Fame that an anthology can signify to so many students who, with no small measure of anxiety, crack it open for the first time and expect to find greatness, profundity, and permanence everywhere. These Native American storytellers and listeners seem to participate in the making of the world by the very act of saying, by repeating reverently and irreverently, and adapting boldly; by conserving lore and visions, dreams and wisdom; and by giving them new shapes for new cultural situations. When and if students eventually consider contemporary Native American writers like Leslie Marmon Silko and Louise Erdrich, they will see writers in a quest to accomplish something akin to what their ancestors did: to keep old tales alive by reconfirming their relevance and making them new. A discussion that entertains such problems can broaden into important considerations for your students as they negotiate these texts and wonder about the process and ritual of the survey course and what they themselves are being asked to do, and are doing on their own, as they infuse these deeply foreign, deeply American texts with their own imagination. That process is going on in everything they read; and if on that level they understand a commonality between this one reading experience and others, they will have a surer and more plausible basis to maintain interest in Native American literary culture and to achieve some measure of passionate engagement with the whole course.

1620–1820

To open this period, you could ask students first to imagine the passage from seventeenth-century England to the New World: the violence and disruptions of the old country and the unknown terrors of the new one; the loss of home, of kinship, of worldly possessions (these ships were very small), of so much that matters to one's personal and cultural identity. It's also a good idea to spend some time on the sheer physical risk of this kind of dislocation. The Roanoke Colony had been wiped out without a trace; a year after the landing at Plymouth Rock, half of the *Mayflower* Pilgrims were dead. Religious warfare raged in Europe; civil war would soon break out in the English homeland, and a succession of religious upheavals and political changes over the previous half century had claimed tens of thousands of lives. If you're hoping that your students will find some way to empathize with the New England Puritan mind, and not regard the whole group as grumpy, hopelessly repressed, inhuman zealots, then it may be a good idea to establish what mortality meant to these people; how very close at hand it was; and how it could affect all phases of life, not just belief but ideas of family, of career, of the worth of any human action or enterprise.

As English separatists, the Massachusetts Bay Colonists were primarily, though not exclusively, Puritan in ideology, which meant that most believed in the literal authority of the Bible. They saw the Bible as a topological model for their own lives (Puritan writers use biblical metaphors to explain the Puritan condition; they often refer to themselves, for example, as Israelites, and the New World becomes Canaan). You will probably need to outline several basic tenets of Puritan thought: original depravity (we are born sinners), limited atonement (no worldly ritual or prayer will ensure salvation; no human action or gesture of faith obliges the Almighty to respond), and predestination (God has chosen his elect before we were born).

For the sake of keeping this a *literature* course and avoiding disappearance into theological arguments that very few of us are competent to handle properly, you might want to approach predestination (if you approach it at all) as an example of the rigorous logic that flourished in Reformation theology, partly as a result of the unprecedented empowerment of the reader and the exhilaration and terror of trying to discern Divine Will on our own. From the perspective of ordinary life and the writing of imaginative literature, predestination is almost a moot point, and students who go round and round with the matter run the risk of doing so at the expense of attention to the texts you are reading together. A few key matters: Puritans viewed the Bible as God's covenant with them; they saw themselves as a Chosen People and identified strongly with the tribes of Israel in the Book of Exodus. In reading both Testaments, they concluded that God, though sometimes arbitrary in His power, was not malicious or capricious. Doers of evil suffer and are destroyed; true believers and doers of good may suffer as well, as worldly misfortune is both a test of faith and a signifier of God's will. In sum, covenant theology taught that although no human being can ever know for certain whether or not he or she is among the saved, the only hope lay in rigorous study of Scripture; relentless moral self-examination; and active, whole-hearted membership in these congregations.

Again, if we are looking for lasting cultural effects, ways in which this theological system, and the consciousness it shaped, continue down through many generations and cultural moments, then it's worth backing away at the end of your summary to ask students to speculate on what those effects might be. The list you come up with might run something like this.

•With the absence of a central religious authority and an expectation that each member of the community should encounter Scripture and theological prose firsthand, New England Puritanism would be strongly influenced by a drive toward solidarity and consensus and by a championing of individual thought. These conflicting values would become clear in the Antinomian controversy, less than ten years after the founding of the Bay Colony.

•An emphasis on individual responsibility, on a direct and personal relationship with God, and on the acquisition of knowledge in anticipation (or hope) of the coming of Divine Grace could be a powerful force for the education of women, and eventually for their political and social equality.

•A belief that salvation required, and would be signified by, the achievement of absolute integrity among faith, worldly conduct, private life, and the spoken and written word would eventually figure centrally in the rise of abolitionist sentiment: race slavery becomes not an economic expediency or a social problem to be overlooked and eventually remedied but a mortal sin, threatening the moral condition of the society and every individual within it. *Uncle Tom's Cabin* is powered along by precisely that assumption.

•A belief in a special destiny and a conviction that what was unfolding in New England was the last and best hope of the Christian world. Cataclysmic changes in London in the middle of the seventeenth century and the erosion of solidarity in the colony after the Restoration and with the passage of years would bring those convictions into crisis at century's end.

•A special emphasis on reading correctly—not only holy texts but commentaries and the events of ordinary life. The New England Puritans were an intellectual people who believed firmly in portents, symbols, and the significance of all that happened in private and public life.

WILLIAM BRADFORD

Of Plymouth Plantation is an excellent foundation for the study of colonial American literature, as it offers a thorough portrait of hopes and expectations central to the New England Puritan mind and it shows us how an idea of destiny, and an expectation that all worldly experience is meaningful and must be "read," organizes Bradford's account of the colony's first years. Everything seems to matter: prosperity, misfortune, natural events, even outbreaks of indecency, which modern readers (including your students) will probably find hilarious. If you are hoping to demonstrate key qualities of the seventeenth-century Puritan consciousness, assumptions and beliefs that echo down through New England literature for hundreds of years, those qualities are strongly evident in Bradford.

The earlier selections from *Of Plymouth Plantation* help students visualize the practical and spiritual concerns of the earliest colonials. In trying to find a harbor (Book I, Chapter X), the "lusty seaman" on board the shallop reminds the pilot to row, "or else they were all cast away." Bradford's account reveals the necessity for self-reliance among the first Puritan settlers; only after they reach "the lee of a small island" can they afford to give thanks to God "for His mercies in their manifold deliverances." Students are surprised to discover how secular and pragmatic the Puritans had to be in the process of creating their spiritual New World. In Book I, Chapter IV, Bradford cites physical hardships, premature aging, lack of control over their children, and only last (if not least) their hope of "propagating and advancing the gospel of the kingdom of Christ" as the Puritans' reasons for "removing" to the "vast and unpeopled countries of America." How does Bradford's text challenge undergraduate students' preconceptions of the Puritans and their literature?

Among the selections from *Of Plymouth Plantation, The Mayflower Compact* deserves close analysis for classroom discussion. Bradford writes that the document was "occasioned partly by the discontented and mutinous speeches that some of the strangers [non-Puritans aboard the *Mayflower*] amongst them had let fall from them in the ship." How does what Bradford calls "the first foundation of their government in this place" establish a Puritan community from the beginning as one that excludes "strangers"? Locate evidence in the *Compact* that even before landing the Puritans defined themselves as an elect group in the secular as well as the spiritual sphere. And what implicit effect does writing and signing the Mayflower Compact have? Putting their first agreement into written form was an act of major significance for the Puritans, who believed in the Bible's literal truth and authority. Written words, from the beginning of American culture, carry the associative power of God's word. What does the writing of the Mayflower Compact indicate about the Puritans' need for divine authority? From the point of landing in the New World, the Puritans were already setting in motion the necessity of inventing for themselves solutions to material concerns that the Bible does not address. In *The Mayflower Compact* we see them trying to create other documents that would, like the Bible of their covenant theology, possess the power to compel respect and obedience.

Students can read later segments as if Bradford's own text were a prefiguring: in what ways do the excerpts from *Of Plymouth Plantation* recall for students later moments or patterns of thought in American history, even in our own time? Compare Book I, Chapter IV with Book II, Chapter XXXII: both demonstrate early attempts to rationalize colonial life, but in the latter, Bradford's own logic breaks down. In his "endeavour to give some answer hereunto," he ends by raising an unanswerable and prophetic question: "And thus, by one means or other, in 20 years' time it is a question whether the greater part be not grown the worser?" As Bradford records successive years in his history, he continues to convey a pattern of rise and fall, of end prefigured in the beginning. In *Proposal to Remove to Nauset,* he describes the split in the church that resulted from the removal to Nauset and characterizes the "poor church" as "an ancient mother grown old and forsaken of her children." Do the selections from Book II in particular suggest a less-than-optimistic view of our colonial origins? Social problems existed from the beginning: corruption, dissent, falling away from the "ancient mother," abandonment, lack of fidelity.

THOMAS MORTON

Morton makes a wonderful pairing with Bradford, especially if you want to focus on relationships between cultural values and literary style. Morton, as the headnote tells you, was anything but a Puritan, and his intentions in settling at Merrymount were worldly pleasure and profit, not the fulfillment of grand destinies or the founding of the New Jerusalem. We know little about his life, but his prose speaks volumes.

Ask a student to read aloud a few opening lines from the Morton selection, and when the student gets lost in the forest of show-off prose and esoteric allusions, offer some reassurances: this kind of writing is *not* meant to communicate clearly but to strike a posture and convey a certain kind of social position and comradeship. Morton seems to know what he is doing, and he is sending his London audience a message that unlike these dour and austere colonists, he is "one of us," an urbane Englishman who loves a good time, fancy dress, courtly manners, and florid writing styles. If your students are coming to you with some experience of Renaissance English literature, urge them to stop worrying about the allusions that break out everywhere in Morton and ask them what this prose *sounds* like. Somebody will say Shakespeare, which is a good connection to build on; you're closer to the mark if they say Sir Toby Belch or Falstaff, affable rascals who escape blame and accusations not by denying the charges against them, but by being charming and by creating farce as an act of self-defense. Morton knows what he is doing: in retelling the taking of his settlement by Standish and the other Puritans, he makes the event a slapstick encounter between good-natured revelers and a sneaking band of Malvolios, who threaten to close down all good times in the New World.

As you move in a bit closer, observe that Morton's allusions and metaphors come from a different storehouse than do Bradford's or Winthrop's. The earlier Puritan writers (with the exception of Bradstreet, whose refreshing independence and range we shall look at it in a moment) have turned away from the classical (favored by Shakespeare, Donne, Jonson, and most of the best writers of the English High Renaissance) and draw their metaphors from Scripture. Compared to Morton's, their prose is as plain and clear as the dress they favored—and a stop with *The New English Cannan* will bring home the fact that the difference between the Puritan sensibility and that of the non-Puritan English middle class affected the choice of words and the workings of the imagination.

JOHN WINTHROP

A Model of Christian Charity gives students the earliest example of a Puritan sermon delivered in the New World (or en route to the New World, because Winthrop delivered it on board the *Arbella*). Students can comment on the image patterns by which Winthrop characterizes the community he envisions, and they can discuss the discursive form of this sermon as an example of the key literary genre of seventeenth-century Puritan culture. If students in a historical survey course are beginning to wonder whether these early writings have any resonance in our own time or show us any literary motifs or imaginative habits that continue to this day, then it's worth spending some time with the City on a Hill metaphor, unpacking its meaning, looking for its analogues in Judeo-Christian history, and noticing where similar core beliefs—that Boston or Chicago or the whole United States is a beacon for humanity and the destiny of the world—continue to show up in our own culture and public discourse.

The Journal offers examples of typology and evidence of the principle of exclusion by which the Puritans founded their New World government. Ask students to assess Winthrop's comments on Roger Williams (possibly asking them to read the selections from Williams) and Anne Hutchinson. How can we account for the fervor of Winthrop's reaction against Hutchinson and her doctrine of personal conscience, which would seem, from some perspectives, quite in keeping with the general religious tenets of the colony? Why does Winthrop go to such lengths to seek evidence that Hutchinson is dangerously wrong and has lost favor with God? What are the implications and possible dangers that can arise from that kind of close reading of worldly experience?

ANNE BRADSTREET

Bradstreet can be a breakthrough moment in a historical survey or major-authors course; after a sequence of historical accounts that may be interesting chiefly as artifacts rather than as living and compelling literature, we suddenly come upon creative genius, a writer whose verse still seems limpid, courageous, and profound and who would command substantial space in any good anthology of Anglo-American verse. As one delighted student recently described the discovery of Bradstreet: "Finally, I can hear one of these writers breathing!"

Bradstreet's poetry may "breathe" because it presents a conflict, a conflict that may have been inherent in living a secular and a spiritual life in a Puritan colony. In the small city of Boston (never more than a few thousand people in her lifetime), she was a public figure, a leader in her congregation, and eventually the wife of the governor. She was also a mother and a grandmother, and as such she had to reconcile Holy Writ with human love, and human fear, for her immediate and extended family. And in Bradstreet's verse we can hear as well the voice of a woman pleased by the richness of non-Puritan English literature, by the sometimes outlandish art of Renaissance verse, and by the whole alluring, and dangerous heritage of the Western imagination.

To begin discussion of Bradstreet, you might suggest that there are two voices operating here, sometimes in harmony, sometimes in conflict. You might call them "Mistress Bradstreet" and "Anne." Mistress Bradstreet is the poet-voice who speaks as she ought, in full accord with religious doctrine, public duty, and conventional belief; "Anne" is the woman who loves, grieves, fears, feels pride, and experiences the full range of emotions and curiosities that the teachings of her faith were supposed to put to rest. In the drama of her poems, sometimes one side of her seems to win out and sometimes the other; sometimes a reassuring harmony is reached, and sometimes not.

Poems that students respond to in line-by-line analysis include *The Author to Her Book,* which has a dangerous metaphor embedded in it; students will want to comment on that. The darkening mood of the three elegies for her grandchildren, a sequence in which the doctrinal consolations seem to console less and less, will also catch the attention of your class and increase receptiveness to the great poems of family love and domestic life: *To My Dear and Loving Husband, Here Follows Some Verses upon the Burning of Our House,* and *Before the Birth of One of Her Children.* Pause over this last one and offer some word about the risk of bearing a child in the seventeenth century, the frequency with which young women died of "childbed fever," and the situation of orphans in a near-subsistence culture with no social services. Students need to know that Bradstreet was looking at very real possibilities.

Students respond to the personal voice and the element of self-disclosure in Bradstreet that make for moving lyrics and can lead into a discussion of the constraints on individual expression in Puritan society. Some additional questions: What does *The Prologue* reveal about Bradstreet's struggle to locate literary authority within herself? Is she really as self-deprecating as a quick first reading of the poem might suggest? How does she assert her own achievement despite the poem's apparent apologetic tone? What are the several meanings of the line "It is but vain unjustly to wage war" in the context of Bradstreet's self-assertion?

Other selections in *NAAL* underscore Bradstreet's self-disclosure and search for personal voice in her work. The contrast between form and feeling in *Another Letter to Her Husband Absent upon Public Employment* emphasizes the radical nature of Bradstreet's writing. Although she builds her verse on a series of closely connected conceits and the conventional forms of iambic pentameter and end rhymes, she writes a deeply personal, rather than conventional, love poem. And in *To My Dear Children,* she further explores her own doubts and perplexities "that I have not found that constant joy in my pilgrimage . . . which I supposed most of the servants of God have."

Even more striking and apparent in *In Reference to Her Children, 23 June, 1659* and in *To My Dear Children,* Bradstreet conveys her sense of God as a mother. She writes in *To My Dear Children* that when she has been troubled "concerning the verity of the Scriptures," she has found comfort in the order of things, "the daily providing for this great household upon the earth, the preserving and directing of all to its proper end." How does the language of "providing" help her view herself in God's image? She, too, has preserved and directed a household and speaks a language of provisions. Here, too, Bradstreet's vision expresses a departure from conventional Puritan thinking. In Puritan typology, it was the father, not the mother, who figured divine authority and power; and the literature of the colonial period noticeably omits references to mothers. In *In Reference to Her Children,* she writes lovingly of her children and gives central importance, at the end of the poem, to the relationship between mother and children: "You had a dam that loved you well, / That did what could be done for young." What students may initially pass over as commonplace in this imagery (as a result of the nineteenth- and twentieth-century institutionalization of motherhood) in effect was Bradstreet's address to the invisibility of mothers in Puritan society and Puritan theology.

Michael Wigglesworth

The Day of Doom may presents difficulties for students unless you suggest what to look for as they read. This was the first New England bestseller, a fact that will astound some members of your class. Ask them to speculate why it lasted so long and did so well. What does it tell us about what New England Puritans thought a poem was *for?* Ask them to find specific evidence of the tenets of Puritan theology, to characterize the contrast between Wigglesworth's sheep and goats, to summarize the portrait of hell in the poem, and to locate passages that suggest the nature of family relationships in Puritan society. And to reveal an important and durable premise in Puritan doctrine, ask students to discuss the poem's refusal to soften at any point, to imagine any last-minute mercy for the hosts of well-intentioned "good" people caught suddenly by death and Judgment, people who simply had not had time (or so they thought) to make ready. No quarter is given—off to hell they go, suddenly and irretrievably.

In some ways this is a tale of terror, making use of some of the same horrifying surprises and rhythms that propel our endlessly popular Gothic fiction. The moment makes a reappearance in works centuries after, like *Uncle Tom's Cabin*, in which St. Clair, as a decent and supposedly Christian and humane sort of slave-holder, is almost ready to free his slaves when without any warning he is stabbed and killed, bringing doom not only to himself, but to his entire household.

In discussion, ask students to contrast Wigglesworth's descriptions of place (heaven and hell) with Bradford's in *Of Plymouth Plantation* and to reread Bradstreet's *Here Follows Some Verses upon the Burning of Our House* (1666) in light of Wigglesworth's 1662 poem.

Mary Rowlandson

A Narrative of the Captivity and Restoration will fascinate students and help them make thematic connections between several Puritan writers. Ask students to speculate on Rowlandson's purpose in writing this narrative: is it a personal account, or didactic, or some mingling of both intentions? Rowlandson's story will come alive for your class, not merely because it includes mayhem and heartbreaking suffering but also because Rowlandson shows us a more conflicted sensibility than does Bradstreet. Her conflict grows straight out of two Puritan premises: first, that the Indians are agents of Satan, emblems of the Philistines, and the unforgivable enemies of her own Bay Colony group; and second, that as a Calvinist she is obligated to look steadily and carefully at worldly experience, and understand fully what it signifies. Therein lies the conflict: though she suffers terribly among her captors and sees much to confirm her impression of some of them as creatures from hell, she encounters others who *do not* seem so, who indeed seem capable of humanity and even of charity.

How does the narrative compare with other Puritan works that show triumph or redemption after suffering? What do the poems of Bradstreet and the *Narrative* of Rowlandson together reveal about the fears, anxieties, and accommodations that shadowed ordinary life for women in Puritan society?

EDWARD TAYLOR

The success by which Taylor works through his extended metaphors to imagery of salvation demonstrates the energy that must have been required for the Puritan to engage in spiritual introspection. Help students focus their attention on Taylor's use of poetic form. Ask them to describe the stanzaic pattern of any of the *Preparatory Meditations,* to locate and examine his use of the extended metaphor, and to discuss the imagery of the poem. *Prologue* works well for line-by-line analysis, especially by way of contrast with Bradstreet's poem of the same title, shows Taylor's awareness that his spiritual salvation and his poetic imagination depend on each other. Taylor's problem as a Puritan is to demonstrate to himself over and over again that he is one of the elect, and he does this by using the metaphysical conceit as a focus for literal and poetic meditation. If he can turn the mark or spot—the poem's central metaphor—into an image of salvation, then he will have proven his election both spiritually and aesthetically. How does Taylor resolve the problem of literary authority? Does he have difficulty seeing himself as God's pen? What does his struggle for poetic inspiration suggest about those who wrote poetry in Puritan society? Examine *The Preface* from *God's Determinations* to elicit Taylor's Puritan vision. What is the relationship between "nothing man" and "Might Almighty"? Ask students to trace the formal as well as thematic cohesion Taylor achieves through repetition of "nothing" and "might," "all might," and "almighty" throughout the poem. Trace Taylor's references to children in some of his poems; analyze his use of erotic and scatological imagery or trace the triumph over death in *A Fig for Thee, Oh! Death,* possibly asking students to compare the poem with John Donne's *Death Be Not Proud.*

Discussing Bradstreet's *To My Dear and Loving Husband* side by side with Taylor's *Huswifery* can demonstrate the contrast between the two poets. Bradstreet is interested in physical life, is aware of love as a physical tie, views heaven as a consequence of human faithfulness, and chooses imagery from daily life and classical mythology; Taylor depicts spiritual rebirth, his dependence on God and love as a spiritual tie and depends on the poetic conceit and biblical imagery to carry the power of his poems. Bradstreet gives us the sense of the individual; Taylor's poetry stifles or subordinates the individual to the spiritual type. Bradstreet's poetry allows her to express her doubts; Taylor tries to contain his within the tight form of the extended metaphor.

SAMUEL SEWALL

Discuss *The Diary* as Puritan introspection in practice. Contrast the form of the diary with Taylor's poetic forms in *Preparatory Meditations.* Weigh Sewall's expressed commitment to "great exercise of mind" in approaching his "Spiritual Estate" with his interest in daily life, "outward causes" of conflict, and public events. Summarize what Sewall's *Diary* reveals about personal life and human relationships in Puritan society.

COTTON MATHER

The headnote to Mather points out that the *Magnalia Christi Americana* "remains Mather's most impressive work" for its portraits of Bradford and Winthrop. Students will find the excerpts from *The Wonders of the Invisible World,* Mather's history of the Salem witch trials, and *Bonifacius,* his discussion of family and community life and child rearing, equally interesting. *Bonifacius* can serve as the thematic culmination for a discussion of what it was like to have been a Puritan child. Ask students to reread Bradford, Bradstreet, and Taylor for references to children and child rearing. It's clear that (1) God's will is more important than the love between parents and children; (2) children are born sinners and must be taught obedience, submission, and fear; and (3) children have the capacity to destroy Puritanism by becoming degenerate and following false teachers. Emery Elliott has written an account of the life of the young Puritan and how life was different for second- and third-generation children (like Mather himself) in *Power and the Pulpit in Puritan New England.*

WILLIAM BYRD

Students need continual reminding that by no means all who settled the New World were Puritans and that we emphasize them as founders by choice, not historical necessity. Ask them to compare Sewall's *The Diary* with Byrd's *The Secret Diary.* How does the Virginian Byrd's view of life differ from that of his New England Puritan counterpart? In form and apparent intention, Byrd's regular writing in his "secret diary" resembles the Puritan practice of introspection and meditation. But students will find it a refreshing contrast. Is Byrd's repetition of his prayers for "good health, good thoughts, and good humor" a cynical response to religion or an expression of well-being that we should take at face value? And what *does* he mean by doing his "dance"?

JONATHAN EDWARDS

The writings of Edwards can be introduced as the highest and fullest achievement in New England Puritan prose but also as the epitome of the male Puritan mind: in New England literature before 1750, only Bradstreet ranks with him in creating, on the printed page, a full, passionate, intellectual, complex, yet integrated sensibility. Students need to understand that 250 years after his death, Edwards still ranks as a pre-eminent American philosopher and theologian. His fire-and-brimstone sermons are more widely read by modern undergraduates than are his careful, systematic readings of scripture and his gentle personal narratives. This can cause a problem: conditioned by scandal-mongering television shows and supermarket tabloids, some students will assume that any preacher with a fiery delivery is automatically a hypocrite. It may be important, therefore, to make it clear from the start that Edwards lived what he believed and preached and that the blameless life (which has stood up to generations of skeptical historical review), the fervent rhetoric, the devotion to family, and the relentless scholarship and theological inquiry coalesce into an integrated self and into the first truly great intellect to emerge in Puritan New England.

A reading of *Personal Narrative* contrasts the Puritan Edwards and the Quaker John Woolman; it also shows us Edwards responding to the opportunity and the challenge of Enlightenment thinking. Edwards took on the challenge of organizing and strengthening Calvinist theology to meet eighteenth-century scrutiny, a scrutiny based in logic, in science, and in a belief that the individual mind, propelled along by healthy skepticism and common sense, could find its way to the profoundest truth. The contrast between Edwards and Franklin, therefore, and the response of Edwards *to* the likes of Franklin, offer a dramatic opposition and a rich way to engage with the transition from the New England Puritans to the secular world of the Federalists.

If you decide not to have students read all of the Edwards selections, you can make a great deal of headway reading *Sinners in the Hands of an Angry God,* not as a work of antisecularist fanaticism but as a breathtaking demonstration of both relentless logic and powerful belief. The earlier sermon *A Divine and Supernatural Light* helps provide a context, a demonstration that those same commingled intentions—to read Scripture meticulously and accurately, to follow logic wherever it might take you, and to believe wholeheartedly—could lead a first-rate Puritan consciousness both to a vision of grace and peace, and to a vision of damnation.

In analyzing *Sinners* in the classroom, it's useful to trace the evolution of semantic meaning in the sermon. Edwards takes a verse from Deuteronomy as his text: "Their foot shall slide in due time." Applying exegetical attention to the verse, he achieves this resounding interpretation: "There is nothing that keeps wicked men at any one moment out of hell, but the mere pleasure of God." Hereafter, the logic moves relentlessly, and the passion of the sermon rises with it. Even in the "Application," in which the attention turns from the "they" of the Old Testament to the "you" of the actual congregation before him, the cool-headed, relentless, Scripture-founded inquiry never subsides or disappears, and the tone of *Sinners* remains one of enlightened compassion, not condescension or wild accusation. This is a way of describing the intellectual genius of the sermon, its rhetorical power, and its commonality with the many far gentler discourses for which Edwards is also remembered.

A Divine and Supernatural Light defines religious conversion; *Sinners in the Hands of an Angry God* instills fear in the unconverted—a subject that students may feel has more varied and interesting literary possibilities than the subject of the earlier sermon. In *A Divine and Supernatural Light,* Edwards tried to find words for his feeling of the infusion of the Holy Spirit, to express an ineffable experience; *Sinners* creates an experience for its listeners, as if Edwards believed that sinners wouldn't have the equivalent sense of being damned that the elect have of being filled with grace.

BENJAMIN FRANKLIN

For your students, the transition to Franklin is easy, because they have known Franklin since the second grade as a benign and grandfatherly American icon and because (for the first time since Morton!) they are now in the company of someone with a modern-style sense of humor. Overall, Franklin is going to seem (in contrast to the Puritans) refreshingly modern; and a good way to begin engaging with him is to ask *why* he strikes us that way.

What would be shocking about Franklin, from the point of view of a Jonathan Edwards or any fervent New England Puritan, is his breezy acceptance of unreconciled conflicts and discontinuities in his own system of values. The Puritan quest for complete integrity among all of one's words, public actions, private life, and cherished principles is replaced by a quest for maximum worldly *effectiveness* and exemplary *citizenship*—and the condition of the soul seems to have little to do with his plan. One can begin with a look at the famous rules that he lays out for himself in *The Autobiography* as a method for achieving a kind of perfection. With delight, students will notice the hedge about "venery"—to be used "rarely" for purposes other than "health or procreation," meaning that it's okay to go on a tear once in a while, provided you do it discreetly and don't disturb others. And they may jump at the world of paradoxes inherent in trying to "imitate" both "Jesus and Socrates," as if there were no fundamental differences between these moral models and as if such "imitation" weren't in itself a problem for someone trying to achieve "humility." When Franklin encounters such dilemmas (as he does here), he escapes with a joke; and students will have much to say about that as an intellectual and moral strategy and about whether or not a Puritan thinker would ever allow himself or herself an evasion of that kind.

Ask students how Franklin's "Project of arriving at moral Perfection" is similar in form to Puritan introspection and meditation. (He writes that "daily Examination would be necessary," and he uses a "little Book" duly lined, "on which Line and in its proper Column I might mark by a little black Spot every Fault I found upon Examination to have been committed respecting that Virtue upon that Day.") Franklin's life and his "instruction" through his *Autobiography* transform daily routine into something resembling a religious practice. Practical life itself seems to become his secular or deistic "religion," governed by more precepts, self-discipline, and a consistent desire for worldly self-improvement, so that Franklin's work both derives from Puritan religious method and is a reaction against it. You might need to make clear that materialism and greed evidently aren't the motives that propel Franklin but an assumption that civic, intellectual, scientific, and charitable *action* constitute the only self worth caring about and the only self that the Almighty (who Franklin imagines as somebody much like himself—busy, intellectual, reasonable, benign, undogmatic, and forgiving) cares about either. Students will have fun considering the implications of Franklin's use of "erratum," in describing moral failings and his refusal to use the word *sin*.

The discussion of Franklin may include the following questions: How does *The Autobiography* reveal Franklin as an eighteenth-century man? In what ways does he adapt what he calls the "Age of Experiments" to political and personal life? What does Franklin's plan for the "union of all the colonies" have in common with his thinking about other matters? Discussion of *The Autobiography* can prepare the way for *The Declaration of Independence*, for which Franklin offered some revisions and influenced Jefferson's conceptual thinking. The title of Garry Wills's book on the Constitution, *Inventing America,* can help students think about what both Franklin and Jefferson are trying to do in their political writings. Franklin is motivated by the advice he receives to "invite all wise men to become like yourself," and students can get a clear picture of Franklin as both a self-made man and a "self-invented" one. Franklin offers his life as a blueprint, a repeatable experiment, evidence that an American can resolve the confusion involved in being a colonial by inventing himself or herself as a new kind of person.

Franklin's other prose both confirms and enlarges on his self-portrait as a rational man. Discuss Franklin's use of satire, especially in *Rules by Which a Great Empire May Be Reduced to a Small One,* as an eighteenth-century rhetorical device. Compare the form of *Rules* with the numbered, discursive, rational forms that William Bradford attempts (see *Of Plymouth Plantation,* Book I, Chapter IV) and Jonathan Edwards perfects (see especially *Sinners in the Hands of an Angry God*) and evaluate the power of Franklin's work. Recast each satirical point into a direct statement and examine the quality of Franklin's logic.

JOHN WOOLMAN

The Journal is well taught in conjunction with Jonathan Edwards, for it allows students to see that Puritanism didn't simply disappear when deism walked in the door but, rather, that the writings by colonial writers (both Puritans and non-Puritans, such as Woolman) reveal stresses on Puritanism from the beginning that foreshadow its own eventual decline as the dominant theology. The Puritan practice of inner scrutiny, the use of the poetic conceit in Edward Taylor's poetry, and the social ritual of executing witches all serve an analogous function: to allow the Puritans to externalize their own inner doubts and confusion and to create a false sense of security concerning their own salvation or election. In reading Woolman's *Journal,* students may wonder what was so terrible about the Quakers that the Puritans felt such a need to pass laws against them and to persecute them. The excerpt will also give students a different view of eighteenth-century religious belief than the one they find in the selections from Puritan writers. Ask them to think about what Woolman means when he writes that "true religion consisted in an inward life." His consciousness of that inward life or the "inner light" of the Quakers may seem more closely akin to the development of individual voice in the poetry of Anne Bradstreet than the didactic poetry of Taylor or Wigglesworth. Woolman's *Journal* suggests that one of the schisms within Puritanism resulted from the discovery, by some colonials, of religious faith that was connected more to feeling than to the purely intellectual "delight" Edwards's work reveals. Are there other ways in which the *Journal* illustrates an increasingly deep split within colonial consciousness? Ask students to think about connections between expressions of self-reliance as early as Bradford's *Of Plymouth Plantation,* Woolman's "inward life," and the popular climate that led to Franklin's great popularity in Quaker Pennsylvania.

In the selection included from *Some Considerations on the Keeping of Negroes,* students can see an excellent example of the logical extension of Quaker values and their application to the question of slavery. Even before the American Revolution and the writing of a Constitution that did nothing to end slavery, Woolman reveals the great sadness concerning the "general disadvantage which these poor Africans lie under in an enlightened Christian country." Ask students to locate the fundamental assumptions of Woolman's argument—an argument addressed to empathy, based on what students will know as the Golden Rule, and derived from the attempt to "make their case ours." In the Age of Enlightenment, Quaker thinkers like Woolman demonstrated that rational thinking must also involve "life guided by wisdom from above," that both individual and social policy decisions must derive from moving beyond "self-love" to considering what is "truly beneficial to society." Woolman implies that rational thinking without moral reasoning leads to a "darkness in the understanding."

Clearly Woolman's position did not prevail, and yet the terms of his plea and his conscious awareness of the politics involved in arguing against slavery remain of interest to twentieth-century readers. He portrays a society more interested in "gain" than in right action, which some students may believe continues to characterize our own society, and he early argues that it becomes necessary to advocate "the cause of some" to promote "the good of all," a principle that implies the interconnectedness of prejudice, oppression, and discrimination. Close readers may find a moment of inconsistency in Woolman's text; he mentions but fails to examine how "the natives are gone from before us," despite his implication that it is as a result of the "disappearance" of the American Indians that he and his contemporaries enjoy "our civil and religious liberties."

SAMSON OCCOM

Occom is a fascinating historical figure, a man who lived in two opposed cultures and became a respected leader in both of them. Though he embraced Christianity at an early age and became an ordained minister and teacher—mastering the theology, the language, and the rhetorical strategies of his chosen faith—he seems to have done all this without losing sight of, or compromising, his identity as a member of the Mohegan people or his understanding that white Christian America would always see him as an Indian.

The writings by Occom that come down to us are sparse: the often re-published *Sermon on the Execution of Moses Paul* (an American Indian hanged for murder in New Haven in 1772), a collection of devotional songs and hymns, and *A Short Narrative of My Life* (which appeared in print only twenty years ago). Because students will want to understand the "literary" dimensions of Occom and his unadorned narrative, you may want to begin there, inviting some speculations on how a representative life, in and of it-self, can become important to our literary legacy and our ongoing conver-sation about who and what we are. As questions of plurality, inclusivity, and multicultural identity abound in the contemporary United States, we can look about for historical forebears who faced such difficult questions throughout their lives and who constructed identities and wrote them with measure and dignity.

At the end of the *Narrative*, Occom writes curtly about the injustice in the compensation he received for a career of ministry and teaching, and the pit-tance he mentions compared with the normal earnings of a white man in similar professional life is astounding—as is the brevity and the matter-of-factness with which Occom describes the difference. Students may want to talk about that understatement as a rhetorical strategy: how dignity is main-tained, how a life thus narrated is not reduced to a protracted grievance, and how Occom's firm and abiding profession of Christian values is not compromised or contradicted by his clear sense of worldly injustice.

Mercy Otis Warren

In an American literature survey course of any sort, *The Group* is going to come as a surprise and as an unprecedented work in the anthology. Sud-denly here is a drama, an all-out, exuberant, venomous satire on the British colonial government and prominent local Tories. The humor is acerbic; heavy handed; and, from a modern perspective, arcane.

The play is a landmark not for its particulars but as a first appearance of a Restoration-style satiric drama by an American woman author. There-fore, you might want to caution your students at the outset *not* to get lost in reading the footnotes or in trying to keep track of who is really who and what specific event in the early days of the Revolution is being alluded to. Encourage them to look at this as a literary artifact, a stage play with an array of characters, a level of intensity, and a cause. Does it still work as a drama? Is there a plot to it? Would a plot in these particular circum-stances be a distraction? Do the characters talk to one another or do they declaim to us as the audience? Are their speeches believable as human speech—not just in language, but in content? In other words, would cow-ardly, corrupt, and villainous people speak so frankly about their intentions and deeds? Are violations of plausibility an advantage in this kind of drama and in this historical time? Are there memorable moments in the work, where the oratory breaks through into something like real eloquence?

What does *The Group* suggest about the intellectual and political role that women could play as writers and thinkers in New England as the Revolution took shape?

J. HECTOR ST. JOHN DE CRÈVECOEUR

Letters from an American Farmer meditates on the now-famous question "What is an American?" If there is a measure of truth in the old adage that one universal American trait is the constant reopening of this very question, then a very long and culturally important discussion may begin here, with Crèvecoeur's attempt to make an answer. Crèvecoeur asserts that in America "the rich and the poor are not so far removed from each other as they are in Europe" and implies that the United States is founded as a classless society. Crèvecoeur also notes the near-barbarousness of some of these pioneers and finds strength and cultural promise in that lack of a European-style sophistication. Indeed, as his narrative reveals in Letter XII, he prefers to accommodate to life with the Indians than with some of the Europeans who have become settlers in the American woods.

A variety of European philosophers and historical crises seem to influence Crèvecoeur's thinking, and it might be worth asking your students to suggest what these are. There are moments when he sounds like Hobbes, like Locke, even like Rousseau—and students may want to discuss this key issue: is this a body of thought that grows out of American experience or is his thinking, and his hope, imposed on American experience or adapted to it from some other culture or body of wisdom? Throughout a discussion of Crèvecoeur, asking students to locate both his assumptions and his contradictions will help them read his letters within Crèvecoeur's own historical context and identify their significance for present-day readers.

Letter IX offers an implicit contradiction to Crèvecoeur's affirmation in Letter III that "we know, properly speaking, no strangers," when he describes coming on the caged African who has been left to die. The letter ends with his report that when he asked why the slave had been punished in this manner, "they told me that the laws of self-preservation rendered such executions necessary." Letter X, in which he writes about the mortal conflict between a black snake and a watersnake, seems a rather gloomy parable, and students may want to speculate on its implications. If we read this parable as being about the relationship between power and corruption, then even within the brief period from the composition of Crèvecoeur's earliest letters (about 1769), to the *Declaration of Independence* and American Revolution (1776), to the composition of his later letters and their publication (1780–82) his altered perception of American life may more accurately reflect the contradictions inherent in the creation of the United States than the utopian vision reflected in Letter III, particularly when Crèvecoeur writes, "we have no princes, for whom we toil, starve, and bleed; we are the most perfect society now existing in the world." In response to Crèvecoeur's question "What is an American?" some students may want to ask, What does he mean by *we*?

WILLIAM BARTRAM

Bartram is a welcome addition to the *NAAL*, because his prose exemplifies an important transition in ways of seeing and writing of the American landscape and human inhabitants. The excerpts from his *Travels* have a different sound, pace, and inherent purpose from narrative descriptions written by the New England Puritans, by writers of the Enlightenment, or by Bartram's Federal Period contemporaries. His prose shows no Puritan urge to find portentous metaphors or meanings in everything that he sees. Unlike Byrd in the Carolina wilderness, Bartram shows no flashes of anger or satire, no inclination to judge otherness; nor do his descriptions suggest the kind of genial and generalizing proprietorship that echo in the style of Jefferson or Franklin. If Bartram is offering us a version of Crèvecoeur's politically healthful back country, where creed and dogma and fervor of any sort are diluted and neutralized by physical distances and hard work, that theme seems muted almost to a whisper.

Bartram's wilderness may have a sacred aura to it, but it is a sacredness different from what Edwards evokes in his writings about natural events, or the consoling gloom that Bryant would find in the forest cathedral of *Thanatopsis*. In helping students to grasp the difference, you might ask them to describe specific scenes in Bartram's narrative as visual experiences. If this work is in some ways a sequence of landscape paintings, then what painterly style are they in? There's usually an art history major or art enthusiast in the room, and he or she can help the group make these connections, especially if you offer some slides of paintings yourself, as suggested below. Bartram seems to be drawing on the Quaker visual and literary archetype of the "Peaceable Kingdom," the modest, untheatrical imaging of a natural world of inherent order and harmony, where even the alligators, as "kings" of the waterways, are rightly where they are. His Seminole Indians are neither dreaded nor scorned nor sentimentalized: in Bartram's telling, they too are what they should be and where they belong. Students may enjoy seeing that Bartram's simple, unpretentious, unassuming prose style, his interest in details (morally reassuring or otherwise), and his gentle acceptance of the world as offered have analogues in painting and that across the arts a revolution was under way in the art of seeing and describing the natural world.

A few well-chosen slides will give students a chance to *see* these differences in ways of *seeing*: the sedate, cultivated, Jeffersonian nature in the background of some Copley portraits; the Romantic gloom and ominousness of some canvases by Thomas Cole or Albert Bierstadt; and the consoling, peaceful natural scenes by George Caleb Bingham, George Inness, and others who carried forward Bartram's patient, trustful way of observing the American landscape.

JOHN ADAMS AND ABIGAIL ADAMS

In the letters of John and Abigail Adams, students can see the rare intersection of public and personal life in colonial America and evidence of an intimate human relationship between two people. Organize class discussion of the letters by asking students to list the various conflicts that each of these writers reveals in his or her letters: Abigail is concerned with smallpox, a lack of pins, and other domestic troubles; she fears war with England; she's afraid that others might read her letters; and she takes pride in her connection with John's work. John is concerned about keeping his private identity alive, even as he attends to the affairs of the new Continental Congress and labors to ensure the survival of a new country. Both are capable of praising and chiding in the same letter and of complaining about the other's lack of attention or expression of feeling. John's letter of July 20, 1776 (less than three weeks after the signing of *The Declaration of Independence*), opens, "This has been a dull day to me," because a letter he had expected to receive from Abigail did not arrive.

Ask students to compare the letters of John and Abigail Adams with those of Franklin and Jefferson. The Adamses use language to communicate with a reader whom they know to be a real person; in contrast, Franklin and Jefferson produce letters that seem written for a general audience. John and Abigail transcend the formal requirements of eighteenth-century letter writing and allow feeling to interrupt form. Indeed, Abigail statedly prefers those letters in which John transgresses conventional form, writing about one of his letters, in hers of July 21, 1776, that "I think it a choise one in the Litterary Way, . . . yet it Lacked some essential engrediants to make it compleat." She wants from John more personal discourse and more words "respecting yourself, your Health or your present Situation." These letters exist within the dual contexts of personal relationship and political change, and the rapid shifts in the discourse reflect the way attention to audience changes the use of language, even in the late eighteenth century.

THOMAS PAINE, THOMAS JEFFERSON, *THE FEDERALIST*, THE DECLARATION OF INDEPENDENCE

Throughout the 1620–1820 period, we have been observing the way in which each shift in thinking retains old forms. The need that the *Mayflower* Puritans felt for a document to clarify and stabilize their shared values is the earliest example of the pattern. In the writings of the Federalist period, the pattern continues. James Madison, in *The Federalist* No. 10, argues that one advantage of union is "its tendency to break and control the violence of faction." By 1787, when Madison wrote his paper, his concern that factions be controlled by means of a union laid out in writing suggests his close kinship with Puritan thought in regard to the authority of the written word.

The Declaration of Independence

Like Franklin's *Autobiography*, *The Declaration of Independence* is a blueprint, an experiment that the French would soon emulate, and another important moment in the invention of an American polity and identity. Yet some students may not do more than skim it out of class, because they read it in high school or because they feel that they are somehow "living" it. It has the aura of a sacred text, and you may find it necessary to discuss, for a while, the legitimacy of looking at *The Declaration* as a literary work, a work with special rhetorical qualities and power, a work that was actually edited by human beings, not dictated from the heavens. Ask your students to consider the way it "invents" history, as Franklin invents his own life in *The Autobiography* Do they see resemblance, in sheer use of the English language, between *The Declaration* and the sermon form, especially in *Sinners in the Hands of an Angry God?* Compare the language with Franklin's in *The Way to Wealth.* Whatever else you choose to teach from Jefferson and the Federalist era, *The Declaration of Independence* can be a central work to read closely with students.

THE ISSUE OF SLAVERY

An approach to teaching American literature that neglects the evidence of dissenting voices within the apparent union makes it difficult for the classroom teacher to explain why anything changed—why writers in any historical period began to think differently, and why they experimented with different genres. Given the principle of exclusion that is our heritage from the Puritans (however far back and from whatever origin we are able to trace our personal lineage) and looking ahead to the Civil War of the 1860s, how our founders saw fit to deal with factions, with social difference, and in particular, with the issue of slavery can help us describe the tensions that have always been, and still remain, a part of American life. In the literature of the Federal Period, then, in addition to discussing major figures and ideas of the Enlightenment, you can also focus on the ways various writers and works address the issue of slavery.

Long before the early nineteenth century, slavery was a national issue; and in failing to resolve it, Jefferson, Madison, and the Continental Congress helped create another "new world" with its own stresses; students of American literature will welcome a discussion of the relationship between liberty and literary authority. The language of liberty that makes Thomas Paine's writing and *The Declaration of Independence* particularly effective suggests that it is the very articulation of the "United States of America" that makes revolution possible and thereby brings the country into being. The documents of the American Revolution achieve their power much as William Bradford does in *The Mayflower Compact:* they focus the nebulous thinking of a larger group and they offer the familiar form of written convenant. The writers of the Federal Period put language in the service of human liberty—for some but not all. And it seems important to point out to students that the unspoken omissions from the language of "all men are created equal" will require other internal revolutions—for the abolition of slavery and the fight for women's suffrage—before the liberty that makes possible the literary achievements of the 1820–65 period will also support the literary authority of black men, white women, and black women.

Students can find discussions of slavery in several writers whose works may otherwise seem difficult to connect. John Woolman, in his *Journal,* records being reluctant to write a bill of sale for a black woman as early as the 1740s, and in *Some Considerations on the Keeping of Negroes* he argues that his listeners must empathize with the plight of the slaves and apply moral reasoning to their "considerations." William Byrd of Virginia writes casually of whipping black houseservants in his *Secret Diary.* Crèvecoeur, in Letter IX, describes the miserable condition of the slaves in Charles-Town. Jefferson, in *Notes on the State of Virginia*, objects to slavery as much for what it does to the masters as for what it does to the slaves and fears "supernatural interference" and even the "extirpation" of the masters—yet makes no concrete proposal for ending slavery (and he himself owned many slaves). *The Declaration of Independence*, in its original version (*NAAL* includes the original document Jefferson submitted to the Continental Congress, with the changes as adopted noted in the margins), clearly shows Jefferson's abhorrence of the institution of slavery. The passage in *The Declaration* that begins "He has waged cruel war against human nature itself," which was completely excised from the document based on objections from representatives from South Carolina, Georgia, and some northern colonies engaged in the slave trade, helps students understand the inherent contradiction in the document's reference to "all men." The textual revisions show that the Continental Congress addressed the issue of slavery, then decided to eliminate it from consideration in *The Declaration*. One essay that can be especially useful in preparing to teach *The Declaration* is Edwin Gittleman's article "Jefferson's 'Slave Narrative': *The Declaration of Independence* as a Literary Text" (*Early American Literature*, 1974).

OLAUDAH EQUIANO

One of the first questions you might raise with students concerns the inclusion of Equiano's *Narrative* in *NAAL*. What makes it interesting as "American" literature? Equiano's *Narrative* gives students a new perspective on life in the American colonies. Although the original version of *The Declaration of Independence* includes a reference to the slave trade (see the changes Jefferson notes in the text included in his *Autobiography*) and although during the writing of the Constitution the prohibition of the slave trade was discussed, stipulations concerning slavery were omitted from the Constitution, and Congress was formally prohibited from abolishing the slave trade for at least twenty years. Equiano's narrative exists within the context of that history and provides a rare and stirring firsthand account of life in Africa, the internal African slave trade (Equiano's own father owned slaves), and conditions on the slave ships themselves.

The American world that Equiano depicts enshrines the merchant. King, the Philadelphia merchant, eventually keeps his promise and allows Equiano to buy his freedom. Equiano does so by becoming a merchant himself. Cargo thus becomes central to Equiano's freedom; he begins as "live cargo," becomes a trader in various goods, and literally reverses his fortunes. Unlike the authors of later slave narratives, such as Frederick Douglass, Equiano does not achieve freedom by finding his voice. Neither does he feel compelled to keep silent. By including his manumission papers in his *Narrative,* he seems to suggest that, indeed, it is only a reversal of fortune, not his own power, that has produced his freedom, for the "absolute power and domination one man claims over his fellow" that allowed Robert King to emancipate Equiano equally allowed other white men to enslave the freeman Joseph Clipson.

JUDITH SARGENT MURRAY

Murray offers a polemic about gender inequality—but before settling in to discuss the underlying logic of her attack, there are some long-term benefits to spending some time with the *tone* and rhetoric of this essay and its epigraph poem. That tone is subtle and blended, and it may take your class a while to hear some of its components, the playfulness and wit mixed in with the aggression and rage. By this point in the course, students should be developing a sense of how to hear various rhetorical strategies, how to listen to verse like this, for example—rhymed couplets and relatively simple language—as opposed to the declamatory classical style put on by Sarah Morton. They may also be able to hear the exuberance and the agility in that first, almost endless onrush of a paragraph, that torrent of rhetoric and rhetorical questions with which Murray overwhelms a supposedly male reader. What stereotypes is she playing with here, in the very structure of her prose? When does she good-humoredly seem to give ground, concede small points or cliché characterizations of women to move around or to pass these minor issues to get to major ones? Where does the tone change—and at what points is the reader, put at "his" ease by the easy flow of this mostly genial and civil argument, caught by surprise? These are important matters to dwell on: when we get to a different sort of argument-by-inundation, with Emerson, students can keep in mind, thanks to Murray, that the discourse of human liberty has more than one tradition within it, more than one way of accomplishing its purpose. When Fuller comes up in the sequence of your readings, be sure to stop and do some comparison to Murray and see how the two of them gang up on the likes of Emerson, offering a Fabian, supremely mobile prose strategy in contrast to his more ponderous forward movement. When you come to talk about differences between male poetics and female (or feminist) poetics in the American tradition, a comparison of these rhetorical styles will serve that discussion well.

TIMOTHY DWIGHT

Dwight's account is a new addition to *NAAL,* and it compares elegantly with the travel writings of Bartram, his near contemporary. Again we can see some of the predispositions and aspirations that would cause Romanticism and Transcendentalism to flourish soon after, in American intellectual and artistic circles. Like Bartram, Dwight shows great faith in the inspirational and healing power of the natural landscape; but where Bartram is consistently mild and detachedly appreciative in his observations, Dwight deals in avalanches of details, statistics, and superlatives. Students will notice the mingling here of names, numbers, and breathless astonishment; and they may want to talk about the core assumptions and didactic intentions at the center of this description of the region around Niagara Falls. Dwight lays those assumptions out quite clearly in the middle of this narrative; his belief that "the house," the immediate physical environment, can expand or confine the sensibilities, character, and motives of the people who live there. The American natural landscape is the best possible house for nurture of the soul, and Dwight's account aims to allow all of us to dwell in it, at least to visit it imaginatively and feel those possibilities vicariously. Dwight's prose is a very interesting stylistic mix, and a close look at one or two of his paragraphs will be time well spent. Students can see on the printed page an attempt to reconcile Enlightenment logic and science with a rising Romantic faith in the sheer mystical and spiritual power of wild nature. Hereafter, a succession of Americans, going into the wilderness for expansion and inspiration, will self-consciously carry with them, at least in mind, intellectual processes, and interests much more suggestive of London, Boston, and New York City than of the bookless outback. Thoreau and Emerson will bring Harvard to the Massachusetts woods; Whitman, Muir, Chapman, Abbey, and Dillard will all work for reconciliations, of one sort or another, between what has been learned in the Anglo-Saxon schoolroom and what is met firsthand in the wilderness.

PHILIP FRENEAU

In a provocative mix of voices, Freneau's poetry addresses the social and historical events of his day and attends to both moral issues and small details from nature, in anticipation of the Romantic poems like *The House of Night* and *On Observing a Large Red-Streak Apple*. *On the Emigration to America and Peopling the Western Country* and *On Mr. Paine's Rights of Man* derive their force from their historical situation. The poems suggest that the American Revolution made the development of American poetry possible; and yet, as Francis Murphy notes in the *NAAL* headnote, Freneau was not "the father of American poetry." Ask students to think about what limits Freneau. Freneau's brand of eloquence as it survives in his poetry (he also wrote political pamphlets) has not appeared to be as lasting in its significance as our country's founding documents; the political covenant and the autobiography absorb almost all of the literary energy available during the Revolutionary and Federal Periods and serve as the major literary genres of the late eighteenth century. Still, Freneau's choice to respond to political and social conditions in *To Sir Toby*, written about slavery (although he addresses a sugar planter in Jamaica rather than a southern slaveholder), demonstrates his faith in the power of language used in the service of political and social change. This faith has its roots in the Puritan belief in the literary authority of the Bible, but it also anticipates the First Amendment to the Constitution and the idea that freedom of speech is the most important freedom, because it is speech that leads to freedom itself.

PHILLIS WHEATLEY

Wheatley is a fascinating poet, for she reflects Puritan influence, wrote poetry that imitates Alexander Pope, and was the first African American to publish a book. Wheatley writes about liberty as an abstract or spiritual condition, rather than as freedom from slavery. In *On Being Brought from Africa to America,* the kind of enslavement she seems most concerned with is that of her former ignorance of Christianity and redemption. Her letters provide a valuable addition to students' understanding of Wheatley's life, documenting her correspondence with abolitionist groups in England and America and with other Africans in servitude in America. The correspondence continues to suggest that she views spiritual salvation as "the way to true felicity," as she expresses in her letter to Arbour Tanner, but also that she is aware of the needs of both Africans and American Indians. Her letter to Samson Occom comes closest to revealing the development of Wheatley's voice as an advocate for the natural rights of blacks.

Ask students to compare Wheatley with Bradstreet. What explains the absence of personal voice in Wheatley? Is her emulation of eighteenth-century British poets a kind of performance or does this poetic style allow her both to achieve and to evade a distinct literary voice? Wheatley does make a connection between achieving exalted language in poetry (or in art, as in *To S. M., a Young African Painter, on Seeing His Works*) and rising on "seraphic pinions." Wheatley resembles the earlier colonial writers (such as Wigglesworth and Taylor) for whom personal concerns and personal voice are largely absent, but the powerful images of "rising" and racial uplift will reappear in black prose and poetry from Booker T. Washington to Countee Cullen.

The two poems newly included in *NAAL, To the Right Honorable William, Earl of Dartmouth* and *To Mæcenas,* can be looked at as a good deal more than polished performances in a borrowed genteel mode, an African American woman working in a form perfected by Pope, Cowley, Lee, and a score of other British Augustans. When Wheatley addresses Dartmouth and Mæcenas, she addresses individuals who achieved (as she says of Mæcenas) a "partial grace," who lived lives of talent and achievement but who somehow exist on the periphery, either of history or cultural memory or the main stream of contemporary action. Terence and Virgil were "happier" in the arts than was Mæcenas; Dartmouth did "once deplore" injustice, but he has taken sides against freedom now, as the revolutionary movement in America rises to what Wheatley portrays as irresistible strength. In each case, as she frames her address, Wheatley reveals something of herself, as if to achieve some commonality with the individual she speaks to. What does she turn to within herself and why?

SARAH WENTWORTH MORTON

Morton is a welcome addition to *NAAL,* as she compares in interesting ways to Wheatley: two American women poets in a complex predicament. They are both writing in a time when the prevailing style of English poetry was very grand; the simplicities of Bradstreet, commonplace language, and metaphor drawn from Scripture and ordinary life have given way to the kind of adornment that Morton had indulged in playfully and that had become fashionable again in London. Classical allusions are back with a vengeance, and Horace, Juvenal, and highly oratorical poets from antiquity are again being celebrated as the highest achievements in formal verse.

The problem for Morton and Wheatley isn't that women can't play the high-style game and match male London court poets metaphor for metaphor; the problem may be instead that even the most accomplished grand-style verse by American women writers could not escape seeming like a performance, like a *tour de force* rather than an expression of any genuine insight or sentiment. Another and more profound problem may transcend even issues of gender and involve instead an incompatibility between this kind of verse and emerging American democratic values. In other words, the high-flown language that was still expected from pre-Romantic poets may have been inherently inappropriate for this new republic, in which much of the power now rested not with hereditary nobles but with scattered yeoman farmers, small-town merchants and tradesmen, and a populace that survived by hard work rather than inheritance or hereditary privilege. America had yet to evolve a poetics that could accommodate the values that were expressed in the *The Declaration* and the Constitution.

Still, it makes little sense to present Morton as some kind of victim of her time, a woman poet born too soon. If the best of eighteenth-century English poetry locks itself in chains and still manages to dance somehow, then where are the moments in Morton where she breaks through the high formality that she accepts and achieves lasting rhetorical power—where, in other words, is she convincing as a poet of feeling? When she writes *The African Chief*, a poem with much in it of the epic and the heroic elegy, is she convincing? Does she convey empathy for the plight of this nameless African? Or is he only an excuse for a grand-style dream, a co-opted Hector for a pocket-sized *Iliad*, safely distanced from our own experience?

Again, you can reach for your slides and bring in some heroic-academic paintings from right around this time (earlier work by David, for example, or any large canvas of handsomely realized dying Noble Romans) to suggest how this kind of extravagant imagining *could* be a mannerism. Students may want to fight about this—and the debate may open up important issues having to do with poetics and tastes in the Federal Period and in the literary eras soon to come in your course.

SUSANNA ROWSON

Charlotte: A Tale of Truth still makes a bumptiously good read; and once students get a few pages into it, they are likely to enjoy it. After all, it has seduction, abduction, sex, betrayal, lots of desperation and misery, a grand *tableau* death scene, and ghoulishly fitting retribution for the malefactors— all the elements of the daytime soap operas that some of your students may be scheduling your course around! Students will be glad to discuss the similarities between this first best-seller of the American republic and pop entertainments of the present day: the discussion will get more complex, and more far-reaching, when you ask whether the overtly didactic tone and intentions of *Charlotte* are justifiably there in the novel or read like hypocritical add-ons, dignifying an essentially sensationalistic text? A question like this can lead in many directions. You may open up interpretive problems relating to differences between intention and effect. You may hear objectives to imaginative fiction having any moral design at all, or to reading it for such designs. As one of the very first American novelists, Rowson was engaged not only in helping invent the form but also in inventing an audience and cultural purpose for the form. She draws on many established traditions and sanctioned habits: the Puritan sermon, suspicion of Redcoats and of women with vaguely French connections, a myth of an innocent America vulnerable to seduction and undoing by European-style deceit and sophistication. This is a literary work that expresses fierce suspicions about imaginative literature, a novel that seems very uneasy about novels and the power they can have over guileless readers. The conversation can radiate outward, therefore, to speculations about America's uncomfortable relationship to its own literary practices and legacy and its habit of turning out powerful works that seem to turn against weaknesses and failings in their own form. As you close, you might suggest that the uncertainty will continue down through Thoreau and Stowe and Whitman and James and onward to the debates in today's newspapers about the worth of the literary arts.

1820–1865

One way of creating a context for discussing early-nineteenth-century authors is to analyze closely with students several works related in theme before proceeding to a more chronological examination. You might ask students to read *Rip Van Winkle* (see discussion of Rip's dream below) in conjunction with *Young Goodman Brown* (another story that shows the male protagonist waking from a dream), *Bartleby, the Scrivener* (where Bartleby's "dead wall revery" becomes a variation on the dream motif), and Thoreau's *Resistance to Civil Government* (in which he describes his night in jail as "a change [that] had to my eyes come over the scene"). Students have heard the phrase *American Dream* used as a cliché; beginning in the nineteenth century with works in which American dreams actually figure in the plot helps them look for new meanings in the theme. In these four works the dreamers share confusion concerning the nature of reality. Your students should keep in mind the larger historical context—the abolitionist movement; early manifestations of the women's rights struggle in the temperance society; the emerging American economic system; the near extinction of the American Indians in the settled Northeast and Midwest; and the various conflicts with Canada, Britain, and Mexico—as they study a literature that explores the power of the imagination and struggles with or evades the conflicts at the center of early-nineteenth-century American social and political life.

As Hershel Parker notes in the period introduction in *NAAL*, by the 1850s "there was some elusive quality about [the country's] new literature that was *American*." Even though many of our early-nineteenth-century writers may have turned inward—to the world of romance, Gothic fantasy, dreams, idealized portraits of the West and the American Indians, or to the microcosm of individual perception, or to the single-sex universe of Melville's sea fiction—even the transcendentalist Thoreau, in separating himself from society at Walden Pond, tries to give imagery of the waking literal—and literary—body. Is an American identity the creation of a few early-nineteenth-century dreamers or does it result from rhythms of dreaming and waking, of separation and engagement, of evasion and confrontation?

As the literature of the 1820–65 period shows, writing helps Emerson, Hawthorne, Dickinson, and others discover who they are in what they see and the language they find to express that vision. What we are exploring, in part, as we read American literature is the development of ways of thinking and seeing the world as well as ways of imagining and creating the self. In rejecting the rationality of the Enlightenment, early-nineteenth-century writers were evolving their own vision. Thoreau, in *Walden*, exchanges Enlightenment thinking for mystical enlightenment. Can students see the early-nineteenth-century writers' rejection of rationality as part of a pattern in American literary history? The Puritans were typological, the eighteenth-century writers exalted reason and logic, but the early-nineteenth-century writers were analogical in their way of seeing. Perhaps the emergence of an "American" imaginative literature in the early nineteenth century may itself be seen as evidence of evolution in epistemology. Once writers became capable of inventing metaphors for their own imagination or for telling stories about either private or public life, they became equally capable of exploring the meaning of their experience and of defining it as "American."

In one sense, Transcendentalism took the separatism of early-nineteenth-century writers to its limit, yet *Nature* and *Walden* both show us that the transcendentalist theory of language is the basis for another American spiritual movement. In fact, every prior moment of separation in colonial and American literary history may be seen in retrospect as a variation on that pattern. When the Puritan reliance on God's word seems in need of strengthening, Jonathan Edwards rewrites the Bible; when theology fails to solve material problems, Benjamin Franklin invents a language with which to address the common people and to create himself as a blueprint; when Britain no longer speaks for the colonists, Jefferson writes a document that enacts the very independence it declares; and in the early nineteenth century, Emerson calls for a literary separation ("We have listened too long to the courtly muses of Europe," from *The American Scholar*) and for an American poet capable of finding the language for the "as yet unsung" American experience ("Yet America is a poem in our eyes," from *The Poet*). The evolution from typology to logic to analogy is progressive, even though the early-nineteenth-century writers were the first to see the pattern. The "forms of being" change and the theories of language change, but American writers become increasingly aware of their powers to name themselves and thus to write themselves into being. From Rip Van Winkle's dream to Adrienne Rich's "dream of a common language," the meaning of both American identity and American literary history are intimately tied to the evolution of an American language.

By the end of their study of the first volume of NAAL, students can see that while American writers may continue after the Civil War to struggle with language and literary forms that will make it possible for them to write an American literature, from the Revolution on they look to themselves for their literary authority and to their own experience for the emotional and aesthetic power of their work. Despite Stowe's comment about taking dictation from God, American writers after the Federal Period no longer have even the illusion, as Edward Taylor had written, "that Thou wilt guide my pen to write aright." Nineteenth-century authors make creative literature out of the economic and spiritual self-reliance of which Franklin and Emerson wrote. Nevertheless, the prohibitions against writing and speaking that American white women and black and Native American men and women suffered throughout the 1620–1865 period in American history would mean that many Americans, then and now, continued to be silenced and that the act of writing for white women and for black writers would reflect acts of heroic rebellion.

WASHINGTON IRVING

Rip Van Winkle is a good place to open the 1820–65 segment, and we can analyze it closely. If this story is the first "American dream" in American literature, we can talk about the implications of that dream. Students make connections between the confused state of mind the earliest colonists must have experienced and Rip's confusion on "waking" to discover that he is a citizen of a new country, an event that must have seemed to many to have taken place overnight. In one central passage in the story that recurs almost as a template in later American literature, Rip asks, "Does nobody here know Rip Van Winkle?" Irving writes, "The poor fellow was now completely confounded. He doubted his own identity, and whether he was himself or another man. In the midst of his bewilderment, the man in the cocked hat demanded who he was, and what was his name?" Rip's reply echoes with contemporary resonance to undergraduate students: " 'God knows,' exclaimed he, at his wit's end; 'I'm not myself—I'm somebody else— that's me yonder—no—that's somebody else, got into my shoes—I was myself last night, but I fell asleep on the mountain, and they've changed my gun and every thing's changed, and I'm changed, and I can't tell what's my name, or who I am!' " The story suggests that, like Rip, we may be deeply confused and years behind in accepting or understanding our own history and destiny. The new country begins in uncertainty; the new American's sense of identity falters, then gains confidence, much as the tale itself shows Rip, by the end, invested with new authority and self-assurance.

But what is the nature of that authority? For Rip, who becomes "reverenced" as a storyteller, a "chronicle of the old times 'before the war,' " is the same person who, twenty years earlier, owned the "worst conditioned farm in the neighbourhood" and was "ready to attend to any body's business but his own." It is only *after* history catches up with Rip, in a sense, and he manages to wake up after the Revolution that he finds his vocation. Is the story in some sense Irving's meditation on imaginative literature before and after the American Revolution? What happens to Rip's cultural identity that makes it possible for the townspeople to produce their first storyteller? The story seems to document the transition between the moment in which the new country had a potential chronicler (Rip Van Winkle) but no history to the moment just a "dream" later when its new identity gave it both a storyteller and a story to tell. Like the moment of the decline of Puritanism and the emergence of enlightenment thinking that we see in Franklin's *Autobiography* (where Franklin respects the general form of Puritan introspection but dramatically alters its content), there is a similar moment of transition between prerevolutionary and postrevolutionary thinking for the new American Rip Van Winkle. In changing only the red coat of King George to the blue coat of George Washington on the sign that used to stand over the village inn (and now advertises the Union Hotel), Irving suggests that the "singularly metamorphosed" country may have undergone radical change in some ways, but that in other ways it may have changed very little indeed.

At the end of the story, Irving turns Rip's confusion into a joke at Dame Van Winkle's expense: "But there was one species of despotism under which he had long groaned, and that was—petticoat government." Here Irving establishes a theme that would become characteristic of much nineteenth-century fiction, in which the male character represents simple good nature, artistic sensibility, and free spirit and the female character signifies the forces that inhibit that sensibility. Dame's "curtain lectures" vie only with Puritan sermons in their severity, and it is her "dinning" voice, her tongue that was "incessantly going," that Irving blames for silencing the budding artist in Rip. ("Rip had but one way of replying to all lectures of the kind. . . . He shrugged his shoulders, shook his head, cast up his eyes, but said nothing.") American fiction seems to begin, therefore, in the silencing of Dame Van Winkle—for Rip's real victory is not the one he wins over the British, but the one he wins as a result of Dame's death. One might speculate that for Irving—as for Cooper, Poe, Hawthorne, and Melville—the real American Dream is of a world in which women are either silent, dead, or in some other way excluded from the sphere of action.

If students are interested in reading Irving for allegorical resonance or for the indication (or betrayal) of certain archetypal fears in the emerging American male author, then *The Legend of Sleepy Hollow* can provide them with more possibilities along this line. What if we read the conflict between Ichabod and Brom Bones as suggesting somehow a larger opposition—between Ichabod as the product of a new-style book-learning that conceals but does not eliminate foolishness and superstition and Brom Bones, who flat-out refuses intellectuality and intellectual pretensions and who makes his way through the world on personal intuitions and common sense? Ichabod reads and reasons and teaches, but he cannot escape his childish fears; Brom says no! in thunder to Ichabod's kind of thinking—is it significant then that this Horseman of his is headless? About two hundred years before Irving wrote this story, Anne Hutchinson was banished from the Bay Colony for trusting her own mind and heart above any printed word or reasoned argument; playfully or otherwise, has her spirit made its return in Irving's story? Does the last line of the story suggest, perhaps, that the story itself celebrates a buoyant distrust of the spoken and printed word? To what extent are latter-day Antinomians and Headless Horsemen heroic figures in American imaginative literature? That is a question to bear in mind and entertain as we move forward from Sleepy Hollow.

After these expertly crafted and vigorous tales, in which Irving enacts a bemused and even condescending air toward his characters and even toward the whole practice of storytelling, the chapters from *A Tour of the Prairies* may strike some students as rather flat and meandering. Which may be the point: in the expanses of the west, Irving finds a world that is utterly different from the tradition-saturated and sedately pastoral Hudson River Valley, which he presents in *Rip Van Winkle* and *Sleepy Hollow*. The cool detachment seems to be gone now, and Irving presents himself as encountering something like what Nick Carraway, in *The Great Gatsby*, calls a place "commensurate to his capacity to wonder." The *Prairies* excerpts may not merit a long pause in a survey course, but they can suggest the challenge facing American imaginative writers—to evolve literary forms and achieve energy "commensurate" with this wilder place and these diverse peoples.

JAMES FENIMORE COOPER

You have small bits here of a writer known for sprawling works, and some special care may be required so that students read him sympathetically. You might want to open with some notes about Cooper's huge popularity in his own time and after—to the extent that later nineteenth-century writers (like Mark Twain) felt that he was a ponderous Romantic legacy that realism had to push out of the way, just as British realism had to rise up against Sir Walter Scott. Cooper remained a rite of passage for young American boys until the middle of this century; and his grander yarns, in which Hawkeye (Natty Bumppo, the old hunter in these excerpts) was young and a superhero in buckskins, did much to shape not only the popular conception of the eastern woods in the French and Indian War and the Revolution but also popular ideas of what Indians were like and how to tell the Noble Savages (mostly Delawares and Mohegans in these tales) from the skulking, villainous Hurons.

Back before academics began to fuss about literary modes and schools, Cooper was engaged in doing several kinds of cultural work at once in these novels about Natty and the early days of settlement in the neighborhood of Otsego Lake, Lake George, and Lake Champlain. He was writing an epic, with the classic purposes of Virgil's epic: to lay claim to a heroic heritage, to infuse a landscape with an aura of grandeur and elegy, to inspire his contemporaries with paragons of various virtues. He was also writing romance, in the manner of Scott, who not only had imbued Scotland with magic, legend, and melancholy beauty but also had made a fortune in the process. And Cooper was also a man of political and social causes: environmentalist ethics burst forth at times in these novels, as do moments of prophecy. It's worth telling your students that these floods of pigeons, slaughtered with cannons and so thick that they blot out the sky, are indeed the passenger pigeons that were driven to extinction in the opening decades of this century. As you read more closely, talk at some length about Cooper's slow-developing sentences; his delight in the carefully composed tableau; and the affinity of such a style to the dark, emotion-charged, ceremonial canvases of the Hudson River School of painters, to which Cooper was closely allied.

THE CHEROKEE MEMORIALS

The *Memorials* themselves were written in response to the Indian Removal Act of 1830, which authorized the removal of Indian groups to lands west of the Mississippi. The *Memorials* reveal inconsistencies in the U.S. government's treatment of the Cherokee: on the one hand viewing them as subjects and on the other negotiating with them as independent people of a separate nation. "The answer must be plain—they were not subjects, but a distinct nation." Furthermore, the *Memorials* hold that treaties enacted between the Cherokee and the U.S. governments were "always written by the Commissioners, on the part of the United States, for obvious reasons: as the Cherokees were unacquainted with letters." In each of these arguments, students can see evidence of awareness on the part of the Cherokee themselves, and reading the *Memorials* may help them recognize that even at the time of their own removal, the Cherokee were articulate analysts of their own situation and of U.S. policies and accurately predicted the disastrous outcome of the Indian Removal Act. In the document dated November 5, 1829, the authors note that the doctrine will be "fatal in its consequences to us" and urge the House and the Senate to take action so that "our national existence may not be extinguished."

The Cherokee had built roads and houses, become Christianized, published books in an alphabet invented by Sequoyah, and adopted a national constitution. In light of these efforts, students may see in the hope that "our national existence may not be extinguished" a double meaning: the Cherokee do not wish to lose either their cultural identity or their new attainments as "civilized" or "national" persons. They doubly express their feelings of betrayal, because they are asked not only to leave their ancestral lands but also to understand that their efforts to "improve" their society have not merited what they had expected—"the voice of encouragement by an approving world." In a literature course, it is particularly important to look at the structure and language of these *Memorials* and understand how they work. They are not a mindless copycatting of language in *The Declaration of Independence* and sections of The Constitution of the United States; they employ those by-now "self-evident" truths and principles, and the language in which they were expressed fifty years previous, to give special emphasis to the facts that "all men" are not being treated equally by the Washington government, and that those most feared sins of the New England Puritans—hypocrisy and deep inconsistency between principle and action—are overshadowing relations with indigenous American peoples.

CATHERINE MARIA SEDGWICK

Think twice before you pass over Sedgwick. For several reasons, she can be an important inclusion in a historical survey course, especially if you are following the development of an American voice, or voices, and looking for vivid accounts of how large-scale doctrines, creeds, and cultural shifts influenced ordinary life. If you are seeking indications of how we got from the magisterial sound of Irving and the rhetorical stodginess of Cooper to the vital vernaculars of Melville, Twain, and Jewett, then Sedgwick marks an important stage in those developments.

Something is happening to American prose and to American ideas of authorship, and *Cacoethes Scribendi* (take a moment and reassure your class that the story under this pretentious-sounding title is anything but pretentious) is a tale that your students will move through with a speed that may surprise them. It a tale of life and love in a small New England town, and in the context of a survey course it can help shift and extend the view of white American experience. You might select a page or two of Sedgwick and do a quick comparison with Irving in *The Legend of Sleepy Hollow*, or Rowson or Cooper, and see if students can hear a difference, hear a prose style that in this case is aptly suited to the context and people which the story is about. This is ordinary America as Sedgwick knew it, and it is also the regular literary scene: the world from which writers and audiences and a literary culture will grow. The story is light-hearted; this is no pastoral tragedy or Thomas Gray lament for talent lost under the bushel of rural life. But there are uncertainties here about how people will write, why they will write, and what they will write; and your class can get a good glimpse of the emerging situation of imaginative literature in America, a situation understood firsthand by one of its most successful authors.

A *Reminiscence of Federalism* is perhaps harder to enter into imaginatively. Sedgwick is writing of an era that for herself was long gone, and she is telling a story that is mustier to your students than a tale of small-town love. There is a distinctly eighteenth-century cast to the plot: the early death of a mother and a great deal of anxiety about inheritance, expectations, family name—the stuff of the English gentry as evoked by the likes of Fielding. There is a timeless quality, however, to some of the central subjects of the story: a struggle between political values, a struggle supposedly far away, is having a local effect on the motives of characters in the foreground and on the reasons and rationalizations that they offer (to others and to themselves) for what they do. It's a reasonable hope that some of your students have been wondering about this, about how the big philosophical and political principles encountered so often in a typical survey course sifted down into ordinary thinking and experience. Sedgwick's astute, cool observations of those effects make her work an important moment in the growth of American fiction as social observation and commentary. For those reasons, the Sedgwick materials make an excellent combination with Alcott's *Transcendental Wild Oats*.

WILLIAM CULLEN BRYANT

More than Freneau, Bryant exemplifies the new "Americanness" of nineteenth-century literature; yet Bryant will not serve as Emerson's American poet. Ask your students why; and ask them to compare *Thanatopsis* with Freneau's *The House of Night*. Which of Bryant's poems look to eighteenth-century values, both in philosophy and in aesthetics? You can closely analyze *The Prairies* in class, for this poem is the most clearly "American" of the Bryant selections in *NAAL*. Even so, memories of Sarah Morton (if *The African Chief* has been read before Bryant) will cause students to wonder what the core intention is here—a mystical breakthrough into understanding of these bygone Indian nations, these enigmatic moundbuilders about whom Bryant has no clues but the landscape and its telltale shapes? Or a pretext to write, on a small scale, an American *Aeneid,* and thus claim for ourselves some reassuring romantic ghosts in our wilderness and some oblique claim to an ancient, heroic, and tragic tradition?

What marks the poem as American? You can discuss the way Bryant draws his imagery from the Great Plains, takes as his subject the "dilated sight" of the romantic perceiver, and associates the source of perception with change in the "forms of being." The mixture of styles, philosophies, and attitudes toward poetry that students find in *The Prairies* helps them see that evolution in thinking and writing takes place slowly. Some might argue that the "British" elements in Bryant's poetry contribute greatly to its beauty and power and that the evidence of continued influence is one valid response to the confusion the new Americans must have felt after the Revolution and also serves as a tribute to the enduring cultural and emotional content of the new country's relationship to things British, despite the change in our form of government.

WILLIAM APESS

Both Samson Occom and William Apess were Christian preachers, and both worked as missionaries of and reformers to American Indian peoples. Furthermore, in both of the texts in *NAAL*, Occom and Apess are addressing a white audience; Apess, however, is much more direct in criticizing the audience he is addressing.

Ask students to comment on the image of the looking glass. In one sense Apess's essay holds a mirror up to his Euro-American audience, but that mirroring also creates a rhetorical form of encounter, thus linking Apess's text with the "Literature to 1620" section of *NAAL* and hinting at several new ways to interpret this trope in light of the history of Native Americans in the nineteenth-century United States.

For the looking glass also shows his audience the reality of the lives of Indians, particularly of women and children in poverty—"Let me for a few moments turn your attention to the reservations in the different states of New England"—thus asking his audience to encounter in a literal sense the lives he describes for them and in a spiritual sense the racism they have condoned and that Apess deems responsible for the material condition of the Indians' lives. The looking glass thus becomes both self-reflexive and reflective of the racialized "others" in American history—a history that for Apess includes the treatment of African Americans as well as American Indians.

In some ways the rhetoric of Apess's text may seem uncomplicated, perhaps partly because the arguments he raises to counter racism may be familiar to students in your class. He argues that Euro-Americans use skin color to racialize the difference and hence the inferiority of both Native Americans and African Americans; he reminds his audience that there are by far more skins of color in the world than white skins (he cites the ratio of fifteen to one), he makes his audience aware of the theory that Jesus Christ and the Apostles were themselves persons of color, and he protests the double-standard that has allowed white men to marry Native American women but has not allowed Native American men "to choose their partners among the whites if they wish." Many of these and other points of his argument actually seem quite forward looking for 1833, anticipating analyses of racial formation in our own time. And Apess cites Scripture to underscore his reasoning.

In another way, his rhetorical strategy is complex and provocative. After all, as a Christian Indian, he is himself the product of a particular aspect of white culture, the aspect he now invokes to affirm his perspective. Thus as he addresses his white audience, he himself becomes a looking glass; in Apess, his Christian audience can see their own creation and their own best selves taken as gospel and then held back up to them. Point out to students that Apess does not base his essay on Scripture and in fact does not even quote from the Bible early in his text. It is only later, when he is looking for support for his own argument, that he quotes. Examine the particular passages he includes; these passages become the ultimate moments of encounter with the self for his Euro-American audience, for they have ostensibly served as models for New England character. When he examines them, he states his purpose, namely "to penetrate more fully into the conduct of those who profess to have pure principles and who tell us to follow Jesus Christ. . . . Let us see if they come anywhere near him and his ancient disciples." The act of examining the principles of Christ—including especially "Thou shalt love thy neighbor as thyself" and "Let us not love in word but in deed"—becomes the rhetorical act of holding up the looking glass, but in effect, the Indians themselves are what Apess wants his audience to see when they look in a mirror. "Thou shalt love thy neighbor as thyself" becomes, in Apess's text, "Thou shalt see thy neighbor as—and in—thyself."

Apess's text thus becomes an emblem of American literature viewed as encounter: without the meeting of Native American and Christian cultures in Apess himself, he would not be speaking texts in a language that can be transcribed (but rather, perhaps, be an orator of native myths or songs). What he has to say, as a product of that encounter, is conveyed by the word *looking glass*. Thus the history of relations between Indians and whites explains the emergence of Apess's text: *encounter* serves as a figure for another creation myth, this one for a Native American's creation of American literature and his implied white reader.

CAROLINE STANSBURY KIRKLAND

Kirkland's brief sketches help jar the notion that realist intentions came to America only after the Civil War, but the interest of this material extends further. These are thoughtful observations, and they ask whether high-flown philosophical premises and Romantic perceptions and sentiments have a life in the outback—a life of their own or as transplants from eastern or European intellectual circles. Crèvecoeur is an obvious figure for comparison here: he hardly mentions women in his imaginative and fairly abstract tour of American rural settlements. Kirkland, in contrast, centers on the experience and space of the woman pioneer and builds her larger formulations out of the particulars and domestic details of life on the frontier; in other words, she seems to work from an opposite direction. To what extent does she arrive where Crèvecoeur does, on the subject of freedom and the moral effects of living in the natural world? Where are the important differences?

LYDIA MARIA CHILD

Child was a prolific and adventurous writer; this excerpt is nonfiction prose from fairly late in her career, after the success of *Hobomok* and much of her work in the cause of abolitionism and women's rights. All of her life, Child was a risk taker, out ahead of other reformers and social critics; and students may respond well to a look at the way she frames her defense of John Brown. There is sustained, high-serious intensity here, and Child's argumentative strategy compares in very interesting ways to the tactics that Fuller and Fanny Fern adopt for arguing important issues connected to principles of liberty and human worth. The best comparison, however, might be with Thoreau's famous *Plea for Captain John Brown*, which could easily be brought in and looked over in class. In defending Brown, each of these writers sees him differently; and those differences open up major comparisons in their temperament, in their social circumstances, and in the motives that shaped their respective careers.

RALPH WALDO EMERSON

If you are focusing on the New Americanness of American literature in the early nineteenth century, one or more of the following essays will help you develop the theme: *The American Scholar, The Divinity School Address, Self-Reliance,* and *The Poet.* If you are interested in discussing Emerson's philosophy and contrasting it with his commentary on social issues of the day, you might want to choose from the list in Chapter 4. Whatever your model of course organization you can ask students to read all of *Nature,* and then spend several class meetings analyzing it. Understanding Emerson may depend on success with this essay, so detailed suggestions are offered below.

Nature

Emerson can lose students in the opening paragraphs of *Nature,* and it might be useful to read the "Introduction" with them during the class period before you turn them loose on the entire essay. One of his opening premises, "Every man's condition is a solution in hieroglyphic to those inquiries he would put. He acts it as life, before he apprehends it as truth," initially can give students difficulty; but as you talk about it, trying to find something in their own experience that will give them some affinity for what Emerson is saying, they begin to see that for Emerson nature includes our own "condition." He breaks down boundaries between self and body, between our own feeling and the natural world, with the result that he achieves a spiritual vision of unity with nature: "I become a transparent eyeball. I am nothing. I see all. The currents of the Universal Being circulate through me; I am part or particle of God."

Pedagogically, the most important single concept in the essay may be contained in the following sentence: "Each particle is a microcosm, and faithfully renders the likeness of the world." Students can see this visually by turning to an example Emerson uses earlier in the essay, at the beginning of "Language," in which he writes, "Who looks upon a river in a meditative hour, and is not reminded of the flux of all things? Throw a stone into the stream, and the circles that propagate themselves are the beautiful type of all influence." Almost everyone in the class, at some point in childhood, will have done just that; and all will remember the series of concentric circles that radiate out from the point at which the stone enters the water. Ask students to reconstruct what happens as we look farther from that central point; they all remember that the circles grow larger but fainter, and some of them will recall from a high-school math class that, theoretically, the circles continue infinitely, even though they might not be visible to the eye.

You can talk about this example as an analogy for Emerson's entire philosophy, for it contains several essential ideas: (1) that our observation of the finite ripples on the water leads us to "see" the ripples that ease out into infinity, (2) that the concentric circles made by the ripples themselves form a series of analogies, and (3) that in the act of throwing one stone we can manage to contact an infinitely enlarging sphere. This discussion helps with the related ideas that "man is an analogist, and studies relations in all objects" and that "the world is emblematic. Parts of speech are metaphors because the whole of nature is a metaphor of the human mind." Each of these points takes time, but the rewards are great. Students begin to see that through analogies we can understand the world and our own relation to it. The chapter "Language" is important to this discussion, because Emerson sees the very process of creating analogies or metaphors as essential to human understanding. Therefore, he can quote Plato—"poetry comes nearer to vital truth than history"—and can state, "Empirical science is apt to cloud the sight . . . a dream may let us deeper into the secret of nature than a hundred concerted experiments." Here you can ask students to compare Emerson with Franklin and Jefferson; Emerson's philosophy is deeply antithetical to the Age of Experiment.

Why do students find *Nature* difficult? Ask them to think about what constitutes the unit of thought for Emerson. Is it the sentence, the paragraph, the section? He uses a linear form, prose, but does not write discursively. Is *analogy* Emerson's basic unit of thought? His ideas seem to move out from an analogical center like the ripples on the pond, even though he is forced to write about them as if he were thinking linearly and logically.

Another concept that students need help with is what Emerson means by *transcendence*. How does an understanding of analogies, or of the microcosm that is nature, help us transcend the limitations of our material existence and our own finite abilities to "see"? Here, understanding Emerson's use of *analogy* as the unit of thought is crucial, for Emerson seems to affirm that if we focus on the analogy and on the single part, we will be able to understand the whole. To this end, he states, "Whilst we behold unveiled the nature of Justice and Truth, we learn the difference between the absolute and the conditional or relative. We apprehend the absolute. As it were, for the first time, *we exist.*" If you have any students in your class who have studied transcendental meditation, or any other Eastern meditative technique, you can ask them to talk about how they have understood and experienced the difference between the "absolute" and the "relative." Sometimes these students can explain what it feels like to begin with a mantra in meditation and then "transcend" into an oceanic feeling of oneness with the universe. (This is also an ideal moment to ask students whether they find any lingering Puritanism in Emerson. Are there similarities in form between Emerson's focus on the analogy as the vehicle for transcendence and the Puritan's search for the black mark or spot?)

Ask students to list some American themes that Emerson touches on or invokes in the essay: reliance on the self; the idea that the possibility of redemption lies within the individual; a belief in the perception of the individual and the intimate connection of human beings with nature (if students have studied the British Romantic poets it will help here); the ability, the imperative, of Americans to "build their own world"; and essential to his philosophy, the conflict between empirical knowledge and intuition, between logic and analogy. You can talk about the way that conflict is apparent in students' own lives, even in their own choice of major fields of study at the university: Do they become technologists or humanists? Do they choose applied or theoretical science? Do they elect courses in computer science or poetry? Emerson is certain to challenge their conception of thinking as linear, for he shows that analogy possesses its own logic, and that poetry and imaginative literature can help us live in the world, perhaps better than science and technology—for, if analogy is the means of transcending, then analogy holds ascendancy over logic and helps us reunite body and spirit, thought and feeling. "What we are, that only can we see" brings the essay back to the beginning, to the idea of "solution in hieroglyphic."

The Poet

Emerson's essay *The Poet* makes an argument for the value of poetry and the significance of language that remains compelling in the late twentieth century. It also reflects a distinctly male sort of poetics that can be contracted to the way in which American women writers from Fuller through Dickinson and onward to Plath and Rich choose to engage with the world.

As the *NAAL* headnote observes, Emerson considered himself a poet, and we can read an Emerson essay as if we were reading the work of a poet; we can respond to individual sentences and to Emerson's specific expression of particular ideas much as if we were trying to close-read a lyric poem. In this essay, we begin with his central idea that all of us "stand in need of expression . . . we study to utter our painful secret. The man is only half himself, the other half is his expression." Asking students to respond to this idea can lead into a discussion of voice, one of their own specific tasks as undergraduates, as well as the ongoing task of American writers throughout our literary history. Emerson suggests that the poet possesses both a complete vision and the tool—language—for expressing what we would all understand if we were just given the analogies for doing so. The poet finds those particular analogies (metaphors, similes, images) that allow us to understand what we might have been just on the verge of seeing but were never able to fully see without the analogies themselves.

Therefore, Emerson writes, "Words are also actions, and actions are a kind of words." Someone who is able to express the inchoate understandings of other human beings allows us to integrate our being and our experience in the world. This idea may generate some controversy for students, unaccustomed to viewing language as action. Ask them to talk about related ideas they find in their reading of the essay, perhaps Emerson's statement that "language is fossil poetry" or that the world is "thus put under the mind for verb and noun." Asking students to explain what it might mean to see the world as "put under the mind for verb and noun" may help them become more conscious about the relationship between words and actions.

Emerson's poet does more than help us create a bridge between what we see and what we can express; the poet also enables us to re-create ourselves. Thus, Emerson writes, "All that we call sacred history attests that the birth of a poet is the principal event in chronology." In direct challenge to particular theologies, Emerson asserts that, as young Americans (whether we interpret him to refer specifically to the young culture of the New Republic, or more loosely to the process of forming American identity in each of us as one of the tasks of undergraduate intellectual development), we look for a poet who will be able to tell us who and what we are. "Poets are thus liberating gods," he writes. "They are free, and they make free," and they keep us from miserably dying "on the brink of the waters of life and truth."

This is a powerful manifesto for poetry in the Transcendental age and after, and Emerson's influence extends down to the present. But ask students to look closely at lines like these: "the man is only half himself, the other half is his expression." "The religions of the world are the ejaculations of a few imaginative men." "Hence the necessity of speech and song; . . . that thought may be ejaculated as Logos, or Word." Here and throughout the essay, Emerson's poetics is aggressively male: all about gaining dominion over experience, playing Adam, naming all things in the natural world, or playing some version of the wild bard that Emerson imagines as powerfully male primordial spirit and force in Anglo-Saxon poetry. It's not just the imagery in the essay that shows this male inflection: it is this assumption that the highest and best engagement with worldly experience is agonistic, a struggle to say the profoundest and most permanent possible thing, and to have the Last Word. What about a poetics based on dialogue with experience, rather than dominion over it? What about a poetics in which each poem is not proffered as the *last* word or the last poem but as momentary perceptions in and of a particular moment? What about a poetics in which a certain mutuality, rather than domination, is the hoped for relationship to the world? Students will want to know what you are suggesting. This is a great time to turn to Dickinson and to read half a dozen poems together, fairly quickly. When students ask whether they "add up" to a consistent theme or aesthetic vision, why not ask where this idea comes from, that all the poems from a complex and changeful sensibility have to add up to some overarching and final profundity? *That* idea comes from Emerson . . . and in Dickinson we see the most brilliant resistance to the idea that Emerson's "Poet" describes *the* Poet, for all times, and for both genders.

Fate

The late essay *Fate* will elicit controversy among your students and give them a glimpse of Emerson responding to the current events and spirit of his own times. Throughout the essay, Emerson variously defines *fate* as the laws of the world, as what limits us, and as unpenetrated causes; he writes that "once we thought, positive power was all. Now, we learn, that negative power, or circumstance, is half. Nature is the tyrannous circumstance." Contrast what he says here about nature with the essay *Nature* itself. How do your students respond to Emerson's position that the "fate" of our limitations cannot be transcended, except by accepting it and building "altars" to the "Beautiful Necessity"? Is there no hope for reform in the world if "the riddle of the age has for each a private solution"? Is Emerson asking us to accept what he himself terms the "complicity" of "race living at the expense of race" because "Providence has a wild, rough, incalculable road to its end," and therefore, it is futile to "whitewash its huge mixed instrumentalities"? Is there no hope for environment or the "nurture" side of Emerson's portrait of nature? He writes of the ditch digger that "he has but one future, and that is already predetermined in his lobes, and described in that little fatty face, pig-eye, and squat form. All the privilege and all the legislation of the world cannot meddle or help to make a poet or a prince of him." Is Emerson's own essay itself an example of "organization tyrannizing over character"? If we accept the "Beautiful Necessity" of things, are we enshrining elitism, the New England Brahminism of ideological caste and class? Allowing your students to challenge Emerson is one way of teaching them to take his ideas seriously, to be critical as well as appreciative; it is a way of allowing them to participate in the shaping of ideological debate that characterizes American cultural history.

Last of the Anti-Slavery Lectures (March 7, 1854)

The March 7 speech is new to *NAAL* and is usually overlooked in the Emerson canon, in part because Emerson came to the antislavery movement rather late and because these speeches were not collected and published in book form in his lifetime. From a literary perspective and from the perspective of the American intellectual tradition, this speech can be read as a testing ground, an experiment in which the Emersonian way of thinking, and of organizing perceptions, had to be reconciled with the needs of a New York City auditorium full of sympathetic listeners and an overwhelming moral emergency. There is a struggle under way here, having to do with self-expression and one's own legacy as a great American author and established philosophical leader; and students can be asked to offer their opinions on how that struggle turns out: Emerson loves the vast perspective, the free range through all Western historical periods, the immense generalization, the durable truth extracted from (we are to suppose) a mountain of reading and long rumination. Race slavery certainly wasn't something abstract and timeless as a human condition; and obviously the institution was the antithesis of everything Emerson called for, and hoped for, in regard to the possibilities of the free human spirit. How well do these long paragraphs work as a speech on this subject? What turns out to be the subject? Is this a speech designed to be followed logically? Is it meant to be persuasive? Is it constructed for an audience that needs to be convinced that slavery is a social and moral evil? Or is something else happening here, an effort, perhaps, to connect Emerson the gray eminence with a movement that has a shape, momentum, and creed already and to which he can provide only added legitimacy, a blessing, and some intellectual grandeur?

NATHANIEL HAWTHORNE

Hawthorne can present a problem for a teacher because students often feel that reading his work is little more than a quest for the "moral" or a game of "find the secret sin." They confuse his use of Puritan subjects and themes with his own values and conclude that Hawthorne is himself a Puritan. They may also need help in understanding the concept of allegory and how it works in Hawthorne and in making distinctions between those stories that seem predominantly or essentially allegories and others in which the allegory is only part of a larger experience or meditation. *Young Goodman Brown, The Minister's Black Veil,* and *Rappaccini's Daughter* all invite students to find allegorical "equations"; but each of these stories ultimately frustrates the attempt. In each of these stories, see if students can identify the "good" character; in every case, they will eventually come around to qualifying their initial response. If students can grow comfortable with the idea that Hawthorne, as an author and a modern human being, asks complex questions rather than deals in prophecy or reductive moral answers, they will enjoy reading him all the more and see his importance to modern American fiction.

Rappaccini's Daughter works particularly well in classroom study of Hawthorne's use of allegory, for students have fun trying to work out the parallels between the Garden of Eden and Rappaccini's garden. The role of the serpent (after the lizard is poisoned by the flower) remains open by the end of the story: who *is* responsible for Beatrice's death? Rappaccini? Baglioni? Giovanni? Hawthorne himself? How does the story, in creating an antigarden, actually affirm the moral universe of the Garden of Eden, despite its attempt to invert those values? Is the story a variation of *Rip Van Winkle*, in which Irving triumphs over Dame Van Winkle's power by silencing her at the end?

Asking students to read Melville's *Hawthorne and His Mosses* can lead into a discussion of the "blackness" Melville saw in Hawthorne's fiction. Is that blackness a reference to Hawthorne's moral universe or a reflection of his use of dream imagery (explicitly in *Young Goodman Brown* and implicitly in the atmosphere of his other work)? Suggest to students that the ambivalence they find in Hawthorne actually expresses the mingled self-confrontation and self-evasion that characterize his protagonists. Rather than try to "solve" the ambiguities one finds in Hawthorne, show students instead that his choice to be ambivalent is deliberate and conscious. You can also talk about the way Young Goodman Brown, Reverend Hooper, Rappaccini, and the speaker in *The Custom-House* (from *The Scarlet Letter*) are all, in part, Hawthorne's self-portraits, or at least portraits of the artist. Unlike Thoreau, who values facing life "deliberately" in *Walden*, Hawthorne goes only so far in trying to see what is there—in his characters and ultimately in himself. Hershel Parker, in the period introduction in *NAAL*, describes the "crucial aesthetic problems" early nineteenth-century writers faced and suggests that Hawthorne's involved his attempt to "strike a balance between the allegorical and the realistic." What might this mean, if we consider the actual moment of confrontation between the writer and the blank page? *The Custom-House* provides a rich opportunity for students to consider the struggles of the writer and to see that these struggles take place within the depths of the psyche, perhaps at the source of the individual writer's (or the culture's) dream life.

New to *NAAL* are *The Birth-Mark* and *The Celestial Railroad*, which make a nice pair, especially if students are moving through the anthology chronologically and reading Hawthorne after an experience with Emerson and Transcendentalism. Students will probably have an easier time with *The Birth-Mark*, as it seems to play by all the rules and themes that became evident in *Rappaccini's Daughter*—the foolhardiness and depravity of seeking perfection or superhuman power; the fatality of mistaking infatuation and idolatry for love; the reduction, in one's own mind, of other human beings into objects to be manipulated, overhauled, or otherwise controlled. In contrast to this dark fable, *The Celestial Railroad* may strike your class as an outbreak of disorder, a refreshing escape from high formality, provided that students, coming to this story after unpacking and appreciating the high formality of the others, don't frustrate themselves in seeking or enforcing a tidiness and a closure that may simply not be there. It might be well to suggest that Hawthorne writes very much as one of us, a passenger on the train being carried into a future that he, like most of us, only dimly understands, even while he listens to the reassurances of bumptious Emersonian optimists. If this narrative of the modern, post-Emerson situation can be read as open-ended, as an eloquent and sometimes funny expression of worry from a fellow traveler, someone like ourselves, then a tour of Hawthorne can close on a high note and with a stronger sense both of the risks that he takes as a writer of fiction and of the big-scale issues that he enters and necessarily leaves open.

The Scarlet Letter

The Scarlet Letter has been interpreted in many different ways, and most of you have probably written about the book at some point, as students or as critics. It helps to remember what it was like to read the book for the first or second time and to give students a chance to achieve some kind of direct and personal relationship with the text before turning them loose on a writing assignment.

The Custom-House: As you move into the text, you might want to observe some peculiarities of *The Custom-House*, a preface which some students will want to dismiss as a time-waster before the real story begins. You might draw attention to the atmosphere of dream or hallucination that accompanies not only Hawthorne's discovery of the letter but also his entire memory of the custom-house itself. Also interesting are (1) the moments in which Hawthorne blames others for his own "torpor" and his consequent difficulty in writing and (2) the image patterns of this opening essay: the meals which he describes, the word-portrait of the Inspector, and Hawthorne's speculations about reconciling "the Actual and the Imaginary." Consider the statement that Hawthorne makes early: "To this extent and within these limits, an author, methinks, may be autobiographical, without violating either the reader's rights or his own." Is *The Custom-House* a revelation of its author or a veil like the one Reverend Hooper wears?

The novel itself (or the romance—ask students to talk about what they think Hawthorne means by the difference in *Preface to The House of the Seven Gables*) raises a lot of related questions. Hawthorne bares Hester; does he reveal or conceal Dimmesdale? Examine the imagery of revelation in the book: Hester's first appearance in the prison door; the scarlet letter itself; the scenes on the scaffold; and Chapter XXIII, titled "The Revelation of the Scarlet Letter." Does Hawthorne's symbol, literally fastened to Hester's breast, allow him to bridge "the Actual and the Imaginary"? Compare Hawthorne's use of tangible symbol with Emerson's use of analogies. Is the scarlet letter also a way of seeing and of knowing, for Hawthorne's characters and for himself? What is the relationship between symbol and stigma? And why does Chillingworth, twice in *The Scarlet Letter,* have the privilege of seeing what is on Dimmersdale's breast, while Hawthorne averts his own eyes—and ours? Who are the "good" or "evil" characters in this book?

What limits Hawthorne's sympathy for Chillingworth? What limits his portrait of Hester? In Chapter II he writes, "The women, who were now standing about the prison-door, stood within less than half a century of the period when the man-like Elizabeth had been the not altogether unsuitable representative of the sex." Even so, Hawthorne implies that, by the early nineteenth century, American women have changed. "There was, moreover, a boldness and rotundity of speech among these matrons, as most of them seemed to be, that would startle us at the present day." Is Hester herself a variation on Dame Van Winkle—silenced by her author as much as by her society? And to what extent is *The Scarlet Letter* not "about" Hester Prynne at all? To what extent does she catalyze the "real" drama of the dynamic and developing association between the minister and the physician? And how does Hawthorne use Pearl, particularly at the end of the book, to affirm a certain view of femininity and to reject others? He writes that her tears "were the pledge that she would grow up amid human joy and sorrow, nor for ever do battle with the world, but be a woman in it." Is *The Scarlet Letter* itself an indictment of Hester? And a vindication of Dimmesdale? And how do we interpret the "moral" Hawthorne "presses" on his readers at the end: "Be true! Be true! Be true! Show freely to the world, if not your worst, yet some trait whereby the worst may be inferred!"

EDGAR ALLAN POE

You might find it useful to open with some observations about the rediscovery, or reinvention, of Poe: the way he faded into obscurity in America for decades after his death; his rediscovery and veneration by Symbolist and Imagist poets in France; and his reimportation to America as an imaginative writer of real consequence, rather than as a maestro of Gothic entertainments and a sort of showoff in the tradition of Romantic verse. Did the French get it right? You might also move into some speculations on how and why Poe has become so influential in our popular culture, the forebear of mountains of gothic novels, slash-and-hack films, gruesome television shows. Poe has changed for us, and has changed us. The largest and most vexing questions are if, and how, we should take him "seriously" and what our efforts to do so say about our notions of seriousness in imaginative literature.

The dream world characterizes Poe's work, of course; and students may study his dream imagery in the poems *The Sleeper, Dream-land,* and *The Raven.* Can we read any of these allegorically, as we might read Hawthorne?

Are these poems about the mind? Is there any connection between Poe's dream worlds and those of *Rip Van Winkle* or Hawthorne's fiction? Many writers in American literary history serve as spokespeople for others; does Poe? What effects does his poetry create in the reader and how? His poetry lacks specific references to American places or American life; is it, like Freneau's or Bryant's, derivative of British poetry? If you read *The Philosophy of Composition* closely with students, and compare it with *The Custom-House*, then how is the act of writing different for Poe and Hawthorne? Ask them to evaluate Poe's description of the composition of *The Raven* against their experience of reading the poem. When Poe asserts that the ultimate subject for a poem is the death of a beautiful women, is he "serious"? Can you complicate their thinking a little by turning to *The Imp of the Perverse*, and to Poe's famous relish for put-ons and practical jokes? Students have a lot of experience with the way that comedy and horror mingle in popular gothic entertainments, their habit of becoming reflexive and self-satirizing. What about here? Is there an element of the absurd about *The Raven* and is that absurdity possibly intentional?

You can also analyze *Annabel Lee* line by line in the context of Poe's statement in *The Philosophy of Composition* that beauty moves the soul best when the subject is sad and that, therefore, the death of a beautiful woman becomes the "soul" of poetry. Why does Poe need to kill off Annabel Lee to achieve the male speaker's maturity and poetic inspiration? And if you are willing to let the conversation rove a bit more, you might ask for observations about how Romantic male writers constructed women as subjects in their poetry and fiction.

Among the tales included in *NAAL*, *The Fall of the House of Usher* and *Ligeia* further demonstrate the effects Poe creates at the expense of his female characters. In either case, is the center of interest with the tormented woman or with the psychological torments of the men who bear witness? If you had any luck with reading *The Raven* as in any sense allegorical, what happens if we try reading *The Tell-Tale Heart* and *The Masque of the Red Death* that way—as allegories for mental states or motions? How does Poe's use of doubling in *The Fall of the House of Usher*, reinforce the effect of the torture and death of Madeline? Ask students to think about the "organic" relationship between human beings and nature, or the supernatural, in Poe, especially *The Fall of the House of Usher*, as another form of doubling. In what other tales does Poe use doubling between characters and events? Does he alter the effects of the dream world by portraying events as nightmares (in *The Tell-Tale Heart*, for example)? From the point of view of twentieth-century psychology, do Montresor and Fortunato in *The Cask of Amontillado* represent shadow elements of the same personality?

Ask students to analyze *The Purloined Letter*, deducing from it some of the conventional elements of the detective story. Compare it with Poe's tales of the supernatural; what are the different effects he achieves in *The Purloined Letter*? How do Dupin's cleverness and rationality go together with his idea that "the material world abounds with very strict analogies to the immaterial"? Consider the statement in light of Emerson's use of the analogy in *Nature*. Compare Dupin's language with Poe's in *The Philosophy of Composition:* is the character a double for his author?

MARGARET FULLER

The Fuller selections are much expanded in this edition of *NAAL*. *The Great Lawsuit* is reproduced in full, along with an unfinished autobiographical work; together, these present a much richer experience of Fuller than would a few short excerpts from her writings about the rights of women. We have a better chance to see how she constructs her most famous prose work, what civilities and audience expectations she accommodates, and which complacencies she attacks head-on.

Fuller's long essay on the oppression and undervaluation of women ranges widely, through contemporary literature, ancient mythology, philosophy, the arts, history, the realities of public and domestic life; it alludes to Shakespeare, Isabella, George Sand, The U.S. Constitution, Spenser's Britomart, a dreamed-up modern Miranda, Orpheus and Euridice, Mosaic law, the French Revolution, Isis, Sita, Mary Wollstonecraft, Mesmerism—it seems that nothing is left out. Are these comparisons and allusions random, stream-of-consciousness? In other words, is *The Great Lawsuit* an accretion rather than an organized essay? Or is there a sequence, and a cadence, to the way that these issues and allusions are raised, and to the style that they are raised in?

The Great Lawsuit takes a while to warm up, and the opening paragraphs are long and ornate, to the extent that modern students may feel like tuning out before reaching the quick, sharp, imaginary exchanges and short incisive paragraphs that constitute the best-known parts of the essay. Why does Fuller start as she does, with paragraphs like the one which begins "But it is not the purpose now to sing the prophecy of his jubilee"? Compare this paragraph with the short one a few pages later, the paragraph that begins, "Yet, no doubt, a new manifestation is at hand, a new hour in the day of man." Who does this sound like? How is Emerson echoed and invoked in Fuller's essay? Is it pure homage? Does a quarrel open up, at some point, with a failure, among Emersonian Transcendentalists, to extend their gospel of freedom and self-reliance to include women? Does Fuller stay with the Emersonian style, as represented in the paragraph we just looked at? Or does she develop a voice of her own?

The Great Lawsuit, especially in its lively "Miranda" passages, is an excellent place to open questions regarding the development of a discourse that escapes certain male predispositions, about formal argument and engagement with experience. Fuller shines as a creator of dialogue, and her tighter, more economical paragraphs can make Emerson's symphonic sentences and grand generalizations seem overbearing. To put it another way, Fuller's style, as it gradually comes clear or breaks away from conventionality and formality in *The Great Lawsuit,* may represent a very different spirit and style in regard to addressing and persuading others and understanding life: there is a delight in give-and-take, in open-endedness, rather than in displays of overwhelming rhetorical force and the "settling" of big questions. Fuller calls the essay *The Great Lawsuit*—why? What were lawsuits like in the nineteenth-century Anglo-American legal system? Were clear, quick victories to be expected? Is there anything sardonic or playful about Fuller's title? In comparison to the way Emerson argues or pleads a case, does Fuller's wit weaken hers, or get in the way somehow? Does it change, or even satirize, the nature of argument itself, as that ritual has evolved over several centuries, under male governance?

Students may wonder why so much space is given over in Fuller's essay to domestic relations, to husbands and wives, especially considering that Fuller was never married and eventually lived (and died) out beyond the pale, as far as Anglo-American matrimony was concerned. Is this section of the essay a gesture of accommodation? Is it subversive in some way, or Fabian (to borrow an adjective from decades later) in the way that it addresses the American domestic scene?

For several reasons, you may find that your students respond more readily to *Autobiographical Romance* than to *The Great Lawsuit,* and not merely because readers tend to like stories more than debate. Fuller's account of her early life resonates wonderfully with several other compelling accounts of growing up and self-creation, the mix of will and hazard that shapes an individual self. Franklin looms here, as both model and adversary, and the relationship that Fuller describes, between her temperament, her intellectual curiosity, and all the received wisdom about the education of (male) children is full of paradox, elements of comedy, and moments of pathos. The opening half of Fuller's account is a comic disaster of good intentions or rather of noble aims dangerously mixed with severity and coldness in family life: At a time when women were denied admission to genuine higher education, Fuller's father sets out to give her a tour of "all he knew," which at least isn't demeaning or diluted down to what an early nineteenth-century middle-class American male might have believed was a "woman's level." The psychological price is high—in part because of her father's harshness, but also because of a larger, culture-based assumption that logic and common sense are the virtues to be cultivated above all others. Like John Stuart Mill (who was driven to a nervous breakdown by a similar sort of childhood education), Fuller has to discover, on her own, other ways of thinking and seeing. The arrival of Ellen Kilshaw, the unnamed "English Lady" who comes into Fuller's life in the second half of this account, allows for a handsome portrait of these opposed sensibilities: the logic and "accuracy and clearness of everything" represented by Fuller's father; the "region of elegant culture" represented by Kilshaw, the reassurance that one could "gratify the sense of beauty, not the mere utilities of life."

Nonetheless, there is nothing reductive about Fuller's account of her upbringing, and once you establish this opposition between the pragmatic and the aesthetic (or the Franklinian and the Romantic) in Fuller's upbringing, you might want to complicate the model a bit, by observing what she draws from these opposed ideals regarding education. The stand-off with her father over Shakespeare makes an amusing center for attention: at the age of eight, she affirms her taste for *Romeo and Juliet* over her father's objections, but how has she been prepared for that rebellion? Does her playfully recounted taste for things Roman show itself in the way she writes, in the character that she presents on the printed page? You might focus on the paragraph containing the following passage, to observe the complex way in which Fuller draws on, modifies, and rebels against the education that her father sought to instill in her: "Thus it was with me,—from no merit of mine, but because I had the good fortune to be free enough to yield to my impressions. Common ties had not bound me; there were no traditionary notions in my mind: I believed in nothing merely because others believed in it: I had taken no feelings on trust. Thus my mind was open to their sway." How did Fuller's upbringing prepare her to enter the Emersonian circle of thought, and to take it farther, in some key directions, than Emerson intended for it to go?

HARRIET BEECHER STOWE

This is a book that was, and is, "big" by any measure. Selling millions of copies in hundreds of editions, and having a real effect on American social and moral thought, it's often known to today's students via myth and misconception. Students can feel some gratification in arriving at a text that, unlike *Moby-Dick* or *The Scarlet Letter,* really shook the world in its own time and achieved vast popular success—but they will want to know what the fuss was about and why the doors of the canon have creaked open lately to admit (after a long lapse) a book that was written for the millions and that plays by so many of the rules of popular fiction.

You might plan to organize class discussion around a few large and important questions:

1. Technologically, socially, and aesthetically, how can we account for the huge appeal of this book? As students speculate about this, you may want to bring up the revolution in printing and in transportation that was taking place just before and during the publication of *Uncle Tom's Cabin.* The Hoe Rotary Press had suddenly raised page production from one thousand sheets per hour to about twenty thousand; the web of railroads now allowed publishers to ship large quantities of printed books farther and cheaper than ever before—and suddenly the smash best-seller, selling hundreds of thousands of copies in a few months, was a possibility. But students will want to speculate about the way that the novel works within and against the popular romantic or sentimental narrative, and they can draw on their own experience (with *Charlotte* or popular modern novels that they have read on their own) to look at the way that these representative chapters exploit and resist expectations.

2. Where does the moral fire of this novel come from? In other words, *Uncle Tom's Cabin* can be read as a point of arrival in a long American quest to evolve a morality out of the Puritan heritage, the words of the

chartering documents of the republic, the ethos of the Enlightenment, the values of Transcendentalism. To put it simply, a suspense had been building: was America going to stand behind what it had been saying about the consequentiality of the individual life, the importance of direct experience and personally acquired wisdom, the equality of all human beings? On what does Stowe's moral fervor seem to be based? In latter-day Calvinism? Concord-style ethics? Franklinian rationalism and self-reliance? Some fusion of all of these sources?

3. What is Tom like as a character that he has been variously admired and vilified for his temperament? This can be a complex question: students may have personal and painful experiences with "Uncle Tom" as an epithet, to the extent that they may be surprised and bothered by the way that Stowe lauds him in this novel. Why this kind of character in the foreground, at this particular historical moment?

4. If students have heard of Tom before, they may have heard of Simon Legree as the villain of the piece—and if they follow the cue of, say, *The King and I*, they may think of the novel as the agon of the final chapters between the stoic and saintly Tom and the self-hating Satanic Legree. The other whites in the novel are remembered less well in the popular imagination, but Stowe spends a great deal of time developing them—more, actually, than she spends in developing Tom and his fellow slaves. Why all of this attention to these genteel whites, who carry no whips and do no violence themselves and who have elaborate and sometimes eloquent excuses for their various degrees of noninvolvement in the issue of race slavery? Ask a question like that, and you may reach an area of real importance in Stowe's novel: the book's sustained wrath about the supposedly good men and women who do nothing. Ask how the portraits of these complacent whites might have a special effect in creating the shock and suspense of the novel and in reaching Stowe's overwhelmingly white, middle-class, churchgoing northern audience where it lives.

FANNY FERN

These brief selections can do more than merely demonstrate, yet again, that women were thoroughly engaged in the battle of words and ideas in the middle of the nineteenth century, including the controversies about various missions of imaginative literature. Fuller and Stowe, however, are hard acts to follow, so you might want to put special emphasis on ways of distinguishing Fern's voice and her strategy as an essayist. Students will notice some similarities, especially to Fuller; and noticing this Fabian, sometimes self-deprecating, highly mobile mode of attack, they may want to think about how this strategy played both with and against conventional male stereotypes of female temperament and intellectual reach. Is this an effective strategy or an accommodation? A discussion of this sort can resonate for a long time and open many perceptions and speculations about how the individual talent interacts with prevailing, and sometimes prejudicial and oppressive, cultural and intellectual habits.

HARRIET JACOBS

The six chapters included here represent a coherent, integrated unit that conveys the power of Jacobs's narrative and shows her raising questions about slavery and particularly the experience of women in slavery. Chapters I and VII focus on family connections. Jacobs contrasts the powerful emotional bonds enslaved families felt for each other and the horrors of a legal system that did not recognize slave marriages or the primary bonds between parents and children. Chapters X and XIV explore what students might term Dr. Flint's sexual harassment of Linda and Jacobs's presentation of Linda's moral right to choose a lover. Throughout Jacobs's description of Linda's relationship with Mr. Sands, she addresses herself to white women readers and is concerned that they will identify with Linda as both a woman and, later, a mother and yet not judge her behavior by their own codes, which prescribed chastity. Jacobs implies that Linda felt she could achieve some measure of protection for children she might have with Sands, and so this proved to be in the short term; later, in part of the text not printed in *NAAL*, Sands marries and, under the guise of taking Linda's daughter Ellen to educate her, turns her into a house servant for his family. Yet she knows that she cannot shelter her child when it is born a girl: "slavery is terrible for men; but it is far more terrible for women." Explore with students differences between Frederick Douglass's *Narrative* and Harriet Jacobs's *Incidents*. Without *Incidents*, would we know much from Douglass's account concerning the sexual harassment and abuse of enslaved women?

After an abortive attempt to run away, Linda hides in the garret of her grandmother's shed; and Chapter XXI will raise many questions for students. In this chapter Jacob uses the intriguing metaphor *loophole;* what does this mean? The image *loophole* seems accurate to describe the garret in which she hides; she lives in a space that would not be visible to anyone who looked. It is as if she had "escaped" slavery by finding a "loophole" within the institution; has she "all but" escaped Dr. Flint by hiding for seven years in her grandmother's shed? If so, her "freedom" does her little good, and her children might have been better served had she escaped to the North. Why does she stay? She implies that she wants to remain near her children, even though for a long time they do not know she is there; does she remain a mother, except for the "loophole" that her children do not know where she is? She compares herself to Robinson Crusoe; ask students to explore the accuracy of this comparison. Chapter XLI, "Free at Last," serves as an ending for Jacobs's narrative; and as she writes, her story "ends with freedom; not in the usual way, with marriage." Ask students to explore what *freedom* means for Linda and her children. "Free at Last" shows Linda still with no home of her own, and her daughter has not received the education she has wanted for her. The chapter hints at the lingering ravages of slavery and the deficits the newly freed persons experienced by virtue of being propertyless, uneducated, and separated from family members.

HENRY DAVID THOREAU

In Thoreau's *Resistance to Civil Government* and *Slavery in Massachusetts* we see him as the prominent exception among his contemporaries to the pattern of evading confrontation with social and political issues of his day. And *Walden,* despite the premise of separation from society on which it opens, emphasizes the practical aspects of transcendentalism. Ask students to locate Thoreau in a tradition of American writers from Bradstreet through Franklin who speak in a personal voice and address the common reader. How do the effects Thoreau achieves in *Resistance to Civil Government* or *Walden* differ from those Emerson creates in *Self-Reliance* or *Nature?* Ask students to compare and contrast *Nature* and *Walden* as literary works: how are they conceptually similar but technically different? Many who found it difficult to find logical discourse in *Nature* will perceive a narrative design in *Walden.* How does Thoreau manage a happy balance between logical and analogical thinking?

Walden

You will probably want to spend several class sessions on *Walden.* Here are some questions and issues that can be raised in sequence:

1. Focusing on "Economy," ask students to address Thoreau's practical concerns. What, for Thoreau, is wrong with the daily life of his contemporaries? What were his motives for going to Walden? What led him to write the book? How does his version of writing in the first person compare with Hawthorne's in *The Custom-House?* Find evidence that he is making a pun on *I* and *eye;* recall Emerson's "transparent eye-ball" in *Nature.* Are Thoreau's criticisms of his own society applicable to ours? How seriously are we to take his suggestion that students ought, quite literally, to build their own colleges? Compare Thoreau's list of materials for his house at Walden with Franklin's list of virtues in *The Autobiography.* Is there evidence in "Economy" that Thoreau is constructing an analogy or is he writing a how-to book in the tradition of *The Way to Wealth?*

2. In "Where I Lived and What I Lived For," students can consider again the creation of analogies in *Walden,* suggesting here that analogy becomes a method of introspection and religious meditation for Thoreau. Stanley Cavell in *The Senses of "Walden"* suggests that *Walden* is a scripture. You can review ways in which American writers before Thoreau achieved literary authority and what different relationships writers have to scripture, especially the Bible. Does Thoreau achieve literary authority by going back to what he sees as the very source of creation, in nature at Walden? Ask students to comment on the following quotation from Hershel Parker's headnote: "The prose of *Walden,* in short, is designed as a practical course in the liberation of the reader." Thoreau's experience at Walden becomes a record of his

way of seeing the world; as it does for Emerson, the process of learning for Thoreau involves making the analogies he discovers as a result of going to the woods. In Thoreau's very ability to create the analogy he has the experience; transcendentalism can thus be seen as the first American spiritual movement based on a theory of language. That theory is Emerson's as well as Thoreau's, but Thoreau is able to find the analogies he wants in the life he is living on an hourly, daily, and seasonal basis at the pond.

Crucial to considering *Walden* as scripture are the frequent references Thoreau makes to Eastern religious experience. He writes that every morning "I got up early and bathed in the pond; that was a religious exercise, and one of the best things I did." How can bathing in the pond be a religious exercise? (He seems to mean that it is a spiritual experience, not just part of his routine that he follows religiously.) Following his own inclination toward analogy, bathing in the pond metaphorically suggests his daily immersion in the meaning of the experience of the pond. To jump into it suggests, by means of analogy, his daily attempt to understand it. It cleanses, renews, wakes him up—provides a rippling effect by which he can reach Eastern enlightenment, "to reawaken and keep [himself] awake, not by mechanical aids, but by an infinite expectation of the dawn." Bathing in Walden becomes an interim "mechanical aid"; when he becomes able to keep himself awake without the pond, he won't need it anymore.

You can ask students, at this point, how Thoreau's meditation differs from Puritan meditation. Thoreau (like Franklin) is also focusing on a single mark or spot—but instead of looking for his theological or economic salvation, he is attempting to transcend the world of literal limits, what Emerson calls the relative world. Yet, there is so much of the literal world in *Walden*. There is a sense in which the very rhythm of working in the physical world, finding an analogy in that work to spiritual life, and feeling—temporarily, at least—at one with the universe becomes cumulative for Thoreau. The process enables him to make successive leaps between relative and absolute worlds, to transcend the limits of material existence, truly to become eccentric (a word that he cites as particularly important at the end of *Walden*). Walden Pond becomes his eye (see the chapter "The Ponds").

3. Beginning with "Brute Neighbors," you can trace Thoreau's deep submergence into the character of Walden Pond as nature's "face." Then the last three chapters, "The Pond in Winter," "Spring," and "Conclusion," all build to Thoreau's description of the transcendent moment in which he has the experience of confronting absolute truths. In "The Pond in Winter," Thoreau makes the analogy between sounding the depths of a pond and "sounding" the depths of the human mind, as one might theoretically do by pursuing Eastern meditation techniques. Thoreau has no mantra but his pond; his "depth" of knowledge of the pond prepares him for an even deeper dive into his own imagination, his own consciousness.

"Spring" heralds new life at the pond and new light in the writer. Here he discovers that "the day is an epitome of the year"; the small scale of

Walden Pond (and ultimately of *Walden* as book or scripture) is what makes it useful as an analogy. He concludes, at the end of "Spring," that "we need to witness our own limits transgressed, and some life pasturing freely where we never wander." Becoming eccentric, getting outside our own limits, trying to transcend the narrowness of our own experience, can give us the vision of larger life, of some life "pasturing freely where we never wander." The exploration of life by means of analogy possesses a spiritual dimension that logic does not.

But he leaves the pond because he has learned its lessons. When the person becomes enlightened, the vehicle of enlightenment is no longer necessary. The religious technique, or the poetic analogy, is viewed not as an end in itself, but as means to an end. The basic idea in *Walden*, then, is that of self-expression, Thoreau's attempt to find a way to make visible and concrete his sense of who he is. His greatest fear, as he expresses it in "Conclusion," is that his "expression may not be *extra-vagant* enough." It's hard to get students to be extravagant themselves, because it means encouraging them to "wander outside" the limits of everything they have learned as received knowledge, prescribed feelings, and "right" and "wrong" ways to think.

FREDERICK DOUGLASS

Douglass wrote his 1845 autobiographical *Narrative* the year before Thoreau began to write *Walden*. Ask students to consider the following quotation from *Walden* in connection with the *Narrative*:

> I sometimes wonder that we can be so frivolous, I may almost say, as to attend to the gross but somewhat foreign form of servitude called Negro Slavery, there are so many keen and subtle masters that enslave both north and south. It is hard to have a southern overseer; it is worse to have a northern one; but worst of all when you are the slave-driver of yourself.

Would Douglass agree? Are there conceptual and thematic similarities between *Walden* and *Narrative of the Life of Frederick Douglass, an American Slave*? Do Douglass's escape to freedom and Thoreau's transcendence at Walden Pond suggest connections between abolitionism and transcendentalism? Both narratives imply that the experiences that are their subjects also confer literary authority on their narrators. Evaluate the *Narrative* as autobiography; what are its formal and thematic similarities to Franklin's *Autobiography*? Is the slave narrative a variation on autobiography or a distinct genre? The central feature to focus on in Douglass's *Narrative* is the way he, like many white writers before him, articulates himself into being, creates an ontological model for black male identity: "You have seen how a man was made a slave; you shall see how a slave was made a man," he writes. And he makes himself a man by refusing to submit to Mr. Covey. Therefore, Douglass achieves ontological freedom before he escapes to actual freedom; and in portraying his own courage in fighting Mr. Covey, he sets himself up as a model for other slaves much as Franklin did in his *Autobiography*.

Ask students to compare Douglass's *Narrative* with Jacobs's *Incidents*. Does Douglass's assertion about the ontological freedom of manhood apply to the experiences of women slaves? Would the quotation work for Linda Brent ("You have seen how a woman was made a slave; you shall see how a slave was made a woman")? Douglass portrays himself as a "heroic fugitive" for others to imitate. Contrast Douglass and Stowe. Might we consider "The Mother's Struggle" a form of the slave narrative? Can the warrior mother be a heroic fugitive? Douglass and other escaped slaves wrote their stories with the encouragement and support of the northern abolitionist press, and there is clear didactic intent in Douglass's *Narrative* (as there is in *Uncle Tom's Cabin*). Does didacticism weaken the narrative as a work of literature? Students may find it interesting to discuss the contrasting effect didacticism has in works produced under the umbrella of a reigning theology (such as Puritan literature) and works that are clearly trying to change people's ideas. From the literary perspective, the year 1845 is as important as 1776 because it shows a former slave writing in his own voice and naming and claiming his own liberty. Douglass's *Narrative* and Fuller's *The Great Lawsuit* suggest that, while going to Walden may be an effective technique for some Americans to achieve transcendence, black Americans and white women must first adopt defiance.

The Meaning of July Fourth for the Negro demonstrates Douglass's rhetorical skills. Students will be powerfully affected by his arguments, both in their historical context (he delivered the speech two years after the enactment of the Fugitive Slave Law of 1850) and in their continuing significance for our own time. Identify with students his rhetorical strategy: first, he lauds the founders, the principles of liberty they espoused, and the language of *The Declaration of Independence* (while subtly maintaining his distance by referring to the United States as "your country," the country of his white audience, rather than his own); then he raises the case of slavery, which totally contradicted the language of liberty and freedom on which this country was founded; and he ends by demonstrating that Americans and their politics are "flagrantly inconsistent," calling for an end to this inconsistency and a return to the principles of freedom: "interpreted, as it ought to be interpreted, the Constitution is a glorious liberty document." Much of Douglass's argument remains relevant to late-twentieth-century American society; and Douglass offers students a model for the way his own words can be applied to ongoing discrimination in American society—against poor people, against African Americans, against white women, and against gay men and lesbians. He writes, "We have to do with the past only as we can make it useful to the present and to the future . . . now is the time, the important time." Ask students to discuss this statement and to find others that might have been written in the 1990s as well as in 1852. Some of the most powerful might include, for many disenfranchised groups, "I am not included within the pale of the glorious anniversary!" and "There is not a nation on the earth guilty of practices more shocking and bloody than are the people of the United States, at this very hour" and "Americans! your republican politics, not less than your republican religion, are flagrantly inconsistent."

WALT WHITMAN

In teaching both Whitman and Dickinson, you can show students how these two poets are pivotal figures, summarizing in their work many of the themes and concerns of earlier writers, yet looking ahead to the twentieth century in their poetic technique and the high level of self-consciousness that each brings to the act of writing. How, in particular, does Whitman express a culmination of American impulses in poetry? Ask students to reread Emerson's *The Poet* and to evaluate Whitman; is Emerson prophesying the kind of poetry Whitman would write, especially in *Leaves of Grass* [*Song of Myself*]? Or are both writers responding to the same cultural need? Ask students to discuss the detailed catalogs of American people, places, and human feelings that Whitman creates in *Song of Myself*. How does Whitman's portrait of human life differ from those of earlier writers? You can introduce the concept and complications of realism here, and suggest elements of realism in Whitman's language, looking ahead to the "local color" impulse of some of the post–Civil War writers that students will read in Volume 2.

You might consider carefully Whitman's idea of the dream, particularly in *The Sleepers*, which illustrates the process by which Whitman works through the "night" of his analogy to "awaken" into a diffused and enlarged sense of self; students can then trace the same pattern through the much longer *Song of Myself*, at the end of which the poet transcends even his physical body, becoming effused flesh that drifts "in lacy jags." How does Whitman's use of analogy compare with Emerson's or Thoreau's? And how does reading Whitman compare with reading earlier writers? What is the conceptual unit of a Whitman poem?—possibly the catalog? What is the effect of the repetitions? What evidence can students find of discursive reasoning in Whitman? Whitman may require a kind of immersion ("religiously," the way Thoreau bathes in the pond). Is *Song of Myself*, like *Walden*, a kind of scripture?

Students understand Whitman better when they locate the same image in several different poems; the imagery shows Whitman's vision of physical life. Harold Aspiz's *Walt Whitman and the Body Beautiful* (1980) is extremely useful reading as you prepare to teach Whitman. Aspiz suggests that "Whitman's physical self is the authentic vital center of *Leaves of Grass*. By idealizing his body, Whitman created a model that his fellow Americans could emulate." Such a reading of the poems makes it possible to suggest pedagogical connections between Walt Whitman and Benjamin Franklin, for Whitman clearly "invents" himself as the American poet in the same way that Franklin invents himself as American man. And it may lead students to see that *Leaves of Grass* is as much a poetry of evasion (Aspiz makes the point that for all of Whitman's pretense to health in his poems, from childhood on he had physical problems, was fascinated by physical illness, and spent many years as a sick man) as it is of self-disclosure (as in "I celebrate myself, and sing myself"), in its own way another *Minister's Black Veil.*

Ask students to examine *Trickle Drops* and other *Calamus* poems included in *NAAL* for evidence that Whitman's analogue for vision is male sexuality. In *Trickle Drops,* they can see most clearly and succinctly the way Whitman views poetry as spermatic fluid; the image is pervasive in his work, including his discussion in *Preface to Leaves of Grass.* Male physical health and robustness, in general, becomes a metaphor for vision. Does that make male sexuality, for Whitman, as much a product of the creative imagination as Walden is for Thoreau? Is the version of sexuality Whitman proposes (and suggests, throughout his work, that women share) another variation on the early-nineteenth-century American dream?

The sequence of poems *Live Oak, with Moss* demonstrates more specifically Whitman's interest in male sexuality and in personal as well as public poetry. The headnote and footnote discussions provide the essential literary context for reading the poems in *Live Oak, with Moss* in their own sequence, as they exist in unpublished manuscript, rather than as Whitman collected some of them in his *Calamus* poems. And, as editor Hershel Parker suggests, had it been published, "the sequence would have constituted a new and highly public sexual program, nothing short of an open homosexual manifesto." Trace with students the various "narratives" embedded in this poem sequence: (1) a love affair begun, then ended, with the speaker abandoned; (2) the speaker's growing wonder, as in VIII, whether there are other men like him; and (3) the narrator's emerging awareness of the relationship between poetry and "manly love" and of how this relationship comes to matter more to him (in V) than being the "singer of songs." In a sense, *Live Oak, with Moss* serves as a revision of what Parker calls Whitman's "tributes to the American people" and, as such, invites comparison with Douglass's question "What to the slave is the Fourth of July?" in *The Meaning of July Fourth to the Negro.* Consider with students the irony that the "good grey poet" who created himself and has been constructed by critics as our first truly *American* poet should also be our first gay poet struggling for freedom of expression both as a poet and as a lover. In Whitman's time, as in our own, *Live Oak, with Moss* suggests the contradictions between free speech and the expression of sexual orientation; as Whitman writes in XI, "I dare not tell it in words—not even in these songs."

Recognizing that some instructors teach Whitman, along with Dickinson, in the second half of the American literature course (when students will be using Volume 2 of *NAAL*), Norton makes available a separate volume, free of charge, *Walt Whitman/Emily Dickinson: Selections from* The Norton Anthology of American Literature, 5th edition.

HERMAN MELVILLE

A few days with Melville can be a high point in a survey course, provided that your students are comfortable about plunging into *NAAL*'s well-chosen selections from *Moby-Dick*—fully aware of what you're asking them to do and what kind of book these chapters are excerpted from. They may wonder whether these pieces from such a thick volume will come together somehow and give them a plausible sense of the whole text; and having heard all the student rumors that this is a Big Hard Great American Novel, they may have their defenses up or come to class expecting that there is some vast profound overarching theme that pervades every sentence and phrase of this dangerous-looking masterpiece. They *won't* expect wit, humor, changefulness, exuberance, breezy vernacular American English, a host of engaging and brilliantly drawn characters—or any of the other qualities that make the book delightful to read and not just a sum total of cumbersome themes.

There are plenty of good ways to enter this novel and escape some deadening expectation that the discussions will be about "Oh, What a Big Deal This Is." One of the virtues of *Moby-Dick* is that it really is about what it is supposed to be about: a voyage on a whaling ship; and you might want to tell your students that what they're *not* reading (the chapters that aren't in the anthology) includes more about the details and bric-a-brac of whaling, sailing, and cetology than most of them would ever want to know. You might start with some facts and speculations about life on one of these whalers— your Greenpeace convictions need not get in the way, as all this happened a long time ago when this dangerous, deadly work was regarded as vital. Take a moment to tell them how small these whaling ships were, how long they went out for, what kinds of crews they picked up (Melville's collection of cannibals, Calvinists, Indians, and seadogs from all over the world is not far from the truth), and what kinds of people would spend a year to three years or more of their lives in such an enterprise? This is life on the edge; and students can sometimes empathize with Ishmael's wildly varied ruminations, his emotional highs and lows, and Ahab's drive to create firm conviction and sublime or monomaniacal purpose amid nothing, if they understand the work that they do and the company that they keep.

Once you are into the book, you might suggest that students suspend one expectation that could foul up their reading and make them unnecessarily anxious—an assumption that every one of these chapters connects smoothly to what comes before and after. Talk about temperament and the motions of the mind before you start taking about *what* Ishmael says or thinks at any given moment. Ask your students whether a book about, say, the struggle to *understand* life wouldn't be different in rhythm and shape, and perhaps more companionable and plausible, than a book that tried to deliver big consistent answers covering every phase and moment of human experience.

When you finally get around to symbols (do think about holding off on all that for a while, until the students gain some momentum and confidence in engaging with the book), you might want to begin with some discussion of what symbols are, not just what they signify about the thing symbolized but about the mind and mood of the individual who creates or gravitates to the symbol. In other words, if symbols can be interesting as provisional *attempts* to penetrate to truth, or express possibly transient perceptions, or seasons of the mind, then the act of reading becomes much less mechanical and deadening than a decoding of the whale or the whalebone leg or any of the gams. These are Ishmael's attempts, over and over, to make sense of what he sees and what he has been through; and if students can keep that understanding in mind, that these are the creations of an eager human being, trying (perhaps with no permanent success at all) to understand the world and his place in it, then connections can be made on which students will be able to build their own.

Bartleby, therefore, makes a very nice pairing with the *Moby-Dick* excerpts, both for its apparent oppositeness as a story (a confined, domestic, claustrophobic urban tale) and for its commonalities (its array of characters, its bizarre humor, its intense and possibly unsuccessful struggle to understand life and fellow human beings, its thorough grounding in actual experience). If you began *Moby-Dick* with a conversation about the realities of whaling, then begin *Bartleby* with some talk about mindless, dehumanizing, mind-wrecking work: students will have plenty to tell you. Bartleby is a human photocopying machine, and most students who have worked summer jobs will be quick to tell you that work this grim has *not* gone away with the mechanized office.

In your class you may have erstwhile roofers, corn detasselers, telemarketers, potato fryers, intelligent young people who spent months in front of a VDT or on an assembly line to pay for college expenses. Ask them to speculate on what a life of such work would have done to them; also ask if they had the experience in those jobs of working with some other individual whom they could never figure out. It can be very hard, in the long routines of repetitive work, to really know the poet from the fool, the tragic figure from the true machine in human form. If students want to jump to full credence in the narrator's conclusion about Bartleby, that he was a sensitive soul brought to grief by his work in a dead-letter office, see if you can loosen that conclusion without driving them into what they might regard as frustrating ambiguity. Again, if this story is in some ways about the sad, funny quest to understand others and to understand the self (to what extent might this narrator be using Bartleby as an evasion, a way of *not* looking squarely at the emptiness of the narrator's *own* life?), then it is certainly about much and not ambiguous at all about the predicament of the sensitive mind amid the demands of modern life.

Billy Budd, not published until thirty years after Melville's death, is a thrill to read, a posthumous treasure and a supremely crafted tale—so well crafted that students may run the risk of allowing the allegorical rumblings of the tale's first half to determine their reading of the story's ending. Again, you might want to spend some time making it clear that Melville had done his homework regarding the predicament of England in the midst of the Napoleonic Wars: most of Europe was in the hands of the enemy, and survival depended on the Royal Navy—and in the navy conditions were brutal and mutiny was a real possibility. It's important to make that clear, especially if students feel an urge to turn the tale into an allegorical chart and to assign stable values to each character: Billy as Adam or Christ or both; Claggart as Satan or one of his minions; and Vere—what of Vere? If they decide that Vere is Pilate they are no more than half right, which means that they deny themselves much of the modernity and human understanding in the story. Vere sits in Pilate's seat, to be sure; but he doesn't "wash his hands" of the case. Quite to the contrary, he insists that his drumhead court convene and judge Billy Budd by the strictest and harshest standards, even though a part of Vere (in our judgment the *best* part of Vere) cries out against doing so.

Students will want to know what's going on here. If you want to get into Hobbes and his constructions of both sovereignty and political identity, you can do so here; but if you fear that this will just muddy the issue, you might open the question of how we can willfully and consciously define ourselves—as students; as leaders; as professionals; as clear, firm, limited creatures of one sort or another, acting to the end on contractual and statutory obligations—and *almost* believe that this public or social "us" is the real us. Vere convinced the court: did he convince himself?

EMILY DICKINSON

There is much in the headnote to guide a discussion of Emily Dickinson and her poetry. *NAAL* includes several of the poems involved in Dickinson's "rebellion against the theology of her town" (for example, 324 and 1068); poems that reflect her deep regard for British writers Elizabeth Barrett Browning (312 and 593), the Brontë sisters (148), and James Thomson (131); and numerous poems that reflect T. W. Higginson's groupings for the first (1890) edition of her work, his response to Mabel Loomis Todd's efforts to secure posthumous publication for Dickinson. Although each individual poem reflects larger formal and thematic interest than grouping it under one heading indicates, the process of creating the thematic groups (according to the categories Higginson created: life, love, nature, time, and eternity) gives students one way of looking for intertextual connections and, indeed, of beginning to create interpretive patterns within which to analyze and appreciate Dickinson's work. Thus one homework exercise you might assign students would ask them to group the poems under Higginson's headings, then, in class, to discuss the difficulties involved in doing so.

Here is a thematic arrangement to consider:

Life: 67, 241, 258, 341, 536, 650
Love: 249, 303, 1078
Nature: 130, 285, 314, 328, 520, 978, 986, 1068, 1138, 1397, 1463
Time: 305
Eternity: 214, 216, 280, 287, 315, 324, 449, 465, 501, 510, 528, 547, 664, 712, 822, 824, 978, 1099, 1125, 1126, 1540

What is interesting about this exercise is less the extent to which individual readers agree concerning which poems to include in each group and more their reasons for inclusion and their interpretations of the categories themselves. The categories may express more about the themes and world-view Higginson reflected a century ago than the themes and interests of our own time.

A follow-up exercise would involve asking students to identify the themes by which they would group Dickinson's poetry, if they were creating their own edition for contemporary readers. As readers still trained to revere modernist and postmodernist aesthetics, some of them may want to include a category that reflects Dickinson's self-consciousness concerning poetic form and practice; the poems they may group together for such a list may include 185, 285, 303, 326, 441, 448, 488, 505, 709, 952, 1129, and 1138. Discussion of this list may also follow from Parker's observation that in a poem like 326, Dickinson reveals her awareness of her own originality, her own "genius."

The exercise also leads into questions of editorial selection. Thomas Johnson's *The Poems of Emily Dickinson* (1955) includes 1775 poems. *NAAL* includes 81 poems, many of which have frequently been anthologized. One question that emerges from the process of editorial selection concerns the role a particular editor's interests or tastes play in such a process. Put one of the Johnson editions on reserve and assign individual students clusters of 75 or 100 poems so that all 1775 are covered. Then ask the students to make a case (either in a class presentation or in a paper) for the inclusion of one or two additional poems. On what grounds would the students argue for inclusion? What different portrait of the poet, or of the body of poetry, would emerge if the poem or poems (and others like them) were included?

Such an approach encourages students to evaluate certain poems as representative of Dickinson's perspective. *NAAL* includes several poems that appear to address women's lives as wives: 199, 732, and 1072. For a different perspective on the life of a wife, students may discover in one of the Johnson volumes poems 154 and 219.

The headnote characterizes Dickinson as "undaunted by her powerful father's domestic tyrannies." While many of the poems—indeed the very existence of the poems—provide evidence that Dickinson remained "undaunted" either by her mortal father or her immortal one, students attuned to the way Dickinson claims to, as she expresses it in 1129, "Tell all the Truth but tell it slant—" will find in other poems, not anthologized here, further complexities concerning Dickinson's view of her relationship to her particular father (Parker describes poem 61, "Papa above!" as an example of her religious rebellion, but it also conveys overtones of rebellion from paternal authority) and of her portrait of white upper-class women's constricted lives in the world of nineteenth-century Amherst, Massachusetts. The first lines of most of the following poems, not included here but worth analysis by students for their challenge to the more mainstream Dickinson often presented in anthologies, hint at Dickinson's critique of the lives her society sanctioned for women: 77 ("I never hear the word 'escape' "), 146 ("On such a night, or such a night"), 178 ("I cautious, scanned my little life—"), 182 ("If I shouldn't be alive"), 248 ("Why—do they shut Me out of

Heaven?"), 439 ("Undue Significance a starving man attaches / To Food—"), 476 ("I meant to have but modest needs—"), 540 ("I took my Power in my Hand—"), 579 ("I had been hungry, all the Years—"), 612 ("It would have starved a Gnat—"), 613 ("They shut me up in Prose—"), 773 ("Deprived of other Banquet"), and 791 ("God Gave a Loaf to every Bird—"). This lists surveys the poems Dickinson wrote between 1858 and 1863; if students read later poems, they will find others that critique the social position accorded to white upper-class women in nineteenth-century America.

The selections include a number of love poems and provide students with background information about the major contenders for Dickinson's "passionate relationships." One of these relationships "may have been with the friend who became her sister-in-law," Susan Gilbert. Students may be interested in reading the selection of poems (not anthologized here) that provide grounds for such an observation. This list includes, from the poems written between 1858 and 1863, the following: 14 ("One Sister have I in our house,") which ends "Sue—forevermore!"), 27 ("Morns like these—we parted—"), 44 ("If she had been the Mistletoe"), 84 ("Her breast is fit for pearls"), 91 ("So bashful when I spied her!", 156 ("You love me—you are sure—"), 208 ("The Rose did caper on her cheek—"), 218 ("Is it true, dear Sue?"), 251 ("Over the fence—"), 427 ("I'll clutch—and clutch—"), 446 ("I showed her Heights she never saw—"), 474 ("They put Us far apart—"), and 704 ("No matter—now—Sweet—"), a poem that may reflect Sue's rejection of her sister-in-law. Bring in some or all of these poems (it doesn't violate copyright to put them on the board, and they are all short enough to do so) and discuss how Dickinson's perspective on same-sex love compares with Whitman's in the *Live Oak, with Moss* and *Calamus* poems included in *NAAL*.

For a more traditional discussion of Dickinson, note that many of her poems are transcendental in theme and style, and ask students to select a favorite and discuss affinities with Emerson and Thoreau. But Dickinson is often considered an early modernist, because of the way her poetic technique calls attention to itself and reflects a high level of self-consciousness (see the specific list of anthologized poems discussed above in connection with poetic form and practice). You can begin discussion of Dickinson by asking students to contrast her with Whitman—and not just in the poets' perspectives on same-sex love. Both poets reverse students' expectations concerning traditional poetic form, and comparing and contrasting the ways they do this leads to an extensive discussion of what each poet might have been trying to do in poetry. Sheer size is one of the most striking points of contrast; see poem 185, in which Dickinson writes, " 'Faith' is a fine invention / When Gentlemen can *see*— / *But Microscopes* are prudent / In an Emergency." Compared with Whitman's "Walt Whitman, a kosmos" and the "magnifying and applying" of *Song of Myself*, Dickinson's small poems seem microscopic. Exploring the freedom with which Whitman creates the vast catalogs in *Song of Myself* and allows himself endless repetition and then contrasting that freedom with Dickinson's 185 or 1099 ("My Cocoon tightens—Colors teaze—") can move the discussion from

formal differences to thematic ones, and to the question of literary authority. Where does Whitman find his? How does it appear as an assumption in
his poetry, although Dickinson, as in 505, must struggle to achieve it? How
does the smallness of her poetry suggest her own assumptions about the nature of literary authority?

Unlike Whitman, Dickinson appears uninterested in the physical body,
grounding many poems in a specific image from nature that she then proceeds either to transcend, as in 328 and 348, or to despair in finding her
own inability to transcend human limitations and the limits of poetry, as in
465. Like Whitman, Dickinson also writes analogically, following Emerson's technique for transcendental vision. Many poems illustrate her use of
analogies to express and contain her vision, particularly the poems that appear to be about death but actually show the poet trying to see beyond the
limits of human vision that death, as life's limit, symbolizes for her. 465,
510, and 754 are just three of the many poems that illustrate this pattern;
and many others write thematically about the process, as 67 and 528.

Many of the Dickinson poems that initially appear so elusive to students
can become deeply revealing of the consciousness of the woman who wrote
them—and of the fact that they were written by a woman, as the list above
(beginning with poem 77) indicates. Poem 1129 also becomes another
Dickinson variation on Emerson's use of the poetic analogy to achieve transcendental vision. But her reasons for choosing analogies that move in
"slant" fashion rather than in concentric circles (like the ripples that result
when Emerson throws a stone) suggest that Dickinson, unlike Whitman,
may have seen herself as self-conceived, self-born—not because she has invented a new kind of poetry but because she has dared, as an American
woman, to write at all (especially in light of the fact that her models were
British women). In inventing herself as woman and poet, how does she differ from other self-inventors: Franklin and Douglass? Does she imagine
setting her life up as model for others? And does the biographical fact that
she published only seven poems in her lifetime imply self-censorship or
feminine reticence? Ask students to reread Bradstreet's *Prologue* and *The
Author to Her Book*. To what extent does Dickinson's use of smallness in her
imagery reflect her sense of inadequacy even as it gives her the analogical
vehicle for transcending that sense?

Finally, for some readings of Dickinson that are certain to provoke discussion in the classroom, and that may provide students with some support
for their own readings, see, in particular, Mary Loeffelholz's *Dickinson
and the Boundaries of Feminist Theory* (1991), William Shurr's *The Marriage of Emily Dickinson* (1983), and essays by Adelaide Morris and Joanne
Dobson in *Feminist Critics Read Emily Dickinson* (1983), edited by Suzanne
Juhasz.

REBECCA HARDING DAVIS

Davis's rediscovered story *Life in the Iron-Mills* can allow you to end
your course by making thematic connections with earlier writers and in-

troducing your students to an early work of literary realism. Ask students to compare the atmosphere in Davis's mill with Melville's *The Paradise of Bachelors and The Tartarus of Maids* and to compare Davis's nightmarish descriptions with Poe's. Students who have read some Dickens in earlier courses (especially works like *Hard Times, Bleak House,* and *A Tale of Two Cities*) will hear a familiar ring to Davis's grim opening panorama and should join a discussion of how Realist and Romantic motives can intertwine.

They may also want to compare Hugh Wolfe's creation of the korl woman with women characters created by Irving, Poe, and Hawthorne and to think about the korl woman's special hunger in light of Dickinson's own poems about yearning. There are also similarities to note between the bondage of Davis's mill workers and Douglass's portrait of race slavery. Comparing the very last lines of *Walden* ("Only that day dawns to which we are awake. There is more day to dawn. The sun is but a morning star.") to the closing of *Life in the Iron-Mills* ("its groping arm points through the broken cloud to the far East, where, in the flickering, nebulous crimson, God has set the promise of the Dawn") can provoke a far-reaching discussion of hope in nineteenth-century American literature: what that hope consists of and what assumptions it is founded on.

Louisa May Alcott

You might want to teach Alcott out of the Norton chronological sequence and include this selection among your Transcendentalist readings. With a deft blend of satire and affection, Alcott writes of her girlhood here, the years in which her family was most under the influence of the philosophical winds blowing out of the Hedge Club, central Concord, and a certain pond one mile out of town. *Little Women* is one of a handful of nineteenth-century American works that students still read enthusiastically, and in great numbers, without any prodding from academe; and a turn to Alcott, in the midst of Emerson's grand formulations and the cool and crankiness of Thoreau's opening chapters in *Walden*, could provide context and a measure of relief. Alcott's subject is eerily modern: the danger of the totalizing formulation, the great idea or ideal imposed not only on one's own thinking and conduct but also on others.

It's probably good to avoid a too-long immersion in the exact historical sources or analogues for this or that moment or character in the story: if students know a little about Brook Farm, the Fruitlands experiment, Robert Owen and the other Utopians, and Bronson Alcott's other misadventures, they will know the important thing—that this was an era in which some people were actually trying to live Emersonian and Romantic doctrines and that the comedy and near-tragedy in Alcott's story are a sometimes whimsical, sometimes hard-edged commentary on the consequences of "-isms" and the dangers of ideas taken too much to heart.

You might begin with one moment that seems modern to you and work outward from there, speculating about whether this story is relevant only to the Concord neighborhood in the middle of the nineteenth century. You can open the tale by means of the dialogue on shoes and lamps: to avoid any moral complicity with any human activity that this little group finds repugnant—the leather trade and whaling for starters—they decide to go barefoot and lightless until a someday when suitable and morally correct substitutes are contrived. The passage about the evils of cotton and wool works much the same way: it's funny and yet eerily familiar. A good point of arrival, however, might be the specialness of the Alcott voice, the rare mix of exuberance, playfulness, pathos, and moral intensity that keeps her novels fresh and flourishing after all this time.

Harriet Prescott Spoffard

Circumstance may seem like a very odd place for Volume 1 of *NAAL* to conclude. The tale is hard to classify, and it certainly doesn't fit neatly into any model of literary development whereby American Romanticism and Transcendentalism give way to Realism and Naturalism. This is in some ways an all-out Gothic, with an aura of symbolic or allegorical intention; and students will probably want to know how to classify it and whether or not pursuing those (possible) symbols is sensible or worthwhile. The story also resonates with that sexuality which got Spoffard into trouble as a writer. Oscar Wilde and the English Decadent writers could get away with this— thirty years later—but here again, Spoffard seems so far ahead of her time as to be something of a literary orphan or lost soul.

With that in mind, you might want to head off the symbolism anxieties at the start and instead ask students what this story is *like*, what it reminds them of—from their assigned reading and from their experience of American pop culture. For the story does belong to a lively tradition of tales of horror, of women in terrible danger threatened by monsters (human and otherwise), of crises of faith in the wilderness. The trail runs from Rowlandson through *Young Goodman Brown* and *The Scarlet Letter* through *The Turn of the Screw* to Stephen King, the biggest-selling American novelist of the past quarter century. Again, this has to work as a Gothic tale, a tale of terror, before it can work as an allegory; and students have much with which to compare it and on which to evaluate it. Even in the welter of American horror fiction, it has a compelling strangeness; and on that basis you can venture out to speculate (do keep it speculative) on the possible implications of these creatures and events that seem to mean something more.

In other words, *Circumstance* may help open a conversation about how American Gothic fiction connects to symbolism within ourselves, giving form and faces to abstract things that frighten us, whether we read Gothic tales or not: the loss of one's way in life, the sudden irresistible rise of passions and drives from within, the loss of love and family, the loss of whatever faith keeps us going and confers our identity. If students venture out from this tale to test the symbolic reverberations of the latest smash-hit horror novel or popular film, so much the better.

Volume 2

1865–1914

Realism and Its Variants: Regionalism, Local Color, and Naturalism

The question of realism and the genre of narrative fiction dominate the concerns of post–Civil War writers. The meaning of the term *realism* is complicated by the fact that, as the period introduction in *NAAL* suggests, there were "other realists" and there were critical categories that seem somehow both related and different: regionalism, local color writing, and naturalism (which at the turn of the century was often termed "new realism"). Furthermore, this is the period for which we have the richest array of surviving Native American texts; how do these texts intersect with critical categories such as realism or regionalism?

The traditional approach to teaching the period is to begin with the triumvirate of Clemens, Howells, and James and then touch on the "others." One of the difficulties with this approach is that American authors (as a reading of *Life in the Iron-Mills* at the end of Volume 1 suggests) began writing in a realistic mode decades before Clemens, Howells, and James published their major works. If we begin teaching the period not with Clemens, but with the realistic literary works that were published in the 1860s and 1870s, we can give students a better sense of the evolution of American literary realism, which began as a mode of perception and a way of thinking about American life. It achieved the stature of "theory" only when Howells (and James) wrote so many editorial columns (and prefaces) in an attempt to define the American "art of fiction."

The earliest writing in a realistic mode begins with Harriet Beecher Stowe and some of her contemporaries: Alice Cary and Rose Terry Cooke (not anthologized) as well as Rebecca Harding Davis. Literary historians also trace strains of early realism in T. B. Thorpe. To understand the evolution of American realism, students need to see what happens to these early strains, and what happens is that a group of writers—mostly women, beginning with Cary, Stowe, and Cooke—develop the genre of regionalism, represented in Volume 2 by Sarah Orne Jewett, Kate Chopin, Mary E. Wilkins Freeman, Charles W. Chesnutt, Mary Austin, possibly John M. Oskison, and Gertrude Simmons Bonnin. In conveying features of the earlier literary tradition, you might want to teach Jewett and Chesnutt before Clemens, even though all of the particular regionalist texts anthologized in *NAAL* were published after *Adventures of Huckleberry Finn*.

What all of the writers in realistic modes share is a commitment to referential narrative. Despite the evidence of invention, the reader expects to meet characters in the fiction who resemble ordinary people in ordinary circumstances, and who often meet unhappy ends. (The pattern of the unhappy ending is much less prevalent in regionalism, however.) The realists develop these characters by the use of ordinary speech in dialogue, and plot and character development become intertwined. Some writers make use of orthographic changes to convey particular speech rhythms and other elements of dialect peculiar to regional life. They all set their fictions in places that actually exist, or might easily have actual prototypes; and they are interested in recent or contemporary life, not in history or legend. Setting can become conspicuous as an element of theme in local color and regionalist fiction. And the realists rely on a first- or third-person-limited point of view to convey the sensibility of a central character or, in the case of the local color writers, the altered perception of the outside observer as he or she witnesses the scene.

REALISM AND NATIVE AMERICAN LITERATURE

The anthologized selections from Native American oratory, songs, legends, fictions, and autobiographical memoirs in one sense belong to a variety of different genres; but they also comment in interesting ways on the intentions and strategies of literary realism.

As the headnotes point out, Native American literature during this period represents an "encounter" between traditional Native American oratory and the new and contemporary demands of the practices of Euro-American culture, namely the occasions at which Indians used both oratory and writing to try to make beneficial treaties, to achieve their land claims, or to adapt their own practices to meet the demands of the whites. Thus the body of Native American literature represented in this period indeed records a particular and quite evidently referential perception of white American life. The larger history of the encounter between Euro-Americans and Indians during the post–Civil War period, or more accurately between 1830 and 1890, does not have a happy ending. Setting is everything in some of these narratives; land becomes the fundamental source of conflict as well as the source of metaphor, spirituality, and identity for large groups of native peoples. Furthermore, read together and interwoven with Euro-American texts, the Native American materials all imply the existence of and looming threat by an outside observer (sometimes equipped with Hotchkiss guns), who, alas, is also the narrator of a conflicting story of events and the narrator who controls not only the guns but also the language of legal discourse.

Once students explore the suitability of terms like *realism* and *regionalism* for Native American texts, they may find them inappropriate; but the terms may have served the function of pedagogical bridge to an enlarged appreciation for Native American literature taught, inevitably in a survey course, as part of literature in the United States.

To help students make connections between the anthologized Native American texts and the much more familiar concept of realism—as well as to understand crucial distinctions between the two—encourage them to view realism as a literary effect as much as, if not more than, a genre or a defined body of narrative strategies.

Then even the Ghost Dance narrative—which incidentally is told by a variety of narrators in a variety of genres, including Wovoka and his tran-scribers, Charles Alexander Eastman, and tribal songmakers—may be viewed as a collectively told "text" of Native American realism, despite its origins in a vision and its survival in songs and legends. This collectively told narrative also serves as a useful corrective to the theory of realism as artic-ulated by Henry James, which focuses on a single stationary observer and his particular perspective from "the house of fiction" (or what he calls "the posted presence of the watcher, . . . the consciousness of the artist" in his preface to the New York edition of *The Portrait of a Lady*). The collectively told narrative of the Ghost Dance and its aftermath, Wounded Knee, can be viewed from several perspectives at once in Native American literature. The realist observer becomes apparent to the reader, "appears" to the reader (as if reader response to Native American texts involved forming a Wovoka-like vision of his or her own), as a collective, or even "tribal," grouping of observations that confirm each other. These observations share a common theme and referentiality (the focus is on the gulch in which the women and children were massacred and buried in snow), emerge from more than one "watcher," are confirmed by more than one pair of eyes, and above all pro-vide a counternarrative to the absence of this story in Euro-American "re-alism" of the period.

The particular mode of realism that seems to assume the closest kinship to the perspective from which the body of Native American literature is spo-ken or written is that of regionalism. While it is certainly true that tradi-tional Native American literature must be viewed as central to itself and not even part of "American literature," American literary history (and canon re-vision politics) has led to the revision of anthologies of "American literature" in the late twentieth century to "include" Native American materials and lit-erary scholarship about these materials. From the perspective of such an-thologies (as *NAAL*), both regionalism and Native American literature are noncanonical, marginal representations of American life; both cannot sep-arate setting from the development of character; and both foreground the contrasting perception of persons on the margins of American life in the nineteenth century with those who own the land and the property, who make (and break with impunity) the laws, and who consign certain persons to separate lands (or separate spheres or regions).

It is no coincidence that the author headnote for Mary Austin refers to Austin's efforts to make a critical and aesthetic connection between what she called "the landscape line" of Native American poetry and early mod-ernism. She also wrote an essay titled "Regionalism in American Fiction" (*English Journal*, 1932), in which she asks, "what is a race but a pattern of response common to a group of people who have lived together under a given environment long enough to take a recognizable pattern?" Austin's sense of the "pattern of response common to a group of people" more ac-curately describes the collective point of view on the "text" of Wounded Knee than James's theory of the single "watcher"; and it is clear that for Austin living together in a "given environment" is a precondition for the pat-tern of response that we know—differently yet with some similarities in late-nineteenth-century American fiction—as regionalism and as Native American literature.

SAMUEL L. CLEMENS (MARK TWAIN)

Adventures of Huckleberry Finn

Why read *Huckleberry Finn* again? It's likely that most of your students have read the novel at least once before, in a high-school English course, in a history course, or on their own; and if they haven't, they have probably seen some of the many films of the story. However, the chances are good that they haven't considered the novel from the perspectives you are developing in your own course: the evolution of an American vernacular, the imaginative transformation of the North American landscape, the Romantic and Realist traditions, themes of individuality and escape, the sources of wisdom and conscience in this culture, and imaginative fiction's address to race slavery and the predicament of minorities and women. *Huckleberry Finn* can be reread from any or all of these perspectives; but it is probably a good idea to avoid too much zeal in imposing one reading at the expense of all others. The reasons are perhaps obvious; over the past ninety years, the novel has weathered one systematic interpretation after another: disturbed Freudian dream, New Deal hymn to the Common People, Symbolist poem, formalist masterpiece, radical (or reactionary) political tract . . . the alternatives stack up high, and few of them have had any effect on the popularity and image that this novel enjoys with a worldwide audience. The problem is complicated by the fact that many readers (including perhaps many of your students) feel that this novel is *theirs,* a freewheeling tale told by an ordinary boy, improvising his way through a world presented as it really was—and a story that is, or should be, out beyond the systems and evaluations of modern academe.

If you sense that your class is uneasy about being urged into some overly systematic reading of *Huckleberry Finn,* then it might be a good idea to present the novel, and Samuel Clemens, as requiring us to do a different kind of close reading than we do on a highly crafted work like *The Scarlet Letter* or a short story by Melville or Poe. *Fenimore Cooper's Literary Offenses* can work well as an hors d'oeuvre before the plunge into *Huckleberry Finn.* Clemens's commentary on Cooper and on Romantic fiction is still fresh and funny (especially if your group has experience with Cooper); and this essay is as close as we can come to a forthright statement by Clemens about the Realism that he supposedly championed. We can see in this comic piece that Clemens's "realism" is reactive, a rejection of the extravagances and illusions of Romantic narrative, and that Clemens's mode defines itself by what it isn't at least as much as by what it is. *Huckleberry Finn* can be read many ways, of course; one such way, which follows naturally from a look into *Fenimore Cooper's Literary Offenses,* is as a book about the impact of Romantic and sentimental fiction, drama, poetry, and illustration on the Mississippi River world in which Huck and Jim try to survive.

But the first order of business, and perhaps the most important objective in rereading the novel as part of an American literature survey, is to help students find ways to engage with literary works that suggest or demonstrate genius and that may please them deeply but that from some perspectives may be formally flawed. To clear the air, it might be worth drifting through the novel's early chapters to look at the evidence of false starts and abandoned intentions. This book did begin as a potboiler, as "The Adventures of Huckleberry Finn, Tom Sawyer's Comrade," and it seems also to have begun as a detective story. If we look at the bric-a-brac in the floating house (Chapter IX), which Huck catalogs at such length, and at all the details that are provided in regard to the faking of his own death, we see some of the remains of the plot that Clemens eventually abandoned. However, if we ignore those detective story relics and try to describe the novel's plot as a flight to freedom and as the quest to free Huck's friend Jim, then we have major problems explaining why the two of them continue to flee southward, after missing the confluence with the Ohio River and the route into free territory. And as for formal symmetry and perfection: though you may hesitate to give Ernest Hemingway any last word about American literature, you might toss into the conversation his famous remark that after Chapter XXX—when Jim is trapped at the Phelps farm—the rest of the novel is "cheating." The ending of the book has been debated for fifty years; and students should know that however they feel comfortable reading it (or ignoring it), their views can find validation somewhere in the welter of published criticism.

Another unsettled controversy also requires some attention: the question of how the book is to be read as a commentary on racism and the appropriateness of including in the canon, as required reading on thousands of syllabi, a novel that uses the word *nigger* freely and dozens of times. A strong and time-honored case can be made that *Huck* is very much about racism, about a culture that instills and enforces dehumanization and prejudice, an ideology that can be escaped only for brief interludes when the human social world fades away and something more natural and innocent can flourish. A good case can also be made that if this were the intended theme of the novel, then Clemens did not stay with it faithfully: the other Tom and Huck narratives that Clemens wrote thereafter fail to show much interest in social justice for African Americans or in Jim as a rounded and interesting character. If students reach an impasse in settling, in some general way, the rightness of listing this novel as an American classic and a must-read for students of all races in all contexts, then see if they want to make distinctions among contexts. When and where would they feel comfortable teaching the novel? To what kind of class? In what sort of historical moment?

As you move into the novel, here are some suggestions for developing a different sort of close reading, a close reading suitable for a work in which high art might be quite different from highly polished formality.

1. The opening page can be read carefully, attending to Huck's language and to Clemens's strategy in getting the novel going. Huck claims no liter-

ary authority; his idea of a story apparently seems to be the simple and un-adorned telling of actual events, moving from one incident to the next, without the embellishment of elaborate commentary or even subordinate clauses. Compare the beginning of *Huckleberry Finn* to the opening paragraphs of *The Scarlet Letter*, and students will see why Hemingway felt that the modern novel begins right here. But if the language and the teller have grown simpler in some ways, the narrative, in a broader sense, has grown more complex, more reflexive, more aware of the paradoxes of writing and reading novels. To introduce himself, Huck refers us back to Mark Twain, who "told the truth, mainly" about two boys who do not exist; but then again, "Mark Twain" does not exist either, does he? Is there a playful address to "truth" and to "realism" here, by a writer who is supposed to be a master of the mode? Is realistic fiction a hopeless contradiction in terms? If such questions are asked in an appropriately light-hearted way, students may be more willing to enter the novel as, in some senses at least, an epistemological funhouse, a meditation on how illusions and ordinary life get intertwined—in ordinary life as well as in narrative fiction.

2. When Tom Sawyer shows up in the novel and Huck acquiesces to being a member of Tom's gang, we see how make-believe, borrowed from Romantic fiction, pervades childhood in this world; soon afterward we will encounter plenty of situations in which adults show themselves susceptible to the same disease. The deeper realism of the novel grows especially clear hereafter, for the nature of the real, of genuine emotion, moral action, and social behavior, all come into vigorous and sustained question. Here and afterward, you can raise questions about Tom's influence on Huck, when Tom is on the scene and when he isn't. Tom, we should remember, is several years younger: do students find Huck's compliance and his occasional admiration, plausible in a fourteen-year-old boy? Does Huck end the novel as morally grown up as we might like him to be?

3. As you move past the point in the novel at which Clemens put aside the manuscript (Chapter XVI, where the steamboat runs over the raft), it's worth stopping to observe what intentions have been abandoned or outgrown and what has happened not only to the plot but to the characters. Jim, for example, has become much more interesting as a moral presence in the work, Huck's "sound heart" has finally brought him to a full recognition of his friend's humanity and dignity, the Ohio River has been missed somehow, and the novel has cut itself loose from nearly every expectation with which a reader might have begun it. *Huckleberry Finn* is often classified as picaresque, as a way of addressing this escape from conventions and from its own opening; but are we witnessing here not just the liberation of one white boy's mind but also of American narrative fiction? The novel may seem loose, but it should not seem strange: students have read works like *The Catcher in the Rye*, *One Flew Over the Cuckoo's Nest*, *Their Eyes Were Watching God*, and *The Bell Jar*, all of which may owe something to the "breakout" of Clemens's novel from prevailing habits of literary

form. Ask students to talk about what has been gained and lost in this act
of escape.

4. The Grangerford-Shepherdson feud is based on actual violence that
Sam Clemens knew about as a young man growing up along the Mississippi.
But these chapters about the Grangerford household, their values, preten-
tions, and impact on their own children, can bring a lot of interesting commentary out of a class, especially now, when the papers are full of senseless
mayhem based on family and pseudo-family affiliations and contorted ideas
of honor and macho behavior. You can have a good deal of fun with Huck's
description of Emmeline's poems and "crayons"—Huck tries comically and
poignantly hard to be respectful of her morbid work, but his similes betray
his real reactions. It's a bravura piece of narrative description; but beneath
the comedy, beneath this struggle between common sense and supposedly
genteel aesthetics, there are hints of a tragedy, a young girl destroyed by the
sickness of the family values around her and the sickness of the sentimentality being shipped into this home from the "sivilized" world.

5. As the duke and the dauphin usurp the raft, some students may wonder if the "cheating" hasn't begun already, in other words, if Clemens isn't
making Huck and Jim into "extras" in a tale of con artists and fools. It
would be worth spending some time, therefore, on the duke-dauphin chapters as a unit in the novel, to observe their overall pattern and the effect on
Huck's thinking. The initial scams of the two conmen may seem relatively
innocuous: if the Pokeville camp meeting is so ignorant and foolish as to believe a wild tale about pirates from the Indian Ocean, perhaps they deserve
to be gulled; and the Bricksville we see (the site of the Boggs shooting and
the Royal Nonesuch) seems so meanspirited, lazy, and cowardly that we may
cheer when the three visitors (for Huck is now an accomplice) fleece them
with a bad stage show. But after this, the tone darkens, and Huck's in-
volvement with the duke and the dauphin becomes morally perilous. When
and why does he decide to take a stand against them? Does he do it on principle? Is he moved by a pretty face? By his "sound heart?" Or by a touch of
that sentimentality or degraded romanticism that have overwhelmed Tom
Sawyer and Emmeline Grangerford? You may expect some lively debate
over questions of this kind.

6. The Phelps farm chapters, with Jim incarcerated and tormented and
Huck and Tom playing children's games with the life and liberty of a
grown man, need to be looked at carefully rather than passed over as
padding or an awkward coda to a narrative that really came to an end
somewhere before this point. Students will want to speculate on Huck's
moral situation and psychological development, on the "realism" of his fall
back into being Tom's sidekick, on the plausibility of his apparent failure
to generalize from the various lessons that Jim and his river adventure
have taught him, and on the thematic value of this final sequence. Is the
last paragraph of the novel optimistic? Indeterminate? A foretaste of the

pessimism that, according to some critics, overtook Clemens in the final decades of his career?

Bret Harte

In *The Outcasts of Poker Flat*, Harte creates central characters who become the object of perception by someone outside the setting or region. Oakhurst is the outsider; and the reader's views of Madam Shipton, Piney Woods, and the others are all filtered through Oakhurst. When Oakhurst kills himself at the end of the story, Harte presents this scene also as a tableau for other outsiders—his readers—to see. Ask students to consider the humor of the story: does Harte achieve it at the expense of any particular characters more than others? Had he tried to depict the experience of western life from Mother Shipton's point of view, would *Outcasts* have been a different story? How much does Harte assume that his readers will find women, in general, and western prostitutes, in particular, laughable? Is he laughing at or with his characters?

W. D. Howells

Novel-Writing and Novel-Reading gives students a chance to read some of Howells's literary theory, and then they can test the application of that theory in *Editha*. Howells's definition of *realism* requires that fiction be "like life," and the central statement in his essay is the following: "The truth which I mean, the truth which is the only beauty, is truth to human experience. . . . It is a well ascertained fact concerning the imagination that it can work only with the stuff of experience. It can absolutely create nothing; it can only compose." For students who come to Howells after studying *Adventures of Huckleberry Finn,* notions of "like life" and "truth to experience" will seem justifiably naive.

For all of the complexities of the world in which he lived, Howells's own view of reality remains a simplistic one: that somehow reality may be verified and agreed on. However, Howells's theory makes more sense if we focus on the word *compose.* He seems to be saying here that the novelist must "place together" elements from real life that he is unable to create, that the novelist's art reveals itself in the relative placement of real things. Later in the essay he draws the analogy of a cyclorama to explain what he attempts in his fiction. He describes beginning "with life itself" and then going on to "imitate what we have known of life." The good writer will *"hide the joint.* But the joint is always there, and on one side of it are real ground and real grass, and on the other are the painted images of ground and grass." The realism of Howells describes the way existing elements are placed together. But composing implies assertion. To pose a question is to assert it, to propound it, to put it forth for examination. Therefore, in the very process of "composition," Howells and his hypothetical realistic writers are trying to set forth reality itself for examination, as if it were the proposition of an argument.

Editha, for all of the realism of its portrayal of sexist stereotypes in late-nineteenth-century American society, is superficial in its attempt to find and define motivation in Editha's character. Is Editha a real person or a "painted image"? And if she is a "painted image," does she project social reality or her author's distorted view of women? Compare her with Dame Van Winkle, Ligeia, Freeman's Louisa Ellis in *A New England Nun*, and James's May Bartram in *The Beast in the Jungle*.

Ambrose Bierce

Occurrence at Owl Creek Bridge is going to be a familiar story to many of your students, as it appears commonly in anthologies and collections for middle- and high-school use. Students will remember the ironies in the surprise ending; and perhaps with a little encouragement, they will remember other surprising and ironic configurations in other stories from this period by Bierce and his contemporaries: Crane, James, O. Henry, Wilde, Wharton, Stevenson. If this was the heyday of Realism and Naturalism, it was also a golden age of the supremely crafted tale; and if conversation about Bierce flags a bit, because the story is an old-home-week return for too many of your students, then you could have an engaging and far-reaching conversation about irony itself: why it came into such vogue around this time; whether it suggests some belief in large forces governing human experience; whether it is a *substitute* for belief, an orderly, and even tidy, suggestion of an inherent disorder or malice controlling the human situation. You might bring in a few excerpts from Bierce's *The Devil's Dictionary*, which will amuse your students: the epigram and the adage were also in vogue, and Bierce was a leading practitioner. A few of his more startling one-liners can provide fuel for a conversation about how he saw the world.

Native American Oratory

In his discussion of Native American oratory, Andrew Wiget (*Native American Literature*, 1985) observes that "from the first centuries of white settlement in America, the oratorical ability of Native Americans, their artful talent for persuasion, was noted by Europeans," and he cites Thomas Jefferson's *Notes on the State of Virginia* (1784) as offering the "moment of highest praise." In preparation for a discussion of Native American oratory, ask students to read the excerpt from Jefferson's *Notes, Query VI. Productions Mineral, Vegetable, and Animal*, (in Volume 1), which includes Jefferson's comments.

Cochise

Cochise's speech makes a plea for the Apaches, although much reduced in number by the wars with the Euro-Americans, to retain "a part of my own country, where I and my little band can live." As the headnote observes, this is an example of oratory addressed to white listeners, and its theme is land. You can make the speech live for readers in a couple of ways.

First, ask students to recall (and reread) the *Pima Stories of the Beginning of the World* (in Volume 1), for the opening sentence of Cochise's speech makes an indirect reference to the emergence myth of creation of some Southwest Indians, a myth in which humans crawl out from a hole in the ground: "This for a very long time has been the home of my people; they came from the darkness, few in numbers and feeble." It's important that students catch this reference, what Euro-Americans would call a literary allusion, but what for Cochise links the spiritual origins of his people with their present predicament (and the occasion for his oratory). It also provides evidence for the headnote's observation that for Native Americans there were no fixed distinctions between the spiritual and the secular.

In light of Cochise's allusion to the emergence myth of the Pimas and the Apaches (locate for students the reference at the end of the Pima *Story of the Flood* to the origins of the Apaches as "the first ones that talked"), you might want to note that Native American literature itself "emerges" with such power during the years 1830–90, when the Indians themselves were losing their battles with the whites. And yet the emergence myth implies the cyclical destruction and reemergence of native peoples as well as their migrations. Perhaps the new "emergence" of Native American literature into the larger canon of American literature through the contest for space or literary "territory" in anthologies represents the triumph, or at least the persistence, of Native American cultures, despite several acts of destruction by the world maker.

Second, trace with students the numerous and pervasive references to land in the speech and all of the different ways in which Cochise configures the meaning of land to his people. Variously, land becomes imaged as "these mountains about us," "home," and "our country," and the Apaches are portrayed as integral to that landscape, as, early in the speech, Cochise compares the way his people "covered the whole country" to the way "clouds cover the mountains." The rhetorical occasion for the speech, namely to arrive at a treaty that would yield "a part of my own country," establishes its form, in the sense that Cochise defines himself and his people as quite "part" of the country. In formal terms, the speech becomes synecdoche: he speaks for all, and the terms in which he speaks establish an identity between people and their land. To take away the land kills the people who are "part" of that land; if the people have been reduced in numbers, then they can survive on "part" of that land, but they must be on that land. Like the deer that flee the hunter in a later image from the speech, the Apaches only exist on the land that has been their home.

Charlot

This speech addressed to Charlot's fellow Flathead Indians lives up to its description in the headnote as "a powerful critique of the white people's ways." Contrast with students the tone and language of Charlot's speech with Cochise's; focus on the evocation of shame in the speech and discuss the way racism attempts to obliterate emotions of shame; compare and contrast this with William Apess's *An Indian's Looking-Glass for the White Man*, another powerful indictment of white treatment of native peoples. Ask students if the rhetorical stance of the speaker reminds them of any historical works in Euro-American literature: for instance, Franklin's *An Edict by the King of Prussia*, Thomas Paine's *Thoughts on the Present State of American Affairs* from *Common Sense*, or especially Thomas Jefferson's *Declaration of Independence*. Without suggesting that the *Declaration of Independence* serves as a literary model (which nevertheless it may—even though the headnote does not indicate this—because Charlot delivered the speech "in the year of the centennial celebration of American independence"), compare the rhetorical construction of King George III in Jefferson's *Declaration* with Charlot's rhetorical construction of "the white man" whom he personifies as an individual power throughout his speech, as in "is his prayer his promise" and "he wants us to pay him besides his enslaving our country."

Another interesting text to examine in such a discussion is Elizabeth Cady Stanton's 1848 *Declaration of Sentiments* (included as an appendix to this Guide), which similarly personifies not "white man" but "man," protests not "shame" but "tyranny," and lists moral and political grievances. In the documents by both Charlot and Stanton, the speaker/writer addresses oppressed people with the sense of being overheard. The press, at least, was present to transcribe Charlot's speech; and after its signing by a hundred men and women supporters of women's rights in 1848, presumably the *Declaration of Sentiments* also became a public document (although its inclusion as part of the Guide instead of *NAAL* itself suggests that it has not yet approached even the neocanonical status of Charlot's speech).

Examining the rhetorical strategy of constructing the oppressor in each of these three political statements designed simultaneously to arouse enmity against "King George," "the white man," and "man" and support for the cause of the oppressed also increases students' perspective on the use of rhetorical devices as part of the process by which writing becomes a form of political action that Native American speakers, perhaps because of their tradition of oral practice and the extent of their own grievances, were quite skillful in employing.

HENRY JAMES

The Art of Fiction shows that James shares Howells's theory of fiction, in part. He writes, "The only reason for the existence of a novel is that it does attempt to represent life." However, what James means by *life* and what Howells means by it are two different things. Unlike Howells, who asserts a reality that is referential and shared, James suggests that creation resides in the author's perception. Without the perceiving eye there is no art. James implicitly links realism with point of view and with the "quality of the mind of the producer." He writes, "A novel is in its broadest definition a personal, a direct impression of life: that, to begin with, constitutes its value, which is greater or less according to the intensity of the impression." Thus reality is subjective for Henry James; and he suggests that, far from being referential, Realism reveals aspects of life that cannot be seen. He insists on "the power to guess the unseen from the seen, to trace the implication of things, to judge the whole piece by the pattern"; and he writes, "Experience is never limited, and it is never complete; it is an immense sensibility, a kind of huge spiderweb of the finest silken threads suspended in the chamber of consciousness, and catching every airborne particle in its tissue."

If, as Howells writes, the reader is the arbiter of a fiction's realism and if "the only test of a novel's truth is his own knowledge of life," then many of our students will have difficulty seeing realism in Henry James. The challenge in teaching James is to try to get students to follow the psychological complexity of the relationships James creates—between Daisy and Winterbourne in *Daisy Miller,* and between John Marcher and May Bartram in *The Beast in the Jungle*—and to see his interest in relationships per se as an aspect of realism that makes James stand out among many of his contemporaries. Compare James's analysis of the complexity of emotional and psychological development with Clemens's in *Adventures of Huckleberry Finn* and with Howells's in *Editha.* The regionalists link emotional development to the development of community—here portrayed by Mrs. Todd's empathy with the French woman in Jewett's *The Foreigner.* And Freeman and Chopin show that the individual develops emotionally within the context of human relationships, but their focus remains the quality and development of individual or shared vision. Only James among his contemporaries focuses on human relationships themselves as the source of experience. The single context within the meaning of human experience may be explored. In the shorter works anthologized here, we see relationships that are primarily dyadic. In the novels, James interweaves pairs of intense personal relationships with each other to form the "huge spiderweb" of his psychological fiction.

The Beast in the Jungle

In this story, James fully develops his theory of the novel as "a personal, direct impression of life," for it is actually such an "impression" that Marcher expects to have and by which he figures his "beast." James's use of third-person-limited point of view to define the unfolding of Marcher's perception serves as a laboratory of the use of technique. Marcher's point of view gives the reader a sense of reality as being bounded by the limits of perception and consciousness; yet James so skillfully creates May Bartram that, without ever entering her consciousness, we know what she is thinking and feeling—even more than John Marcher, despite the fact that he sees and hears everything the reader does.

Ask your students "what happens" in this story. The wide range of responses creates a spectrum of the kinds of experience that constitute "reality" for James. Some will reply that nothing happens—which, in a sense, is true enough. Others will wonder whether Marcher dies at the end of the story—a valid speculation. Some will reply that he discovers he has been in love with May Bartram all along—an assertion that seems both true and false in light of the story. A few will focus on the developing portrayal of character as "what happens" for James. You can help them see what interests James in the relationship between his two characters by asking them which character they, as readers, most resemble. They will certainly align themselves with May, for, in a sense, Marcher and May are acting out the ideal relationship between author and reader. He is his own author, like many American male protagonists before him; she is his ideal reader—she grants him his *donnée*—as, James states in *The Art of Fiction*, the reader must do for the novelist. So that when the two meet again after ten years' time and May Bartram remembers Marcher's old impression, he asks, " 'You mean you feel how my obsession—poor old thing!—may correspond to some possible reality?' " "Corresponding to some possible reality" is the precise problem of the story, of James's other work, and of Realism itself. If reality is only "possible" and if two different characters within the same story, in which nothing else happens but their relationship, have such different perceptions of what is real, then what happens to realism itself?

James's interest in convention and social forms in *Daisy Miller* is apparent in *The Beast in the Jungle* as well. Marcher's very "unsettled" feeling about the nature of reality makes it difficult for him to go along with social forms. And so he lives with his "figure" of the beast as the hypothesis by which he understands his life. When the beast springs, in a sense, he will be able to live; until then he can't consider marriage. The beast becomes his disfiguring quality—he calls it "a hump on one's back"—and it is necessary for May to "dispose the concealing veil in the right folds." James, here, continues Hawthorne's fascination with the contradictions between apparent self-confrontation (Marcher tries to think of himself as courageous) and actual self-evasion (even when the beast finally springs, he turns "instinctively . . . to avoid it" as he flings himself, face down, on May Bartram's tomb).

Ironically, his relationship with May contributes to that process of self-evasion. For she helps him "to pass for a man like another"; with her, Marcher appears to be conventional and to be living an ordinary life. He says to her: "What saves us, you know, is that we answer so completely to so usual an appearance: that of the man and woman whose friendship has become such a daily habit—or almost—as to be at last indispensable." Although they aren't married, Marcher believes that he has the "appearance" of it. He uses May to "cover" his apparent deficiencies. But certain kinds of experience and certain kinds of psychological development cannot be acquired by what "passes for" living, and neither can they be taught; they must be lived. Therefore, although the reader perceives that May Bartram understands much more of Marcher than he does of himself, she restrains herself, as James restrains himself, from telling him what it all means. He has to figure it out for himself—or not know it at all.

The story ends "happily" in a sense, because, although Marcher discovers the limitations of his fate, James manages to achieve his own goal—namely, that of portraying a character having a "personal, direct impression"—a literal *impress* of "letters of quick flame." The question becomes, How does Marcher finally achieve that impression? What is responsible, what is the catalyzing moment? Students will remember the scene in the cemetery, when Marcher sees the ravaged mourner, who is apparently a widower and whose manifestation of grief makes Marcher ask, "What had the man *had,* to make him by the loss of it so bleed and yet live?" The apparent answer, and perhaps the only "right" answer, is that the other man has been touched by passion, has loved, whereas Marcher "had seen *outside* of his life, not learned it within." And he concludes, "The escape would have been to love her; then, *then* he would have lived."

But it seems curious that the other man at the cemetery seems—possibly, to Marcher—aware of an "overt discord" between his feelings and Marcher's. The significant thing, to Marcher, is that the other man showed his feelings, "*showed* them—that was the point." And he is aware of his own presence as "something that profaned the air." Perhaps James is more interested in Marcher's inability to find the appropriate *form* for his feeling than in his inability to feel at all. He describes Marcher at May's funeral as being "treated as scarce more nearly concerned with it than if there had been a thousand others." As the author of his own fate, Marcher has failed in its execution. He has failed to find any manifest form for his own "personal, direct impression" that would have allowed him to "learn from within." And James links that failure with Marcher's refusal to make "real" what is only "appearance"—his "daily habit" of relationship with May Bartram. For James, consciousness requires a social context. Therefore, "it was as if in the view of society he had not *been* markedly bereaved, as if there still failed some sign or proof of it." James's characters may defy convention, as Daisy Miller does, but they don't escape having to confront it. The intrusion of convention in James's fiction establishes its social realism, the limitations within which his characters may establish themselves as conscious.

The Jolly Corner and The Great Good Place

If the students have been reading the James materials chronologically, then some questions may have been forming in your class regarding all these situations in which protagonists and raptly attentive narrators find themselves terribly and sometimes fatally deceived: they have looked at the truth, and for the truth, and they have failed to see it. Somebody may have made the observation in your group that the higher forms of Realism, as practiced by people like James, Wharton, Clemens, and even Howells, often deeply question the nature of the real. If that hasn't come up as a speculation, then you might open it as you move into both of these stories, in which even one's own identity becomes suspect.

It is also an old adage—about sheer storytelling, not specifically about Realism—that to tell a good horror story an author has to find something that scares himself or herself. If that is true, then the ghost story dimensions of these two tales can lead into a very fruitful discussion of what it is that would scare the daylights out of a confirmed realist, an artist who gives his life and his career over to "seeing"—to a belief in a stable self; a coalesced and perhaps transcendent consciousness; and the validity of any quest to understand who we are, where we are, and what we are. A conversation like this can expand outward beyond all of these tales, so that students will be better prepared to read the longer James works and to understand what urgencies, compulsions, and fears underlie all the social maneuverings on the surface of those great texts.

Joel Chandler Harris

The "Uncle Remus" tales depend for their narrative success on the contrast between black storyteller and white audience. Harris includes in his work "instructions" to his readers, writes for a white audience, and yet manages to avoid caricaturing his black characters or turning them into mere entertainment. In his extensive use of southern black dialect and African American folktales as the source of his subject matter, Harris might easily have been perceived in his time, and in ours, as a local-color writer. With your class, you might speculate about the usefulness of distinctions between "regionalism" and "local color." One difference might be that the regionalist narrator looks *with* the regional protagonist, whereas the local-color writer looks *at* regional experience; ask students to consider the location of Harris's own perspective on his characters.

Sarah Orne Jewett

In the traditional presentation of late-nineteenth-century American fiction, Sarah Orne Jewett and Mary E. Wilkins Freeman are often grouped with the local-color writers, and *regionalism* becomes a descriptive term for the entire group. A closer look at American literary history reveals that regionalism and local color writing developed as distinct but parallel genres and that if we look at chronology, regionalism was the first of the late-nineteenth-century fictional genres to emerge. Harriet Beecher Stowe published *The Pearl of Orr's Island*, the work that influenced Jewett's own development, five years before Clemens's *The Notorious Jumping Frog of Calaveras County*; and during the same decade that Hawthorne and Melville were publishing their most significant work (the 1850s), Alice Cary, Rose Terry Cooke (not anthologized here), and Stowe herself were establishing regionalism as a genre. By the time Jewett published *Deephaven* (1877), she already had a regionalist tradition to write within; and although by the chronology of birth order she and her work appear to follow Twain, Howells, and James, the publication of *Deephaven* precedes that of *Adventures of Huckleberry Finn*, *The Rise of Silas Lapham*, and *The Portrait of a Lady*.

A White Heron

In this story, Jewett chooses as her center of perception a character who lives within the region she is writing about. In *A White Heron*, Sylvy (whose name means "woods") is indigenous to the setting (even though she has moved there from the city), because she speaks the language of nature; it is the ornithologist who is the outsider, implicitly resembling the local color writer in his quest to come into the rural scene, shoot and stuff a bird, and bring it back for urban people to see. In refusing to reveal the secrets of the white heron's nest, Sylvy protects the regional perception from exploitation.

The contrast between Sylvy's desire to allow the bird its freedom and the ornithologist's desire to kill and stuff the bird provides a focal point for a discussion of the contrasts among regionalism, Realism, and local-color writing. Consider Bret Harte's story *The Outcasts of Poker Flat* and James's *The Beast in the Jungle* in conjunction with *A White Heron,* and ask students to describe differences in point of view, the extent to which the story includes the perspective of other characters, and the text's depiction of female characters. Ask them to imagine that *The Outcasts of Poker Flat* included the perspective of the Duchess, Mother Shipton, or Piney Woods, instead of turning them into caricatures, or to imagine that *The Beast in the Jungle* included May Bartram's perspective and gave her a voice, and you will begin to convey some of the particular features of regionalism as a genre. In *A White Heron,* Jewett shifts the center of perception not only to a poor, rural female character but also to a nine-year-old child and makes it possible for her reader to understand the disenfranchised perspective.

The Foreigner

The Foreigner depicts the relationship between the female narrator of *The Country of the Pointed Firs* and her guide in that novel, Mrs. Todd; but Jewett wrote *The Foreigner* after publishing the novel and the story stands alone. In this text, students can experience the power of the earlier, longer work. Like Clemens, Howells, and James, Jewett as regionalist also experimented with storytelling, but *The Foreigner* adds empathy to the requirements of relationship between storyteller and reader/listener/audience. In characterizing the tale Mrs. Todd relates in *The Foreigner* as a "ghost story," Jewett's narrator invites us to contrast her approach with James's narrators in *The Turn of the Screw.* For James, the "impression" the teller makes on the listener becomes the standard of the tale's success. For Jewett, the tale becomes a medium for relationship between teller and listener; and although the narrator of *The Foreigner* says very little while Mrs. Todd tells her story, her choice to remain silent at crucial points in the narrative establishes her as a partner in the telling. The listener/reader has a role to play in Jewett that goes beyond the reader response James's narrator tries to teach in *The Turn of the Screw.* Without relationship between teller and listener, there is no text. The power of Jewett's narrator is that she does not attempt to "read" the meaning of Mrs. Todd's narrative but allows the other woman to tell the story as its meaning deepens and dawns on her. The appearance of the "ghost" at the end is not Mrs. Todd's attempt to frighten her listener or to create a narrative effect but to move beyond her storm fear for her aged mother, who, with Mrs. Todd's brother William, lives on one of the "outlying islands."

The story begins with Mrs. Todd separated from her mother by the raging gale and dramatizes her use of storytelling to ease her anxiety and to regain inner peace. By the end of *The Foreigner,* Jewett has taught her readers how to feel a different kind of suspense than they might have expected in a ghost story. The story's climax occurs not with the appearance of the ghost but with Mrs. Todd's recognition that Mrs. Tolland has been reunited with her mother. In the larger story, the narrator also feels the strengthening of her ties to Mrs. Todd; and fiction, for the regionalist Jewett, becomes reparative and inclusive. Neither Mrs. Tolland nor Mrs. Todd is a caricature set up for readers to laugh at; the comedy of *The Foreigner* makes possible the continued "harmony of fellowship" that eases separation anxiety and social isolation.

KATE CHOPIN

At the 'Cadian Ball

This story was Chopin's first significant regional publication, and it establishes an interest in hierarchies of southern society according to categories of race, class, and gender that would characterize much of her regionalist fiction. In the southern Louisiana locale of her work, her characters establish superiority for the Creoles, descendants of the original French settlers of Louisiana, and lower-class status for the Cajuns, descendants of the French Acadians exiled by the British from Nova Scotia in the late eighteenth century. Black characters occupy the lowest social position in this society; and within the rank of Cajuns (" 'Cadians"), status is granted according to racial characteristics that are viewed as European rather than African. Helping students sort out the social codes among the characters will help them understand the way class power and sexual desire are constructed and become interconnected. For example, Calixta, a Cajun woman with a Spanish Cuban mother, has more "status" than other women because she has blue eyes and flaxen hair, even though it "kinked worse than a mulatto's"; but she has no power at all against Clarisse, the upper-class Creole woman, "dainty as a lily." The racial codes in this society are complex. Bruce, the black servant, does not go to the 'Cadian ball, but the 'Cadians are not apparently considered white; for Chopin writes, when Alcee Laballiere arrives, that "anyone who is white may go to a 'Cadian ball, but he must pay for his lemonade. . . . And he must behave himself like a 'Cadian." Once students sort out the intricacies of power and hierarchy in this story, it becomes easier for them to understand Calixta's attraction for Laballiere and yet her decision to marry the "brown" Bobinot. The story leads to a more general discussion concerning the way racial and class status construct sexual desire and even sexual attractiveness in American society.

The Awakening

In seeing Edna Pontellier as yet another American on a quest to become self-reliant and to establish her identity within a hostile society, students might consider whether *The Awakening* could be titled "Adventures of Edna Pontellier." This can lead into a brief discussion of *Huck Finn*, and students can see essential differences in design between the two novels. Briefly, Edna Pontellier is not a "picaro," and Chopin does not present her awakening as a linear series of adventures but rather as an interwoven account of the relationships Edna has with other characters and the way in which her awakening becomes her own "education." Conversely, you may ask students whether Clemens might have subtitled his book "The Awakening of Huckleberry Finn," and the incongruity of the two portraits of nineteenth-century life becomes even clearer. (If you have taught Volume 1 to the same group of students, you can also make connections between Chopin's novel and earlier American dream fictions, especially *Rip Van Winkle, Young Goodman Brown,* Thoreau's *Resistance to Civil Government,* and certainly to Jim's dream in Chapter XV of *Huckleberry Finn.*) In Chopin's successful attempt to present Edna's life from her own point of view—so that students can see that even physical sex is not an end in itself for Edna but rather only one aspect of her artistic and spiritual awakening and her struggle to achieve autonomy—she uses the technique of shifting the center, which characterizes the best of regionalist writing. One essay that will help students place Edna's attempts to reach toward limits that seem radical for women in her time is Elizabeth Cady Stanton's 1896 *The Solitude of Self,* which is brief enough to circulate as background reading.

But Edna's attempt to achieve her own limits is thwarted—by her husband; by the attitudes of men, like Robert, whom she respects; and by the society in which she lives. In describing the limitations Edna constantly comes up against, Chopin writes literary Realism, because in *The Awakening,* Edna's identity is finally so contingent on her social context that it becomes impossible for her to reconcile her sense of her own individual identity with society's expectations. But does she commit suicide? Some students may want to argue that her death is not actually suicide, but rather the consequences of Edna's choice to immerse herself quite literally in a context (the sea) that is the only place she can transcend her own limits (with connections here to Thoreau's "immersion" in Walden Pond). To put it another way, if Edna's death is suicide, then Huck Finn's choice to evade the conflicts of civilization is suicide by other means.

You might want to closely read one scene in the novel (the closing scene of Chapter XXIII, in which Edna and Leonce have dinner with Edna's father and Dr. Mandelet) as a way of demonstrating Edna's inability to transform the world she lives in into one that will seem real to her. In this scene, each of the four characters tells a story that reveals a great deal about the teller's character. Leonce tells an antebellum tale of "some amusing plantation experiences" and casts himself as a paternalistic Huck Finn, Edna's father depicts himself as a "central figure" in the Civil War, Dr. Mandelet tells a tale of a woman who moves away from her husband but whose love returns "to its legitimate source," and Edna tells a romantic story of two lovers who paddle away one night and never come back. What is interesting about the scene is that only Edna's story engages the imaginations of her audience. Despite its romanticism, the story possesses some compelling truth. Ironically, the anecdotes the other three relate are equally romantic projections of themselves or, in the doctor's case, of his ability to "cure" Edna; but in each case, the society has provided mirrors that appear to confirm the self-portraits. Leonce can depict himself as Huck Finn without seeming ridiculous, the colonel can aspire to having a war hero's reputation without attracting scorn, and the doctor can presume to understand the nature of women without losing patients. But Edna cannot find in her culture—except in the invention of her own imagination—any ratification of her self-concept.

Edna's confusion can be viewed as a variation on Du Boisean "double-consciousness," for throughout the book she constantly lives in a state of tension between her emerging sense of self and the limitations her society imposes on her. You might ask your students if Chopin is portraying Edna as the victim of social forces over which she has no control and if the novel can, therefore, be viewed as naturalistic. To call sexism a social force, in the same way that Darwinism might be seen as a social force at that time, obscures the fact that theories of separate spheres were viewed as the underpinnings of American culture, rather than as new "discoveries." The force over which Edna has no control leads her to look for some other form within which to manifest her double-consciousness. In the "real" world of Edna's family and society, the only person capable of understanding her death on its own terms might be Mlle. Reisz, another woman who has engaged in a similar struggle and taken the life of the artist as her own form within which to express the tensions of the solitude (also the title of the piece of music she plays) of self. From a realist's view, Edna's last act appears to be meaningless suicide. From a regionalist's view, however, it becomes the only form of expression available to her.

Yet, perhaps the novel's limitations partly reside in Chopin's limited vision of what an American woman might achieve. Edna isn't strong enough or talented enough to live like Mlle. Reisz, and Chopin doesn't even present this as a serious possibility for her. Neither does she perceive the possibility of extending her own desire for awakening to the countless, and generally nameless, women of color in the novel. Neither Edna nor Chopin herself seems to perceive Edna's concerns as applicable to women of color or different social class. Perhaps Edna's limitations are Chopin's own: for Chopin, implicitly viewing sexism with the naturalist's eye, cannot achieve the full shift of the center of perception that would be necessary to produce works of regionalism in the nineteenth century or modernism in the twentieth, a shift that in Chopin would have to focus on Edna's perception as normal and the perceptions of other characters as skewed. The only nineteenth-century work by a woman writer that really accomplishes this is Sarah Orne Jewett's 1896 The Country of the Pointed Firs (not anthologized in NAAL but available in paperback in a Norton edition).

Mary E. Wilkins Freeman

Like Jewett, Freeman wrote in the genre of regionalism, and also like Jewett, Freeman places women's lives and regional vision at the center of her stories. Freeman's A New England Nun makes a useful companion story to Jewett's A White Heron. Ask your students to evaluate the motivations and final choices of Louisa Ellis and Jewett's Sylvy. Compare and contrast A New England Nun with Bret Harte's The Outcasts of Poker Flat. Although Freeman focuses on Louisa Ellis's experience, she portrays her male character, Joe Dagget, more sympathetically than Harte or Hamlin Garland do their female characters. A *New England Nun* presents Louisa Ellis's vision and decision not to marry as valid and normal; but Freeman doesn't earn the reader's sympathy for her female character at Joe Dagget's expense. She portrays Joe as well meaning and honorable, if typical of his time and place (many young men left New England to make their fortunes elsewhere in the years following the Civil War). Some critics have called Louisa sexually repressed. A lively discussion will follow if you ask your students whether they agree.

The *Revolt of "Mother"* earns Freeman a place in the humorist tradition, with a difference. Once again, she includes "Father's" perspective in her story of "Mother's" revolt, and suggests "Father's" ability to enlarge his own capacity for empathy. Unlike writers of the Southwest humorist school, for whom local color implied acceptance of off-color jokes about women, Freeman does not elevate Sarah Penn by caricaturing Adoniram and making him the object of ridicule. Like Jewett's A *White Heron, The Revolt of "Mother"* may be read as Freeman's response to local-color writing. From the opening line of the story, what Sarah Penn seems to want most of all is to engage her husband as her audience and to find acceptance for her own voice. *Revolt* may be too strong a word to describe Sarah Penn's attempt to make herself heard; she remains within the family structure, even if she has managed to redefine its terms; Nanny's impending marriage, not Sarah's own frustration, moves her to act.

Freeman contributes to the development of regionalism by collapsing narrator and female protagonist. Ask students to consider the absence of narrators in Freeman's stories and to contrast this with the reliance on narrators by her contemporaries, most notably Jewett and James. Where Jewett makes it possible for a reader to empathize with a regional character and to imagine that character speaking in his or her own voice, Freeman actually stands back from her own regional canvas, allowing her characters' voices, not a narrator's perspective, to create their own stories. Unlike Jewett, Freeman does not dramatize a shift in the center of perception, from, say, the ornithologist of A *White Heron* to the nine-year-old rural child; instead, Freeman writes from a position where such a shift has already occurred. She frames her stories carefully—Louisa Ellis's window and the Penns' barn door carefully limit the world she depicts—but within that frame, she creates a fictional territory in which characters can articulate the perspective of marginal women as central. The tight form of her fiction both fences out and fences in; she writes as if regionalism both opened up and protected that small space within which late-nineteenth-century women were free to express their vision.

BOOKER T. WASHINGTON

In this edition of *NAAL* the Washington materials are much expanded; and they give us a real opportunity to talk about the construction of an American identity, of an autobiography, and of a text that converses with other important documents in our cultural history. Writing at the very end of the nineteenth century, Washington was deeply aware of the historical and literary moment in which he was working: Benjamin Franklin, Harriet Jacobs, Frederick Douglass, Walt Whitman, Ulysses S. Grant, and many other autobiographers had already done much to establish the pace, subject matter, and general configurations of an American life set down on paper. Your students have probably engaged with some of these forebears (or competitors) in the craft and art of American-style autobiography; where do they see suggestions that Washington is echoing or resisting moments or assumptions that we associate with these other writers?

You might focus on the opening pages of *Up From Slavery* and the way it continues and departs from traditions developed by Douglass; you might spend some time with much-later passages in Washington's book that describe the mature leader's daily schedules, work routines, and conceptions of success, recreation, and personal contentment and compare these to procedures and values laid out by Franklin or Thoreau. Does Washington conceive of his audience as similar, somehow, to Franklin's? Do themes or tones emerge here, in *Up From Slavery*, that might account for the way that Washington's book, which was hailed as a classic for decades, fell into eclipse in more recent years? In what spirit does he distinguish his own upbringing from middle-class conceptions of childhood? When he talks about his strategies as a public speaker, what assumptions might be indicated about complexities of maintaining personal integrity and Emersonian-style honesty, while also striving (as Washington affirms that he does) to please an audience so thoroughly that not one listener would ever leave the hall?

Charles W. Chesnutt

It would be a mistake to present Chesnutt as just another local colorist, an African American working faithfully in the mode and fashion pioneered and dominated by white authors. His situation is in some ways much more complex, and his handling of it is worth our attention—not as a way of excusing him somehow but as a way of recognizing the breadth and depth of what he achieves. In several ways, Chesnutt's situation was supremely paradoxical: he was a black writer narrating black experience into a context already well supplied with narratives of black experience; written by white people. Moreover, the situation of African Americans in the United States had obviously changed immensely in a thirty-year period, to the extent that the perceptions, personal histories, and identities of this minority had never been more scattered and diverse. Chesnutt was a realist by conviction—in which direction did "the real" lie: back in the rural South and the plantation life or as far from it as one could flee? There were also profound ironies having to do with his situation as an artist, working in a mode in which the flashy counterfeit could often strike a reading audience as more "true" than the true article.

Chesnutt, therefore, speaks in a chorus of voices, and he violates expectations, not just in terms of plotting but in terms of the realist mode itself.

The motive may be to return his readers to a condition of wonder, of the rapt attention that can come with seeing things freshly or for the first time. Like Clemens, like James, like Wharton, Chesnutt will throw plausibility out the window at times, in pursuit of a more important or larger sort of "realism." His frame-tale narrators (as in *The Goophered Grapevine*) don't serve merely to give Chesnutt himself some safe distance, or social removal, from the story he tells; the strategy allows us to approach, in stages, something unfamiliar, where (as your students might say) all bets are off—an American reality where the conventional white turn-of-the-century audience would find very little that was familiar to it and where, in a sense, anything could happen.

The Wife of His Youth, included for the first time in this *NAAL* edition, is a story with a twist, somewhat like an O. Henry tale; but the twist has the resonance that a plot twist might have in a Hawthorne romance. An old woman wanders by chance into the life of a man who believes, to his core, that he has left his old life and his old self behind and has achieved full amalgamation into sophisticated urban life, or at least into this new African American gentility, where Tennyson's poems have replaced the spirituals that Du Bois lauds in *The Souls of Black Folk*. Is Liza's return, then, the return of Ryder's soul? Is the transformation that simple? What will happen next, after the last page of this narrative? Does Chesnutt offer some forecast here about the future of his people? Or does he puzzle over that future, as Hawthorne does when he engages with present-day New England?

CHARLES ALEXANDER EASTMAN (OHIYESA)

In light of the headnote's assessment of Eastman's assimilationist tendencies, read the chapters from *From the Deep Woods to Civilization* with particular awareness of Eastman's references to whites; to other Sioux, such as Blue Horse, who claim to be "friends" with white men; and to Sioux who are intolerant of relationships with whites. Then recall Charlot's speech, in which "the white man" is portrayed as a monolithic villain. Does Eastman's narrative confirm or refute Charlot's speech? To what extent would students argue that Eastman's assimilationist perspective is the product of his white education in the Indian boarding schools of the period? Is it possible for Eastman to be both an assimilationist and a spokesman for Native Americans? He summarizes the ambivalence of his position at one point early in the excerpt when he writes about the difficulty parents had separating from their children who were attending government boarding schools and about how they would ask him to write letters excusing their children on account of illness: "I was of course wholly in sympathy with the policy of education for the Indian children, yet by no means hardened to the exhibition of natural feeling." Yet later (in Chapter VII) he seems to give meaning to the phrase he is called, "the Indian white doctor," when he writes, "I scarcely knew at the time, but gradually learned afterward, that the Sioux had many grievances and causes for profound discontent, which lay back of and were more or less closely related to the ghost dance craze and the prevailing restlessness and excitement." Eastman speaks the Sioux language, has power vested in him by the U.S. government, and yet does not completely understand the Sioux point of view.

Eastman's powerful narrative conveys details about the day-to-day workings of the Pine Ridge Agency. Explicate with students the apparent role of the agency in the lives of Native Americans and the power the agency could exercise; explore the significance of such "games" as the buffalo hunt on "issue day"; consider the role of the Indian police force at Pine Ridge Agency. Consider as well the meaning of the placement of the doctor's offices: "the assembly room of the Indian police, used also as a council room, opened out of my dispensary."

For the larger narrative of the story of the Ghost Dance religion and the Wounded Knee massacre, Eastman's narrative offers a powerful eyewitness account of impending conflict and of the aftermath and consequences of the massacre. Trace references to the "new religion" that has been proclaimed at about the same time as Eastman's arrival at Pine Ridge. Read the anthologized versions of Wovoka's *Messiah Letters* and compare them with Eastman's careful paraphrase of Wovoka's teachings in Chapter VI (Captain Sword's account of the Ghost Dance religion). Examine Eastman's narrative for evidence that might explain the resistance of white settlers to the Ghost Dance religion.

Then examine carefully Eastman's account of the Ghost Dance war itself, including the U.S. government's use of black soldiers against the Sioux. While not an eyewitness, Eastman is an "ear-witness," for he hears the sound of the Hotchkiss guns. Yet what he sees of the wounded and dead when he visits the battlefield, although it tests his assimilationism, does not ultimately change his course of action: "All this was a severe ordeal for one who had so lately put all his faith in the Christian love and lofty ideals of the white man," he writes—and sets his day of marriage to a white woman for the following June. Recall here, once again, the words of William Apess's *An Indian's Looking-Glass*; in Eastman, we see at least one Sioux who manages to avail himself of the possibilities of cross-racial marriage. The times—and the terms of the discourse—are different for Eastman than they were for Apess sixty years earlier.

HAMLIN GARLAND

Garland's *Under the Lion's Paw* usefully contrasts with both Jewett's *The Foreigner* and Freeman's *The Revolt of "Mother."* Although Stephen Council initially helps Haskins get a good start, Garland focuses on the futility of Haskins's labor; and the concluding scene creates a tableau similar in effect to the end of *The Outcasts of Poker Flat*. Haskins is "under the lion's paw," and Butler (and Garland) leave him "seated dumbly on the sunny pile of sheaves, his head sunk into his hands." The reader views Haskins—like Mother Shipton, Piney Woods, and ultimately Oakhurst as well—from the outside. Contrast this with the perspective Jewett offers in *The Foreigner*, in which she depicts the growth of sympathy between characters and in which Mrs. Todd explores and tries to repair the social exclusion of Mrs. Tolland; Haskins ends as an object of exclusion, viewed from outside the story, whereas Jewett's characters expand their circle of community. Or contrast the poverty of the homeless characters in *Under the Lion's Paw* with the inadequately housed Sarah and Nanny Penn in Freeman's *The Revolt of "Mother."* Garland bases the power of his story on its portrait of the bleakness of poverty; Freeman bases hers on her protagonists' awareness of their own strengths.

CHARLOTTE PERKINS GILMAN

Like *The Awakening, The Yellow Wall-paper* shows a woman trying to find some alternative context for self-expression. The speaker in the story looks in vain for any referential reflector of her own reality, until she is incarcerated by her husband in a room with yellow wallpaper and, over the course of the story, comes to identify with or project herself onto the figure of a woman who stoops down and creeps about behind the pattern on the wallpaper. Gilman presents her narrator's "double-consciousness" as the tension the woman artist must live with in a context that refuses (with absolute denial of her husband) to mirror her self-concept. Like Edna's suicide at the end of *The Awakening*, Gilman's narrator's madness becomes understandable as her only means of self-expression. Ask students to contrast the story with Poe's *The Fall of the House of Usher* and James's *The Beast in the Jungle*. Consider the narrator as a type of the artist and apply to her Howell's dictum that the imagination "can work only with the stuff of experience." Does the narrator "compose" elements from real life; and if so, are both her madness and her work of art—the story itself—realistic? What happens to a writer when she wants to write referentially about experience that the world refuses to recognize? What does the story tell us about the prevailing medical attitudes toward women in the late nineteenth century? Reading *Why I Wrote "The Yellow Wall-paper"?* in conjunction with the story makes it clear to students that Gilman was self-conscious about the possibilities for fiction to intervene in the medical treatment of women as well as in women's understanding of the relationship between their own madness and their lack of social autonomy and intellectual choice.

EDITH WHARTON

Souls Belated is in some ways a period piece, a story about the institution of marriage and the relatively recent innovation of divorce, as these were construed by members of the Anglo-American upper classes—including people who thought of themselves as independent minded and thoroughly self-aware. But if students can find their way past the historical surfaces of the story, they can follow Wharton into an absorbing contemplation of what "love" means and how our inmost feelings and aspirations can be inextricably tangled up with cultural and social influences. Veteran Wharton readers in the group (students who have already encountered *Ethan Frome, The Age of Innocence,* or *The House of Mirth*) will recognize patterns here:

the woman in a socially constructed predicament; the leading man thought-ful, sensitive, self-scrutinizing, but given to destructive and self-destructive irresolution. But within this general pattern, *Souls Belated* can stand out.

You might open by asking a broad question about the tone of the story and about how, finally, we read it: as a tale of star-crossed lovers, a bourgeois tragedy? Is there humor here or an element of bemused detachment in the way Lydia and Gannett are presented? Why open the story with that odd vignette of the nameless "courtly person who ate garlic out of a carpet-bag"? Amid the condescension in that brief description, is there any element of yearning for a life constructed in some other way—other than the genteel and frustrating civilities that keep Lydia and Gannett in their predicament?

If you sense that students are having some trouble believing in these two people as *people*—that is, as individuals with plausible motives and inhibi-tions—it might be well to center on one of those cadenza passages in which these lovers try to articulate their values and fears. The paragraphs after the surprising line, " 'But I don't *want* to marry you!' she cried," will offer plenty to talk about—eloquent explanations (chiefly by Lydia) of the way that love and marriage are understood in their world, and the resistance and ac-commodation that each of them is forced into to be together. The conver-sation may veer outward into a contemplation of Realism as a mode: the supposed implausibility of this pair of lovers in our own time may be a function of their perfect plausibility in theirs. And what of these stifling pro-prieties? Are they unmitigatedly awful, in Wharton's portrayal of them? Or do they offer identity as well and the matter of life—without which there would be the "nothing left to talk about" that Lydia dreads in the opening of the story?

The Eyes will open up for a class much more successfully if they have read *Souls Belated* first or seen Wharton in her guise as a realist. To start a conversation about *The Eyes* you might open with speculative questions: why is it that the golden age of Realism and literary Naturalism gives us so many of our most durable ghost stories and Gothic horror stories, and why is it that so many of these supposedly certified realists (Twain, James, How-ells, Wharton, etc.) try their hand repeatedly at the mode? Conjectures may take your group in a number of different directions: when the time is right, you might go back to the old adage that for a good, successful horror story, the author has to scare himself or herself in the process—that he or she must find a way to dramatize or articulate something genuinely and per-sonally frightening. What would scare a realist? What, given what we have seen of her in *Souls Belated* and *The Eyes*, would frighten Edith Wharton? The danger of the erosion of the self? The destruction, in subtle, almost un-traceable stages, of one's ethics, one's identity?

Ask students to look at the way that the eyes are first described, as be-longing to someone who has not fallen into theatrical "evil" or Romantic-style villainy but rather into some more modern sort of moral decay, a con-dition of lassitude, negligence, and covert exploitation of others. That passage should provide the basis for a lot of dialogue, about Romantic and modern conceptions of depravity and self-destruction.

MARY AUSTIN

Austin's writing combines attention to natural detail with the themes and forms of literary regionalism. *The Walking Woman* possesses some of the mystical and visionary qualities of Jewett's Mrs. Todd in *The Foreigner;* and like that story, Austin's portrays a narrator who learns from the character who is her subject and perhaps sees this character as a model for her own life. In the Jewett story, the narrator describes Mrs. Todd telling her own story about the Frenchwoman; and thus in both Jewett and Austin, regionalism becomes an exercise in listening, reading, and storytelling across lines of difference. One of the features of late-nineteenth-century American life was the increasing independence of American women. James portrays his own version in *Daisy Miller,* where Daisy violates social conventions in an Italian sense but in other ways conforms to American conventions for a middle-class, white, heterosexual woman. In some of the portraits of independent women included in *NAAL*—Jewett's Sylvy and Mrs. Todd, Chopin's Mlle. Reisz, Freeman's Louisa Ellis, Austin's Walking Woman, and the autobiographical persona of Gertrude Bonnin—regionalist writers present rural, working-class, or poor women; the story line either conflicts with or occurs after any heterosexual interest; and in the case of Bonnin, the narrative presents the experience of a Native American.

Students may find that Austin's Walking Woman has so "walked off all sense of society-made values" that she herself has moved into a different "race" of women and class issues have become irrelevant to her vision; indeed, the narrator writes that "the word she brought about trails and waterholes was as reliable as an Indian's." Living in the desert has given her "both wisdom and information" that are not characteristic of white and nondesert societies. And she certainly tells some truths about the place of (hetero)sexuality in her life and her ultimate independence from men who place her in a liminal category of turn-of-the-century women. The Walking Woman, like the fiction in which she exists, possesses an intimate relation to the desert landscape that promotes the "fullest understanding" between her and her narrator. Help students contrast Austin's narrator's approach to the Walking Woman's difference and to western life with Bret Harte's local-color approach in *The Outcasts of Poker Flat.* Some students may insist that this difference is gendered in some way and that regionalism approaches "different" characters with more empathy and respect than do the writings of the local-color writers represented in *NAAL* (Harte, Garland, even Clemens).

W. E. B. DU BOIS

The moral and political problems, and the problems of personal and cultural identity, raised so eloquently by Du Bois in these selections, can fuel plenty of discussion—about race, politics, and painful, continuing differences between professed national values and actual social practice. You may not, however, have to make an either-or decision as you plan your classes in regard to teaching this from aesthetic or political perspectives. Du

Bois was an uncommonly skillful writer, and a fully respectful reading of *The Souls of Black Folk* should take note of his sense of pace; his analogies and extended metaphors; and his expert understanding of when to make use of the rhetoric of the pulpit and when not to, when to reach into the cultural experience of an educated audience and when to turn to the details of ordinary life as experienced by African Americans after the Civil War.

You might select an especially strong passage—strong not just in the complexity of its content but also in the energy of its prose—and work backwards, toward the beginning of the chapter, to observe how Du Bois prepares the way for a rhetorical adventure of this sort. The two paragraphs beginning with "The history of the American Negro is the history of this strife—this longing to obtain self-conscious manhood, to merge his double self into a better and truer self" can provide such a starting point. What are the connections—both logical and intuitive—between these paragraphs and the song selection that opens the chapter and the personal memories that come soon after it? If the long conceit about the "mountain path to Canaan" returns the reader to the familiar imaginative territory of the Calvinist and Evangelical traditions, how has Du Bois prepared us to accept this old (and perhaps time-worn) analogy as something relevant and fresh? How would students describe an overall strategy of *The Souls of Black Folk,* the discernment, in the lines of supposedly simple African American spirituals, of complex ideas of selfhood and self-fulfillment? Is this a writerly *tour de force,* a display of wit, mental agility, and (perhaps) late-Victorian sentimentality by one author working in a mainstream tradition? Or does Du Bois make this venture into cultural anthropology ring true and convince us of the deep wisdom within the ordinary and the plain?

The necessary two-ness of Washington and the "double-consciousness" that Du Bois expresses allow students to see the emergence of real stress points in the concept of a referential, universal, or reliable reality. While it would not be accurate to say that the double-consciousness of American blacks and of American women, beginning with Elizabeth Cady Stanton's address to the Seneca Falls Woman's Rights Convention and the *Declaration of Sentiments* in 1848 (reprinted as an appendix in this Guide), led to ways of thinking that would produce modernism, it was one aspect of the social environment that made and continues to make central concepts of modernism seem relevant to American experience. While neither a naturalist nor a modernist, Du Bois can be interpreted as a transition thinker— someone who observed the social forces at work in his own moment, who wrote to move common people, and who located his vision within the increasing sense that reality and identity might not be inherited or myterious but rather, like myth, invented.

FRANK NORRIS

Norris, as one of the promising naturalistic American writers who (like S. Crane and Harold Frederic) died very young, leaves us a conundrum in *A Plea for Romantic Fiction.* It gives us an oblique look at the workings and intentions of *McTeague;* but more important, it pleasantly complicates our thinking about realism and romanticism and their modern permutations. If your students are sufficiently prepared now to tell the difference between an interesting paradox and a frustrating muddle, and to enjoy aspects of a complex and unsolved question regarding representation of the real, then this short, lively essay can open some contemplations that can extend beyond the reach of your course. Norris makes the case that naturalism isn't the stepchild of realism but the completion of a circle, a swing back around to Romanticism, a journey virtually required by the coming of the supremely limited protagonist. It isn't doctrine that takes the writer back to Romance, but the subdoctrinal demands of sheer storytelling: start with a dull and limited character—somebody who lacks self-awareness and power and the capacity to change—and the plot will invariably need to be exotic and extraordinary, if *anything* is going to happen in the narrative. So the naturalistic writer, beginning with a naturalistic character—a stupid inert man like his notorious McTeague—will end up writing a Romance.

Is Norris just being clever here? Or is he onto a permanent problem having to do with the timeless demands of narrative and the inevitable stylizations of naturalism? Is he sensing the limits of the mode? Is the implication this: that when a character becomes capable of seeing himself or herself and his or her situation clearly, then the fabric of a story can tear as that character gains the capacity to escape from the confinements of a naturalistic fable, in which experience always overwhelms the individual? A conversation like this can very well jump to Chopin, to Fitzgerald, or Mamet or be recalled when these writers are raised in subsequent classes.

STEPHEN CRANE

For Crane, even our most intimate self-concepts are contingent on our social context and on the forces of natural environment. The selections in *NAAL* allow students to see the variety of forces against which the protagonist in the Crane universe must fight. *The Open Boat* presents the forces of nature as the elements against which the characters are pitted, and *The Blue Hotel* reveals the rage and ultimate lack of control that govern human behavior. *The Bride Comes to Yellow Sky* is anomalous in the collection. Where does the story get its humor? What are the local color elements in the story? Crane suggests that marriage itself is a force; how does the story suggest that each character is controlled by that force?

THEODORE DREISER

Dreiser's fiction conveys his sense of forces ranged against the individual; and in most of his work, these forces act directly. In *Old Rogaum and His Theresa,* students see a more subtle text, for the forces Theresa and her father must battle are revealed to them indirectly. Unlike other women in Dreiser's fiction, such as Carrie Meeber of *Sister Carrie,* Theresa is not "ruined" during her night out but is given a glimpse of how she might be. And Old Rogaum does not lose "his Theresa," but the blond girl who shows up groaning on his doorstep gives him a glimpse of how the night might have turned out. Dreiser reveals the forces within the family as well. Old Rogaum himself is both a force for his daughter and is taken over by forces of rage and powerlessness beyond his control. His wife is no force at all; compare her with the bride in Crane's *The Bride Comes to Yellow Sky.*

JOHN M. OSKISON

The Problem of Old Harjo may be discussed both as a Native American text and as regionalist fiction, and the two readings complement each other.

In the context of other Native American works anthologized in the 1865–1914 section of *NAAL*, begin by comparing Miss Evans with Charles Eastman's wife-to-be, Elaine Goodale; for Miss Evans is the prototype of the young, white, well-meaning, and often female Christian missionary to the Indians. Unlike the more experienced and less idealistic Mrs. Rowell, who expresses racism in her attitude toward "the old and bigamous" among the Creek Indian population (stating that "the country guarantees [Harjo's] idle existence" even though the truth is that he is materially solvent on his farm), Miss Evans is capable of seeing Harjo's situation as he sees it himself and withholds moral judgment. Harjo mutely questions her; she questions Mrs. Rowell, then her old pastor in New York, even implicitly church doctrine when she is tempted to say to him, " 'Stop worrying about your soul; you'll get to Heaven as surely as any of us.' " Yet the "problem of old Harjo" becomes Miss Evans's problem; and although the story seems unresolved at the end, since the problem remains insoluble, her "solution" (if not "solvent") is to recognize that circumstances have somehow tied her to this particular mission station to this particular "impossible convert." Tied to Harjo "until death . . . came to one of them," does Miss Evans become in effect yet another "wife" to the bigamist? Even if not, Oskison is nevertheless suggesting that the real agenda of the Christian missionaries is to suppress Creek culture in the young until the old men die off. What is this agenda but a continuation of the Ghost Dance War in another form?

Readers familiar with Native American literature may recognize Harjo as a figuration of the trickster (archetype, which they may have encountered in the Native American Trickster tales in *NAAL* Volume 1: a transformative character who represents the dilemmas of change—change for the old Creek but also change necessarily in the Christians, if anyone is to achieve genuine salvation. The story's apparent lack of resolution—"And meanwhile, what?"—conveys the disruptive effect of the trickster figure but also the process of highlighting trouble in the prevailing moral order. Old Harjo brings into relief the basic contradiction inherent in the encounter between the Christian missionaries and some Native Americans, which perhaps might be summed up in Mrs. Rowell's (long) wait for the "old bigamists" to die out. Yet as the story's ending attests, Harjo's powers include tenacity; and he engages Miss Evans in a temporal "problem" for which the only solution would be genuine change in the moral order of things. She becomes his "wife" to the extent that the trickster figure who appears in some Native

American legends may represent sexuality and desire; and her wish to assure him of salvation is humorous within a Native American tradition, for the trickster (as students may recall from the *Pima Story of Creation*) is already Coyote, the divinely powerful child born when the moon became a mother. So Coyote is another version of the Messiah of the Ghost Dance religion in the sense that, in a "trickster" mode, Coyote—or here, Harjo—becomes incarnate to point up moral failings in the creation.

Read from the perspective of regionalism, the story's portrait of the relationship between Harjo and Miss Evans becomes an exercise in empathic exchange. Miss Evans is capable of moving into Harjo's moral and affectional universe because she is able to look with, not at, the "problem" Harjo presents. At the same time, her sympathy for him works implicitly to challenge the moral, political, and religious control Mrs. Rowell represents. Although Oskison's story may not on initial reading appear to be as sophisticated as Charles Chesnutt's *The Goophered Grapevine*, both involve powerless and disenfranchised persons (old Harjo and Uncle Julius) creating a situation that will force whites to reveal their own moral limitations. In both stories, it is the cunning of the powerless that sets up the "looking-glass" to white society; in posing his "problem" week after week in the church, Harjo is indeed expressing his cunning, for has Miss Evans converted him or has he converted her?

As a fictional representation of Apess's critique, *The Problem of Old Harjo* has much in common with the work of Chesnutt and other nineteenth-century regionalists. Or, to put it another way, regionalist writers invented the white characters (like Miss Evans) capable of responding to figures like Harjo, whether we view him as a Native American trickster or as a "realistic" problem occasioned by the encounter of cultures, in this story represented by the conflict between the Christian missionary and the "old and bigamous" Creek.

JACK LONDON

London's *To Build a Fire* is a standard in English courses as early as the eighth grade, and some of your students will probably have keen memories of its graphic description of the stages of freezing to death in the Yukon wilderness. If you are approaching the story in the context of literary naturalism, however, you will have new things to talk about: for example, the subtlety or self-evidence of the themes in the tale and the open question of whether the story is inherently a fable advancing the loosely Darwinist doctrines that gave literary naturalism its force around the turn of the twentieth century. Why do works by London and S. Crane make use, so often, of protagonists with limited imagination and intellect? Are they, therefore, representative of the typical human being or of the human condition in general? Or would an extra measure of self-awareness and intelligence spoil the drama somehow by affording the protagonist the power to escape from the vast, indifferent, yet hostile context that provides the world of this tale, Crane's *The Blue Hotel* and *The Open Boat*, and London's *The Call of the*

Wild? If you feel that the habits and limitations of naturalism might wear thin as a subject, you could escape the "-isms," at least for a while, and speculate on why this kind of narrative, compelling and memorable and powerful as it is, has become the stuff of popular fiction, while supposedly serious fiction has turned in other directions? If Henry James, as a consummate realist, held that literature should be (in his words) "a celebration of life," then what of *To Build a Fire*?

NATIVE AMERICAN CHANTS AND SONGS

Although teaching the chants and songs may not take the central position in your presentation of Native American literature, they are significant because they give the instructor a way to illustrate the truth that there was an American literature on this continent before there was English here. With this brief set of examples of chants and songs, students can learn that there was also literary form on the North American continent before there was formal literature, indeed, that there was drama, in the ceremonial performance of the nine-day *Navajo Night Chant;* there was dance as a form of language, as the Comanche and Sioux drawings of the Ghost Dance recall; and there was music, particularly represented by drumbeats and tonalities. Chants and songs gave poetry breath, considered by some Native American groups to link human life with the hole from which the earliest people emerged (as in the *Pima Stories of the Beginning of the World,* reprinted in Volume 1).

Teaching the Native American chants and songs invites some transformation from the linear to some other mode—whether it be spatial (asking a group of students to enact at least part of the staging directions for the Navajo *Night Chant,* perhaps without sand!) or aural (asking others to prepare one or two of the songs for presentation). If you have a student talented enough (or courageous enough) on the recorder or flute, you might ask him or her to perform a few such songs in class. These songs must be heard to be appreciated for the way they alternate time signatures. In the Ghost Dance songs of the Arapaho in particular, there seems to be some correlation between elongated time signatures and the address to the gods. In *Father, have pity on me,* the singer takes longer measures to address the "Father," and the singer does the same thing in *When I met him approaching* when re-creating the moment of trance vision. According to Andrew Wiget (*Native American Literature,* 1985), the songs or prayers in ritual Native American poetry seek "to re-create a state rather than an event" and achieve "substantiality and duration in time and space by repeating many different short songs in sequence." Perhaps the alternation of time signatures or rhythmic meters within these short songs also contributes to achieving this "substantiality and duration in time and space."

Students may feel on most familiar ground in reading the English translations themselves, and certainly the Ghost Dance songs will be evocative if you have discussed the Ghost Dance religion and the Wounded Knee massacre previously. These songs convey the losses of the native peoples and their hopes for revelation and salvation. The two excerpts from the Navajo *Night Chant* may produce the most extensive formal analysis of the (translated) language of the chants and songs.

The Navajo *Night Chant*

The headnote points out that the chant is a healing ceremony, focused on an individual rather than society as a whole—but clearly understood to be inclusive and relevant to the audience-participants. The patient of the first chant comes onto the "trail of song"; prays to ("walks with") the gods; and follows the rainbow (their promise of salvation, associated with rain) progressively to, then into, then within the "fore part of my house with the dawn," where he meets the gods that symbolize generative and regenerative powers. Upon sitting with these gods, the patient experiences restoration of his own powers ("Beautifully my fire to me is restored") and walks a new trail at the end of the prayer, one marked by the pollen, grasshoppers, and dew that represent generativity (and the dawn).

The second chant, according to the notes, represents the prayer for salvation as the prayer for rain. The progression in this chant moves from the repetitions of invocations to the "male divinity" to bring the rain, to the chanter's association of rain with individual healing, to a joyful acknowledgment that healing has taken place ("Happily for me *the spell* is taken off. / Happily may I walk"), and to a section of the chant leading up to the benediction and conclusion of the ceremony that widens the circle to include others ("Happily may fair white corn, to the ends of the earth, come with you") and ends with the patient's inhalation of "the breath of dawn," signifying the patient's emergence into health. This chant focuses both on an individual's healing and on transforming the social order. The patient's healing symbolizes the well-being of all those who live the Navajo "way" or walk with their gods.

Wovoka

For Wovoka's vision, offered here in two versions as "Messiah" letters, the headnote is as important as the text to the classroom reception of the entire range of Ghost Dance/Wounded Knee narratives included in *NAAL*. Spend time going over the details of the Ghost Dance religion and the subsequent massacre at Wounded Knee. Explore with students the statement from the "Native American History and Literature" segment of the period introduction that "armed action against the settlers and U.S. troops had failed. . . . Many American Indians turned to spiritual action as a means of bringing about desired ends. From this impulse arose what has been called the Ghost Dance religion." The implication here is that some northern Plains Indians knew that they could no longer defend themselves in battle and, therefore, turned to spirituality to save themselves and give themselves hope. Read the two *Messiah Letters* carefully with students and identify specific aspects of the letters that link them with Native American traditions and with Christianity. Ask students why Euro-Americans seem to have had such difficulty imagining the concept of religious freedom for Indians. Recall Apess's *An Indian's Looking-Glass for the White Man*, and apply his strategy of eliciting shame in his white Christian readers to the white settlers' resistance to the practice of a Christian-inspired religion by a few defeated bands of Indians.

GERTRUDE SIMMONS BONNIN (ZITKALA ŠA)

Bonnin's three autobiographical essays invite comparison with other autobiographies by women writers. Students may find it interesting to read Mary Rowlandson's *Narrative* (in Volume 1), in which Rowlandson describes her capture by the Wampanoag Indians against Bonnin's narrative of "capture" by the "palefaces." Suggest that Bonnin's account of her removal from the reservation and attempted assimilation into white culture provides a twist on the Indian captivity narrative of the colonial period. It's also interesting to think about Bonnin as a Native American Daisy Miller.

Although Bonnin's work does not, strictly speaking, belong to the genre of regionalism—it is autobiography, not fiction—nevertheless, there are elements of fictional form, especially in *Impressions of an Indian Childhood*. She uses images—learning the "art of beadwork" or the cropped and "shingled hair"—that characterize both her own life and the larger plight of other Native Americans. *Impressions of an Indian Childhood* also possesses an aesthetic distance that students might associate with fiction. At the end of the third selection, *An Indian Teacher among Indians,* Bonnin herself acknowledges that "as I look back upon the recent past, I see it from a distance, as a whole." Perhaps the reason for this distance is that, at least in *Impressions of an Indian Childhood,* she writes about a developing child whose path of development as a Sioux becomes so pinched off that the older child and adult narrator cannot even repair the discontinuity.

She also writes in English about events that took place when "I knew but one language, and that was my mother's native tongue." The act of rendering her Sioux childhood into English creates its own fiction, for she writes about herself at a time in her life before speaking and writing in English was even imaginable. Like the regionalists, Bonnin depicts a female-centered universe and her own refusal to be silenced, and she triumphs on behalf of the disenfranchised "squaw" when she writes of winning the oratory contest; but unlike the separation of Mrs. Todd from her mother in Jewett's *The Foreigner,* a separation that can be eased by telling a comforting story, Bonnin's estrangement from her own mother only deepens as she proceeds with her autobiography. She loses her connection with the world of nature, becoming a "cold bare pole . . . planted in a strange earth."

HENRY ADAMS

Whether or not Henry Adams ever read or heard W. E. B. Du Bois, for pedagogical purposes we can see the excerpts from *The Education* as thematic variations on the Du Boisean theme of "double-consciousness." Like Du Bois, who summarizes nineteenth-century black thinking in 1903, Henry Adams writes as one born in 1838, yet wanting "to play the game of the twentieth" century. *The Education* is another book in the tradition of

Franklin's *Autobiography* but interesting because of the new directions Adams takes:

> As it happened, he never got to the point of playing the game at all; he lost himself in the study of it, watching the errors of the players; but this is the only interest in the story, which otherwise has no moral and little incident. A story of education—seventy years of it—the practical value remains to the end in doubt.

The development of self-reliance in the American writer and thinker leads Adams to write that "every one must bear his own universe." Unlike Franklin, Adams does not become a politician but rather finds literary symbols that, as the headnote to Adams in NAAL asserts, make *The Education*, to many readers, "the one indispensable text for students seeking to understand the period between the Civil War and World War I." Students can see this clearly in Chapter I, where Adams writes, anticipating modernism, that the twentieth century is a world without design: "Often in old age he puzzled over the question whether, on the doctrine of chances, he was at liberty to accept himself or his world as an accident. No such accident had ever happened before in human experience. For him, alone, the old universe was thrown into the ash-heap and a new one created." And Adams traces his perception to early events (railroad and telegraph) that presented his six-year-old eyes with a "new world." Even as a boy, he developed "a double nature. Life was a double thing. . . . From earliest childhood the boy was accustomed to feel that, for him, life was double."

Chapter XXV, "The Dynamo and the Virgin," crystallizes the doubleness he feels, presaging modern life, in the symbols that express the split between technology and spirituality. Adams writes clearly; students could easily prepare a summary of the argument of this chapter. In class, you can continue to focus on Adams's early modernist ideas: what happens to human energies—symbolized by the force and power of the Virgin and of ancient fertility goddesses—in an age and in a country that replaces human with technological power and is it possible to state, "with the least possible comment, such facts as seemed sure" and to "fix for a familiar moment a necessary sequence of human movement"?

1914–1945

In moving forward to the moderns, you probably face at least three different questions right away:

How and why these writers saw the world differently from writers in earlier periods and centuries—what we might call a thematic approach to understanding modernism.

How and why they chose their images and their narrative and poetic forms.

How their gender, ethnicity, or class might have influenced their writing—how pluralism, both within American culture and as it derives from international influence (particularly by Joyce, Woolf, and Yeats), emerges as a determining factor and a consequence of modern literature.

Selections from Native American and African American writers allow students to explore these questions, and you can also perceive continuing colonial attitudes (in both white and minority writers) that manifest themselves in racial segregation and discrimination.

BLACK ELK

In opening discussion on the excerpts from this work, begin by asking students questions that will help them explore the very interesting narrative form. To the question "Who is speaking?" they will answer, Black Elk. But who is narrating? Black Elk or John Neihardt? Make use of the *NAAL* headnote, especially the fact that Black Elk could neither read nor write and spoke little English when he told John Neihardt the story of his great vision, and talk about the context within which *Black Elk Speaks* was created: Black Elk telling his story to his son, Ben Black Elk, who then translated it into English for Black Elk's "adopted" son, John Neihardt, while Neihardt's daughter, Enid, wrote it all down and other Sioux elders contributed their memories of events. Then, later, Neihardt worked from his daughter's transcriptions to produce *Black Elk Speaks*. How do the circumstances of composition affect students' perception of authorship of the work? Discuss differences between Neihardt's work and the work of early-twentieth-century social scientists who often paid Native American informants to tell their stories. Neihardt was himself a poet; in agreeing to tell his story to Neihardt, holy man Black Elk was recognizing a kindred spirit.

Even so, there had to be limits to that kinship, and the long account called "The Great Vision" requires some careful preliminary discussion if we are going to engage with it effectively in an American literature course. We have to decide, at least tentatively, what we are reading, or listening to, or overhearing: this is a personal experience (spiritual, religious, psychological, carefully allegorical, or some combination of them all) related across a considerable cultural and linguistic divide to a white listener who constructs a written, printed narrative which is subsequently collected into a literary anthology and read by ourselves. A lot of transformations—so many, in fact, that recovering the original intention and texture of Black Elk's narrative, and its cultural and historical moment, may be impossible for nearly everyone except an expert in the Sioux peoples in the last century. Still, we can value the way in which this narrative extends and enriches our collective sense both of the nature and possibilities of North American storytelling and of the individual self. Though your students will have some familiarity with the cultural importance of the Vision Quest among native peoples of the Western Plains, can they speculate about how the pronoun "I" is used in Black Elk's account and what that pronoun signifies? When he presents himself as one chosen to receive special wisdom from the Six Grandfathers (most of us have only four), how are these nameless teachers and their young pupil presented to us? Why don't all these grandfathers have names? Is this a "spiritual" education in the European or New England sense of the word? Are power and wisdom achieved through creating or discovering "identity" as a thing apart? When Black Elk becomes "the spotted eagle floating" and then moves to the bay horse and finds himself "painted red all over," are these self-aggrandizing representations? Why might there be so much emphasis on "the earth," the ground, in Black Elk's vision?

Black Elk Speaks records only the first twenty-seven years of Black Elk's life, ending with the battle of Wounded Knee. Neihardt ends *Black Elk Speaks* with an image of drifted snow in "one long grave" at Wounded Knee. Although Black Elk himself lived another fifty-nine years, Neihardt closes his text with what some readers have described as Black Elk's spiritual death and the end of tribal independence; for as Black Elk himself states, after the end of Sioux freedom, he and his people become simply "prisoners of war while we are waiting here."

Black Elk Speaks, therefore, shapes the form of Black Elk's story as Neihardt works to create the full effect of Sioux tragedy "in" his white readers, just as Black Elk himself was capable of feeling "in" himself the pain of the people. The act of the bicultural collaborator creates empathy in the modern reader. Furthermore, the act of teaching *Black Elk Speaks* places the instructor also in the position of bicultural translator, using the classroom and discussion of the text as a way to complete the circle between the American undergraduate student and the text that "writes" Black Elk's name in our canon of collective attempts to define the American identity.

WILLA CATHER

Cather remains a strongly popular author, a centerpiece on many school reading lists, and a favorite among younger students; many of your students will have encountered *My Ántonia* before and will remember it fondly. The various ways in which Cather has been classified by critics and literary historians, however—as a latter-day realist, naive regionalist or local-colorist, pioneer of an American lesbian sensibility, anti-Freudian sentimentalist, austere modernist of the Great Plains—will strike some of your students as confining or inadequate, based on their reading of this novel or other Cather stories that they have encountered and appreciated before. You might begin there—with this question of whether there is any real need, anything to be gained, by maneuvering Cather into some aesthetic position next to Fitzgerald or on some literary family tree with Clemens, Howells, and Crane down below and, say, Anne Tyler or Grace Paley or Ann Beattie or others branching out at the top.

If students don't like the idea of locating Cather in this way, then the conversation can move out into a different kind of likening: how this book achieves a unique feel by being a bit like other works that students have encountered and yet very different—and one difference that will come to the surface is the reserve (not detachment, not aloofness, but reserve) with which Cather creates this chronicle of the passions and fortunes of working-class immigrant girls and women. For *chronicle* might be the right word, or at least a better word than *novel*, because compared to the fiercely judgmental, overtly controlling novel narration that distinguishes so many realists and naturalists before Cather and the self-dramatizing modernist narrators who came soon after *My Ántonia* (Fitzgerald, Hemingway, Faulkner, and Wolfe), Cather can seem almost invisible, watching the lives and the action unfold with dignified empathy and a sustained disinclination either to judge or to transform the individual life into the grand parable or myth.

Students will want to talk about characters here, and with this novel they may have more trouble than usual in talking about them as artistic creations rather than as actual people. That is a high tribute to Cather's skill as a novelist and as an observer of human nature but is potentially an awkward situation when you're making some effort to talk about this art as art, rather than as personal account or a kind of microhistory. One way through the problem: given all of the overarching formulations about the human condition that were rife during Cather's career—Marx, Freud, the various Darwinisms; all the aesthetic manifestos and promulgated totalizing statements about what art and fiction should do and what the human condition inexorably was or should be—is Cather's poise, her commitment to a narrative that looks (deceptively) like sheer storytelling, a kind of resistance, a refusal to see and portray the world as less complex and minutely interesting than she understood it to be? If we are going to understand the durability of Cather and her heartening intractability as a writer in any ex-post literary school or movement, then some thought about this issue might be a good contribution to that understanding.

Amy Lowell

Following chronologically from poets Edgar Lee Masters and Edwin Arlington Robinson, Lowell will continue to beguile students into believing that the poetry in the 1914–45 period is accessible. Explore both the accessibility and the inaccessibility of imagism by reading Lowell in conjunction with H. D. and Pound. Examine *Meeting-House Hill, Summer Night Piece,* and *New Heavens for Old* as imagist poems. Lowell's inclusion in *NAAL* does not fully resolve the question about which critics remain divided: Is Lowell's poetry any good? Is it too sentimental to be good poetry? And in using the word *sentimental* against her are we mistakenly accepting devaluation of the very concept of the sentimental and its legitimate role in poetry?

Whatever the verdict among your students, including Lowell's voice in your syllabus will make room for early discussions of female mythological characters that will inform much poetry by women and men in the twentieth century (in *The Captured Goddess* and *Venus Transiens*), and will introduce what Baym calls "appreciations of female beauty" in poems by women. Indeed, a few of the poems included here may be considered love poems to specific women or to women in general: *Venus Transiens* and *Madonna of the Evening Flowers*.

GERTRUDE STEIN

The Stein entries are going to be a train wreck for students who approach them with their close-reading methodologies fully engaged and hot from deep-meaning searches that they may have conducted with various realists and modernists that have come before in your course. In reading Stein, they don't get it; and some students can become anxious or angry or (worse) quietly demoralized, like those visitors to the Cabaret Voltaire in Zurich, where Dadaism had its birth in the midst of World War I, who couldn't figure out what was going on because they tried too hard to decode the words and action on the stage. Actually, the problem with Stein, in this particular context, can be just as bad, or worse—because enshrined in an anthology, discourse that might otherwise beguile, or pleasantly dislocate, becomes academic text that must be sounded and understood or else all is lost!

Perhaps a way to grow comfortable with Stein, and to get much farther in reading these selections, is to back up a bit, and converse about those many sorts of cultural experiences in which things *don't* make sense but in which you can have a good time anyway and not worry about "getting it"— because from somewhere you get the message that getting it isn't the point at all. Your students listen to plenty of music and see plenty of video and film, which in a strict sense they can't decode or fathom and would feel absurd trying to do so. The pictures don't fit the words; the words are sometimes nonsense. Why is it (you might ask) that they—or rather, we—can accept uncertainty and even complete mystification in some art or entertainment experiences, but not in others? Can we take pleasure in adventures such as this, adventures into prose and poetry that seem to escape the usual chore of making sense and being clear? When your students have gone home after a day of classes, barraged by tomes of deadly earnest, highly rhetorical argumentative prose—showing us this and telling us that and proving to us something else—can a yearning arise for an escape into a freer sort of writing, where meanings (in a Victorian or standard modern sense) are less important than the intellectual and psychological refreshment of getting lost?

An approach like this tends to make Stein seem a contingent writer, responding to and in a sense resisting certain mainstream Western habits of prose and poetry (and the perhaps artificial categorical differences between the two), but understanding first what Stein is *not* doing is an an effective way of opening a discussion of what she accomplishes as new American writing.

ROBERT FROST

Like Cather, Frost retains elements of realism, and like her, he portrays moments in which his speaker's perception changes as central to his poetry.

Several class periods can be spent on individual poems and representative poems by other twentieth-century poets through the fulcrum of our analysis of Frost. You can prepare for a discussion of *The Oven Bird* by reading *Nothing Gold Can Stay*, with its allusion to Eden and human mortality. *The Oven Bird* deserves an important place in our discussion because Frost's other poems, his essay *The Figure a Poem Makes*, many other works of literature by modern writers, and even the concept of Modernism itself seem contained and articulated in the poem's last two lines: "The question that he asks in all but world / Is what to make of a diminished thing." The bird and the poet ask questions that express the central modernist theme: How do we confront a world in which reality is subject to agreement or lacks referentiality altogether? How do we express the experience of fragmentation in personal and political life? How do we live with the increasing awareness of our own mortality—whether we face the prospect of human death (as the speaker does in *Home Burial*; *After Apple-Picking*; or *"Out, Out—"*), the death or absence of God (as Frost considers in *Desert Places* and *Design*), or mere disappointment at our own powerlessness (as in *An Old Man's Winter Night* or *Stopping by Woods on a Snowy Evening*)?

In regard to *The Oven Bird*, ask students to hear contrasting ways of intoning the last two lines. You might read the lines first with emphasis on the phrase "diminished thing," and the pessimism in Frost and in his conception of modern life receives most of our attention. But read them again, emphasizing the infinitive "to make," and the poem seems to reverse its own despair, to create the possibility that creative activity can ease the face of the lessening, the "diminishing," of modern perception.

Other works offer this positive response to the bird's question. In *The Figure a Poem Makes*, Frost defines the act of writing poetry as "not necessarily a great clarification" but at least "a momentary stay against confusion." Students who have studied the Volume 1 material may see Frost's solution to his own metaphysical problem as one more variable in Edward Taylor's attempt to sustain a metaphor through the length of one of his *Preparatory Meditations* to arrive at the language of salvation. Frost emphasizes, though, that he wants to be just as surprised by the poem as the reader. And his description of the thought process that a poem records applies to our own endeavors in the classroom as well—whenever we try to engage students first and then teach them how to order their engaged perception. When Frost contrasts scholars, who get their knowledge "with conscientious thoroughness along projected lines of logic," with poets, who get theirs "cavalierly and as it happens in and out of books," most students prefer to identify with the poets. And Frost might, indeed, be describing an American epistemology, as it works best with students: "They stick to nothing deliberately, but let what will stick to them like burrs where they walk in the fields."

No study of Frost, at any class level, is complete without close analysis of the great poems *Birches* and *Directive*. Students at any level profit from line-by-line discussion of *Directive*, particularly in contrast with the earlier poem *After Apple-Picking*. In this poem, the speaker's troubled sleep results from his realization of the imperfection of human power to "save" fallen apples (or fallen worlds) or to fully complete any task as someone with god-like power (or any "heroic" human being before the modernist era) might have been able to do. *Directive* transcends those limitations, offers a specific path to take ("if you'll let a guide direct you / Who only has at heart your getting lost"), and arrives at a vision of spiritual regeneration unparalleled in any of Frost's other poems: "Here are your waters and your watering place. / Drink and be whole again beyond confusion."

How does Frost contain *both* American dream and American nightmare? How does his poetry, as he writes in *Two Tramps in Mud Time*, allow him to "unite / My avocation and my vocation / As my two eyes make one in sight"? How do Frost's images suggest that, long after the apparent decline of transcendentalism, the analogical thinking of Emerson and Thoreau would become a permanent part of the American imagination?

SHERWOOD ANDERSON

If students have been reading chronologically through *NAAL*, they will be ready to see Sherwood Anderson as writing in the fresh wake of Realism, of Naturalism, and of the Regionalist and Local Colorist traditions. These are traditions which he both respects and resists in achieving an individual voice. Anderson wants to know where it all begins, to focus on a particular house in a particular street, and to try to figure out, by examining origins, who he is and who we are. Anderson's life before he declared himself a writer illustrates a classic theme in nineteenth-century fiction by white male writers; ask your students to recall Irving's *Rip Van Winkle*, or Clemens's *Huckleberry Finn*. Like the characters in that earlier fiction, Anderson also seems to have suffered a form of amnesia, sudden disappearance, or inexplicable departure, one day, from his life with his wife and his job at the paint firm. In leaving his life in Ohio so abruptly, Anderson expressed the incompatibility of living conventionally and also writing an American book. How does this define the role of the writer, for Anderson? *Winesburg, Ohio*, though fiction, emerges from an autobiographical impulse; and the reporter in that work, George Willard, experiences the young writer's conflict. Later in life, Anderson would write a memoir titled *A Storyteller's Story; Winesburg, Ohio*, which tells the story of Anderson himself still within the eggshell, before his "hatching" as a storyteller.

Several related themes characterize the anthologized stories from *Winesburg*. Anderson portrays conflict between inner emotions and outward behavior; Alice Hindman and Elmer Cowley share this conflict although they express it differently. Sexual repression and displaced aggression enter American fiction in *Winesburg*, and each of the anthologized stories shares this theme. In Elizabeth Willard, sexual repression and repressed identity become interconnected, and in *Adventure*, Anderson hints at "the growing modern idea of a woman's owning herself and giving and taking for her own ends in life," although his own fiction explores the stunting of women's lives, not their "modern" alternatives. Writing itself becomes the American passion for George Willard; the "queerness" that interests Anderson in some of his characters (Elmer Cowley and Mook in *"Queer"*) suggests an American illness caused by inarticulate inner lives that the fiction writer might be able to "cure."

At the end of *Rip Van Winkle,* Rip takes his place as the "chronicler" or storyteller of the village and thus moves from margin to center in his position in the town. Anderson's portrait of the American storyteller—in his character George Willard and in the events of his own life—addresses the marginality of the white male writer. Anderson's marginality is central to his vision; despite his portrait of the way American life has twisted and thwarted individual development, he chooses to portray it from without, not envision recreating it from within. Like Huckleberry Finn, George Willard escapes Winesburg and, in the process, becomes capable of telling a story.

WALLACE STEVENS

Poems such as Frost's *The Oven Bird* and *Desert Places* allow students to experience modernist feeling; Stevens translates the central thematic concern of modern writers into an intellectual framework. We can begin by reading *Of Modern Poetry* line by line and make connections between the idea of "finding what will suffice" and making something "of a diminished thing." This poem links modernist thought to World War I, breaks with the realists' "script," and ends with actions that appear referential ("a man skating, a woman dancing, a woman / Combing") but can be understood only as manifestations of what is spoken "In the delicatest ear of the mind," not as semantic symbols.

Students' greatest difficulty in reading Stevens is to move beyond the apparently referential quality of his language and to learn to read it as dynamic forms of abstract ideas. *Anecdote of the Jar* works well to analyze closely. This poem forces them to push beyond the referential features of the language, for its meaning resides not in the jar but in its placement and in the larger design the poem creates and imposes. But that larger design is an arbitrary creation of the poet, not the manifestation of divine presence in the universe; and we can work through other Stevens poems that illustrate the poet's power to make his world's design. *Thirteen Ways of Looking at a Blackbird* can help students see the problem of perception in a modern world in which there is no shared reality; in *The Idea of Order at Key West,* the woman makes order out of the diminished thing by singing, thereby becoming "the self / That was her song, for she was the maker"; and *The Emperor of Ice-Cream* proposes as the modernist's reality a world that lets "the lamp affix its beam" to show, as *The Snow Man* states, "Nothing that is not there and the nothing that is." Ask students how the idea that nothing is there—except what the imagination invents—becomes a manifestation of American self-reliance. For Stevens, all forms of order are created by human perception; nature itself reflects human values only as we project our image onto the natural world.

Stevens responds to the oven bird's question in the first line of *A High-Toned Old Christian Woman:* "Poetry is the supreme fiction." Nina Baym directs the reader's attention to two repeated activities in Stevens's poems: (1) looking at things, and (2) playing musical instruments or singing. Ask students to identify poems in which these activities appear (for the first, see in particular *The Snow Man, The Emperor of Ice-Cream, Thirteen Ways of Looking at a Blackbird, Study of Two Pears, An Ordinary Evening in New Haven,* and *The Plain Sense of Things;* for the second, see in particular *A High-Toned Old Christian Woman, Peter Quince at the Clavier, The Idea of Order at Key West, Of Modern Poetry,* and *Asides on the Oboe*), and we identify as parallel concepts making music or singing and writing poetry, and perceiving or observing and giving existence to reality. These parallel activities replace the Christian God, create new gods or mythological forms (see *An Ordinary Evening in New Haven*), and allow us to devise our own supreme fiction. The new mythology or fiction, for whom the poet is both creator and secular priest, explains the presence of so much continually unexpected imagery in Stevens. Furthermore, Stevens's own poetry provides an answer to the woman's musings in *Sunday Morning*.

In *Sunday Morning,* Stevens creates a dialogue between a woman and a narrator, or a dialogue of one that shows the woman thinking within her own mind, and he alters the meaning of Christianity. The poem transforms the religious connotations of Sunday into those of a human-centered "day of the sun," in which, since we live in an "island solitude, unsponsored, free," we invent as our supreme fiction, our god or our explanation for the way the universe works, the very mortality that is the only "imperishable bliss" we know. Stevens proposes making ritual of the diminished thing, creating fellowship "of men that perish and of summer morn," and seeing "casual flocks of pigeons" not as "homeward bound" but rather as nature's "ambiguous undulations." Nature has no message for us; but in the act of writing (and reading) poetry, we can create our own order, one that becomes more beautiful because it is the projection of "man's rage for order" and, therefore, as fragile as human life. "Death is the mother of beauty" for Stevens because it intensifies the act of "arranging, deepening, enchanting night" (in *The Idea of Order at Key West*), the act of taking momentary "dominion" (in *Anecdote of the Jar*), or the "old chaos of the sun." Poetry serves Stevens (from his book of collected lectures, *The Necessary Angel*) as a "means of redemption." What should we make of a world in which there is not external order? Project onto it human mortality and make art out of the moment of sinking "Downward to darkness, on extended wings," create a "jovial hullabaloo among the spheres."

The images of the sun that form the focus for the woman's meditations in *Sunday Morning* also provide Stevens's central image in other poems. Build class discussion around a group of these poems (*Gubbinal, A Postcard from the Volcano, The Sense of the Sleight-of-Hand Man, An Ordinary Evening in New Haven*), and examine the way Stevens builds his real image of what the supreme fiction might look like on the sun itself. In *Sleight-of-Hand Man,* he writes, "The fire eye in the clouds survives the gods," and in *New Haven,* he calls "imagining of reality, / Much like a new resemblance of the sun." The supreme fiction takes the form of human flesh in

Peter Quince at the Clavier. Give students time to work through the experience of Stevens's concept of the supreme fiction. For many, reading Stevens will seem like heresy, a fundamental challenge to their own religious practice. Allow them to compare notes on their various perceptions of Stevens's work. Use class discussion as an exemplum of modernist thought; a class of any size may approach "Thirteen Ways of Looking at Stevens," or "a visibility of thought, / In which hundreds of eyes, in one mind, see at once."

ANGELINA WELD GRIMKÉ

The Closing Door is a powerful story that should cause a lot of comment from the class regarding its strangeness and its familiarity. Students who are reading backwards into the African American literary tradition, coming to Grimké after encounters with narratives such as *Sula, Native Son,* or *The Color Purple* may find this story oddly genteel, and even flawed in its avoidance of the dialects featured in these more-modern tales of black experience. If that objection is raised, it would be well to spend some time establishing the cultural and literary context of *The Closing Door*—what kind of audience was out there to receive it, what the conventions and prevailing modes were in the first decades of this century regarding good fiction, and what political and moral work a minority writer might have faced in those times as opposed to now. If good stories implicitly dialogue with other stories and speak to questions raised in other powerful texts, then is Grimké engaged in that practice here? Ask students to think about the way that "darkness" is raised here: it turns up repeatedly and perhaps most remarkably in the following passage:

> There was a roaring in my ears. I seemed to be a long way off. I was sinking into a horrible black vortex that seemed to be sucking me down. I opened my eyes and saw Jim dimly. His nostrils seemed to be two black wide holes. His face was taut, every line set. I saw him draw a great deep breath. The blackness sucked me down still deeper. And then suddenly I found myself on my feet struggling against that hideous darkness and I heard my own voice as from a great distance calling out over and over again, "Oh, my God! Oh, my God! Oh, my God!"

Even if students have not read Conrad, they will know the kind of color symbolism favored by writers in the decades before *The Closing Door.* How does Grimké's "darkness" respond to, or quarrel with, those conventions? How do the opening pages of the story, pages that tell a mild tale of ordinary domestic life with small-scale troubles and delights, prepare us for the tale's conclusion?

ANZIA YEZIERSKA

Yezierska writes powerfully about the contrast between immigrant expectations and immigrant reality and between the rhetoric of democracy and its broken promise for the immigrant poor. *The Lost "Beautifulness"* raises these issues painfully and clearly and promotes extensive discussion in the classroom. Ask students to derive two sets of assumptions from the story. The first set includes assumptions about class that Hannah Hayyeh makes, for example: (1) that poverty doesn't mean a person can't also have beauty in life; (2) that even though someone is poor doesn't mean she can't have a rich friend, that friendship can cross class lines; and (3) that "making money ain't everything in life." Explore how Hannah comes to hold these assumptions, what happens to disillusion her with respect to each one, and whether students share any of them.

The second set includes assumptions about America and the meaning of democracy, for example: (1) "democracy means that everybody in America is going to be with everybody alike"; (2) it's possible to assimilate into American values—as Hannah tells her husband, "so long my Aby is with America, I want to make myself for an American"; (3) merit is recognized, as in "such a tenant the landlord ought to give out a medal or let down the rent free"; and (4) even a "hungry-eyed ghetto woman" can be an "artist laundress"—the American Dream takes many forms, but even a ghetto laundress can have her dreams. The second set will be harder for students to dislodge, in terms of their own dreams and their assumptions about their own future. However, in the 1990s, even middle-class students are more realistic about the hollow ring of some of these assumptions and will observe the validity of the landlord's corrective truth: "in America everybody looks out for himself."

Compare the ending with the narrator's behavior in Charlotte Perkins Gilman's *The Yellow Wall-paper,* and ask students to comment on the effectiveness of the course of action Hannah chooses to follow. Examine the final scene as a moment of imagistic prose, in which the insignia of the Statue of Liberty, the gold service stripes, and the "assurance of the United States Army" that Aby Safransky possesses contrast with the image of broken Hannah in her eviction from her apartment, from her dreams of beauty, and from all things she believed were American.

WILLIAM CARLOS WILLIAMS

How does Williams answer the question, What to make of a diminished thing? We can begin with *A Sort of a Song,* which directs its reader to write a poem about the thing. Make nothing of it but the thing itself. Because there may not be meaning, don't insist on it. And we can talk about characteristics of Williams's poems, trying to elicit, in discussion, some of the central features of imagism: exactness, precision, compression, common speech, free verse. *The Red Wheelbarrow, The Widow's Lament in Springtime,* and *Portrait of a Lady* work well for this discussion. We can analyze *Spring and All* closely, suggesting that the process Williams describes becomes, in part, analogous to the creation of a poetic image. Some students have difficulty understanding the concept of the image; and in teaching Williams, you might take time to talk about the eidetic faculty—what happens in the mind when we read a visual description. *Portrait of a Lady,* read aloud with appropriate emphasis ("Agh!"), can help them "hear" another kind of image.

You can then talk about some themes in Williams—love and death—and how the poems strip those themes of sentimentality. What happens to Williams's view of human life in poems such as *Death, The Dead Baby,* and *Landscape with the Fall of Icarus?* compare Williams and Frost; students may suggest that, despite his objectivity, Williams lacks the pessimism of some of Frost's poems. How does Williams's use of poetic technique develop his themes? Critics often compare Williams with Whitman. Ask students to discuss this connection. Several modern poets try to write longer poems, perhaps with the epic form in mind.

EZRA POUND

We read a few Pound poems to see how he uses the image: *In a Station of the Metro* and *The River-Merchant's Wife: A Letter* work well; although students sometimes have difficulty actually seeing Pound's image in the first poem. Does the poem's second line work only if one sees a contrast between the faces and the black bough? Does Pound assume light-skinned faces? *To Whistler, American; A Pact;* and *The Rest* are easily accessible to students; but what response do they have to *Hugh Selwyn Mauberley (Life and Contacts)* or *The Cantos?* How do students without a classical education understand Pound's dictum to "make it new"?

H. D. (HILDA DOOLITTLE)

Several strategies for reading H. D. may enlist student interest. With editor Baym's comments about imagism as a guide, trace H. D.'s formal uses of the image in her poetry, and compare her work with that of A. Lowell, Williams, and Pound. Alternatively, move ahead to other women poets whose work reflects H. D.'s influence. For example, Susan Gubar (in "The Echoing Spell in H. D.'s *Trilogy,*" in *Shakespeare's Sisters,* 1979) suggests comparing H. D.'s use of the seashell image to Marianne Moore's *To a Snail.* (See also Moore's poem *The Paper Nautilus.*) The last stanzas of *The Walls Do Not Fall* are clearly echoed later in Adrienne Rich's poem *Diving into the Wreck.* Even further, Gubar suggests that really to understand H. D., we need to move beyond discussions of Imagism and Modernism (and psychoanalysis) to exploring "H. D.'s sense of herself as a woman writing about female confinement, specifically the woman writer's entrapment within male literary conventions, as well as her search for images of female divinity and prophecy." Reading H. D. as a feminist modernist and a poet who is trying to express her discomfort with male-defined representations of women and of history may give students another approach to her poetry.

Because H. D. has been fully appreciated only by recent feminist critics who write about Modernism, you or your students may find useful Susan Stanford Friedman's critical biography *Psyche Reborn: The Emergence of H. D.* (1981), in which she traces H. D.'s development as a feminist modernist and in particular H. D.'s interest in a woman-centered mythmaking. From *Leda* to *Helen* to the goddesses Isis, Aset, and Astarte in *The Walls Do Not Fall*, students will at least find the female figures to counterbalance the presence of the all-father and Osiris. H. D.'s closing lines of that long poem ("we are voyagers, discoverers / of the not-known, / the unrecorded") have particular resonance for women in a modernist world.

ROBINSON JEFFERS

Jeffers's poetry contrasts sharply with that of both Frost and Stevens; ask students to discuss his ways of transforming poems about nature into philosophical meditations. Jeffers appears to have disdained Modernism; is his poetry traditional? Compare Jeffers's use of free verse with Williams's poetic line. How is Jeffers's poetry unique? Discuss his use of the physical landscape of the central California coast. Is Jeffers a regional poet? Identify the source of his cynicism and compare it with Frost's pessimistic poems. Jeffers seems to suggest that "what to make of a diminished thing" is to diminish it still further: "We must unhumanize our views a little." Consider what he means by this.

Shine, Perishing Republic can be discussed line by line—or alternatively assigned to students to explicate in an essay. The poem stands out in contrast to many of the modernist works we read, both in what it lacks (any sense that classical mythology holds the key to understanding our present) and for what it offers (as a view of twentieth-century American life and values). This poem and others (*November Surf* and *Carmel Point*) seem to some students to comment on our own contemporary life. How does *Shine, Perishing Republic* suggest what it means to be an American in the twentieth century?

MARIANNE MOORE

In *Naked and Fiery Forms: Modern American Poetry by Women* (1976), Suzanne Juhasz describes Moore as "the leading American woman poet" of her generation but not the "leading American poet" and comments on the contrast between Pound, who "does not have to deny his masculine experience, because it is all of mankind," and Moore, who makes "a neat division between 'woman' and 'poet,' with art and artistry belonging to the domain of the latter." Juhasz's framework is useful for reading modern American women poets; she suggests that the second generation (in which she includes Muriel Rukeyser, Elizabeth Bishop, Louise Bogan, and Gwendolyn Brooks, all anthologized in *NAAL*) continued to separate "woman" and "poet" but that writers at mid-century (Denise Levertov, Sylvia Plath, and Anne Sexton) begin to function as both "woman" and "poet."

Teaching Moore following Juhasz's framework will help contextualize both Moore's avoidance of women's experience in her poetry and the increasing attention to women's experience by poets later in the century. Indeed, students will find it difficult if not impossible to locate any gendered experience in Moore. She writes either with a gender-neutral first person (in *Poetry, In Distrust of Merits,* "Keeping Their World Large," and *O to Be a Dragon*) or about generic "man" (as in *A Grave* and *What Are Years?*). Only nature is feminized (as in *Bird-Witted* and *The Paper Nautilus*).

Editor Nina Baym comments in her headnote that in Moore "the reader almost never finds the conventional poetic allusions that invoke a great tradition and assert the present poet's place in it." In Juhasz's framework, this is because women of Moore's generation could not find or present themselves as part of a great tradition. What Moore does do, like many of her contemporaries, is to reinvent poetry for herself or to find a new form for what she thought poetry should be. Locate and discuss Moore's statements on the act and art of poetry. Analyze in such a discussion *To a Snail.* What happens to poetic language when there is an "absence of feet"? Also analyze closely the frequently anthologized *Poetry.* Often students have difficulty understanding why a poet such as Moore would write with such passion about the nature of poetry itself. Build on previous discussions of the image to help them find the contrast, in the poem's middle stanzas, between the discursive statements Moore makes ("we / do not admire what / we cannot understand" and "all these phenomena are important") and her use of images drawn from precise observation of the animal world, such as in the poem *The Paper Nautilus.* What does she mean in trying to create "imaginary gardens with real toads in them"? Analyze *Bird-Witted* and *Nevertheless* to see what Moore does with form in poetry.

Comment on the kind of stanza she creates in *Nevertheless* and ask students to locate rhyme in *Bird-Witted* and *The Mind Is an Enchanting Thing.* Most will not have discovered rhyme (as students, in reading Frost, do not immediately perceive rhyme in *After Apple-Picking*). What is the effect of the use of rhyme? Compare *Bird-Witted* with Frost's poem. Is *Bird-Witted* a poem about birds or about poetry? What is Moore's "uneasy new problem"? Does one possibility cancel out the other for her?

Which poems illustrate Moore's response to the modern way of seeing the world? Compare *In Distrust of Merits* with Jeffers's earlier *Shine, Perishing Republic.* Which poem seems to be more referential? Discuss Moore's views of war as an "inward" struggle in *In Distrust of Merits.* How does her image of the world as an "orphans' home" comment on the modernist themes of her contemporaries? Ask students to extend Moore's discussions—of enslaver and enslaved and our being "not competent to make our vows" about not hating—to our own contemporary social and global conflicts, to the resurgence of nationalism in the world, and to the significance of "I inwardly did nothing" in the context of bias incidents and hate speech on college campuses and in U.S. society as a whole.

EUGENE O'NEILL

Long Day's Journey into Night demonstrates that one of the strong features of twentieth-century American literature is the continuation of what O'Neill's Edmund calls late in the play "faithful realism." But O'Neill's realism differs from that of the late-nineteenth-century writers, even as it seems to extend some of their concerns. In fact, O'Neill's play sometimes seems a compendium or a spectrum of American ideas that long precede the late nineteenth century, for he presents the Tyrones both as deeply conditioned by their past and as characters who face in their daily life (in this classically unified one-day's play) the fragmentation that is one symptom or consequence of modernist sensibility.

Mary's descent into the madness of morphine addiction becomes the play's emblem; and although O'Neill is writing, in part, about his own mother here, he is also sensitive to Mary's position as woman in the American family and in American history. As the play unfolds the history of Mary's medical treatment and of her husband's attitudes toward her condition, students will make connections between Mary Tyrone and both Edna Pontellier and the narrator of *The Yellow Wall-paper*. O'Neill suggests that modern life is more difficult for women than for men: Mary might have played the piano, but married instead, thereby depriving herself of the coherence of vocation; in marriage, and especially in marriage to the peripatetic James Tyrone (rootlessness itself becomes a modern condition), she cuts herself off from having woman friends with whom she might ease her loneliness (O'Neill adds early scandal to the fact of marriage as a way of doubly cutting Mary off from other women); and in choosing to ease her loneliness by following Tyrone on his tours, she is forced to reject even the traditional solace of making a home for her children, so that the series of choices becomes irreversible, and her need for something to ease her emotional pain and to dull her perception of her own meaninglessness increases.

Within the family structure, Mary also suffers the anachronism (in the twentieth century) of not being able to move beyond the scrutiny of external forces that seem to control her. When she tells her husband, "You really must not watch me all the time, James. I mean, it makes me self-conscious," she is experiencing the radical emotion that led the deist Founding Fathers to revolution in the 1770s. But, unlike the deists, who experienced a fundamental shift in worldview when they accepted the idea that God might not be watching them all the time and fought for self-determination from the system of divinely ordained British monarchy, Mary Tyrone is only made "self-conscious" by Tyrone's scrutiny.

She suffers self-consciousness and is not inspired by it. She is not self-conscious in a way that leads other modernists to insight; she is only increasingly made aware of her own worthlessness. O'Neill underscores that worthlessness by presenting the role of wife as one based on constant humiliation and defined by Tyrone's need to feel he has made "good bargains" in life—he makes others pay the price he won't pay.

Throughout the play, O'Neill presents Mary as someone living in a dream (especially as she becomes more and more detached by the effects of taking morphine) that might have made sense for Rip Van Winkle but, protracted into the twentieth century, simply increases her sense of disorientation and alienation. She says at one point, early in the play, "None of us can help the things life has done to us. They're done before you realize it, and once they're done they make you do other things until at last everything comes between you and what you'd like to be, and you've lost your true self forever." For students who have studied Irving, the language Mary uses here will seem reminiscent of Rip's "identity crisis" when he returns to the village after his twenty-year sleep. Later in the play, thinking aloud to the hired woman, Cathleen, Mary ties that disorientation to the death of what students might see as her own American Dream. She says, about the fog, "It hides you from the world and the world from you. You feel that everything has changed, and nothing is what it seemed to be. No one can find or touch you any more." Her language clearly echoes Irving's here, but it also conveys the isolation of American self-reliance carried to its historical extreme and epitomized in the role of twenty-century American wife and mother—Mary must be self-reliant to survive and must do so in a world devoid of human context other than her own family. She asks the play's central question: "What is it I'm looking for? I know it's something I lost."

Her son Edmund, the autobiographical voice for O'Neill himself, is the only character who understands his mother's drug addiction as the play progresses and who suffers the consequences of trying to articulate the kind of pain she feels. In Edmund's statements, students who have read twentieth-century European literature will hear connections to Camus and Beckett. Edmund also feels the absence of home; and referring to his nebulous, nameless lack of power to control his life, he says, "They never come back! Everything is in the bag! It's all a frame-up! We're all fall guys and suckers and we can't beat the game!" Later he calls himself "a stranger who never lives at home." Like Mary, he would like to "be alone with myself in another world where truth is untrue and life can hide from itself," but he chooses poetry rather than morphine to ease his own pain, and then must confront his own failure as a poet. In a scene with his father, Edmund says, "I just stammered. That's the best I'll ever do. I mean, if I live. Well, it will be faithful realism, at least. Stammering is the native eloquence of us fog people!" In depicting Edmund's "stammering," O'Neill underscores both the need to express modern consciousness and the difficulty of finding the words for it. Other twentieth-century writers will take some comfort in making the attempt; Edmund's "faithful realism" prevents him from idealizing his "stammering." In brother Jamie's cynicism ("The truth is there is no cure") and father James's despair ("A waste!, a drunken hulk, done with and finished!"), O'Neill completes his portrait of the disintegration of the American psyche and American family life and yet presents that portrait within the conventions of literary Realism.

T. S. ELIOT

The Love Song of J. Alfred Prufrock works well to read closely with students. Find images in the poem that serve as Eliot's "objective correlative" for Prufrock's particular emotions and for the state of feeling in the modern world (as Eliot saw it). *The Waste Land* raises a problem students have with Modernism generally: that so many twentieth-century poets make extensive use of classical allusions or interweave references to Renaissance painters or quote writers in languages other than English. Berating students for not having a classical education doesn't help them much. Discuss the poem in context with *Tradition and the Individual Talent,* in which Eliot defends his own method and describes the good poet as the one who is able to "develop or procure the consciousness of the past."

Although Eliot presents a "waste land" as his variation on the "diminished thing" that symbolizes human personality and culture in the modern world, his answer to the oven bird's question is not to make something (entirely) new or to show Stevens's snow man confronting "the nothing that is not there" and inventing a "supreme fiction," but rather to surrender the individual personality of the poet. The poem becomes a medium that expresses the essential history of the culture. Eliot writes in his essay, "Impressions and experiences which are important for the man may take no place in the poetry, and those which become important in the poetry may play quite a negligible part in the man, the personality." How does Eliot depersonalize the poet in *The Waste Land?* He combines traditions from mythology and legend, anthropology (with references to vegetation myths and fertility rites), classical literature and culture (including Shakespeare and Wagner), the Tarot, and comparative religious cultures; and he juxtaposes these traditions with images of isolation, fragmentation, uncertainty, and waste, hoping to use "these fragments" to "shore against" the ruins that are Eliot's variation on Frost's "diminished thing."

CLAUDE MCKAY

McKay is a strong inclusion in any survey of modern American literature, especially if the course is intended to look into complex relationships between form and content in verse. McKay's form choices may come as a surprise, for the notion still seems to run deep (not only among students but also among critics and teachers) that "free verse" or at least unrhymed, loosely metered verse signifies honesty, spontaneity, and emotional intensity; whereas sonnets, rhymed couplets, and other traditional patterns all suggest accommodation to social practices, conventional beliefs, and ordinary values. McKay is a passionate writer and a political radical, and he writes sonnets, uses rhyme royal, and frequently employs forms reminiscent of Pope, Wheatley, and Longfellow. What's going on here? Does compression and control in such forms diminish the strength of their intention? Or does confinement, in some way, seem to increase their heat? Is there an element of defiant performance here, reminiscent of Equiano perhaps, or of Ellison? In other words, does McKay's demonstration of such expertise, in what has been predominantly a white European literary practice, parallel or support some purpose that can be found in the content of these verses?

KATHERINE ANNE PORTER

Porter's fiction shows a vast range of subject, and the two selections in the anthology seem so different as to defy comparison. *Theft* is set in the professional world of New York City; *Flowering Judas* is about life on the edge, dangerous complicity with an apparently doomed revolutionary movement in Mexico. But look at the predicament of the woman at the center of each story and a deep harmony will emerge. The Porter world, whatever the specific scene, is often a world of dislocation, of the self in the predicament of being, or feeling itself to be, a nearly helpless witness to one's own life; the barriers to action or to direct engagement or even to any vital feelings other than profound loneliness can seem too great to cross. If students seem puzzled by a connection of that sort, you might have them look at certain key paragraphs in each tale. Here is a classic Porter-moment from *Theft*:

> In this moment she felt that she had been robbed of an enormous number of valuable things, whether material or intangible: things lost or broken by her own fault, things she had forgotten and left in houses when she moved; books borrowed from her and not returned, journeys she had planned and had not made, words she had waited to hear spoken to her and had not heard, and the words she had meant to answer with; bitter alternatives and intolerable substitutes worse than nothing, yet inescapable; the long patient suffering of dying friendships, and the dark inexplicable death of love—all that she had had, and all that she had missed, were lost together, and were twice lost in this landslide of remembered losses.

This is a *tour de force* of explication, and Porter is remembered as a courageous explainer of the deepest and most complex pain endured by her protagonists. Students may realize that this paragraph could appear in either tale and possibly also in *Miss Brill* and other often-anthologized Porter stories that they may have encountered before. That recognition can serve as a starting-point for other comparisons and speculations. To help them understand the specific strategy that Porter adopts and her strongest recurring themes, you might ask them to compare this kind of narration with Fitzgerald's in *Babylon Revisited,* with Cather's in *My Ántonia,* or (to go back to the heyday of American Realism) any of the stories by Henry James. Does any of these seem more like Porter's voice than the others? What are the similarities? The differences?

ZORA NEALE HURSTON

Hurston worked as an anthropologist as well as a writer and wrote *The Eatonville Anthology* after graduating from Barnard College and returning to her birthplace in Eatonville, Florida, to transcribe the folktales and folkways she remembered from childhood. Like her later *Mules and Men* (1935), both the *Anthology* and the essay *How It Feels to Be Colored Me* explore origins of consciousness—both collective and individual—that Hurston transforms into mythology, her attempt to explain the creation of the universe, to understand why the world is the way it is. Mythology does not overpower Hurston's fiction; rather, it empowers her use of folk history. Ask students to locate suggestions of mythology in *The Eatonville Anthology*; see, in particular, the opening of Section XIV: "Once 'way back yonder before the stars fell all the animals used to talk just like people." Are there important differences between Hurston's handling of talking-animal folk-tales and the way Joel Chandler Harris told them in the previous century?

Their Eyes Were Watching God

This selection illustrates Hurston's reliance on folklore as a source of lit-erary authority and creates a black woman, Janie, as a powerful speaking voice. Ask students to describe the narrative context in Chapter 2. Who is telling the story, and to whom? Although Pheoby does not emerge as a clear character in this excerpt, she does become the "hungry" listener who helps Janie tell her story. By implication, the presence of a sympathetic ear makes it possible for Janie to discover her own literary authority; and Hurston also suggests, in using the word *hungry*, that Janie's story serves an essen-tial need of Pheoby's. The relationship between narrator and listener—which replicates the relationship between Hurston and her own reader—is one of intimate friendship, self-disclosure, and mutual need. Women turn to each other's stories for understanding and consolation.

Before Janie can begin her own story, she must first tell her mother's and grandmother's stories. Discuss the statement "She thought awhile and de-cided that her conscious life had commenced at Nanny's gate." Hurston is one of the first American writers to write fiction about the origins of African American women's consciousness. You might note again connections be-tween mythology and fiction for Hurston, and then discuss the many ele-ments that create Janie's "conscious life," her attempt to locate herself in a universe that has "a personal answer for all other creations." Hurston weaves together in Chapter 2 the source of Janie's burgeoning sexuality, her connection with the natural world as a way of knowing, her recognition of Nanny as a "foundation of ancient power," the history of black women's op-pression during slavery by white men and women, the burden of sexual as well as racial oppression for Janie's mother, the impulse (in Nanny) to ac-commodate to a world in which " 'de nigger woman is de mule" by finding "protection" in a responsible man, the imperative (in Janie) to strike out on one's own in a world in which "the familiar people and things" have failed.

We can discuss the novel as Hurston's "sermon"—Nanny had envisioned herself as a preacher—and the act of writing fiction as akin to making a sa-cred text. After Leafy runs away, Nanny thinks to herself about Janie, " 'Ah said Ah'd save de text for you.' " Janie finds herself in telling Pheoby the story of her life; "saving the text" is precisely what Janie learns to do for her friend and what Hurston does for the black and white women writers who would come after her. Hurston focuses on a black woman's need to write stories that mirror her own image—unlike the first photograph Janie sees in which she cannot find herself—and in this way she expresses a black woman's modernist concern. What happens to a black woman, or to a woman of any color, when the "familiar people and things" fail? As long as Janie has not discovered for herself that what her grandmother wants her to believe is a lie—that in marrying Logan Killicks she will come to love him—she is willing to go along with another's script or formula for her life. But when she walks out to the gate a second time (in Chapter 3) she has a more realistic view of the road. Hurston suggests that it is only by rejecting the conventional scripts that Janie "became a woman." And for Hurston, *woman* is synonymous with "independent person." In *Their Eyes Were Watching God*, Hurston creates a modernist myth of origins; the process of becoming a woman for Janie involves making her own dream, her own story.

The Gilded Six-Bits

Like most of the African American women writers represented in *NAAL*, Hurston was a risk taker—so much so that her reputation has gone through some dramatic swings in the past forty years. In this story she steers very close, perhaps dangerously so, to certain stereotypes that have been widely exploited over the years. Students who have followed recent controversies about BET and the "Def Jam" comedy forms will already be aware of the complexities of telling this kind of tale: how it is interpreted can depend very much on who is reading it, and in what context. Where are the stereotypes in *The Gilded Six-Bits*? Is Hurston playing along with them? Subverting them? Correcting them? What kind of audience is this story implicitly intended for and in what kind of political and moral context? Does the story take unexpected turns—not in plotting but in tone? In what ways does Hurston distinguish her own voice, her own perspective, from that of Missy May and Joe Banks?

DOROTHY PARKER

Parker has been experiencing renewed attention in recent years, but more as a victim of an odd literary context and period than as a writer whose talent came to full flower. If students show interest in the Algonquin Round Table and the *New Yorker* group of the twenties and thirties, you might recommend that they look at the film *Mrs. Parker and the Vicious Circle* (1995) or consult James R. Gaines's *Wit's End: Days and Nights of the Algonquin Round Table* (1977), a highly readable short book that describes Parker's world as one in which talent was suborned into superficial display. Students may want to talk about wit and irony (by Parker or other modern practitioners) and whether these strategies take a reader, or a writer, anywhere worth going. Does Parker's humor have connections to the general tradition of American humorist writing? Can students talk about the ways in which Parker achieves her linguistic effects, both in her short poems and in *The Waltz*. What kind of audience seems implicit here? Can they comment on the suggestion that in Parker's poems, "wit and elegance costume moods of emptiness and despair." What happens if we compare Parker's *The Waltz* with Charlotte Perkins Gilman's *The Yellow Wall-paper*? Where does the Parker legacy show up, in contemporary American humor and satire?

GENEVIEVE TAGGARD

If you have brought Juhasz's framework into your presentation of women poets (see discussion of Marianne Moore), Taggard's poetry will seem quite in advance of her generation, because much of her poetry derives from women's experiences (as in *With Child, Mill Town,* and *To My Mother*), and particularly women from poor and working-class origins. Indeed, Taggard's poetry poses a challenge in defining aesthetic Modernism. In response to Frost's famous question in *The Oven Bird,* "What to make of a diminished thing?" Taggard would seem to answer: sing! strike! move! In Taggard, poetry and politics become intertwined and women participate in both (as in *At Last the Women Are Moving* and *Mill Town*). Even more startling in Taggard is the presence of class politics. More than any other poet in the 1914–45 period (with the exception of black poets Sterling Brown and Langston Hughes), Taggard's poetry addresses class issues; indeed, her poetry gives voice to working-class women and men, and like Brown and Hughes, she privileges "everyday" experience (as in *Everyday Alchemy*).

To demonstrate the contrast between a white male poet's apolitical approach and Taggard's interweaving of one woman's experience with the experience of class and with politics, read *A Middle-aged, Middle-class Woman at Midnight* against Frost's *An Old Man's Winter Night.* In Taggard's poem, age, cold, and anxiety about the state of the world allow her "middle-class woman" speaker to cross class boundaries and align her own struggle to sleep ("A woman took veronal in vain") with the "stink of poverty": "I hope the people win."

As part of your discussion of Taggard, ask students to think about the relationship between poetry and politics. In Latin America, poetry has long served political ends and has a vital life among people outside the college classroom. In the United States, many people believe that poetry (and all art) should have nothing to do with politics. Taggard is herself aware of her departure from convention in this regard. For Taggard, poetry must move people, and must move them collectively.

E. E. CUMMINGS

Consider what it would mean to ask whether Cummings is a "serious" poet. Describe the ways in which he experiments with language in poems such as *anyone lived in a pretty how town* or *my father moved through dooms of love,* and consider their effects. Ask students to read *Buffalo Bill's* or *"next to of course god america i* out loud and discuss what happens to poetry that is meant to be read, not spoken. Locate modern themes in Cummings; place him in context with Frost (compare *pity this busy monster, manunkind* with Frost's *Departmental*), Jeffers (*i sing of Olaf glad and big* with *Shine, Perishing Republic*), or Moore (*Poem, or Beauty Hurts Mr. Vinal* with *Poetry*).

JEAN TOOMER

Discuss *Georgia Dusk* as a variation on Emerson's call for an American poet a century earlier. What, for Toomer, will be the characteristics of that "genius of the South"? And what will be the literary tradition for that "singer"? Locate Toomer in the context of other black writers or writers about black experience in *NAAL,* for example, Joel Chandler Harris and

Charles W. Chesnutt. What does it mean, in Toomer, to make "folk-songs from soul sounds"?

Analyze *Fern,* first from the narrator's point of view and then focusing on Fern herself. What is happening within the speaker as he imaginatively recreates Fern? What is the literary analogue in Toomer for Du Bois's "double-consciousness"? How does Toomer evoke "the souls of black folk" in this excerpt from *Cane?* Place Fern herself in the context of other works by American male writers, such as Poe's *Ligeia* or Anderson's *Mother.* Toomer gives Fern a moment of speech when she asks, "Doesn't it make you mad?" and then his narrator interprets what she means. Does he give her voice? Consider the last sentence in *Fern:* "Her name, against the chance that you might happen down that way, is Fernie May Rosen." What, in this sentence, gives the reader more clues to Fern's identity than Toomer's earlier idealization of her? Is there any "real" Fern beneath Toomer's portrait of her as his narrator's muse? Note Toomer's reference to the black woman who "once saw the mother of Christ and drew her in charcoal on the court-house wall." The allusion is one piece of evidence to suggest that black women, as well as men, have tried to record their visions; they have been artists as well as inspirations for art.

F. SCOTT FITZGERALD

Many of your students will have read *The Great Gatsby*—many of them will have read it more than once. You might want to begin by seeing who in your group is familiar with Fitzgerald, and whether they have liked the experience, and whether they see the sense of teaching his stories (sometimes the *same* stories) at every level from ninth grade to graduate school. You can help the class consider how the comfort and style of various American decades helps determine which canonical authors get attention: as the fair-haired boy of the opulent twenties, Fitzgerald went into eclipse during the Depression, for his agonized patricians, working out their fate in mansions, exclusive clubs, and expensive hotels, meant nothing to a desperate populace. When times got better, so did Fitzgerald's posthumous reputation—perhaps because our attention has shifted from the pains of basic need to the pains of having what we thought we wanted.

Babylon Revisited comes from an array of stories about men and women who have made it, people who have lived beyond the year or two of glory that Gatsby achieved before he died, perhaps mercifully, in his own West Egg swimming pool. These are stories of people who move unhappily through glorious locales: the Riviera and Paris, the comfortable private places in midtown Manhattan, the exclusive resorts of Switzerland. An opening question for your class: what differentiates this kind of story from the modern trash novel, the kind sold in drugstores or beach-supply shops, about the woes of being a supermodel, a Hollywood sex star, a magnate in fashion or the perfume trade? If students grope for an answer, you might grab a paragraph or two and suggest the difference: no matter how dissipated or dislikeable the Fitzgerald protagonist or how unsympathetic—or voyeuristic—we might feel toward the general situation that the story offers us, there are gorgeously phrased moments of insight about human nature, the mingled emotions of going back and coming home, the internal conflicts of wanting and *not* wanting in the same instant. As flush times and bad times come and go, Fitzgerald's reputation will have to rely on his prose to carry him through, and with the sound and pace and agility of his prose your discussion can begin and end.

WILLIAM FAULKNER

As I Lay Dying

As students begin to read *As I Lay Dying* they experience fragmentation and dislocation. After assigning only the first five or ten monologues, you could spend much of the first class period allowing them to discuss the expectations they bring to a novel as readers, and how *As I Lay Dying* disrupts those expectations. The initial confusion they feel as a result of Faulkner's disparate narrative sections and points of view can help them understand Modernism as a challenge to their ways of seeing the world. If allowed to express their own disorientation, they begin to use Faulkner's novel as an exploration of ways of knowing (epistemology) as well as of ways of being (ontology) in a disordered universe.

We begin with a preliminary discussion of the book's title in light of earlier thematic discussions of Modernism. What does the reader expect, given this title? And how does the novel, from its opening sections, thwart those expectations? Who *is* the "I" of the title? Just Addie Bundren? What or who else does that first-person point of view include? And how does the past tense of the title create a preliminary absurdity before the reader begins the novel? In eliciting students' initial confusion about opening sections, try to give them the experience of posing Faulkner's own questions as he lets his characters speak. What do they know as they read, and how do they know it? You might closely read Darl's opening section. Where does Faulkner "locate" the reader? Part of what "lies dying" for readers new to Faulkner is any reliance on the author as someone who will facilitate knowing. Faulkner shows readers only what his characters know, not what readers may feel the need to know.

As students proceed through the novel (over the span of an additional two or three class periods), you can spend class time describing what Faulkner is doing. A class might want to consider novelistic conventions—character development, plot, use of a narrator, chronology, narrative form—and assess the extent to which Faulkner adheres to or deviates from traditional elements of the novel. In the collective act of description, students make numerous statements about *As I Lay Dying*: they note the number of narrators (fifteen by the novel's end) and sections (fifty-nine separate monologues); they distinguish among the narrative voices by making descriptive observations: Darl has, by far, the most sections; some central characters—Jewel and Addie—have only one monologue; monologues by Darl, Jewel, Dewey Dell, Anse, Vardaman, Cash, and Addie create a nexus of family dynamics;

other characters—Cora, Tull, Peabody, Samson, Whitfield, Armstid, Mac-Gowan, Moseley—express a wide range of possible social responses to the Bundrens. These descriptive statements may make some students feel that they have "figured out" the novel; and you may observe that their attempts to "solve" the novel may be premature and may actually be covering over their uneasiness as readers, lest they become lost in a work without omniscient authority.

They also establish collective understandings about the characters in the novel that become shared facts and that serve as a prelude to interpretation. The attempt to bury Addie becomes the family members' ostensible reason for the journey to Jefferson, which provides Faulkner with his novel's narrative structure; but most of the Bundrens also have other reasons for the trip. Cash wants the free ride back to Tull's, where he is supposed to work on his barn, and he dreams of a "talking machine." Vardaman remembers something in a store window (the toy train) that Santa wouldn't have sold to town boys. Anse wants to get some new teeth. Dewey Dell hopes to buy a drug-induced abortion. Darl twice narrates events at which he could not have been present and in other sections appears to "know" things that others have not told him (he knows Dewey Dell is pregnant and that Anse is not Jewel's father). Among all of Addie's survivors, Jewel seems best able to feel the depths of his connection to his mother, to mourn her death, and to achieve emotional resolution. (At the end of Cora's section just preceding Addie's monologue, Addie tells Cora that Jewel "is my cross and he will be my salvation. He will save me from the water and from the fire," and indeed, Jewel first saves Addie's coffin in the ford, and later from the fire Darl has set to Gillespie's barn.)

The group effort to figure out what can be known in reading the novel becomes a pedagogical analogue to the Bundrens' own journey. The parallel tensions of burying Addie (for the Bundrens) and figuring out what is happening in the novel (for the members of the class) comment on the act of modernist reading: without the storyteller/guide of traditional narrative, the task of arriving at an understanding of Faulkner's text (analogous to bringing the coffin to Jefferson) places much of the burden of creation on the act of reading itself.

As a result of description, students move toward interpretation. The elements of form they observe lead to their perceptions of character. For example, they note the repetition in the form of the images Jewel and Vardaman create as a way of grieving for Addie: "Jewel's mother is a horse" and "My mother is a fish." Then they can ask, which image works best to help the character resolve grief? In responding to the question, they explore the relationship between image and feeling, between word and meaning, between the novel as a form and the attempt to order the fragments of human consciousness.

Central to exploring Faulkner's search for theme, meaning, and order is Addie's single monologue, placed off-center in the novel in the second half, long after Addie has died and the Bundrens have begun their journey to Jefferson. To what extent does Addie exist in the novel? Although she gives the other characters their ostensible reason for action, she herself does not act. Neither does she speak, except to acknowledge Cash as he builds her coffin. Her monologue in the novel may appear to give her a voice, but her death has already silenced her and prevents her from making her genuine presence known. She exists for others as their own projected need. Interestingly, what occupies her thinking in her monologue is the uselessness of words. Discuss Addie's various statements about words: "words dont ever fit even what they are trying to say at"; a word is "just a shape to fill a lack"; a name is a "word as a shape, a vessel . . . a significant shape profoundly without life like an empty door frame"; words are "just sounds" that people have "for what they never had and cannot have until they forget the words." In the narrative structure of Faulkner's novel, Addie is herself "just a shape to fill a lack."

The visual image of the coffin that appears in Tull's third monologue typographically disrupts, once again, the reader's expectations; for although Faulkner has violated readers' expectations of linearity and wholeness in narrating *As I Lay Dying*, he at least uses words. With the visual image of the coffin, followed later by Addie's description of words, Faulkner creates a series of concentric visual images or shapes that serve both to contain his novel's meaning and to express the limits of narrative form. In Faulkner's thinking, each of the following is associatively synonymous: the visual figure of the coffin, the name *Addie,* the narrative form he has chosen for the book (it is spatial, a world laid out by compass and rule), and the book itself. *As I Lay Dying* effectively becomes Addie's coffin, a fiction in which she is silenced by the title; and like her family in Jefferson cemetery, she might be listening to the other fifty-eight monologues, but she'll "be hard to talk to."

As I Lay Dying can have a profound effect on students who are themselves struggling to emerge from silence and to explore the world's order and form, to discover whether it has any or whether they must join the human collective task of making form and meaning. Students may empathize with Addie's silence and may find it reflected in Vardaman's obsession with his mother as a fish or in Cash's inability to speak except to focus on the coffin's construction or need for balance. *As I Lay Dying* demonstrates the novelist's own struggle to emerge from silence, and students may believe that it is only partly successful or that Faulkner is saying that it is possible to achieve only partial success.

In evaluating the relationship between the construction of form—as a coffin or a novel—and of meaning, ask students to think about Darl. Is he crazy? If so, what makes him crazy? Interestingly, Darl has by far the least difficulty with silence; he can speak for others as well as for himself. Is he a mere scapegoat at the novel's end? Do the other members of his family believe he "knows too much"? Or has he failed in some basic way to create a form for what he knows? Darl is the only character who cannot make a connection between himself and some concrete object. He has no coffin, horse, fish, abortion, or reason to go to town. Students may find it difficult to believe that Darl "goes crazy" at the end of the novel, in part because, in many of his monologues, he closely resembles a traditional omniscient narrator, one whose own identity does not intrude. Who then is Darl? If he cannot express his connection in terms of an image, a form—coffin or novel—his knowledge and creativity become destructive. Darl simply cannot "be contained" in a form; therefore, as Cash realizes at novel's end, "this world is not his world; this life his life." In Darl's failure to achieve a form for human consciousness, Faulkner implies his own struggle for meaning. What to make of a diminished thing?—make something of it, find a word to fill the lack, write a novel that will reconcile human need for form with the formlessness of human consciousness. Cash's briefest monologue locates *As I Lay Dying* in the progression of Faulkner's career as a novelist: "It wasn't on a balance. I told them that if they wanted it to tote and ride on a balance, they would have to." *As I Lay Dying* rides precariously, a book about silent knowing necessarily told in words. Expecting to be told, students emerge from *As I Lay Dying* with the uneasy knowledge that words no longer—for the Modernist—carry ultimate authority. As Addie expresses it, "the high dead words in time seemed to lose even the significance of their dead sound." Perhaps literary authority itself is at least a part of what "lies dying" in Faulkner's modern fictional universe.

LOUISE BOGAN

Bogan is hard to categorize, which may be an inconvenience for critics but is possibly a testament to her versatility, her range of voices and tastes, and her quest to express the many dimensions of modern experience by using a variety of vocabularies and forms. By this point in the course, students will have a number of strong American poets in mind already; and if their experience does not include much Auden or Yeats (writers whom Bogan admired), they may have fresh recollections of Dickinson and Whitman—who are often played off as opposites in later nineteenth-century American verse. When does Bogan sound like Dickinson? When like Whitman? When the voice is reminiscent of Dickinson, are the themes similar as well? When she works in the long, free-verse lines of Whitman, is she playing ventriloquist or is she adapting Whitman's free, buoyant voice to a different purpose? In sum, does Bogan seem like an imitator of yesterday's poetry? Or does she transform these established voices into something unique and new?

HART CRANE

Crane can be hard to engage with in a quick-moving survey course. His prosody varies; as a visionary poet and a twentieth-century bard, he takes on immense subjects; his verse presents a first-time reader with a bewildering range of moods and temperaments; and the story of his short, turmoiled life can shadow the poetry so much that the verse can become subordinate to the biography, mere exhibits in an investigation of the man. If you want students to appreciate, on the fly, Crane's ambitions as a poet and the variety of voices that he mastered, the best beginning might be to take two extended stanzas from two different part of *The Bridge* and examine them closely and comparatively. For instance, you might have students read carefully, perhaps aloud in class, the first stanzas of *Powhatan's Daughter* and *Cutty Sark*—rhymed, formal, grand-style verse, and Cummings-like, unpredictable, wide-open lines. Why the difference? Do other voices resonate in these different stanzas? In other words, are these different voices in some ways a kind of incantation, calling up not just different historical moments, but different eras in the history of the American imagination? Can a poet or a poem encompass such diversity? Whitman tried to embrace all of American experience, but his prosody did not show this kind of variety. What do students think of Crane's experiment, not just in seeing but in creating one long poem in such a variety of styles?

ERNEST HEMINGWAY AND THOMAS WOLFE

Hemingway and Wolfe are neighbors in this edition of *NAAL*, and there is much to be gained in looking at them together if one of your objectives is to help students increase their awareness of the variety of literary styles that were applied to modern experience. Students can see here a spectacular contrast, opposite ways of refreshing American narrative catching the feel of contemporary life: Hemingway the minimalist, the stoic, the great doubter of emotional and intellectual display, and Wolfe, the ecstatic describer, the lover of adjectives and unending periodic sentences, the believer in saying. Judging by the post-1945 prose fiction that is included in *NAAL* and other canon-making anthologies, Hemingway seems to have won the face-off: Vonnegut, Carver, Beattie, Silko, and many other contemporary writers show his influence. Why did the Hemingway style prevail? What was it about modern experience that made minimalism appropriate or more so than Wolfe's ebullience? If students need some coaxing to engage in these speculative questions, you might ask them to compare the closing paragraphs of *The Lost Boy* and *The Snows of Kilimanjaro*. They are both elegiac in a sense, both about loss, death, and the problem of understanding the meaning of one human life. But the tonal and thematic differences will be strongly apparent, and contrasting the passages can open up a broad discussion about saying, and *not* saying, as literary and artistic values.

STERLING A. BROWN

Brown chooses the principle of contrast between white man and black man as his subject in *Mister Samuel and Sam* and *Master and Man*. In these poems, the differences between white and black are settled by the common denominators of death and harvest time; and yet as the poems appear to resolve differences, they also end by highlighting the inequalities within those common denominators (both Samuel and Sam may die, but the harvest is more bounteous for the Master than for the Man). Other poems (such as *He Was a Man*) also derive their form from the principle of contrast; but the holding back of detail in early stanzas typical of a ballad about the life of a man yields to more detail, and the ballad's "story" turns out to be the progress by which this "man" is reduced to not a man in the eyes of white people. The promise of unfolding in the ballad form is negated (and demonstrated by the poem's consistent use of negatives— "It wasn't about," "Didn't catch him," "It didn't come off")—by the poem's ultimate irony, that it's impossible to write a story of a man's life when he isn't viewed as a man. Thus the title's assertion (*He Was a Man*) becomes the poem's primary message. *Break of Day* continues the ballad/blues form and a variation on the same theme: "Man in full" becomes "Long past due" by the poem's end.

LANGSTON HUGHES

Before the Harlem Renaissance writers of the 1920s (Angelina Weld Grimké, Zora Neale Hurston, Jean Toomer, Sterling Brown, Langston Hughes, and Countee Cullen are all associated with this period), most black writing took the form either of the slave narrative of the mid-nineteenth century or of "racial uplift" literature or polemical writing characteristic of the turn of the century (and represented in *NAAL* by Booker T. Washington and W. E. B. Du Bois). While most African American writers wrote for white audiences, Langston Hughes may be the first African American writer to view his white reader's interest, and his role as speaking voice, as a form of encounter not unlike those early encounters between Europeans and native peoples during the period of exploration and colonization. You can begin teaching Hughes with *Visitors to the Black Belt* and discussing the two-sided perspective this poem gives about Harlem. More than an exercise in language ("Across the tracks" versus "here on this side of the tracks"), the poem ends with a simple question and answer that resonates with the problem of postcolonialism. "Who're you, outsider? / Ask me who am I." In these lines, the poet teaches the reader, by means of the expected question, how to ask the speaker who he or she is rather than to assume he or she already knows. If the outsider learns to know his or her place as outside, then the person on the inside ("To me it's *here* / In Harlem") has room to define himself. So Hughes is pleading with his white audience not to draw conclusions about black life without asking him, without allowing him, to define its reality and meaning and—in other poems (such as *I, Too; Refugee in America; Madam's Calling Cards;* and *Democracy*)—what it means to be an American.

The other side of the experience of encounter involves the responsibility it places on the poet. Echoing Whitman in *I, Too* and self-conscious about both calling for a black American poet and responding to that quasi-Emersonian call in *Note on Commercial Theatre*, Hughes responds very simply: "I reckon it'll be / Me myself! / Yes, it'll be me." From the perspective of literature of encounter, if Hughes can imagine a white readership "encountering" black experience and black art with genuine interest (perhaps for the first time on a large scale during the Harlem Renaissance), then he has the responsibility to make certain that experience and that art don't become "colonized," commercialized ("You've taken my blues and gone—"). The person who recognizes that colonization is taking place must struggle against it, especially by resisting being appropriated in a white someone else's image. Thus Hughes moves beyond Brown, whose poetry stresses contrast and counterpoint, to include contradiction and the two-way experience of encounter.

Students will also find in Hughes's work an appreciation for black women's struggles and an attempt to represent women's experiences. In one of his greatest poems, *Mother to Son,* he also connects his own answer for the modernist question to a woman's voice and a woman's experience. If you read this poem closely with students, you might focus on the contrast between the mother's description of the stairway itself and the image she arrives at ("Life for me ain't been no crystal stair") as a controlling metaphor for her vision. The poem shows the mother arriving at modernist order in the chaos of "sometimes goin' in the dark" by making this particular image. Ask students to consider the numerous connotations of the image of the "crystal stair" as well as the way Hughes is experimenting with levels of diction, in effect raising the level of diction in this phrase. Raising the level of diction and "racial uplift" become ground notes in his work; see, for example, *Genius Child,* in which Hughes moves beyond protest to a transcendent belief in the "genius" of black life (*"Kill him*—and let his soul run wild!"").

And in the Alberta K. Johnson poems (here represented by *Madam and her Madam* and *Madam's Calling Cards*), Hughes demonstrates the complexity of the relationship between black woman and white woman. When Alberta responds to her Madam's profession of love by saying "I'll be dogged / If I love you," Hughes is making a simple statement of fact: if relationship with the Madam means that Alberta Johnson has to work even harder, she will indeed be "dogged," for it will kill her; and indeed, Alberta must stop short of "loving" the woman she works for if she is to love herself at all. And that she does love herself is clear in *Madam's Calling Cards:* "I hankered to see / My name in print." Both like and unlike Yezierska's characters, Alberta Johnson wants to be an American but doesn't consider herself an immigrant: "There's nothing foreign / To my pedigree."

RICHARD WRIGHT

Discuss what "being a man" means to Dave Saunders. Why does the gun represent manhood to him? Does a black boy in the 1930s South automatically get "to be a man like anybody else" or does he have to make that happen? Why does he want the power to "kill anybody, black or white"? How does Dave Saunders move beyond Booker T. Washington's views of black identity in *Up From Slavery*? Is Dave another heroic fugitive, like Frederick Douglass? Does he have a destination at the end of the story?

MURIEL RUKEYSER

As the headnote points out, Rukeyser "denied that there was any conflict between poetry written at a high level of technical and textual sophistication and poetry that was politically motivated and dedicated." Ask students to evaluate their response to her poetry, compared with their response to Taggard or Hughes. Does it work (do they believe) to write political poetry at a "high level"? Does Rukeyser reach the audience she might want to reach (and can we tell who that might be)? *Who in One Lifetime* is emblematic of Rukeyser's work, the one poem in the anthologized sequence that can integrate her various styles and concerns. She has seen "all causes lost" and yet has tried to make poetry out of those defeats (in yet another answer to Frost's modernist question, "What to make of a diminished thing") to explore the contradictions both biographically and poetically in her self-portrait as "a childless goddess of fertility." Read her images of coming to voice (in *Suicide Blues* and *"Long Enough"*), of coming to sight (*The Poem as Mask*), of healing fragmentation (*Who in One Lifetime*).

Poems, for Rukeyser, seem to be one way of making sense of all of the wars she has lived through; see *Poem,* with its transformation from historical moment ("I lived in the first century of world wars") to contemporary dilemma ("I lived in the first century of *these* wars" [emphasis added]). And notice, with students, the considerable range of Rukeyser's historical and political themes. The questions which may draw the most interest, however, have to do with her development as a stylist, as a creator of poems, over such a long career. It's a sad fact that for convenience critics often classify a poet on the basis of what he or she publishes in the first collections and alter that classification only slowly, and sometimes grudgingly, as an artist matures and takes on new voices and experiments. Ask students to compare the last three poems in the *NAAL* selection with the first two or three—not with regard to theme or embedded politics, but as assemblages of words and sound. What has changed in Rukeyser's voice? Are those changes interesting and possibly important?

American Prose since 1945

INTRODUCING STUDENTS TO CONTEMPORARY AMERICAN DRAMA

An introductory course in American literature, especially in twentieth-century or contemporary literature, offers students a unique opening into the experience and meaning of drama as an American literary form. American writers have certainly produced great plays before the contemporary period; and drama served a vital function for Americans as early as Royall Tyler's *The Contrast,* when delighted audiences flocked to view Jonathan's comic rendition of what an "American" in 1787 might look like. Few of your students, however, will have thought much about the uses of drama in their own lives.

One way of beginning is simply to ask students to talk about drama in general. What do they associate with drama? Some may reply, Shakespeare. Almost all of them will have read Shakespeare in high school; they may have learned, as a result, that drama belongs to an elitist category of literary forms. Are any students willing to challenge that impression? Others may recall acting in less serious high school plays: comedies, musicals, or plays written especially for high school acting. A few may have written and/or acted in original plays as children or may have parents who participated in community theater groups. Others may associate a family trip to New York City to view a Broadway play as some initiation rite into adult life and culture. Some may associate drama with television situation comedies. Even with this limited range of responses to the experience of drama in their lives, you can begin to explore the variety of functions drama serves. What are some of the differences between literature that one reads, often alone in a room, and a play that may be "taking place" before the viewer's eyes, as that viewer sits in a group with others? Is a play "shown" or "told" when the performers stage it? What kinds of effects does the stage play make possible? And what does it mean to dramatize?

Contemporary drama may elicit students' ability to engage in the reading process more readily than contemporary American poetry, which often seems deliberately to distance the reader with its private meanings, idiosyncratic uses of language and imagery, and sense of barriers between speaking voice and reader of the text. Drama, however, seems to require a viewer; a play creates audience in the process of making character, situation, scene, and dramatic effect; the student, in the act of reading, becomes a collaborator in creating a visual image of the scene.

The plays included in Volume 2 of *NAAL*, by their very choice of subject matter and realistic treatment, may particularly elicit the student's capacity to become engaged, to become created or re-created as audience. When Eugene O'Neill explored American family life in *Long Day's Journey into Night*, he did not exhaust our increasing fascination for the function and fate of the American family. Perhaps the crisis in family life for late-twentieth-century Americans has brought on the crisis of consciousness that earlier in the century we associate with World War I and the question of the death or absence of God or design in the modern world. Family life provides a central focus in the work of Tennessee Williams and Arthur Miller. If the American family is dead or absent, who or what "mirrors" an American identity that continues to evolve?

EUDORA WELTY

Analyze the relationship between Leota and Mrs. Fletcher. Does Mrs. Pike exist? What function does Leota's fantasy life serve? Discuss the undercurrent of violence in *Petrified Man*. How does Leota's story show her attempt to gain control over her life? Is she successful? Who is Billy Boy, why is she taking care of him, and where does he get his own power at the end of the story?

TENNESSEE WILLIAMS

The loss of "Belle Reve" seems to establish the tarnished American dream as one of Williams's central themes in *A Streetcar Named Desire*. Some students may see Blanche DuBois as a conventional symbol for the loss of that dream: as an unmarried, aging belle, she worries about her clothes, her appearance, and her ability to attract men and uses alcohol to ease her loneliness. But is the loss of desirability, or desire itself, the play's subject? Does Blanche want to find an object for her desire or to be a desired object?

Williams might have made desire itself a symbol; instead, throughout the play, he focuses our attention on explicit sexuality. What particular scenes define desire as sexual in the play? Ask students to discuss in particular the relationship between Stanley and Stella. Their attraction for each other is sexual, and most students will equate sexuality with heterosexuality and, as it is presented in this play, with a hierarchy of physical dominance (the men in the play, especially Stanley, use physical abuse as part of sexual power; see Stanley's comment to Blanche, " 'Oh! So you want some roughhouse!' ").

But this play revolves around that moment in Blanche's past when she married a "young boy" who tried to find "help" in Blanche for his homosexuality. When she discovers him with "an older man who had been his friend for years," and that day tells him how much he disgusts her, he blows his head off. For most students, presuming that heterosexuality is "normal" and homosexuality "deviant," this moment will establish Blanche's tragedy as a conventional one—she has loved young and lost—and the moment in which homosexuality enters the play will quickly recede. Raise the possibility that from this moment on, Blanche's sexual identity becomes ambiguous, despite the fact that Williams has made her a woman in the play, and suggest also that although Stanley and Stella both seem secure in their gender identities, their very insistence on continuing to reaffirm their sexual relationship by means of violence—thereby asserting Stanley's "manhood" and Stella's "womanliness"—begins to raise the question of the origins of gender determination as well.

What would it mean to say that Blanche's sexual identity becomes ambiguous in the play? Near the end she tells Mitch, " 'I don't want realism, I want magic! . . . I don't tell truth, I tell what *ought* to be truth.' " What are Blanche's props for her "magic"? Ask someone to study her array of furs, costumes, jewelry, and perfume in the play; she wears all of the trappings of gendered femininity, like the legendary Mae West (the statuette Mitch wins for Blanche at the amusement park). But her success in establishing her appearance depends on her avoiding the sun and even electric light. Without the costumes, who would Blanche be? What would it mean to call her a "woman"? And who are her consistent objects of desire? Williams is exploring the way female identity is made, not born.

Ask students to think about Stanley's response to Blanche. What motivates Stanley to rape her? What does she represent that makes him want to humiliate her? Blanche sees Stanley—with his phallic "genius"—as subhuman; Stanley sees Blanche as undermining his control over Stella (" 'You remember the way that it was? Them nights we had together? God, honey, it's gonna be sweet when we can make noise in the night the way that we used to and get the colored lights going with nobody's sister behind the curtains to hear us!' "). But Stanley is also acting out of a variation on homophobia—or is homophobia a variation on misogyny? Stanley hates Blanche because she insists on wearing women's costumes and yet refuses to define herself as degenerate or to excuse her sister for her submission to Stanley.

In raping Blanche, he is raping the wearing of women's costumes, the flaunting of sexuality by women (or by men who refuse to be "phallic"). No wonder that Stella tells Eunice, " 'I couldn't believe her story and go on living with Stanley.' " The sexual "stories" Blanche and Stanley tell totally contradict each other. Blanche exhibits desire without violence; Stanley achieves his through violence and humiliation.

Ask students to talk about Stella's grief at the end of the play: " 'What have I done to my sister?' " How has she betrayed Blanche? Has she also betrayed herself? In what version of sexual desire does the "truth" lie? The play ends with Stanley and Stella, having eliminated Blanche from their world, returning to their hierarchical heterosexual roles: Stella weeps in luxurious abandon, Stanley unbuttons her blouse. Is this desire? or a more destructive lie than Blanche's "magic"?

JOHN CHEEVER

Cheever makes an excellent foil for Williams, and he offers a demonstration of how postwar American literature has brought us a proliferation not only of regional works but of different possibilities regarding the presentation of temperament. Rightly or otherwise, Williams has become associated with hot climates, hot passions, overt sexuality, and spectacular (if not always eloquent) breakdown scenes in which primordial desire and deep pain are exhibited and confessed. Cheever's associations are in some ways the opposite: his landscape, physically and psychologically, is often the suburban landscape of southern Connecticut and Westchester County, New York—upscale neighborhoods two hours or less by train or car from New York City, landscapes where urban comforts blend (sometimes attractively, sometimes grotesquely) with a real or contrived pastoral setting, and where people may try to balance and sustain their inner lives in part by keeping their lawns, houses, and outward personalities well tended.

The classic Cheever breakdown, so strongly contrasted with Williams's, is of a sort he associated with prep-schooled, Ivy League–trained professional men and their facade-conserving wives: a sudden wave of anomie, of deracination, an unexplained compulsion to take on or persist in some bizarre or self-destructive activity, or to quietly tear the fabric of the artificial life that surrounds them and their families. Students can work back and forth between Cheever and Williams, strengthening their own powers to compare and discuss works in light of one another and musing on how deep the class differences and region differences still run in contemporary America. Does even madness have its local rules, its cultural shape, its regional identity?

BERNARD MALAMUD

The Magic Barrel also works well with *A Streetcar Named Desire*, because there are similarities between the works that help students formulate their questions. Salzman's idea of Paradise is to find a good woman for Leo, the rabbinical student, and to keep Leo away from his own daughter, Stella, a "fallen woman." (Is Williams's Stella also "fallen"?) When Leo falls in love with Stella's picture and arranges to meet her at the end of the story, Malamud depicts their meeting in "fallen" terms: Stella is dressed like a streetwalker, Leo runs forward "with flowers outthrust" (or as if he and Salzman had exchanged places, and Leo is now a cupid or the FTD florist's winged messenger bearing flowers), and Salzman, convinced that there is no good man, chants prayers for the dead. But Leo pictures in Stella "his own redemption"; and Malamud suggests that although Leo becomes less than a rabbi by the end of the story, he becomes consequently more of a man, more of a human being. Simply loving, in this story, does re-create Paradise because it makes it possible, once again, for Leo to love God—and even to create God in a human image. In Malamud's terms, Leo's love for the fallen Stella makes him a good man; and although Salzman mourns, the story has a happy ending. Less is more for Leo. As he becomes the "diminished thing" in Salzman's eyes, he is more capable of human love. In short, this is a parable, and students will enjoy speculating on Malamud's connections to some of the oldest kinds of storytelling in the Western tradition.

RALPH ELLISON

Here too we have a parable, a novel chapter that works as a story saturated with symbolism, even with allegory. Students by this point in your course will have a lot to say about the use and abuse of symbolism; and to draw them into the power of this tale and to encourage them to read the whole novel, it's worth pausing to see how this chapter works both as an allegory and as a splendid piece of realistic narrative. Compare Ellison's protagonist with Dave Saunders in Wright's *The Man Who Was Almost a Man.* The two might seem incomparable in educational background and social possibilities; yet, how are they up against similar barriers? In the Prologue to *Invisible Man* the older protagonist writes, in retrospect, "responsibility rests upon recognition, and recognition is a form of agreement." How is this observation relevant to his experiences as a young man in Chapter I? How does the boy's attempt to deliver the speech he himself has written comment on the literary tradition of American black writers? What are the symbolic and real obstacles he must overcome in trying to find his voice and to express his point of view? What might it take for the white men at the smoker to "recognize" and "accept" the invisible man? Is the white woman in a better position than the black boy? Does either have power in the world of the back room?

SAUL BELLOW

One of a handful of American Nobel Prize–winners, Bellow has a reputation for being dauntingly intellectual: in a Bellow story, one ordinary-looking man, not especially successful or even known, walking down one New York street on an ordinary day will open up as a cosmos an inner world where Conrad, Marx, Hegel, Henry James, Condorcet, and a mob of other thinkers and public and private personalities will riot and conjoin in amazing thought patterns. The worst and saddest mistake to make in reading Bellow, or in presenting him to a college class, is to take cadenzas of this kind as some sort of showing off, for usually the opposite is true: throughout his career, Bellow has been writing good-natured, human satires about the seductions of the intellect, how we hunger to know so much, and how little good it does in handling the streets of modern America or the big questions about the human condition. At the end of his most celebrated novel, *Herzog,* a compulsive professorial letter-writer, arguer, and last-word-seeker decides to just shut up and not even tell his cleaning lady what to do; other Bellow heroes resort ultimately to one sort of silence or another, yet rarely is it a silence of defeat or of contempt for other human beings. James's old adage, that literature is a celebration of life, is strong throughout the Bellow canon; and *Looking for Mr. Green* has comic dimensions that need to brought out along with a celebration of ordinary experience: that even in the most absurd human jobs and errands and activities, wonderful things can take place.

ARTHUR MILLER

Death of a Salesman gives American family life itself the power to create character—almost as if the play were about the inability of any playwright to invent roles he or she has not already played or watched in the tragedy of family life. The family is both the play and the playwright. And in this play the family prescribes certain roles for each of the four main characters that they continue to reenact in the process of discovering what they are. Students, following Linda's cue, will focus on Willy Loman himself: " 'Attention must be finally paid to such a person.' " Why doesn't Loman accomplish anything? Why does he have such trouble really talking to his sons? Neither of his sons is able to "catch on." How do they all get derailed? Unlike Mary Tyrone or Blanche DuBois, Linda Loman has no identity of her own. Is *Death of a Salesman* realistic in its portrait of Linda? What was her role in Loman's decline? Miller implies that Linda has kept her husband from going to Alaska and "conquering the world"; is she to blame or has she seen inadequacies in her husband that he was unable to recognize in himself? Does she never criticize Loman or want to defend Biff against his father? Who raised these children, anyway? Is the role of American father as provider a myth without basis in fact? Who *does* "provide" in this play? And what is Miller indicting? Capitalism? Family life in general? American fatherhood?

GRACE PALEY

A conversation about Paley can range far: into modern writers and American politics, the status of women in urban cultural and professional contexts, the transformations and development of realist motives as they interconnect in various ways with ideas associated with Modernism and Postmodernism. If you are uneasy about classifying Paley in one clutch or another of contemporary writers (and she resists classification), you might enter this tale as a story about storytelling—not a self-indulgent or self-promoting exercise about individual genius or the supposed magic of fiction but about writers and intended audiences; about whether any mode of narration can achieve simple and profound truth; and about whether all this making of fiction really serves any purpose in a world grown so complex, changeful, and forgetful of the struggles and the rich inner life of the private self. Some of your students have probably been wondering about such issues all term, and Paley can bring those concerns eloquently into the open.

It's a disarming tale that students will probably like very much, as it respects and celebrates creative intentions that in other circumstances are scorned or condescended to: pleasing people whom you love, sharing the heartfelt perception with a father or mother, respecting the life and thoughts of fairly ordinary human beings—people who may not belong in art films but who nonetheless are capable of powerful insight. There is a kinship evident here not only between Paley, Malamud, and Bellow, but also between Paley and American writers at least as far back as Rebecca Harding Davis, and students will help you speculate on those relationships.

Kurt Vonnegut

Vonnegut's vogue may be somewhat diminished; he was *de rigeur* reading among college students in the 1960s, when his simple prose style and his bizarre plots and puppetlike characterizations were seen as refusals of a clumsily elaborate tradition in American fiction, a fiction as hard to penetrate and as irrelevant as most other social and artistic traditions were seen to be in those times.

This speech by Vonnegut is an effective introduction to the Vonnegut style, and specifically to his attempts to adapt an American humor tradition, exemplified most handsomely in the speeches and sketches of Mark Twain, to outrageous realities in the modern condition. You might open by making note of the impossibility and absurdity of the actual situation of the speech: a talk about the evils of nuclear weapons, delivered to a liberal New York audience, is literally preaching to the choir. These people have heard it all before, been scared, or numbed, by the accounts of the devastation and long-range consequences of atomic warfare. How is anyone to reach them and how is anyone to say anything about this subject that would not be a waste of time? Vonnegut veers outward from the immediate subject, however, to muse about many other human brutalities, old and new. What ultimately proves to be the intention and subject of his talk? What familiar strategies from the American humor and satire traditions does he make use of in this presentation?

James Baldwin

Going to Meet the Man is an imaginative leap as well as a political risk: an African American writer exploring, from the inside, the mind of a Southern white racist. Furthermore, brutal as he is, Jesse is not portrayed without a measure of sympathy: Baldwin presents him as the victim of an upbringing in a deep, inescapable culture of race hatred, culminating in a lynching that, for all the talk around him and *from* him about the nonhumanity of black people, terrifies him and awakens in him a human empathy that he seems to be spending the rest of his life trying to suppress. The small-town world that Baldwin creates is rich and intense; and sexuality, racist dogmas, direct firsthand experience, and deep, almost wordless anxiety and guilt seem to contend in the consciousness of this protagonist. Nonetheless, we now read in an era when writers and directors are regularly chided for straying too far from home territory and for presuming to imagine the psychological life of someone from the other gender or from a different race or culture. Does Baldwin succeed at this difficult and dangerous artistic feat? Is a bold act of understanding like this, published in the very midst of the civil rights struggle of the 1960s, an important political or moral act or a gesture that resonates beyond the usual reach of imaginative fiction?

FLANNERY O'CONNOR

In *Good Country People* Mrs. Hopewell says, " 'Everybody is different. . . . It takes all kinds to make the world,' " but she doesn't really mean it. She would prefer that all the world, and especially her daughter, be "good country people" like herself. What would it mean for Hulga to take her mother as her model? Contrast the two sets of mothers and daughters depicted in the story. What are Hulga's "crimes"? What makes her unforgivably "different" to her mother? What is Hulga looking for in Manley Pointer? What does she find? Look at the mother-child imagery of Pointer's "seduction." What do Manley and Mrs. Hopewell have in common? As unlikely as it might have seemed, Hulga has chosen as a love object a person who both infantilizes her and tries to idealize her—someone whose psychological connection with her resembles her mother's own. And what is the story's final betrayal? Is it possible for Hula to escape being her mother's daughter?

GORE VIDAL

This is early work by Vidal, and you might want to caution students against assuming that the simple, confessional style of this short story is indicative of Vidal's subsequent and longer works, the urbane, witty, iconoclastic, history inspired novels that have brought him popular success, Hollywood connections, and celebrity as a kind of latter-day Oscar Wilde. It might also be a good idea to caution against reading this story as an unmediated personal and confessional account. Simply written, it has the ring of a fable, an archetypal story about a kind of coming-of-age. But how does it reverse the usual direction and flow of such tales? Is it about a passage from innocence into experience, or is it in some sense about a move in the opposite direction, a growth from fantasized, "innocent" brutality and cruelty into a sensitive, compassionate, maturity, necessarily private because in the schoolboy world of patrician America, becoming a man meant becoming something very different?

URSULA K. LE GUIN

Students who have been moving through the fiction chronologically, worrying over the symbolic dimensions or pretensions of various writers before this point, may panic when they get to this story; so it's a very good idea to try to relax them and suggest that *Schrödinger's Cat* may be a tale about *not* knowing rather than a story with all sorts of concealed profundities. Le Guin is writing about a paradox that shadows the life not only of the writer interested in science, science fiction, and fantasy but of any sentient person who tries to understand worldly experience: that there are powerful and seductive theories out there that are imaginatively almost ungraspable or that threaten to overthrow or render absurd any attempt to make sense of our own situation. The story is in some ways "about" quantum physics, a body of thought that most of us outside that discipline do not understand at any level beyond the superficial. The story is about that puzzlement, about what can happen to our imaginative life when we try to grasp the principles of uncertainty, of the inherent instability or contingency of what (for several centuries) we had taken (again, perhaps without much real understanding) as the fixed laws by which the universe operates.

Nonetheless, this story (as well as the other Le Guin selection, *She Unnames Them*) seems lighthearted, playful: this is not a portentous allegory, but something like a giddy hallucination or reverie of a sort that an informed modern consciousness might undergo in a hypnagogic state or a daydream. You might ask students to toy with the first long paragraph—what's going on there? What is the tone? What kinds of expectations are set up in this moment? What kinds of expectations and readerly habits do we need to drop to move on into the story? If students seem tense, draw them into a recognition that they deal with surrealism, crazy visual situations, and narrative discontinuities all the time: in rock videos and in big-budget films that they queue up to see on summer weekends. If they can surrender their interpretive anxieties in those situations, then why not here? The answer, of course, is that when a narrative moves into a classroom or an anthology, it becomes a "text," and what would beguile and a muse before becomes threatening now. That's an idea very much worth developing, in regard to Le Guin and many other "texts" that you have been encountering this semester.

PAULE MARSHALL

Marshall's *Reena* is about several different kinds of isolating conditions: being a single professional woman in America, being black, having Caribbean roots, and living in a borough of New York. The narrative has a remarkable arrangement, with the narrator maintaining a Cather-like reserve, withholding judgment and generalization, and the main character talking at length and eloquently about herself and life as she has seen it. Part of the connection between them, the teller and the hearer, has to do with a shared loneliness, a failure to find lasting love. This is a powerful theme in works by Morrison and Walker as well: so powerful that controversies have broken out from time to time about whether America's prominent black women writers are somehow unjust in portraying men in their culture or revealing problems and discords that should not be made public in this way, in imaginative fiction that can be read widely, and perhaps predominantly, outside that culture.

What are the major themes of the story? Is Reena heroic in some way, a casualty of the American urban black experience, or a victim of some kind of modern dislocation that is presented here as transcending culture and race? Does the story seem an act of sharing, celebrating the commonality we may have in feeling lost and having to create value as we move along through life? Or does the story emphasize the essential privacy and specialness of the experience of being black and a woman in the modern United States?

DONALD BARTHELME

Before you launch into Barthelme, it might be a good idea to prepare students to be puzzled and encourage them *not* to feel frustrated if they get lost in *A Manual for Sons* and lose track of any intention or controlling idea of this story, sketch, or whatever it is. Times change: Barthelme's heyday was during the period of happenings, put-ons, and general resistance against notions that logic, literary and artistic conventions, official analyses and histories, and other attempts to guide cultural conduct or individual thought were really worth anyone's time. This selection may keep its freshness if it is looked at first as a freewheeling satire: the how-to books and the "marriage and family" and "parenting" guidebooks take up enormous space in American commercial bookstores; and a substantial literary industry runs on the faith that the printed word can help anyone through the messiest and most personal problems pertaining to relationships with other human beings.

The title of Barthleme's mock-instructions suggests to us that this guidebook industry is the satiric target, but what else is satirized here? The cultural identity that we accept as parents and children? Deadpan, supposedly detached and *in*human descriptions of human behavior? The rituals of cultural anthropology? The idea that any personality, with its melange of habit, intellect, emotion, and general unpredictability can be caught in any sequence of observations and words? Does Barthleme's longish narrative go anywhere? Or does the length itself become part of the satire and contribute to the comic effect?

TONI MORRISON

You may find that your students have previous experience with Morrison, because *Sula* and *Song of Solomon* have become regulars in advanced high-school courses and freshman English sections. It is likely, however, that they haven't previously read a work as concise as this by Morrison. For at least twenty years her work has defied easy categorization; so rather than begin with possible connections between this story and American Realism and Naturalism, you might ask what other narratives *Recitatif* reminds them of—other works by Morrison or works by other fiction writers, dramatists, or screenwriters. The tale has many kin in contemporary American literature: after all, it is a story of two women, formerly childhood friends, who meet by chance and struggle to rediscover some key memories, evade some other ones, and find grounds for intimacy and empathy despite the effects of time and personal experience. There are stories and films in profusion that cover such ground, but rarely in this way and with the themes that Morrison emphasizes here.

Twyla and Roberta don't struggle to impose meaning on life, but rather to find meaning within their personal experience, to accept and engage with the realities that have overwhelmed them since childhood and to discover, as Twyla puts it, "How to believe what had to be believed." Circumstances change and they change again: the late sixties culture gives way to the materialism of the seventies and eighties, and each of these people is carried along and to some extent transformed. Can students see any connection between that general theme and Twyla's emphasis on food and her interest in matching up "the right people with the right food"? Why does she stay at the demonstration, carrying her sign, even when the disorder of the group has made her own placard meaningless? Words seem to fail her, and cultural correlatives (like Jimi Hendrix) keep changing, and people not only shift social classes but shift values and attitudes along with those classes. But is this a pessimistic story? Or do identity and friendship show themselves as transcendent somehow, undamaged in their essence by change? And why is the story called *Recitatif*, which, as the headnote observes, is a narrative that is sung in a free-form way? Is there a suggestion, implicit in this title, that the music of experience is more important than wordy, prosy explications?

JOHN UPDIKE

Updike will be well known to you not only for his best-selling novels and respected short stories but also for his enormous literacy and accomplishments as a critic of art, film, poetry, fiction, and American culture. The challenge in teaching one short work by him lies in conveying the range of cultural experience that can make itself felt within a fairly conventional-looking tale of middle-class trouble. To show how this story might stand apart from a legion of tales about "middleness," separations, divorce, and the failure of love, why not start from the beginning and end and work toward the middle? Turn to the last paragraphs and talk a little about the risks inherent in closing a story with a question like *"Why?"* Can a story about a middle-class family bear the weight of a question like that? What does the young boy mean by that question, and what does his father hear in it? This is a breakthrough moment, but a breakthrough from what kind of confinements? Turn to the opening pages, then, and look at two passages: one of descriptive narrative and one of human speech. What kinds of details does Updike pack into his opening paragraph, and *why*? What kinds of language—what vocabularies—are Joan and Richard using when they speak to each other? What are the effects of those word choices? If this is a couple encumbered, and perhaps undone, by the bric-a-brac of ordinary routine, acquisitions, and professional aspirations, are they encumbered also by a baggage of English words? If your students have read Wharton's *Souls Belated*, ask them to review that story with an ear for the words that are used there in tense, important conversations—and then to speculate on ways in which American realists, bygone and contemporary, understand language as central to the fabric of reality.

AMIRI BARAKA (LEROI JONES)

The headnote to this selection describes Baraka's connections to the Greenwich Village literary scene of the fifties and sixties, an experience that, as an African American, he both gained from and eventually resisted. His relationship with experimental writers and writing in those decades was complex, and *Dutchman* might be read as a commentary on that that strange, unpredictable mix of intimacy, exploitation, and hostility that, as a black artist among white artists and literary camp followers, he experienced firsthand. However, some of the continuing power of the play is that it looks at many more dimensions of urban and interracial experience than just the literary. Quick, false pretenses of mutual understanding, racial stereotyping, hostility lurking just below the relative quiet and businesslike onrush of New York life—they are all here, and they suggest strong connections to the tradition of literary naturalism.

To engage with this play, students might want to start with its cadenza passage, the long burst of eloquence from Clay just before Lula stabs him and the others in the subway car throw his body off the train. Is this mere street-talk brutality, or does the language and cadence of Clay's rage have its literary kin and comparisons? Baraka is a poet as well as a dramatist, and his personal artistic rebellion is an informed and thoughtful one. Have students read a few selections of Ginsberg's *Howl*, or other high intensity poetry from the Beats, and see if there isn't a resemblance there—a resemblance that can help locate *Dutchman* in a particular period of American letters and set it apart from the work of Baraka's contemporaries.

N. SCOTT MOMADAY

In the selections from *The Way to Rainy Mountain*, Momaday interweaves a Kiowa past to which he is connected by his bicultural memory, family, and tradition and a Native American literary future (or "renaissance," in the terms of critics) that recreates in words a culture that exists only "tenuously," in memory. It proves to be Stanford-educated Momaday's thorough acculturation in what his nineteenth-century predecessors would have called "white" or "government" education as well as his command of the English language that makes both possible at once: the preservation of the past and a vision of a future for Native Americans. Unlike most of the Native American texts included in *NAAL*, Momaday's is not transcribed from a non-English language or from an oral performance—although he collects Kiowa tales and myths, with his father as translator—and he is writing simultaneously to native peoples and Euro-Americans. He is also writing for himself, and for others like himself who want to hold onto a Native American heritage. This can include students, even white students, in the American literature classroom.

In some ways, *The Way to Rainy Mountain* becomes a "final exam" of the new Native American materials in *NAAL*, a way of testing students' knowledge and integration of their earlier readings. For understanding the form of the poem requires at least some acquaintance with American Indian myths and history. The poem begins with Momaday's contemporary rendition of the Kiowa myth of creation—an emergence myth, like that of the Pima *Story of the Creation* included in Volume 1. He traces the migration of the Kiowas and the legends they make, such as the legend of Tai-me, and their relation to other gods in the sky; he gives his grandmother, Aho, a position of reverence and a godlike voice from Kiowa history; he relates the development and loss of the Sun Dance ritual, what his grandmother remembers as "deicide"; he works through (with his father's help in translation) a series of Kiowa myths, counterpointed (or as if in "encounter" with) other voices—a voice of family and cultural history, and a third personal voice of reflections on his place in the schemes of history and myth; and he ends with a poem, *Rainy Mountain Cemetery*, which conveys his own vision. The Native American poet in the late 1960s has been to the mountain, an Indian Moses, and has brought back his vision of "the early sun," on the mountain that "burns and shines," in an image of a new dawn approaching "upon the shadow that your name defines"—an unmarked dark stone that must serve as the marker for the beautiful woman buried in an unmarked grave near his grandmother's house, for all of the unmarked dead Kiowas, for the end of Kiowa culture itself. It is as if, for Momaday, the end of the Sun Dance ritual—like the end of the Ghost Dance religion (both of which occurred in 1890)—required a new vision a century later, and the Native American poet writes a version of the *Messiah Letter*, one that combines myth, song, and rituals of ceremonial prayer.

GERALD VIZENOR

Written with humor and reserve, Vizenor's story is in some ways about words and about living in two different cultures, in which the relationship between language and identity is entirely different. Vizenor portrays reservation life as a world of near silence, where words are spoken rather than written or read, and where utterance has great importance and sometimes mystical power. To go into the outside world, however, is to enter a gale of talk and print, where people "talk and talk" like the blond anthropology student, and where everything is analyzed verbally. Even the "sovereign tribal blank books" sold by mail order from an abandoned car transmogrify once they enter the white world: schooled in Samuel Beckett and the supposed eloquence of empty pages, professors do critiques of the books and teach them in California classrooms.

The comedy here is broad, but it may touch on an abiding predicament of being a Native American *and* a writer, a member of a group that understands the power of silences and not saying, and the practitioner of an art that believes in saying endlessly. The paradox is real: language itself, any language, can get in the way of true expression and the culturally based inner life. Students will know the stereotype of the silent Indian all too well; he appears in forms ranging from Tonto through Kesey's Chief Bromden. This story can open some new perspectives, not only on cultures that favor reticence and silence but on the transcultural problems inherent in seeking always to penetrate the unsayable with torrents of words.

Stephen Dixon

The headnote to Dixon draws attention to the cultural moment in which he situates himself as a writer: a resemblance between his work and Beckett's, and Dixon's association with both phenomenology and the so-called literature of exhaustion. However, some of your students may want to affirm (as they may have affirmed in other highly theorized literary periods) that a work of imaginative literature has to do more than demonstrate an esoteric and possibly transient literary or philosophical doctrine. To look for the life and originality in Dixon, you might consider pushing beyond the proffered guidance and considering how he compares to other writers who have put such heavy emphasis on dialogue and so little stress on interior monologue or careful, overt analysis of family relationships and other ordinary human situations. Dixon's analogues in American literature run back at least as far as Norris and Stephen Crane and the other naturalists, and come forward through Hemingway, Vonnegut, and Mamet. In such company, how does Dixon establish an individual voice and perspective?

Clarence Major

Major's career is described in the headnote as influenced by some of the same forces and motives that shaped Dixon's work; the great difference is that Major is African American with blue-collar experience, whereas Dixon comes from a comfortable New York white professional background. They have both been regarded as cutting-edge writers; but are the same issues at stake for both of them in regard to the representation of Postmodern realities, their personal ethnic and cultural experiences, and the establishment of new voices and literary forms? If you encourage your students to start a conversation about such matters, you might want to take care to ensure that it doesn't deteriorate into a debate about who is more hip than who. The more interesting and fruitful question is if, and how, ethnicity and personal circumstances can move experimental writers in different directions, no matter what allegiances they might have in common, to certain prevailing and abstract principles having to do with narrative and literary aesthetics.

Thomas Pynchon

The short story *Entropy* includes some classic Pynchon themes and strategies: the high-intensity anxiety about nearly everything in human experience, from worldly human foibles to frightening laws of physics and uncrackable conundrums in epistemology. We also have the fast-moving, sometimes eloquent, but essentially flat characters orating and tearing about in the foreground: if asked for analogues, and encouraged to be free-wheeling, some of your students will suggest similarities with the Simpsons, other dark-toned comics by Matt Groening and Berke Breathed, and some of the more bizarre Hollywood dystopic comedies. Pynchon has been around long enough and has been popular enough to have had his admirers and imitators in television and film.

After students recognize that Pynchon operates on certain wavelengths familiar to them from popular culture, you might ask what he adapts from conventions of narrative and what he resists. For instance, it's a common-place assumption that good stories run on characterization; that personages presented to us should be compelling somehow, or complex; and that what they do and how they fare should matter to the reader. Is that true for this Pynchon story? If it doesn't play by the conventional rules, then what does it do instead to hold the reader's attention. To approach the question from a different side: it's often (and rather gloomily) observed that Henry Adams's law of acceleration has proved true for human culture, that sheer speed and change have caused us to blur distinctions that used to be respected, and that motion and metamorphosis have taken the place of substance in art, in letters, in the self. Is that a Pynchon theme? In other words, does this tale seem to be a symptom of such a problem, a commentary on that problem, or somehow both?

JOANNA RUSS

A story like *When It Changed* has the ring of an old *Twilight Zone* episode, a short what-if reverie or a quick visit to a world where everything is backward or different from our own. Science fiction has its rituals, its rules, and a vast accumulated stock of stories; and part of the challenge for a science fiction writer is to achieve originality and meaning when so many clever ideas have already been contrived and exploited by other writers. Students will have lots of pop-culture experience to compare this with: they have seen futuristic dystopias on the screen and have narratives (of various qualities) that take the battle of the sexes to outer space or ask what things would be like if men or women were not around. Let them loose with this tale to test its originality and thoughtfulness, not compared to other *NAAL* materials but compared to that plethora of speculative fiction in which they are amazingly literate.

RAYMOND CARVER

The headnote points out that when he died in 1988, Carver's work was widely admired and imitated in academic circles; but since critical attention has focused on Carver as a refuser of many narrative conventions and a practitioner of a "stripped down" minimalist sort of realism, students may wonder what is going on here beyond a gesture of resistance against other kinds of fiction that were in favor in the seventies when Carver began to publish his collections. Your class is not likely to be interested in a transient and parochial dispute, and the challenge may be to open up *Cathedral* as a story that does take chances and that affirms the validity of engaging with the world imaginatively.

Since Carver is usually classified as a latter-day realist, students may be reluctant to see any symbolic dimensions to the key action in the story: the rediscovery of the majesty of a cathedral, not by seeing but by moving the hands and feeling. A little nudging of the story to bring out those dimensions will open up the possibility that even a work as austere as this can resonate in this way and can be about the recovery of the capacity for wonder, even in times of disbelief. The magic, if we can call it that, may lie in how we perceive and how we refresh our own ways of examining the world.

Toni Cade Bambara

You can expect that your students will come to Bambara with other African American writers and stories in mind: there's a good chance that some of them will have read James Baldwin's *Sonny's Blues,* Toni Morrison's *Sula,* Zora Neale Hurston's *Their Eyes Were Watching God,* or other works favored in high-school classes and entry-level college courses as glimpses into modern African American experience and experimental literary forms. An opening question, therefore, about the form of *Medley* could bring out generalizations (half-remembered from some other context) about resemblances between this tale and the forms and improvisations of modern jazz. An observation like that can be helpful, but it can also beg some important questions having to do with the Realist tradition and certain basic expectations and practices in storytelling. To be absolutely true to life as we know it, true to the meanderings, cadences, and interludes of ordinary experience can be to tell no "story" at all. Analogues from the world of music may not answer the question: does *Medley* go anywhere or say anything?

If students find that problem interesting, then a good way to proceed might be to start with a specific, limited passage and work outward. *Medley* is in some ways a story about telling stories, and there are several moments when Sweet Pea, our narrator, muses on the talents of other people as tellers of tales, and of the worth of any story, told badly or well. The paragraphs about Hector as a "bad storyteller," omitting and blurring the details of his reminiscences from the funeral business, offer much to talk about, especially if some attention is paid to Hector as "an absolute artist on windows," clearing the dirt away so that something, however mundane, can be seen clearly, as if for the first time. To what extent is that the experience of reading *Medley*? If some readers find the pace and direction of the story puzzling or exasperating, are they missing what the story is really about— the commingling of a lot of different experiences (emotional, aesthetic, mundane) in one consciousness and the way that these apparently miscellaneous experiences create one identity and voice?

Maxine Hong Kingston

Kingston's *Trippers and Askers* can work exceptionally well in your class, if you are opening questions about how to create a distinct voice and a coherent identity out of the vast array of experiences in modern American culture. Kingston's thinking about this problem is anything but reductive: she recognizes that the contemporary artist, whatever his or her ethnicity and cultural preferences, constantly engages with high art and pop, the classic and the transient, the subtle and the banal. Wittman may be a Chinese American, but he lives in a vibrant city; and its changefulness, color, and life appeal to him deeply. His problem—funny and perhaps tragic in the same moment—is finding a way to speak, to love, and to be within a culture that both inundates him and marginalizes him. One good place to start might be with the title of the chapter—a phrase from Whitman's *Song of Myself*—and with the resonant pun in Wittman's name: is he a latter-day Walt Whitman also seeking to weave a song of himself out of everything he has seen and experienced as an American? What are the risks to this would-be bard? Part of the suspense in this story lies here, in the risk that Wittman faces of becoming nothing as a result of his trying to say and encompass everything. Is this a noble artistic quest? A mad one? An act of artistic courage? Of cowardice?

The headnote points out a Joycean quality in the narration, reflecting the melange of vocabularies and experiences with which Wittman tries to speak to himself and to create himself as an artist and as a lover: you might ask your students whether this wide-ranging, all-mixing vernacular suggests personal chaos, or the possibility of some kind of resolution, a composite and resilient identity well suited to life and writing in a composite and quick-changing American landscape.

DIANE GLANCY

It is possible that because of previous experience with contemporary writers who address a Native American ethnicity students may be puzzled by Glancy's work, which may seem to violate borders among literary modes and between private experience and publishable art. The most important border crossing—or violation, as some of your students might see it—may involve the moral and political predicament of a Native American writer and the kind of license usually accorded to poets of white ancestry and middle- or upper-class schooling. Glancy doesn't avoid or soft-peddle the paradoxes and problems within contemporary Cherokee and Native American culture; she talks about alcohol abuse and sexism within those communities and mordantly about the pretentiousness she sees among other Native American writers, who "play Indian" (in Scott Momaday's phrase) to awe and profit from a largely white American literary culture. She is particularly tough on "Indian intellectuals" and their "surreal coyote tales" in *Jack Wilson*; and students may want to talk about their own predicament as readers, as they eavesdrop on this open-ended and important quarrel among Native American writers. Who is Glancy implicitly writing to and for? Do we hear her? Or do we *over*hear her? Do your students think that the time is right for such internal conflicts to be explored in the open, i.e., in the bookshops, colleges, and literary journals of mainstream America?

BARRY HANNAH

Any college undergraduate or advanced high-school student will have plenty of experience with narratives of Vietnam, to the extent that these students may want to speculate on the legitimacy, ethics, and authenticity of some of these works. If you are ranging through some of these Volume 2 entries more or less chronologically, you may have already opened questions about relationships between war and imaginative literature: when does high-spirited narration become exploitation? When does empathy become voyeurism? Some students may land hard on the fact revealed in the headnote that Hannah did not serve in Vietnam and that like many other contemporary writers he makes his professional home in a college academic department. The problem is not a trivial one: what credentials do we require, or should we require, of fiction writers, screenwriters, dramatists, and directors who try to engage with a large-scale historical crisis. In regard to Vietnam, one motif that has become standard is a contrast of the knowable "home" world with the surreal or nightmarish world of combat on the other side of the planet. To what extent does Hannah escape that convention or work within it?

ALICE WALKER

Walker's depiction of her mother-daughter bond differs considerably from O'Connor's. While Mrs. Hopewell defines herself and her daughter by listening to the voices of conventional "good country people," the mother who narrates *Everyday Use* listens to her own inner voice and creates her own values. How are Dee and Maggie different? What explains Dee's decision to rename herself Wangero? How do the quilt's values change for her and what do they mean to Maggie and the narrator? What does Walker mean by valuing "everyday use," even though the quilts may be, as Dee claims, "priceless"?

ANNIE DILLARD

Like Thoreau, Dillard writes of nature and of solitude; but *Holy the Firm* and much of her other prose can be read as a friendly quarrel with *Walden* rather than as modern-day homage to it. Dillard's experiment in nonfiction prose is important. And students can enjoy the quickness, austerity, and variety in her prose style; the vast but unpretentious array of knowledge and experience that she brings to the page; and the innovations in the way in which she observes detail in the natural world. Thoreau celebrates his isolation, delights in his solitude, and finds benign purpose and wise design everywhere; Dillard's narrative is aware of others, sometimes even hungry for empathy and companionship, and much more skeptical about whether nature and human experience are suffused by Emerson's "over-soul." As far back as Judith Sargent Murray and coming forward through Fuller, Dickinson, and Jewett, we speculated on the rise of a female aesthetic, a reply or alternative to a strongly male discursive and forensic style. You could return to that speculation, and do some interesting comparisons between a Thoreau paragraph—one of those long ones that opens with, say, hooting owls and arrives at a dismissal of human complainers and doubters—and passages in Dillard in which powerful, sharp-focused perceptions are not rounded up into a grand overview but allowed to gather in a mosaic of speculation. *Is* this a way of quarreling with, modernizing, or feminizing Thoreau or of escaping his shadow altogether? What other American writers resonate in this essay (Whitman? Eliot? Plath?) and how are they accommodated or resisted?

ANN BEATTIE

Beattie's *Weekend* alludes to the film of the same name by Jean-Luc Godard, and what violence takes place in this *New Yorker* story takes place only in the language and as disjunction. Houseplants play a significant role in this story (the contemporary writer's concession to the loss of the external green world?), and Lenore projects and simultaneously contains her own violent fantasies when Beattie writes about her that she "will not offer to hack shoots off her plant for these girls." Otherwise, "nothing happens" in this story; Lenore, the "simple" character, asks Beattie's quintessential contemporary question, "Why do I let *what* go on?" Ask students how they interpret Lenore's statement that she is "simple." What does it mean to be simple in contemporary life? "It is true; she likes simple things." Yet Lenore's life and Beattie's *Weekend* are more complex than that; does the word *simple* for Lenore allow her to defend against noticing the full extent of the lack of communication between her and George? *Weekend* presents a simple world of women, in which women are out of place; all of George's guests are "girls," and living with George without being married offers Lenore only the illusion of choice.

George joins a large list of contemporary characters who drink their way through their fictions; and as George drinks, Beattie shifts to passive voice: "another bottle has been opened." The point of the sentence seems to be that no one knows who has opened the bottle; agency unknown reflects the postmodern dysfunction.

How do students respond to Lenore's last action in the story, as she moves next to George on the couch? Beattie writes that Lenore leans her head on George's shoulder "as if he could protect her from the awful things he has wished into being." Lenore ends by giving George credit for "wishing" the existence of "awful things" in the world. Is this what Beattie means by simple? Does Lenore stay with George because she can attribute to him the agony of not being in touch? Because she can listen to him teach that "there can be too much communication between people" and, therefore, not have to look too closely at herself? Does *simple* mean attributing the state of the contemporary world to some other, human, agency, rather than focusing more clearly on the unknown agency of passive voice?

David Mamet

Students will find Mamet familiar territory for several reasons. Several of his plays and screenplays have been made into successful films, which have been in the video stores for years. *House of Games, Glengarry Glen Ross, The Verdict,* and a number of others were box-office successes—to the extent that the Mamet style of hard-boiled language, laconic conversation, and un-principled, ruthless action have been widely imitated in Hollywood films and television dramas. The proliferation of Mamet imitations, in fact, may cause students to wonder what is special about Mamet.

If you have been doing a chronological survey of the past century, then your students will recall the heyday of literary Naturalism, and they will have no trouble seeing a relationship between Mamet's work and selec-tions from Dreiser and Stephen Crane. You may want to have a freewheel-ing conversation about whether the usual dates assigned to Naturalism (c. 1890–c. 1920) make sense at all, if Naturalism went to the movies and entered pop literature and culture rather than gave way to other literary movements. You can also return to the dilemma raised by Norris: that a nat-uralistic narrative or drama isn't a breakthrough from art into truth but a mode that is stylized in a variety of different ways.

Have two students read, with some conviction, a page or two of dialogue from this play, and see if they hear the odd cadences of a classic Mamet ex-change—the repetitions, the little rituals that sometimes make his suppos-edly realistic characters seem to speak like creatures from some other planet. This will lead into broader speculations about whether the literary arts can ever, in any mode, represent things as they really are and human behavior as we really know it.

You can open some long-lasting perceptions if you come at this Mamet play comparatively—as a colder, more cynical reprise of Miller's *Death of a Salesman* or as a modernization of the themes in *Babbitt* or even *The Great Gatsby.* If you are feeling daring at this point in the course, you might ask about recent films that students have seen, films that seem somehow to bor-row Mamet-type characters, speech patterns, and situations. You may hear about a number of films that you haven't seen, haven't heard of, or simply don't want to see: *Clerks, Chasing Amy, Pulp Fiction, Blue Velvet, The Com-fort of Strangers,* and others that, as the students describe them, might as-tound you. But the conversation will be worthwhile if students become more aware of modern cross-pollinations between the supposedly separate worlds of art and popular culture.

Leslie Marmon Silko

At that point early in *Lullaby* at which Ayah does not want to think about her dead son, she thinks instead "about the weaving and the way her mother had done it." Craft defends against sorrow, for Ayah, and for Silko, who weaves the loss of Pueblo culture into Ayah's lullaby at the end of the story. Yet the promise passed down from generation to generation of Pueblo chil-dren from their mothers has been broken: "We are together always / There never was a time / when this was not so." Ask students to explore thematic similarities between Silko's story and others in the post-1945 section. Like Walker and Beattie, Silko also portrays the family in dissolution; however, Ayah has lost her children to the Bureau of Indian Affairs and to cultural assimilation with white people. It is not possible for her to reclaim them or to restore her sense of family. The loss of the possibility of family affects the relationship between Ayah and Chato; and Chato and many other Native American men in *Lullaby* turn to alcohol to numb their despair. Ayah does not drink; her experience makes the men afraid of her and to look at her "like she was a spider crawling slowly across the room."

Ask students to compare Ayah with the mother in Gertrude Simmons Bonnin's *Impressions of an Indian Childhood* and to compare Bonnin's portrait of the removal of Sioux children from their reservations with Silko's, almost a hundred years later. Ask students to examine the problems in the mother-daughter relationship that Alice Walker portrays in *Everyday Use* when Dee also "emigrates" to another culture.

DENISE CHÁVEZ

Chávez also writes about loss, but she sees in loss some potential for growth, choice, and humor. Although references to Mexican and Chicano culture pervade *The Last of the Menu Girls*—the "half lost melodies" of "Cielito Lindo," the illegal alien Juan Maria the Nose—Rocio Esquibel seems to see her own life as a menu, herself on the verge of making "that awesome leap into myself." When she does begin school and a new life, then has an accident that makes her a patient at Altavista Memorial, she experiences firsthand how rapidly things change: "No one took my menu order. I guess that system had finally died out."

Despite the humor of *The Last of the Menu Girls*, Chávez also hints at some serious questions. Will it be Rocio's and Chávez's goal to expand the choices on the Chicana "menu"? Do "wetbacks and healthy college students" represent the two extremes of possibility for young Mexican Americans or are there other models? If Rocio refuses to nurse the dying, will she find a living Chicano culture to nourish? When she returns to Altavista as a patient, Rocio's sister thinks she has lost part of her nose in the accident. What does link Rocio with Juan Maria the wetback? If Rocio emigrates beyond the world of Altavista Memorial, will she return to her childhood culture only as an alien? Is the Chicana writer who chooses to write in English, and thus becomes accessible in the American literature classroom, a kind of literary "wetback"? Or is she creating a model of assimilation into biculturalism?

SANDRA CISNEROS

A bit like Chávez, Cisneros is crossing borders as a writer: writing in English for an English-speaking audience and writing about a world that is in some ways between worlds, the experience of growing up Hispanic in various places in the United States. She takes risks in other ways, writing from *within* that world and entirely within the consciousness of her protagonist, whose sensory experiences and clipped phrases and clauses can convey (at the outset) a sense that she does not really understand her own cultural situation. As story follows story, however, the voice grows and changes, and the perceptions expand. Ask students to do some comparing of paragraphs in the final story with passages from the opening pages of the selection. How is the growth and change conveyed? What stays constant, conveying some continuity of self? Are these stories nostalgic in some way for the experience of girlhood? As Cisneros presents it, what are the costs and the gains of growing up and coming to terms with your own ethnicity in a world that both is and is not your own?

LOUISE ERDRICH

Erdrich is one of the most widely respected contemporary Native American writers; and this story is packed with incident: violence, natural catastrophe; tense confrontations; and at the center, a woman of mystery. So much is going on here that a reader can go with the flow and drift into an assumption that *Fleur* is an unspooling of personal experience, raw narration, whose only source—for event, character, and form—is Chippewa life in northern Minnesota. Part of the challenge of teaching Erdrich, therefore, is to encourage perceptions that this is a highly literate writer, "literate" not just in Native American lore, history, and contemporary experience but in techniques of modern American fiction, the predominantly white traditions of telling. Cather is here, and Faulkner, and O'Connor, and Hemingway, and many others as well—but to discuss Erdrich's implicit conversation with such other writers is not to present her work as ancillary to this tradition. In looking into Erdrich's originality and understanding how her voice, by building on other voices, becomes strongly her own, you might look at the long card game in the middle of the story, which can seem an extended calm. What is it doing there? What suspense does it create? What mysteries does it raise? What does it suggest about life in this place and the consolations and frustrations of living this way as woman or man? What about the final section of the story, the last paragraph block, which, like some closings in Conrad, seems to suggest that truth disappears under a cloud and that no amount of imagining or telling can ever recover it. If that's so, then what is a story like this for in the modern Native American tradition and in Erdrich's dialogue with her predominantly white audience?

WILLIAM T. VOLLMANN

Students will probably feel that they are in familiar territory with Vollmann, even if they haven't read Pynchon, who helped pioneer this kind of storytelling. The fast forward motion, the "torn-from-today's-headlines" topicality, the disinclination to pause (as Porter might) to offer some meditation about human motives, the implication that action matters more than thinking because the inner life is either irrelevant or hopelessly impenetrable. Students have seen this before in screenplays. And they may enjoy and benefit from a conversation that moves outward from Vollmann, once you have spent a few minutes with specific passages, observing what is there and what isn't. When fiction merges with gonzo journalism and the quick jumps and superficiality of the screenplay or the rock video, what is gained and lost? Is this a legitimate accommodation to, or reflection of, life as we know it? Is this kind of writing contingent somehow or refreshing or remarkable for what it isn't rather than for what it is or contains? Are we in the world of literary fad here, the sensational but finally transient gesture that offers little more than its own contemporaneity?

American Poetry since 1945

You will find the general introduction to this section useful in your own preparation for class. After building the introduction on the work of three generations of poets—postwar, 1960s and 1970s, and 1980s and contemporary—the editor, Patricia Wallace, comments on "the distinctive work of individual writers" who produce dazzling poems apart from major trends. She writes, "The living world of contemporary poetry changes: new poets emerge, and existing poets, previously inaccessible or neglected, make themselves heard." In the interweaving of individual poems and groups of poets who wrote in the context of each other's work, of poetic influence that crosses generations and ethnic boundaries, and of shapes and sizes of poems, the introduction recalls for me the experience of wandering down the spiral ramp inside the Boston Aquarium, or watching the vertical tanks in the Monterey Bay Aquarium.

The anthology section can be seen as such an aquarium, with poems and poets representing the broad array of life and creativity now flourishing as American verse. We may continue to associate some of these poets with particular "schools"—Vanderbilt, Black Mountain, Iowa, the confessionals, the Beats, the neo-formalists. We should bear in mind, however, that relationships among these various writers and schools often were (and are) stronger, more complex, and less tidy than categorical models of the postwar poetry landscape usually allow. No single class or course can teach undergraduate students all there is to know about "American poetry since 1945," but with the help of the period introduction, the author headnotes, the anthologized selections, and your own personal preferences, you may at least give your students an experience of certain poets in the "tank" and encourage a more extensive reading of any that catch the eye.

As Wallace observes, "Many American poets do not want to think of their work as the fragments of modern literature." The period introduction pulls the fragments together, and you can make use of that introduction as a starting point for class discussion. The editor describes the generalizations as provisional; the classroom can become, in part, a testing ground for what we can say about a body of literature that continues to change shape almost as we read it; and students should know that all professional and academic evaluations of these poets and their poems are tentative and wide open to their participation.

The author headnotes will also help you manage your task of introducing students to the works. When in doubt about your own familiarity with a poet, work from the headnote, asking students to place the editor's statements against individual poems to see whether they agree or disagree with them.

As the period introduction observes, many of these writers learned their craft while majoring in English or studying with professors of English in colleges and universities. Contemporary poets have created their own industry and their own markets for their products by giving readings, teaching in writers workshops, staffing creative writing programs, and writing book reviews and media commentary to promote the readership for their work. Both as students and as consumers, then, we are all likely to encounter living poets; indeed, we may argue that our poets are made and not born, and that for reasons we may not yet understand our poets serve a socially and culturally useful function. Ask students to consider whether as consumers and present or future taxpayers (who fund some of the grants that keep poets alive), they are getting anything that is useful to them. What are, or ought to be, the "uses" of poetry in contemporary American life? If you read *Rip Van Winkle* with students a semester ago, ask them to consider whether the role of the American writer has changed since Washington Irving's time (see the discussion of *Rip Van Winkle* in this Guide). Do we still need poet-chroniclers to tell us where we have been, where we are going? Do we trust them? What might we plausibly want our poets to do for us, that they seem not to be doing at present?

You might begin by asking students to survey the table of contents for the "American Poetry since 1945" section and to identify poets and poems they recognize. Those works can become useful starting points for the rest of us, and you can then ask students to identify the points of contact they may have with the large body of texts included here. You can then work from their responses to the question concerning the "uses" of poetry to help match them up with unfamiliar poets or poems. If someone believes, for example, that poetry should make us aware of the fragility of our environment, you might encourage them to try Gary Snyder or Galway Kinnell. If students want to hear a strong woman's voice, Adrienne Rich or Audre Lorde can be presented. Much as contemporary poets from all ethnic and regional backgrounds may be said to write for all of us, it can seem helpful to students interested in finding common ground to know what regions or ethnic groups individual poets represent.

Or they may identify with biographical details. Does it interest students to know that Robert Duncan never met his mother because she died at his birth, or that Elizabeth Bishop lost both parents by the time she was five and was raised by relatives? That Berryman, Plath, and Sexton committed suicide? That Robert Lowell and Roethke suffered nervous breakdowns? That Niedecker wrote "on the margins" of literary culture? That Robert Hayden was raised by foster parents? That Rich, Lorde, Duncan, Ginsberg, and Merrill made lesbian and gay choices in their personal lives? That in the midst of the civil rights movement, Baraka changed his name from LeRoi Jones? Assign students the task of reading one new poet carefully based on biographical information; then ask them to write briefly, perhaps in class, about their reading experience. To what extent does familiarity or strangeness motivate or influence their choice?

Consider also your own training and tastes in the very diverse world of contemporary American verse. What works for you? Having been taught to close-read individual poems, be sure to pass that skill on—and the all-important balance of confidence and uncertainty that ought to go along with it. What kind of training did you have and what would you like your students to have if they are to continue to be vigilant, sensitive, open-minded readers? Do you want them to be able to move beyond close reading to see larger intersections between poems and poets, between poetry and prose, between poetry and contemporary culture, between poetry and politics? Are any students willing to challenge your own approach with their own? Do any wish to read their own poems to the class?

Because several contemporary poets are new to *NAAL,* we include some teaching notes specifically about their work:

MARY OLIVER

Because Oliver is very much a New England pastoral poet, it makes sense to encourage students to read her with other such poets in mind. The long, rich tradition of Anglo-American pastoral poetry can actually be a burden for the individual modern artist, if the quest is to achieve an original voice among so many other writers, living and dead, working in similar modes. Students who are comfortable with the overt control and polish of Frost, Wilbur, and Bishop may be disconcerted by the apparent freedom and spontaneity of Oliver's lines. If the objective is to distinguish Oliver's voice, you might begin with *The Black Snake* as a rewrite of or response to William Stafford's famous short elegy *Traveling Through the Dark,* which takes similar risks with a similar situation: an animal found dead along a highway, a poet trying to bear witness without descending into bathos or forced consolations. In some ways, Oliver goes farther with her contemplation than Stafford does, saying things that he left unsaid. Does that pattern, of venturing into the unsayable, continue in Oliver's other poems? In *In Blackwater Woods* she opens a pastoral poem with prosody adapted from William Carlos Williams— not a poet known for conspicuous spirituality or for general truths garnered or glimpsed from observations of nature. How does Oliver transform the Williams voice for her own purposes? If we set Oliver's *Landscape* alongside Richard Wilbur's *The Beautiful Changes,* what differences emerge having to do with the way nature is imagined and poems are made?

ROBERT PINSKY

The headnote for Pinsky suggests relationships between his work and poetry of Elizabeth Bishop and William Carlos Williams; but what students may find most striking—and initially daunting—about Pinsky's work is his vast range of associations and allusions, his apparent faith (a bit like Saul Bellow's) that everything is connected somehow to everything else and that finding and relishing those connections is a source of consolation and hope.

A contemplation of an ordinary imported shirt will take you, imaginatively, to the other side of the world, to moments in American history, to other American and British poets—and from George Herbert to "a Black / Lady in South Carolina." Students can enjoy a ride with Pinsky if they first can see that his leaps and allusions are *not* pretentious, not proffered to make students feel ignorant and small and to give professors something to footnote. These poems celebrate the act of thinking and the motions of the informed, experienced mind. A good way to proceed, therefore, might be to ask students to read passages from the long poem *At Pleasure Bay,* aloud and with a bit of feeling, *not* stopping to worry about "Ibo dryads" or "the Soviet northernmost settlements" but thinking instead about a poetry that tries to cross boundaries of culture, time, and private experience. A poem like this finds its subject and its metaphors everywhere, as if the speaker were a bard for the whole human race. Does the poem succeed? Does Pinsky take us places, imaginatively and intellectually, where other contemporary poets fear to go?

LOUISE GLÜCK

If Glück is read in a clear context, as a poet establishing one voice self-consciously amid a chorus of postmodern American verse and within a well-established and academically sanctioned poetry tradition, your students will probably have much better luck with her work than if she is read alone or in a scattering of American poets from the late nineteenth century into the late twentieth. Glück writes very much in the wake of other writers—Dickinson, Williams, Plath, and Lowell—and her strategy of *not* saying, of closing a poem with a mysterious and personal image or an emotion only partially expressed, achieves importance as a kind of resistance, as a rejoinder to the Lowell-Plath way of closing poems with a kind of crushing finality. To be mystical, Glück leaves things open-ended: hers is a kind of agnostic mysticism. Students may want to talk not only about the contextual specialness of her vision, to compare it to contemporaries (Wilbur, Dickey, and Rich would work well for contrasts), but also about whether they find this kind of indeterminate spirituality convincing and sufficient as poetic discourse. In other words, Glück can be a very good mirror to the reading self, as it considers what it requires from contemporary poetry.

JOY HARJO

Because Harjo is a young writer, and a new presence in *NAAL,* students can be encouraged to join us, as teachers, in developing a conversation about her. The first inclination of the class, perhaps, will be to talk about Harjo's prosody as a continuation or modernization of Native American songs and chants of the sort represented in Volume 1. This is a starting point; but you may want to help students see that there is a broad and paradoxical literacy behind and within Harjo's poems and that these poems, though private in their demeanor, speak to a varied audience. She is writing contemporary poetry in English; and like Kingston, Glancy, Bambara, and others, she seeks to achieve a voice reflecting the totality of her experience as an American of mixed racial and cultural heritage.

Some questions to get the conversation moving can center on the variety in Harjo's prosody: do these variations reflect shifts in mood, subject, and voice? There is considerable emphasis on sound—as an effect but also as a subject. Talk, radio noise, church voices, sudden silences—all are accorded special eloquence and spirituality. Does a pattern of hopes and beliefs emerge among these poems? Or do they read as a preamble to a spiritual breakthrough, rather than as a breakthrough in themselves?

CHAPTER 8

Exam Questions and Essay Topics

The teaching notes contain many questions that you may easily adapt as topics for writing. In offering additional exam questions and essay topics, we have tried to suggest further directions for student thinking and research that may or may not emerge directly from class discussion. Similarly, the exam questions and essay topics are also easily adaptable to questions for discussion, either for the class as a whole, or for small groups.

The first and most extensive set of questions addresses literary, historical, and genre connections among authors. These are followed in each period by questions related to the interpretation of individual authors and texts. The second set of questions includes problems and topics that emerge from examining authors within their own literary traditions or that promote comparisons of authors across traditions.

Part I

Volume 1

LITERATURE TO 1620

General Questions

1. Wayne Franklin calls this period a "many-sided process of influence and exchange." He also writes that "much of what was new . . . came about through struggle rather than cooperation." Choose either statement and write a short essay in which you comment on its accuracy by citing references to specific writers and narratives included in the period.

2. The period introduction identifies three purposes of European colonization. Recall at least two of these and cite texts that specifically reflect European purpose.

3. Much of the literature of encounter and discovery rests on inventories of one kind or another. Choose inventories from three of the writers we have read. From the perspective of a postcolonial world, identify their rhetorical purpose for the writer, what they reveal about the author's assumptions about the New World and its inhabitants, and how the language in each inventory serves to enhance the inventory's rhetorical effect.

4. Many European reporters from the Americas rely on lists or inventories to convince their readers of the value of the land. Discuss the idea that inventories become a textual form of mapping. Making specific references to texts, comment on the relationship between landscape or geography and human beings or their artifacts.

5. From a Eurocentric perspective, historians once discussed the "Age of Discovery" but now instead refer to the "era of encounter." The narratives in the Literature to 1620 section may accurately be viewed as narratives of encounter. Choose several significant moments of encounter from different narratives included in this section and identify the different positions from which the Europeans and native peoples view each moment.

6. Research the myths of Doña Marina and Pocahontas and report on their cultural survival in Mexico and North America.

7. Based on several specific accounts or passages in the Literature to 1620 section, reconstruct and interpret several specific moments of encounter between arriving Europeans and indigenous peoples. Viewing the encounters as moments of communication, interpret how each side views the other and what messages they convey in their own behavior. Ground at least part of your reconstruction in a reading of the *Stories of the Beginning of the World*.

Questions on Individual Authors and Works

CHRISTOPHER COLUMBUS

1. Discuss how Columbus's expectations, "thinking that I should not fail to find great cities and towns," reflect the contrast between European ideas of greatness and a more indigenous perspective on "great" civilizations in the New World.

2. Despite the facts that this material is translated and that five hundred years have passed since Columbus's voyages, can you discern a voice here or an imaginable personality? What moments in his letters give you those clues?

BARTOLOMÉ DE LAS CASAS

1. Write an essay about the moral outrage which Casas shows in his *Very Brief Relation*. Where is it grounded? Is it based in a traditional faith? In a kind of secular or nonsectarian humanism? Look at the details that he offers, and the adjectives he uses, and try to describe his moral position.

HERNÁN CORTÉS

1. Throughout the narratives of Cortés, he conveys the sense that the Spaniards believed they could create their own laws in the New World, or conquer with full

moral justification based on what they saw of Aztec culture and life. Are rationalizations explicitly or implicitly offered for the conquest? Where do you see them?

2. Find an account of the conquest of Mexico by a twentieth-century historian and compare that account with Cortés's own version of events.

BERNAL DÍAZ DEL CASTILLO

1. Write an essay about irony in *The True History of the Conquest of New Spain*. Where do you see it? Does it seem intentional or inherent in the enormous events that the *True History* relates?

2. More than other narratives of encounter, Díaz del Castillo's becomes a narrative of witness. Locate and discuss several moments in the narrative where he demonstrates his self-consciousness and responsibility about his role as witness.

ÁLVAR NÚÑEZ CABEZA DE VACA

1. Focusing on the texts of Cabeza de Vaca and Díaz del Castillo, write an essay that brings into focus the lives of native women in North America.

STORIES OF THE BEGINNING OF THE WORLD

1. Locate and read another Native American creation story and discuss it in light of the Iroquois and Pima stories included in *NAAL*.

2. The Judeo-Christian accounts of the beginning of the world place emphasis on a grand design and purpose and on an essential order in the natural world. Do these Native American creation stories put similar importance on the centrality of humankind and on an overall plan? Where do you see similarities and differences in regard to this theme?

ARTHUR BARLOWE AND THOMAS HARRIOT

1. Demonstrate the contrast between Barlowe's and Harriot's descriptions of the native peoples with whom each comes in contact. Locate moments in Harriot in which his intentions seem to be in conflict as he reports of the encounter between the English and Native Americans.

SAMUEL DE CHAMPLAIN

1. Read Champlain's descriptions of American Indian agricultural life. Summarize the portrait of native life (food, customs, housing, activities, manners, relationships between men and women, domestic arrangements) that Champlain offers. What are the indications that Champlain is looking at this culture objectively or empathetically?

2. Evaluate the narrative voice in which Champlain describes the Native Americans he encounters. Can we trust his account? What evidence might you offer to support your position?

JOHN SMITH

1. The settlement of the Middle Atlantic lands is often contrasted with the settlement of Massachusetts Bay: the Virginia colonies are described as secular and

materialistic in their purposes, rather than religious and spiritual. Where are the indications of Smith's motives and aspirations, as he describes the Jamestown area to
an English audience? What specifically excites him about the prospect of colonies
in this region?

2. Near the beginning of the excerpt from *The Third Book,* Smith writes: "Such
actions have ever since the world's beginning been subject to such accidents, and
everything of worth is found full of difficulties, but nothing [is] so difficult as to establish a commonwealth so far remote from men and means and where men's minds
are so untoward as neither do well themselves nor suffer others." What is he talking about? What assumptions is an observation like that based on? Can you think
of modern intercultural misunderstandings that parallel the problem that Smith believes he is facing here?

3. At the end of the excerpt from *The Third Book,* Smith writes, "Thus you may
see what difficulties still crossed any good endeavor; and the good success of the
business being thus oft brought to the very period of destruction." Locate other passages in which Smith expresses his concern for the reputation of the business endeavor in which he is engaged or in which he uses metaphors from the world of work
or business to describe his activities.

NATIVE AMERICAN TRICKSTER TALES

1. Write an essay in which you imagine the intended audience of these tales, and
compare their culture-based expectations to those of a specific storyteller from the
European tradition: Bradford, Mather, Franklin, or some other white writer who
narrates with a specific purpose and to a particular culture.

2. There are comic moments in these tales; but comedy and fear are often closely
connected—sometimes we laugh at things that in some dimension frighten us.
What might be frightening about these tales? What in the cosmology of the Native
American teller and listener might be threatening about the trickster and the trouble he causes?

3. Write an essay about the mingling of total irreverence and the sacred in two
of these narratives. What does the bawdiness accomplish? Is it "comic relief" as in
a Shakespeare drama or other European-style narrative? Or does the mingling of the
irreverent, the scatological, and the sacred work in a different way?

1620–1820

General Questions

1. Describe some of the central principles of Puritan ideology and illustrate their
significance in specific literary works. Choose from among the following: (1) "New
World" consciousness, (2) covenant theology, (3) typology, (4) innate depravity, and
(5) irresistible grace. A few of the writers who address each of these concepts, and
whom you will need to discuss, include (1) Bradford and Bradstreet; (2) Bradford,
Wigglesworth, and Edwards; (3) Bradstreet (in *Here Follows Some Verses upon the
Burning of Our House*), Taylor, Winthrop, and Wigglesworth; (4) Taylor, Wigglesworth, and Edwards; and (5) Winthrop and Edwards.

2. Trace the connection between the Puritan reliance on written covenant, as in
The Mayflower Compact, and their uneasiness, in their literature, regarding personal
vision.

3. Compare Bradford's metaphors to Morton's. Why does Morton resort to a different trove of analogies than Bradford does? What do these choices say about their temperaments and belief systems?

4. Consider secular consequences of Puritan theology: the Puritan's attitudes toward Native Americans, the structure of ordinary life in the Bay Colony; the fear of witches and demonic possession; and attitudes regarding servants, slavery, and infant damnation. Choose two of these topics and explore their treatment in literary works from the period.

5. Identify and discuss literary texts that reveal stresses on Puritanism or that illustrate schisms within Puritan and colonial consciousness.

6. Describe the contrast between the personal and the didactic voice in Puritan and early colonial literature.

7. Identify the literary forms available to colonial American writers. What limited their choice? How did they invent within these forms? What forms would survive for later writers to work within?

8. Cite some differences between Puritan thinking and eighteenth-century deist thinking. Analyze specific literary works that illustrate these differences.

9. Describe the way the concepts of the self and of self-reliance develop and find expression in colonial and early American literature. Identify those specific figures or works that you see as significant and explain their contributions.

10. Trace the power of the written convenant in colonial and early American literature, beginning with *The Mayflower Compact*.

11. Describe the ways in which Benjamin Franklin and Thomas Jefferson reflect the legacy of Puritan thinking.

12. Slavery is an issue of conscience for some colonial and early American writers; from others it brings an ambivalent response. Discuss the issue with references to several specific texts.

Questions on Individual Authors and Works

ANNE BRADSTREET

1. Write a close reading of a single lyric poem. Depending on how much analysis you have already done in class, choose from among the following: *The Prologue, The Flesh and the Spirit, The Author to Her Book, Here Follows Some Verses upon the Burning of Our House,* and *As Weary Pilgrim*.

2. Analyze a related series of stanzas from *Contemplations,* and discuss the relationship between these particular stanzas and the entire poem.

3. Compare and contrast the imagery of *To My Dear and Loving Husband* with Taylor's *Huswifery*. How does the imagery characterize each poet's work?

4. Discuss the extent to which Bradstreet's poetry reflects Puritan thinking. Analyze in particular the way Bradstreet reflects her own spiritual and metaphysical fears in the process of describing an actual event in *Here Follows Some Verses upon the Burning of Our House*.

5. Analyze the contrast between form and feeling in Bradstreet's work. In what ways does she use self-disclosure as a challenge to Puritan theology?

6. Trace imagery of nurturance and provision in Bradstreet's lyrics. Reread with particular attention to maternal and paternal imagery and references.

EDWARD TAYLOR

1. Write a close reading of any of the poems from *Preparatory Meditations*. Identify the central metaphor or series of related metaphors and describe the process by which Taylor converts the terms of each metaphor into an address to the question of his own salvation.

2. If you have experience with the major English Metaphysical Poets, choose an interesting poem by one such poet, and compare its theme and structure to a similar poem of Taylor's.

3. Trace Taylor's use of objects from the natural world or of secular experience in *Upon Wedlock, and Death of Children; Upon a Wasp Chilled with Cold;* or *A Fig for Thee, Oh! Death* and examine the relationship in the poem between earthly life and spiritual salvation.

4. Discuss the extent to which Taylor's poetry reflects specific concepts of Puritan theology.

WILLIAM BYRD

1. Write an essay in which you compare Byrd's *The Secret Diary* with a work by any of his New England contemporaries. What relationship does Byrd assume between the private and the public self? Between the worldly and the religious self? How do those relationships contrast with ones you see in major Puritan writers?

JONATHAN EDWARDS

1. People often see *A Divine and Supernatural Light* as coming from a completely different sensibility than does *Sinners in the Hands of an Angry God.* Do you agree? Do these works resonate with one another in any important way? Do they give indications of coming from the same theology and individual mind?

2. Discuss Edwards's manipulation of biblical language in *Sinners in the Hands of an Angry God.* What specific transformations does he perform? And how does his use of language in the "Application" section of the sermon differ from and comment on the earlier doctrinal section?

3. Jonathan Edwards and Benjamin Franklin were contemporaries. Explain, with specific references to their works and more general comments on their ideas, why this fact might seem startling.

4. Write a brief comparative analysis of form and function in Edward Taylor's poems and Jonathan Edwards's sermons. (Students need to see the way each of these Puritans tried to demonstrate or even "prove," in Edwards's case, spiritual salvation and the way each associates being saved with the authority of being able to find the right language.)

BENJAMIN FRANKLIN

1. Explain why the eighteenth century was called the Age of Experiment and consider the relevance of this term as a description of Franklin's writing.

2. Analyze metaphors that Franklin uses in Poor Richard's maxims in *The Way to Wealth*. Count and categorize the metaphors; summarize your findings. What are their origins, and how does he use them?

3. What is the "religion" Franklin "preaches" to his readers in Father Abraham's speech? How do you explain Franklin's use of religious metaphors in his writing?

4. Discuss several permanent contributions Franklin made to American life, ranging from the practical to the ideological.

5. Choose any single section or aspect of *The Autobiography* as the basis for analysis. Or contrast Franklin's choice of focus in its four parts; consider the significance of his choice to address the book to his son; read closely the letters that begin "Part Two" and comment on their significance to *The Autobiography* as a whole; discuss Franklin's various practical attempts to alter his moral character.

6. Following notes from class discussion, explain the various ways in which Franklin's *Autobiography* may be seen as "self-invention."

JOHN WOOLMAN

1. Compared to Edwards's *Personal Narrative*, Woolman's *Journal* pays more attention to ordinary experience: family, town life, the details of growing up. How does Woolman give importance to these details? Why would they matter to him but not to Edwards?

2. Choose two paragraphs from Woolman and two from Edwards, and compare them for language use and rhetorical style. Like the Puritans, the Society of Friends emphasized simplicity in ordinary life and personal deportment. Why then the differences in vocabularies and sentence structure?

SAMSON OCCOM

1. In his account of his life, Occom writes from two perspectives: as a minister and as a member of a minority group in the larger culture. Do these perspectives come into conflict in his narrative? Where and how?

2. Occom's narrative has come back into print only recently. In your opinion, what is the best way to read it: as a stand-alone work or as a work that converses with or responds to other autobiographies and personal narratives of the eighteenth century? If you feel that the work stands alone, then offer a close reading to support your position. If you see it as part of a conversation, then choose another autobiographical account and show how that dialogue enriches the reading of both authors.

MERCY OTIS WARREN

1. Because of its Roman roots and its familiar forms in England and France, satire was often described in the eighteenth century as a masculine mode—aggressive, combative, boisterous, reductive. In *The Group*, does Warren achieve a voice and

perspective of her own? Does she express her gender somehow, in the course of this attack?

2. What kind of audience does *The Group* seem intended for? Is it a text designed to persuade? To reinforce views that are already strong in the community? Does it confront its audience or does it accommodate the thinking of that audience?

J. HECTOR ST. JOHN DE CRÈVECOEUR

1. Witnessing slavery firsthand leads Crèvecoeur to lament the "strange order of things" in Letter IX from *Letters from an American Farmer*. How does he reconcile his view of slavery, and of the great contrast between lives of plantation owners and slaves in Charles-Town, with his portrait of America as a place where humankind can be renewed.

2. Crèvecoeur was one of the first writers to see America as a place where dogmatic disputes and sectarian violence could be permanently overcome—not by other idea systems but by the landscape and life within it. Describe his argument, the evidence he offers, and the European historical experience that he turns to for contrast.

3. Compare and contrast Woolman's and Crèvecoeur's understanding of "strangers" and their place in "American" society.

WILLIAM BARTRAM

1. Bartram is writing in a time of transition, in regard to viewing the American wilderness and its inhabitants. Very soon, the Romantics would begin to sentimentalize a landscape that had been viewed, in the midst of the eighteenth century as a place of material opportunity or political therapy (Crèvecoeur). In that time of transition, does Bartram achieve a distinct voice as a describer of the American natural scene? Where do you hear that voice most strongly?

2. Compare Bartram's description of the Seminole villages with Champlain's descriptions of Native Americans or with Franklin's commentary on "the Savages of North America." How does Bartram's perspective distinguish itself as a narrative of a firsthand experience by a white man?

JOHN ADAMS AND ABIGAIL ADAMS

1. Compare one of Abigail Adams's letters to John with one of Anne Bradstreet's poems to her husband, "absent upon public employment." How are sentiments expressed and constrained in both of these texts?

2. The letters that pass between John and Abigail Adams offer us a private view of the writing and signing of *The Declaration of Independence*. Examine the hopes these writers have for independence, and describe those that are not explicit within the document itself.

3. Discuss the accuracy of the following statement: "The frequent intrusions of personal feeling into the letters of John and Abigail Adams reflect more than the intersection of personal and public life; they also suggest a change in values that would inspire other political and cultural revolutions at the turn of the nineteenth century."

THOMAS JEFFERSON

1. Analyze specific ways in which *The Declaration of Independence* demonstrates the influence of eighteenth-century thought.

2. Based on class discussion, recapitulate the ways *The Declaration of Independence* uses rhetorical style to achieve its power.

3. Describe the evidence of Franklin's interests in "self-invention" in *The Autobiography* and suggest ways in which Jefferson, with the assistance of Franklin, carries these interests into the political sphere of *The Declaration of Independence*.

4. Write about the rhetorical strategies used in the antislavery grievance from *The Declaration of Independence*, a section that the Continental Congress eliminated from its final version.

5. Edwin Gittelman has called *The Declaration of Independence* a slave narrative, for in the colonial period, the only precedent for such a form was the Indian captivity narrative, represented in *NAAL* by Mary Rowlandson's *Narrative of the Captivity and Restoration*. Explore the extent to which *The Declaration of Independence* may be read as a variant of a captivity narrative.

OLAUDAH EQUIANO

1. Equiano's prose style is powerful. Choose one or two paragraphs and write an essay about the ways in which he structures his sentences, chooses analogies, and selects vocabulary. At times his prose is highly formal, even ornate. Why? How might his style reflect his situation, or predicament, as a writer?

2. For many years, Equiano lived in a paradoxical condition: as a slave in North America and virtually as a free man on his voyages and sojourns abroad. Do you see this strangeness reflected in the personality that he constructs in his *Narrative* and in the language and style with which he writes it?

3. Reread the early chapters of Bradford's *Of Plymouth Plantation* and contrast the portrait of life aboard the *Mayflower* with Equiano's account of life aboard the slave ship. Consider the various meanings different colonial authors attribute to the word *removal*.

TIMOTHY DWIGHT

1. Choose a substantial passage from Dwight, and write about the ways in which eighteenth-century scientific thought and an early Romantic faith in nature and the institutions blend or conflict in his narrative.

2. Like some of the early explorers, Dwight offers us a wealth of facts: inventories, statistics, and details. Does he do so with the same intentions as in those narratives of exploration? Where and how do Dwight's intentions become clear?

PHILIP FRENEAU

1. Although Freneau's *To Sir Toby* is ostensibly about a sugar planter on the island of Jamaica, examine the poem for evidence that Freneau is also writing about southern slavery. Locate references to slavery in his other anthologized poems and

summarize the way slavery, for Freneau, contradicts eighteenth-century principles of reason and human rights.

2. Evaluate the language of Freneau's historical poems in comparison to specific passages in Paine or Jefferson, and speculate on the relative effectiveness of political and poetic voices within the context of American revolution.

PHILLIS WHEATLEY

1. Locate and discuss imagery in Wheatley's poems that directly or indirectly comments on her experience as a freed slave.

2. In the Wheatley poems that address others—students, General Washington, a painter, the earl of Dartmouth—how does Wheatley present herself? How does she create or suggest a personality within the formal context of these poems?

3. Should Wheatley's poetry be considered an important point of origin for African American verse? Why or why not? Can you talk about specific qualities or moments in Wheatley's poems to support your position?

SARAH WENTWORTH MORTON

1. Does Morton succeed in resisting or individualizing the highly formal style that she has inherited from the eighteenth-century English poets and within which she works? Is she able to express her gender or her American identity in her verse? Discuss specific poems and passages in answering this question.

2. Read carefully Morton's poem *The African Chief*. Does the poem achieve or convey empathy for its subject? Or is it what Randall Jarrell called (in another context) "just an excuse for some poetry"? Talk about specific moments in the poem in answering this question.

SUSANNA ROWSON

1. How would you account for the enormous popularity of this novel, which went through two hundred different editions before 1900? Does it successfully merge the sensational with the didactic? Where, for you, are the novel's best moments? Where are its worst ones? Discuss one scene in detail and comment on its dramatic power and its rhetorical strategies.

2. Is *Charlotte* a feminist document? Why or why not? Discuss specific chapters that influence your thinking about this question.

1820–1865

General Questions

1. Why were the American landcape and political experiment especially suited to a flowering and transformation of European-style Romanticism? What problems did artists and writers face in adapting English romantic themes and tropes to the American scene?

2. Discuss the following statement with reference and relevance to specific literary works: the Puritans were typological, the eighteenth-century writers were logical, but the early-nineteenth-century writers were analogical in their way of knowing and expressing what it means to be an American.

3. Discuss changes in the concept of the American self in the early nineteenth century. Locate your discussion within specific works by Sedgwick, Bryant, Emerson, Thoreau, Hawthorne, and Melville.

4. Cite some key differences between early-nineteenth-century writers and their eighteenth-century predecessors. Focus on the concept of self-invention and, in specific literary works, discuss the early-nineteenth-century evolution of this concept.

5. Examine the work of one or more American Romantic and nineteenth-century painters (Thomas Cole, Albert Bierstadt, George Caleb Bingham, George Inness, Frederic Church), and discuss stylistic and thematic similarities that you see, between the work of these painters and literary works of the period.

6. Consider literary portraits of women engaged in heroic struggle or of escaping slaves portrayed as heroic fugitives. Compare and contrast portraits by Stowe, Fuller, Jacobs, and Douglass with Hester Prynne in *The Scarlet Letter* or Thoreau's autobiographical narrator in *Walden*.

7. It may be possible to sort major writers of this period into two groups: those who advance particular doctrines and systems of thought, and those who question or critique those doctrines or who suspect any systematic or totalizing view of the world. Which of these writers seem to you most interested in arriving at some coherent view of experience? Which are temperamentally more interested in questioning such coherent views—and the possibility of seeing the world through what Fitzgerald would later call "a single window"?

8. American realists made different choices of language and genre than did their contemporaries and immediate predecessors. Write about a text by any of the following authors, and explore elements of realism in their work: Stowe, Thorpe, and Davis.

Questions on Individual Authors and Works

WASHINGTON IRVING

1. What kind of relationship does Irving suggest between himself and the stories that he tells? Compare the end of *The Legend of Sleepy Hollow* to the end of Rowson's *Charlotte*, and write an essay about the different ways in which these stories are offered to the American public. Why do you think Irving takes the stance that he does?

2. Compare Freneau's and Irving's uses of the historical situation as the subject of imaginative literature.

3. Discuss several different ways in which *Rip Van Winkle* addresses versions of the American Dream.

4. Compare Rip Van Winkle with Franklin's Father Abraham in *The Way to Wealth*. What do the two have in common?

5. *Rip Van Winkle* is an early work that casts the American woman as the cultural villain. Analyze the character of Dame Van Winkle in the story and discuss the significance Irving attributes to her death.

6. What happens if we try reading *The Legend of Sleepy Hollow* as an allegory—about city ways and country ways, about common sense and "education"? Is that

pushing the story too far for the sake of literary analysis? If the story does work as an allegory, in what spirit is it offered?

JAMES FENIMORE COOPER

1. In the Leatherstocking Tales (of which *The Pioneers* is one novel) Cooper is often said to be doing the traditional cultural work of an epic writer: helping a new culture to lay claim to an ancient or dying tradition. Where do you see this under-way in these excerpts?

2. Write an essay about Chapter III (the pigeon massacre) as a critique of Old World and Native American ways of living in a natural context.

THE CHEROKEE MEMORIALS

1. Based primarily on direct references or inferences you can draw from the *Cherokee Memorials,* write an essay in which you describe the Cherokees' particu-lar economic, cultural, and political situation in Georgia at the time of the writing of these *Memorials.* If you consult any historical source(s) to verify your inferences, provide appropriate citations.

2. Summarize the argument or arguments that the *Memorials* urge on members of the Senate and House.

3. What are the rhetorical strategies of the *Memorials?* Why might those strate-gies be especially effective in speaking to a white audience in Washington, D.C.?

CATHERINE MARIA SEDGWICK

1. Compare Sedgwick's prose style to Cooper's. In the evolution of a vernacular suited to portraying ordinary American life, what are the advantages of Sedgwick's strategy? If you compare her portraits of domestic life to Rowson's, what differences become clear?

2. In Sedgwick's work, do we see indications of the inadequacy of literary eras and "ages" (like the Age of Romanticism and the Age of Realism) for classifying and de-scribing individual talents? In what ways might Sedgwick be ahead of her time? In what ways does she seem very much a writer of the early nineteenth century?

WILLIAM CULLEN BRYANT

1. In his essays, Emerson calls for the emergence of an American poetics. Fo-cusing on Bryant's *The Prairies,* describe ways in which Bryant might meet Emer-son's demand. In what ways does Bryant move away from imitating British poetry and address American themes? In what ways does he play by the familiar rules of the epic tradition?

2. Bryant is writing about a wilder and less imaginatively tractable landscape than Wordsworth and Coleridge wrote about in the early years of English Roman-ticism: the woods and prairies were not domesticated and were not haunted by "ghosts" of a kindred race and culture. Describe ways in which this situation proves advantageous to Bryant and difficult for him to work with.

WILLIAM APESS

1. Write an essay in which you explore *An Indian's Looking-Glass for the White Man* as an American work. To what extent does it address familiar American themes? To what extent does the emergence of a Native American literature in the English language coincide with and contribute to the emergence of an indigenous (as distinguished from imitative) American tradition?

2. Compare and contrast Apess's *Indian's Looking-Glass* with Frederick Douglass's *Meaning of July Fourth for the Negro*.

3. William Cullen Bryant wrote his poem *The Prairies* within a year of Apess's *Indian's Looking-Glass*. Read *The Prairies* with Apess's perspective and comment on Bryant's portrait of "the red man" in light of Apess's text.

CAROLINE STANSBURY KIRKLAND

1. Write an essay comparing Kirkland's prose style and treatment of subject matter to Sedgwick's. In what ways do these two writers resist modes of description and narration that you see in Irving and Cooper?

RALPH WALDO EMERSON

1. Discuss what Emerson means in one of the following statements from *Nature*: (1) "The use of natural history is to give us aid in supernatural history. The use of the outer creation, to give us language for the beings and changes of the inward creation" or (2) "A man is a god in ruins. When men are innocent, life shall be longer, and shall pass into the immortal as gently as we awake from dreams."

2. Trace Emerson's thinking, image patterns, and particular forms of expression in one of the poems.

3. Compare an Emerson paragraph with an Edwards paragraph. What are the differences in structure? In argumentation? Does Emerson play by the rules that you were taught in composition classes? If not, then how does Emerson make his own strategy work?

4. Explain why the poet is so important for Emerson, summarizing his argument in *The Poet*. Does his idea of a "poet" have a certain gender? Where do you see indications that it does or does not?

5. Discuss the way Emerson uses analogies. Choose several analogies he creates in *Nature* and explain their significance.

6. Explore any one of the following central concepts in Emerson's work in the context of your reading: the spiritual vision of unity with nature, the significance of language in achieving spiritual vision, basic differences between thinking and writing by means of analogy and by means of discursive logic, the theme of self-reliance, and the significance of self-expression.

7. Explain how Emerson's philosophy, as he expresses it in *Nature*, represents a culmination of what it means to be an American in his time and place.

8. Explore what Emerson says, explicitly or implicitly, about race, class, or gender in American culture, and analyze Emerson's position in light of subsequent

American history and political thought. If you choose to interpret Emerson from within an ideological position, define the terms of that position and analyze the way it distorts at the same time that it illuminates Emerson's work.

NATHANIEL HAWTHORNE

1. Explicate character, theme, language patterns, style, use of point of view, setting, or design in any particular short story or in *The Scarlet Letter*. (The problem with assigning one of these topics, of course, is that you then have to deal with the standard interpretations students are likely to find if they go straight to the library. If you use a version of this question, you might use it in in-class writing where the only book available is *NAAL*.)

2. What are the problems with assigning any of the following classifications to Hawthorne's work: Puritan, anti-Puritan, transcendentalist, antitranscendentalist, romantic, realist? Cite specific works, characters, and passages to frame your answer.

3. Are some Hawthorne stories more fablelike than others? Choose two stories that illustrate your response to this question and write about them.

4. Explain what Melville means by Hawthorne's "blackness" in his essay *Hawthorne and His Mosses* and discuss it with specific reference to any two of the stories in the text (or any three or with reference to specific characters in *The Scarlet Letter*).

5. Explore the moral ambiguity in any given Hawthorne character or work. What does reading *Rappaccini's Daughter* (or *The Minister's Black Veil* or *Young Goodman Brown*) do to the reader's ability to discern "good" and "evil" characters?

6. Consider Hawthorne's presentation of women in his fiction. What attitudes inform his portraits of Beatrice Rappaccini or of Hester Prynne?

7. Consider the relationship between *The Custom-House* and *The Scarlet Letter*. Where does the narrator stand in each work? In what ways might we consider *The Custom-House* an integral part of the longer fiction? Consider the particular use of *The Custom-House* as a way of "explaining" or delaying the fiction: might *The Custom-House* serve as Hawthorne's "black veil" in facing his readers?

8. Given the autobiographical references in *The Custom-House*, consider the possibility that each of the major characters in *The Scarlet Letter* might also be aspects of the narrator's own persona. Discuss ways in which Hester Prynne, Arthur Dimmesdale, Roger Chillingworth, and Pearl complement each other thematically.

9. Given your earlier study of Puritan literature, trace elements of Puritanism in Hawthorne's stories or *The Scarlet Letter* and discuss the extent to which Hawthorne himself embraces or critiques Puritan ideology. (Compare actual Puritans you have studied with Hawthorne's fictional characters: Anne Bradstreet with Hester Prynne; Edward Taylor with Arthur Dimmesdale; Jonathan Edwards with various ministers in Hawthorne, or with the narrator himself.)

10. Locate references to childhood in *The Scarlet Letter* and, focusing on Pearl, discuss Hawthorne's portrait of what it might have been like to be a Puritan child.

11. To lighten up the class a bit, screen a few scenes from the recent Hollywood film *The Scarlet Letter*. Ask students to comment on whether certain big (and un-

intentionally hilarious!) scenes catch the spirit of Hawthorne's novel. Viewers' note: the novel that you know doesn't start until about an hour into the film. The final ten minutes—featuring a big Indian fight, a bit of New Age catharsis by Dimmesdale, and an ending that you won't believe—can be a good place to start a lively conversation and inspire some comparative essays about characterization and major themes.

HENRY WADSWORTH LONGFELLOW

1. Longfellow sought to be a poet for the American people: to inspire his nation, unite it, and help it imagine itself as a coherent culture with a historical legacy. Write about two of his poems in detail and talk about ways in which they make his poetic mission clear.

2. Write an essay comparing *The Slave's Dream* to Morton's *The African Chief*.

EDGAR ALLAN POE

1. Summarize Poe's theory of aesthetics as he expresses it in *The Philosophy of Composition* and discuss his application of that philosophy in *The Raven*. Given Poe's delight in wit and practical jokes, do you think that he means everything that he says in *The Philosophy of Composition?* Are these elements of self-parody in *The Raven?*

2. Explicate a short lyric *(To Helen)* and discuss Poe's creation of a persona.

3. Discuss *The Sleeper, The Raven, Annabel Lee,* and *Ligeia* in light of Poe's statement in *The Philosophy of Composition* that "the death, then, of a beautiful woman is, unquestionably, the most poetical topic in the world—and equally is it beyond doubt that the lips best suited for such topic are those of a bereaved lover."

4. Explain what Poe means by his attempt to achieve "unity of effect," and trace the particular ways he manages this in *Fall of the House of Usher, The Man of the Crowd,* or *The Masque of the Red Death.*

5. Poe almost never writes about American settings or cultural contexts. Why not? Write an essay distinguishing his kind of Romanticism from that of Bryant, Whittier, or Longfellow.

ABRAHAM LINCOLN

1. Lincoln's prose style changed permanently the nature of American public speech. In the American literary tradition, what roots does he draw on and what traditions does he break from? Find passages from earlier public or political prose (Winthrop, Paine, Jefferson, Edwards) to make the comparison clear.

MARGARET FULLER

1. Read Margaret Fuller's *The Great Lawsuit,* published the year before Emerson published *The Poet.* Focusing on comparison with Emerson, discuss Fuller's critique of the masculine assumptions of her generation of intellectuals.

2. At one point in *The Great Lawsuit,* Fuller writes prophetically: "And will not she soon appear? The woman who shall vindicate their birthright for all women; who shall teach them what to claim, and how to use what they obtain?" Why was the

time right for Fuller to expect an appearance "soon" of this new empowered woman? Had literary culture in some ways prepared the way? Had it created obstacles that Fuller's new woman would have to overcome?

3. Write an essay comparing Fuller's expository style to Emerson's or Thoreau's. Where does she draw on Transcendental modes of discourse? Where does she break radically from those modes, and why?

HARRIET BEECHER STOWE

1. Write an essay about Tom, whose fame underwent dramatic changes from the middle of the nineteenth century to the middle of this one. Why might Tom have been an appropriate "hero" for the historical moment in which Stowe created him? Are the other African American characters in *Uncle Tom's Cabin* constructed in similar ways, for similar purposes? How do you account for variations?

2. Write an essay about the whites in *Uncle Tom's Cabin*. Why would this particular array of characters serve Stowe's purposes?

FANNY FERN

1. Compare Fern's rhetorical strategies to those of Fuller, or compare both of them to Emerson. Is Fern implicitly criticizing a style of argument, as well as the subjugation of women? Cite and discuss specific passages in Fern's essays to support your answer.

HARRIET JACOBS

1. Compare and contrast Linda Brent with Hester Prynne in *The Scarlet Letter*. See especially the following quotation from *Incidents*, which equates unwed motherhood with stigma: "My unconscious babe was the ever-present witness of my shame."

2. Write a paper comparing Jacobs and Douglass and based on the following central quotations from each narrative: "Slavery is terrible for men; but it is far more terrible for women" (Jacobs) and "You have seen how a man was made a slave; you shall see how a slave was made a man" (Douglass).

3. Explore the particular obstacles Linda Brent faces and their significance for women at the end of the twentieth century: sexual harassment, poor mothers' legal rights, and difficulties for advancement when faced with responsibilities and care for children.

4. Jacobs ends her narrative "with freedom, not in the usual way, with marriage." Comment on the implication here that freedom matters more to Linda Brent than marriage. To what extent does *Incidents* suggest that the "life story" is different for enslaved women than for free (white) women?

5. Identify the contradictions implied in Dr. Flint's promise to Linda that if she moves into the house he has built for her, he will "make her a lady."

T. B. THORPE

1. Without explaining the humor of *The Big Bear of Arkansas*, can you describe it as a literary experience? Does it seem to be written from within the culture it talks

about, or from the loftier view of an outsider? How well does this narrative stance work? Write an essay offering speculative connections between this early work of Southwestern humor and comic styles in modern America.

HENRY DAVID THOREAU

1. Discuss one of the following statements from *Walden*: (1) "Every morning . . . I got up early and bathed in the pond; that was a religious exercise, and one of the best things which I did"; (2) "I fear chiefly lest my expression may not be *extravagant* enough, may not wander far enough beyond the narrow limits of my daily experience, so as to be adequate to the truth of which I have been convinced."

2. Cite several points of philosophical and stylistic connection and divergence between Emerson's *Nature* and Thoreau's *Walden*.

3. Discuss in detail one point of significant resemblance between Franklin's *Autobiography* and Thoreau's *Walden* and one point of contrast.

4. Explain specific ways in which Thoreau's *Walden* may be considered a "practice" of Emerson's theory. Emerson, whose philosophy influenced Thoreau, wrote that "words are also actions, and actions are a kind of words." Write an essay on *Walden* in which you demonstrate Thoreau's insistence on the truth of this statement or apply the same quotation from Emerson to *Resistance to Civil Government*, paying particular attention to the relationship between self-expression and personal conscience.

5. Explore any of the following central concepts in Thoreau: the spiritual vision of unity with nature, the significance of language in achieving such a vision, the theme of self-reliance, the use of analogy as meditation (perhaps contrasting Thoreau with Edward Taylor), and the significance of self-expression.

FREDERICK DOUGLASS

1. Discuss the extent to which Douglass may be considered a Transcendentalist in his view of human nature and the future of the United States.

2. Compare Douglass's *Narrative* with Franklin's *Autobiography*, narratives about self-creation and about the possibilities open to the individual man or woman.

3. Douglass writes parts of his slave narrative as a series of incidents or adventures. Discuss ways in which those various incidents and adventures are made to cohere.

4. Compare Harriet Jacobs's *Incidents in the Life of a Slave Girl* with Douglass's *Narrative*. Was the model of "heroic fugitive" possible for female slaves? Jacob's *Incidents* depicts the network of relationships within the slave community and between black and white communities. Look for evidence of such a network in Douglass's *Narrative*. What explains Douglass's lack of attention to emotional connections?

5. In his prefatory letter to the *Narrative*, Boston abolitionist Wendell Phillips compares Douglass with the signers of *The Declaration of Independence*: "You, too, publish your declaration of freedom with danger compassing you around." Does the *Narrative* share formal similarities with *The Declaration of Independence* as well as rhetorical ones? Compare Jefferson's characterization of the British king and his itemizing of grievances with the design and structure of Douglass's *Narrative*.

6. Compare and contrast *A Narrative of the Captivity and Restoration of Mrs. Mary Rowlandson* with *Narrative of the Life of Frederick Douglass, an American Slave*. What formal, thematic, and historical continuities exist between these indigenous genres?

7. In *The Meaning of July Fourth for the Negro,* Douglass writes that the reformer's heart "may well beat lighter at the thought that America is young" and that "were the nation older," its "great streams" may dry up, leaving "the sad tale of departed glory." Explain why Douglass takes hope from America's youth, and contrast this expression with the twentieth-century poet Robinson Jeffers's sentiments in *Shine, Perishing Republic*.

8. Trace Douglass's views concerning the role of reform and dissent in the American republic in *The Meaning of July Fourth for the Negro*.

WALT WHITMAN

1. Write an essay in which you describe the place and effect of *Facing West from California's Shores* within the context of *Leaves of Grass [Song of Myself]*.

2. Focusing on the following two quotations, discuss thematic, philosophical, and technical connections between Emerson and Whitman: from *Nature:* "I become a transparent eyeball. I am nothing. I see all"; and from *Preface to Leaves of Grass:* "[the greatest poet] is a seer . . . is individual . . . he is complete in himself. . . . What the eyesight does to the rest he does to the rest." Where does Whitman break with Emerson's practice, if not from Emerson's ideals and theorizing?

3. Compare Emerson's *The Poet* with *Preface to Leaves of Grass*. In what ways does Whitman claim to embody Emerson's idea of the American poet?

4. Choose one of the following quotations from *Leaves of Grass [Song of Myself]* and discuss it by suggesting several ways in which it describes what Whitman is attempting in the poem: (1) "I know I am solid and sound, / To me the converging objects of the universe perpetually flow, / All are written to me, and I must get what the writing means"; (2) "I am an acme of things accomplish'd, and I am an encloser of things to be"; (3) "I know I have the best of time and space, and was never measured and never will be measured."

5. Discuss Whitman's poetry as a culmination in the development of American identity. How does Whitman contribute to the ongoing evolution of self-reliance? Of human freedom? Of concepts of democracy?

6. Write an essay about *Out of the Cradle Endlessly Rocking* and the traditions of the Anglo-American elegy. What rules and expectations does Whitman follow here? Which rules does he break, and how and why?

7. Trace Whitman's various responses to the Civil War throughout the poems anthologized from *Drum-Taps*. Compare and contrast Whitman's war poems with the anthologized lyrics from Melville's *Battle-Pieces*.

8. Do a study of Whitman's use of the catalog as a poetic device. Then illustrate, by means of close analysis, the effects Whitman achieves in a particular catalog from *Leaves of Grass [Song of Myself]* or in the poems *There Was a Child Went Forth* and *The Sleepers*.

9. Alternatively, study and illustrate Whitman's use of parallel construction as a poetic device in the same poems listed in questions.

HERMAN MELVILLE

1. Write an essay about *Benito Cereno* as expressing that "power of blackness" that Melville ascribes to Hawthorne's work. In pursuing that "blackness," what happens to the treatment of black slaves as characters in fiction?

2. Writing about *Benito Cereno*, Newton Arvin noted that "the story is an artistic miscarriage, with moments of undeniable power." Evaluate the fairness of this statement given your own reading of the story.

3. Write an essay about the array of characters on the *Pequod*. Why does Melville give us such a broad range of races, creeds, and personalities?

4. Write about comic moments in *Moby-Dick*. Do the novel's patches of broad humor injure its "seriousness" or allegorical dimensions? Make the darker and more meditative moments more tolerable? Have other sorts of effects?

5. Write an essay about Ishmael as a thinker. How does he move from idea to idea? Is he systematic? Should he be? Why have somebody like him tell most of the story?

6. How well is *Bartleby, the Scrivener* grounded in the actualities of modern-style work? Is the narrator himself a victim of the same misery that may have undone Bartleby? Write an essay about this story not as about "ah, humanity!" but as about the frustrations and balked emotions of the modern urban workplace.

7. Part of what fascinates the reader (and possibly Melville himself) about Bartleby is his inscrutability—and possible banality. Describe various "walls" that Bartleby may be trapped behind and explore ways in which the story's structure or design reinforces the reader's inability to penetrate those walls.

8. Choose any one of the following moments of dialogue in Melville and use it as a prism through which to "read" the work in which it appears: (1) " 'Ah, Bartleby! Ah, humanity!' " (2) " 'Follow your leader.' " (3) " 'God bless Captain Vere!' "

9. If in some ways Billy is Adam or Jesus Christ and Claggart is Satan or the serpent, then is Vere to be understood as Pontius Pilate? What are the limits and complications of reading him that way?

10. Explore the two kinds of justice Melville sets in opposition in *Billy Budd, Sailor*, and discuss the moral, political, and thematic implications of Billy's execution.

EMILY DICKINSON

1. Write an essay comparing Whitman's *A Noiseless Patient Spider* with Dickinson's 1138. How do these two poems reveal differences in the way that these poets engage with experience and in their idea of a poem.

2. Read carefully a group of Dickinson poems with related themes—the natural world, death, traveling, private experience, art and its value—then write an interpretation of one of the poems that includes your expanded understanding of the way Dickinson uses the theme in other poems in the group. Some specific groupings: (1) poems of loss and defeat: 49, 67, 305; (2) poems about ecstasy or vision: 185, 214, 249, 465, 501, 528, 632; (3) poems about solitude: 280, 303, 441, 664, 754, 1099; (4) poems about death: 49, 67, 241, 258, 280, 341, 449, 510, 712, 1078, 1732; (5) poems about madness and suffering: 315, 348, 435, 536; (6) poems about entrapment: 528, 754, 1099; and (7) poems about craft: 441, 448, 505, 1129.

3. Dickinson's poems 130, 328, 348, and 824 all contain images of birds. Trace and analyze the image from poem to poem. Or study one of the following groups of poems and trace the related image pattern: (1) a bee or bees in 130, 214, 216, 348; (2) a fly or flies in 465; (3) butterflies in 214, 341, 1099; and (4) church imagery or biblical references in 130, 216, 258, 1545.

4. Locate images of size, particularly of smallness, in Dickinson's poetry. Working out from 185, trace evidence that Dickinson perceived a relationship between "size" and literary authority. Alternatively, locate images of authority in the world (king, emperor, gentlemen) and contrast these with images Dickinson uses to create her own persona as poet.

5. Many Dickinson poems illustrate change in the consciousness of the poet or speaker. Choose a poem in which this happens and trace the process by which the poem reflects and creates the change.

REBECCA HARDING DAVIS

1. Compare the relationships between Hester and Dimmesdale in *The Scarlet letter* and between Hugh Wolfe and Deborah in *Life in the Iron-Mills.*

2. Recall what Thoreau has to say in *Walden* about the "lives of quiet desperation" most men lead. Might Hugh Wolfe, like Thoreau, have chosen to simplify his life and retreat to a pond outside of town? Compare and contrast the conditions under which Wolfe makes his art with those Thoreau describes.

3. Study Davis's references to Deborah, who is generally depicted as being a "thwarted woman" who leads a "colorless life." Contrast her with the korl woman. Discuss the distance Davis creates between the real and the ideal woman in Wolfe's life.

HARRIET PRESCOTT SPOFFARD

1. Write an essay comparing Spoffard's *Circumstance* to other works in the American gothic tradition: consider works by Poe and Hawthorne especially. Does Spoffard take chances that these earlier writers did not?

Volume 2

1865–1914

General Questions

1. Compare the humor in Clemens's *The Notorious Jumping Frog of Calaveras County,* Harte's *The Outcasts of Poker Flat,* and Freeman's *The Revolt of "Mother."*

2. Writers following the Civil War put irony to new thematic uses. Compare the way in which irony is used in Bierce's *Occurrence at Owl Creek Bridge,* James's *The Jolly Corner,* S. Crane's *The Open Boat,* and Wharton's *The Eyes.*

3. Although frequently grouped together as local-color writers, Bret Harte and Hamlin Garland reflect different concerns in their work than do Sarah Orne Jewett and Mary E. Wilkins Freeman. Examine the use of point of view in a male and a female writer from this group. Does the narrator look at or with the characters?

What characters are excluded from sharing the point of view? What effect does this have on the fiction?

4. Choosing specific characters on which to base your analysis, discuss differences in the portrayal of women characters and women's experience in local-color writers Harte and Garland and regionalist writers Freeman, Jewett, Chopin, and Austin.

5. In each of the following stories, the female character behaves in an unconventional way: Freeman's *A New England Nun*, James's *Daisy Miller*, and Dreiser's *Old Rogaum and His Theresa*. Analyze the female characters in such a way as to explain some of the similarities and differences between regionalism, realism, and naturalism.

6. Despite the fact that this period was the heyday of Realism and Naturalism, many writers continued to use dreams and fantasy as important elements in their work. Discuss Bierce's *Occurrence at Owl Creek Bridge*, Jewett's *A White Heron*, Gilman's *The Yellow Wall-paper*, James's *The Jolly Corner*, and Wovoka's vision of the Messiah, focusing on how the use of dream, vision, or altered perception affects the realism of the fiction.

7. Many late-nineteenth-century writers wrote in response to contemporary social conditions. Present a composite picture of their concerns by discussing the following group of texts: Charlot's *He has filled graves with our bones*, Garland's *Under the Lion's Paw*, and Washington's *The Atlanta Exposition Address*.

8. Discuss one of the following groups of works, with the goal of explaining differences between regionalist, realist, and naturalist writers: (1) Freeman's *A New England Nun*, James's *Daisy Miller*, and Dreiser's *Old Rogaum and His Theresa*; (2) Jewett's *The Foreigner* and S. Crane's *The Blue Hotel*; and (3) Austin's *The Walking Woman*, Howells's *Editha*, and S. Crane's *The Bride Comes to Yellow Sky*.

9. Research literary history of the post-1865 period and find other poets besides Whitman, Dickinson, and S. Crane. Write an essay analyzing individual poems and describing the larger context of work by a white woman such as Lydia Huntley Sigourney or a black woman such as Frances E. W. Harper.

10. Examine political writing by Cochise, Charlot, Washington, and Du Bois in the context of political writing in earlier periods of American literature. Does it share the same form? Does it innovate within the form? Does it combine forms? To what extent does it comment, implicitly or explicitly, on other literary genres of the late nineteenth or early twentieth centuries?

11. Read literary historians (Fred Lewis Pattee, V. L. Parrington, Robert Spillers) for their discussions of local-color and regional writing. Analyze any story in the text by Jewett, Chopin, Freeman, Austin, Chesnutt, Harte, Garland, or Oskison in light of the historical commentary.

12. Research a regional writer from your home state or region. Write an essay analyzing one of the sketches or stories by this writer.

13. Reread Howells's *Novel-Writing and Novel-Reading*, Clemens's *Fenimore Cooper's Literary Offenses*, and James's *The Art of Fiction*, and construct a theory of Realism that accommodates premises in all of these texts.

14. Turn-of-the-century critics used the phrase *new realists* to describe the work of naturalists S. Crane, Dreiser, Norris, and London. Choose a work of fiction by any

of these writers and consider the accuracy of the phrase. Based on your analysis, would you identify Naturalism as a new genre or a derivative one (a "new" Realism)?

15. Whether in anticipation of or in the general climate of Freud's *The Interpretation of Dreams* (1900), sexuality concerns several writers of the 1865–1914 period. Analyze sexual imagery or attitudes toward sexuality in several of the following works: Howells's *Editha*; James's *The Jolly Corner*; Jewett's *A White Heron*; Chopin's *The Awakening, At the 'Cadian Ball,* or *The Storm*; Freeman's *A New England Nun*; and Wharton's *Souls Belated*.

16. Locate and read Mary Austin's introduction to George Cronyn's *The Path on the Rainbow* (1918). Then analyze the imagery of the Native American texts included in the 1865–1914 section, with particular emphasis on the imagery in the songs as a test of Austin's critical theory.

Questions on Individual Authors and Works

SAMUEL L. CLEMENS (MARK TWAIN)

1. Many readers of *Adventures of Huckleberry Finn* consider the ending flawed—Hemingway, for example, said that Clemens "cheated"—while others have praised it. Write an essay about the appropriateness of the novel's ending, focusing on Huck's treatment of Jim and on Huck's moral complicity with Tom.

2. The theme of pretending is one that unifies *Adventures of Huckleberry Finn,* although the word *pretending* takes on several meanings and levels of significance as the novel unfolds. Describe three of these, and illustrate each by analyzing a specific character, scene, or incident from the novel.

3. If one were constructing a list of "classic" American books, *Adventures of Huckleberry Finn* would probably appear on it. Write an essay about ways in which Clemens explores American experience in new ways.

4. Explore the relationship between the possible symbolic importance of the river and the design and structure of the novel.

5. Analyze Clemens's portrait of Jim in light of your reading of Frederick Douglass. Is *Adventures of Huckleberry Finn* in some ways a slave narrative? Does Clemens use the discussion of slavery as a pretext to write about other issues?

6. Explore the novel as a presentation of mid-nineteenth-century attitudes toward children and child rearing.

7. Write an essay about Clemens's humor, focusing on *The Notorious Jumping Frog of Calaveras County* or *Fenimore Cooper's Literary Offenses* and one or two incidents from *Adventures of Huckleberry Finn.*

8. Analyze Huck Finn's language in the opening passages of *Adventures of Huckleberry Finn.* Discuss how Clemens uses Huck's style as a way to construct his character.

9. Analyze evidence of dialect in Huck Finn's speech and compare it with dialects spoken by several other characters in the novel. Compare Clemens's depiction of dialect in general with that of Bret Harte, Joel Chandler Harris, or Sarah Orne Jewett.

10. Analyze Clemens's portrait of Tom Sawyer. Is he model, rival, alter ego, or mirror for Huck? Does he develop in the novel?

11. Analyze Clemens's portrait of Jim. Does he have an independent existence in the novel or does he merely reflect the way others see him? Compare his portrait with portraits of black characters in the Joel Chandler Harris tales or in Charles Chesnutt's *The Goophered Grapevine*.

12. Study the female characters in the novel. What stereotypes does Clemens use? Do any of his female characters transcend stereotype?

W. D. HOWELLS

1. Analyze Howells's *Editha* in terms of his assertions in *Novel-Writing and Novel-Reading* that "the truth which is the only beauty, is truth to human experience," and that "the imagination . . . can absolutely create nothing; it can only compose."

2. Study *Novel-Writing and Novel-Reading* for what it tells us about Howells's attitudes toward gender and class. Consider whether the character Edith reflects those attitudes or the referential experience of late-nineteenth-century women. Contrast Edith with Freeman's character Louisa Ellis in *A New England Nun*.

NATIVE AMERICAN ORATORY

1. Compare and contrast Charlot's critique of Euro-Americans with William Apess's *An Indian's Looking-Glass for the White Man*.

2. Compare Charlot's rhetorical construction of "the white man" with rhetorical constructions of "King George" in *The Declaration of Independence* and "man" in *The Declaration of Sentiments* (in the Appendix to this Guide).

3. Explore and comment on the Christian base of Wovoka's vision and the Ghost Dance religion.

HENRY JAMES

1. Examine Howells's *Novel-Writing and Novel-Reading* and James's *The Art of Fiction* and discuss points of convergence and divergence.

2. In *The Art of Fiction*, James writes, "A novel is in its broadest definition a personal, a direct impression of life." With this quotation as your point of reference, analyze the particular "impression" James is trying to create in *Daisy Miller, The Real Thing*, or *The Beast in the Jungle*.

3. James has often been called a psychological realist who was more interested in the development of consciousness than in portraying character types and social reality. Discuss the extent to which this observation holds true in *Daisy Miller* or *The Beast in the Jungle*.

4. Analyze *The Real Thing* as a story in which James explicitly chooses to define the word *real* and show how James's characterization of the Monarchs evolves a theory of fiction.

5. Although *Daisy Miller* appears to focus on the portrait of Daisy herself, a reader might argue that James's real interest is in Winterbourne. Rethink the events of the story as Daisy herself might have viewed them, and suggest ways in which the author of *A White Heron* or of *A New England Nun* might have differently handled both the story and the portrait of Daisy.

6. Bring together evidence of James's interest in convention and social forms from all the anthologized James stories, and analyze a particular scene from one of them that illustrates James as a minute observer of social reality.

7. James perfected the use of point of view as a narrative device. Choose one incident from *The Beast in the Jungle* and analyze his use of point of view in that story. What does it reveal? What does it conceal? How does it achieve its effectiveness? What is its significance in terms of the story's themes?

8. Write an essay about James as a writer of horror stories. As a realist, what Gothic or horror traditions does he draw on? How does he transform and modernize the idea of evil?

SARAH ORNE JEWETT

1. Compare and contrast Jewett's Sylvy in *A White Heron* with May Bartram of James's *The Beast in the Jungle*.

2. The tree, the hunter, the cow, and the heron all seem to possess mythical significance in *A White Heron*. Choose one to discuss in relationship to Sylvy and explore the way Jewett combines elements of folk or fairy tale and literary realism.

3. Read T. B. Thorpe's *The Big Bear of Arkansas* (in Volume 1). Viewing the Southwest humorists as precursors of the late-nineteenth-century local-color writers, contrast Thorpe's attitude toward the bear hunt with Jewett's attitude toward Sylvy's search for the bird in *A White Heron*. Or imagine *A White Heron* told from the point of view of the young ornithologist and explain why this other story might have been accepted for publication in the sporting magazine of the Southwest humorists, *The Spirit of the Times*.

4. Unlike Clemens, Howells, and James, Jewett did not write essays about writing or reading. Fill in the gap in literary history, using the two anthologized stories as a foundation, and write the essay that wasn't: "How to Tell a Story," by Sarah Orne Jewett. You may also choose to title the essay "Fiction-Writing and Fiction-Reading" or "The Art of Fiction."

5. Research other writers in the regionalist tradition and write about work by Alice Cary, Rose Terry Cooke, Harriet Beecher Stowe (*The Pearl of Orr's Island*), or Mary Austin, all of which are available in paperback texts

KATE CHOPIN

1. Kate Chopin writes in *The Awakening,* "The children appeared before her like antagonists who had overcome her; who had over-powered and sought to drag her into the soul's slavery for the rest of her days." Using this quotation as a springboard, discuss it with respect to Aunt Sally from *Adventures of Huckleberry Finn.*

2. Consider alternative titles for Clemens's and Chopin's novels: "The Awakening of Huckleberry Finn" and "The Adventures of Edna Pontellier." Comment on the incongruity of each of these alternative titles in terms of the novels' designs, themes, and development of the central character.

3. Analyze the character of Mlle. Reisz in *The Awakening* and compare her with Louisa Ellis in Freeman's *A New England Nun*. How does Chopin limit Mlle. Reisz's possibilities and influence on Edna in her novel?

4. Edna Pontellier is caught in the contradictions between the way others see her and the way she sees herself. Identify several moments in which this becomes apparent and show Edna's growing awareness of the contradiction.

5. Count, characterize, and analyze the numerous women of color in *The Awakening*. What does their presence and their treatment in the novel suggest about Edna's (and Chopin's) attitudes toward human development for nonwhite and poor women?

6. Some readers have described Edna's death in *The Awakening* as suicide; others view it as her attempt at self-realization. Argue the relative truth of both interpretations.

7. *The Awakening* contains elements of Regionalism, Realism, and Naturalism. Identify these by choosing exemplary characters or scenes from the novel and basing your distinctions on close analysis.

8. Compare the relationship between Edna Pontellier and Mlle. Reisz in *The Awakening* with the relationship between the narrator and Mrs. Todd in Jewett's *The Foreigner*.

9. In *At the 'Cadian Ball,* Chopin explores the dimensions of sexual power and desire conferred by racial and class status and marked by dialect. Identify the numerous relationships among the characters that can be understood in terms of power dynamics and explicate those dynamics.

10. *The Storm* serves as a sequel or companion story to *At the 'Cadian Ball.* Describe the ways Chopin differently constructs Cajun ('Cadian) masculinity in Bobinot with Creole masculinity in Laballiere and the way she differently constructs sexuality in Cajun Calixta and Creole Clarisse.

MARY E. WILKINS FREEMAN

1. Identify the common theme (or themes) that link *A New England Nun* and Chopin's *The Awakening* and briefly discuss the way each work develops its theme.

2. One central theme in nineteenth-century American literature portrays the individual in conflict with the community. Discuss the specific ways in which Louisa Ellis enacts this conflict.

3. Both *The Revolt of "Mother"* and *A New England Nun* portray women who triumph over the material conditions of their existence. Describe the nature of that triumph and the process by which they achieve it.

4. Examine the use of the window and the barn doors as framing devices in the two anthologized stories. Compare form in Freeman's fiction with form in Howells, James, or Jewett.

5. Compare and contrast Oakhurst in Harte's *The Outcasts of Poker Flat* and Freeman's Adoniram Penn. Do they triumph or are they defeated men?

CHARLES W. CHESNUTT

1. Explore the way in which Chesnutt manipulates point of view in *The Goophered Grapevine* and the effect this has on the story's ending.

2. Read the anthologized "Uncle Remus" stories by Joel Chandler Harris. Compare and contrast Chesnutt's use of the folk tale and the folk narrator with that of Harris.

3. Compare and contrast Irving's use of folk materials early in the nineteenth century with Chesnutt's use of folk materials in *The Goophered Grapevine*.

4. Write an essay about *The Wife of His Youth* as a possible act of resistance by Chesnutt against the relative innocuousness of the "local color" tradition in which he usually worked and with which he was commonly associated. In what ways is this story a critique or confirmation of the idea that place determines identity? What difficult problems does it raise regarding the migration of African Americans to other regions and the establishment of new identities and social orders?

CHARLES ALEXANDER EASTMAN (OHIYESA)

1. Research Elaine Goodale (perhaps by reading *Sister to the Sioux: The Memoirs of Elaine Goodale Eastman*, 1978, edited by Kay Graber) and construct a portrait of the young white women who became missionaries to the American Indians in the West.

2. Calling the adherents of the Ghost Dance religion "prophets of the 'Red Christ,' " Eastman writes about what he calls this religious "craze": "It meant that the last hope of race entity had departed, and my people were groping blindly after spiritual relief in their bewilderment and misery." Set this comment against Captain Sword's account of the Ghost Dance religion and evaluate it in terms of the confusion that becomes evident among "hostiles" and "friendlies" during the Ghost Dance War.

HAMLIN GARLAND

1. Compare and contrast Garland's portrait of the women in *Under the Lion's Paw* with Freeman's in *The Revolt of "Mother."* How does each author present women's ability to confront poverty?

2. Garland's narrator views his characters from the outside. Analyze specific scenes in the story to show how this outsider's view predetermines the reader's understanding of the characters' actions.

3. Are the characters in *Under the Lion's Paw* individuals or types? What would be the advantages or disadvantages of stereotyping in a story with these intentions? Compare the story with Howells's *Editha*. Does the use of types or stereotypes limit the effect of realism?

CHARLOTTE PERKINS GILMAN

1. How does Gilman's Realism differ from that of Howells? Does the narrator of *The Yellow Wall-paper* recognize any correspondence between her own perception and external reality? In what ways does Gilman violate Howells's proscriptions in *Novel-Writing and Novel-Reading*?

2. Consider *The Yellow Wall-paper* as Gilman's portrait of the American woman as writer. What does the story suggest about the literary authority of the woman writer? What obstacles stand in the way of her creation? What is her ultimate work of art?

3. Compare and contrast Gilman's narrator and Chopin's Edna as potential artists. What kinds of perceptions empower them? What stands in their way?

EDITH WHARTON

1. For much of the twentieth century, critics regularly regarded Wharton's short stories as exercises in the mode of Henry James. What are the significant differences between *Souls Belated* and James's *The Jolly Corner* or *The Beast in the Jungle*. Write an essay comparing Wharton and James as prose stylists, and as presenters of interactions between men and women.

2. In *The Eyes*, Wharton tries her hand as a writer of horror stories—and the old adage about horror stories is that to write them well an author has to locate something that he or she genuinely finds frightening. What is the essence of the horror in this tale? Why would this fate frighten a writer who was ostensibly dedicated to the values and intentions of American realism?

MARY AUSTIN

1. A number of fictions by writers in the late nineteenth century are "studies" of women. Compare Austin's *Walking Woman* with other "studies," such as Howells's *Editha* or James's *Daisy Miller*.

2. Austin writes western literature from the perspective of the insider. Compare and contrast her portrait of the West with that of Bret Harte in *The Outcasts of Poker Flat*, Gertrude Simmons Bonnin in *Impressions of an Indian Childhood*, or Stephen Crane in *The Bride Comes to Yellow Sky*.

3. Interpret the narrator's final perception of the Walking Woman at the end of Austin's story. What does she believe she learns from her moments of contact with this woman? How does the Walking Woman confound the stereotypes others hold of a woman's life?

4. Read Austin's introduction to George Cronyn's collection of Indian poetry, *The Path on the Rainbow* (1918). Summarize her perspective on Native American poetry and apply it to the images in the songs and chants included in *NAAL*.

5. Read Austin's fiction that focuses on Native American protagonists, either *The Basket Maker*, from *The Land of Little Rain* (1903), or her play *The Basket Woman* (1904). Analyze her representation of Native American characters in light of the anthologized texts in *NAAL*.

W. E. B. DU BOIS

1. Explore points of conflict between Du Bois and Booker T. Washington, as illustrated in the anthologized selections from both writers. What reality do African American people face, according to Du Bois? Do they inherit it? Can they change it? And in what way is their identity contingent on that reality?

2. In *The Souls of Black Folk*, Du Bois takes a number of political and organizational chances. Describe these experiments in connecting subjects unconventionally and comment on the success that Du Bois has in creating a coherent text and a powerful argument.

FRANK NORRIS

1. By a somewhat roundabout argument, Norris links Naturalism not to Realism but to Romanticism. Write an essay that evaluates this argument. Do you find it profound? Clever? What are its strengths and limitations?

2. What are the inherent limitations or confinements of naturalistic fiction, as Norris describes that mode? Do you find that his description makes sense when you apply it to narratives by naturalistic writers: S. Crane, Freeman, Chopin, Garland?

STEPHEN CRANE

1. Compare *The Open Boat* to *The Blue Hotel* as fables about the human condition. Which one seems to you more like a fable or a lesson? What differences do you see in the way in which irony is presented and handled in each narrative?

2. Despite the apparent irrationality of its characters, *The Blue Hotel* moves logically and inexorably toward its conclusion. Study the evidence of irrationality in the story's portraits of human behavior; then describe the linear progression by which the Swede's initial comment—" 'I suppose there have been a good many men killed in this room' "—comes to control events.

3. In *The Bride Comes to Yellow Sky*, Jack Potter's marriage appears to alter forever Scratchy Wilson's perception of reality. Argue that for Crane marriage itself becomes an external force. Does the story's humor mitigate the oppressiveness of this force?

4. Explore relationships between Crane's poems and his fiction. Does Crane's choice of the lyric poem allow him to develop aspects of his major themes that his fiction does not fully explore? How do his choices in language and form reflect his temperament and prevailing themes?

THEODORE DREISER

1. Describe the portrait of family life that Dreiser presents in *Old Rogaum and His Theresa*. Would it be legitimate to categorize this story as a work in the naturalistic tradition? What are the problems or limitations in doing so?

JOHN M. OSKISON

1. Write a research paper in which you locate *The Problem of Old Harjo* in the history of Christian intervention in the lives of Native Americans in the nineteenth century. Cite evidence from other anthologized texts, including William Apess's *An Indian's Looking-Glass*, Charles Alexander Eastman's *From the Deep Woods to Civilization*, Wovoka's vision, and Gertrude Simmons Bonnin's *Impressions of an Indian Childhood*.

2. Explore Apess's figure of speech, the "Indian's looking-glass," as it applies to *The Problem of Old Harjo*. To what extent does Harjo possess the cunning of the powerless? To what extent is Harjo the powerless character in the story?

NATIVE AMERICAN CHANTS AND SONGS

1. For most students writing about these transcribed oral works, the best strategy might be to read them in a broad context, rather than isolate them from each other or as a group away from the other materials in this volume of *NAAL*. In many cultures, chants and songs have done similar important kinds of cultural work: they can encourage resolve, peace of mind, a sense of group identity, connection with the past and with the divine. They also can provide solace or other sorts of escape from the verbal and psychological turmoil of ordinary life and the moment of order and a con-

solation that can come from saying and hearing the same things again and again. What, then, are the resemblances between some of these chants and nineteenth-century poetry by white Americans? Are some New England poets seeking these same values? When Du Bois turns to the "chants and songs" of African Americans as a focus for his meditations on being black in a predominantly white America, does he search for qualities similar to ones in these Native American texts?

HENRY ADAMS

1. Henry Adams writes in his *Education* that "From earliest childhood the boy was accustomed to feel that, for him, life was double." Explain the significance of Adams's particular kind of "double vision." Compare it with the internal contradiction Edna Pontellier feels in *The Awakening* and the "double-consciousness" of Du Boisean black identity.

2. What happens to Adams's perception of design and order in the universe over the course of his *Education*? How does it happen that "he found himself lying in the Gallery of Machines at the Great Exposition of 1900, his historical neck broken by the sudden irruption of forces totally new"?

3. Explain and comment on the following statement from *The Education*: "Adams began to ponder, asking himself whether he knew of any American artist who had ever insisted on the power of sex, as every classic had always done; but he could think only of Walt Whitman; Bret Harte, as far as the magazines would let him venture; and one or two painters, for the flesh-tones. . . . American art, like the American language and American education, was as far as possible sexless."

4. The anthologized chapters from *The Education* contain much evidence that Adams viewed himself as a transitional figure. Identify several points at which he "broke his life in halves again," and trace his progress from his early sense that the eighteenth century was his companion to his entrance into the twentieth century at the close of Chapter XXV.

5. What, finally, does Adams mean by an "education"? Is he seeking the same kind of experience and wisdom that Emerson or Thoreau sought? Do his expectations determine his self-described "failure"?

6. In American literary culture, trace the sources of Adams's habit of organizing experience into dualities and oppositions. Adams thinks in dialectics. Who else in the American traditions thinks that way? How might this habit of mind predetermine what he sees when he looks at modern technological power?

1914–1945

General Questions

1. At the end of Frost's poem *The Oven Bird*, we find the following lines: "The question that he frames in all but words / Is what to make of a diminished thing." With reference to works by other poets and prose writers, explain how this statement expresses a common theme in twentieth-century American writing.

2. Compare an early-nineteenth-century poem (such as Bryant's *Thanatopsis*, in Volume 1) with an early-twentieth-century poem (Frost's *Directive* or Robinson's *Luke Havergal*). Discuss the way both poems reflect shifts in perspective and in ideas about what constitutes poetry.

3. Choose three twentieth-century works and show how they implicitly respond to the following quotation from Wallace Stevens's *Of Modern Poetry*: "The poem of the mind in the act of finding / What will suffice. It has not always had / To find: the scene was set; it repeated what / Was in the script."

4. Explain the parallel concerns in the following statements: (1) "The poem is a momentary stay against confusion" (Frost, *The Figure a Poem Makes*), (2) "These fragments I have shored against my ruins" (Eliot, *The Waste Land*), and (3) "Poetry is the supreme fiction, madame" (Stevens, *A High-Toned Old Christian Woman*).

5. Examine twentieth-century modernist lyric poems in traditional forms by Robinson, Frost, Millay, Bogan, Parker, McKay, and Moore. How do these poets reconcile traditional forms with twentieth-century themes?

6. Many modernist lyric poems are themselves about poetic form and intention. Compare some of these poems by Frost, Stevens, Williams, Bishop, Wilbur, and Dove.

7. Examine the modern use of traditional metric forms. Analyze what Frost does to and with iambic pentameter in *Desert Places* or how Stevens uses it in *The Idea of Order at Key West*.

8. In the introduction to Marianne Moore in *NAAL*, Nina Baym writes, "Pound worked with the clause, Williams with the line, H. D. with the image, and Stevens and Stein with the word; Moore, unlike these modernist contemporaries, used the entire stanza as the unit of her poetry." In an out-of-class essay, choose poems by each of these writers that will allow you to further explain the distinctions Baym creates in this statement.

9. In British poetry, Robert Browning developed and perfected the dramatic monologue. Find and discuss dramatic monologues by several American modernists. Evaluate their uses of, or variations on, Browning's form.

10. Although American poets have not yet—according to critical consensus—produced an epic poem, several twentieth-century poets have made the attempt. Research features of classical epic poetry and identify epic characteristics in Pound's *The Cantos*, H. D.'s *The Walls Do Not Fall*, Eliot's *Four Quartets*, and H. Crane's *The Bridge*.

11. Locate and read one of the following Modernist poetic statements and then analyze one of the author's anthologized poems in light of what he has written about craft: Frost, *The Figure a Poem Makes* (included in *NAAL*); Stevens, from *The Necessary Angel*; W. C. Williams, *Edgar Allan Poe*; Pound, *A Treatise on Metre* or another essay from *The ABC of Reading*; and H. Crane, *General Aims and Theories*.

12. Compare and contrast the Realism of a twentieth-century story with the Realism of Clemens, Howells, James, or Wharton. Analyze William Faulkner's *Barn Burning* or Ernest Hemingway's *The Snows of Kilimanjaro,* paying particular attention to the twentieth-century writer's innovations in point of view or use of symbolism.

13. In Suzanne Juhasz's framework for twentieth-century women poets (see the discussion of Marianne Moore in Chapter 7 in this Guide), she suggests a progression from Moore to Muriel Rukeyser to Sylvia Plath and Anne Sexton to Adrienne Rich in terms of the particular writer's willingness to write about women's experi-

ence in poetry. Choosing specific poems for your focus, trace this progression and comment on its usefulness as a framework.

14. Although traditionally the period 1914–45 has focused on Modernism, numerous writers during the period wrote political poetry that may have been influenced by Modernism but reflects other artistic intent. Analyze representative poems by Genevieve Taggard, Muriel Rukeyser, Sterling Brown, and Langston Hughes for evidence of political intent in poetry and comment on the relationship between this poetry and what we call Modernism.

15. Although the modernist poets do not explicitly concern themselves with gender, race, or class issues, there are exceptions to this statement. Discuss the relationship between Modernism and gender in H. D., race in Langston Hughes, and class in Muriel Rukeyser.

16. While writers like Pound and Eliot were concerned with tracing the origins of modernist consciousness in classical mythology, other writers were more interested in becoming assimilated into American society. Identify and discuss issues of importance to writers, fictional characters, or lyric voices who concern themselves with issues of immigration and assimilation.

Questions on Individual Authors and Works

BLACK ELK

1. Arnold Krupat (in "The Indian Autobiography: Origins, Type, and Function," *American Literature*, 1981) has written that "to see the Indian autobiography as a ground on which two cultures meet is to see it as the textual equivalent of the 'frontier.' " Write an essay in which you comment on this statement and its significance for understanding *Black Elk Speaks*. In writing your essay, pay particular attention to the way this text challenges the expectations of a white listener or reader.

2. In the second (1961) edition of *Black Elk Speaks*, John Neihardt changed the title page of the text from "as told to John Neihardt" to "as told through John Neihardt." Explain the significance of this change and interpret the relationship it suggests between Neihardt and Black Elk, and between Neihardt and *Black Elk Speaks*.

3. Compare this excerpt from *Black Elk Speaks* with two other American texts: Benjamin Franklin's *The Autobiography* and *Narrative of the Life of Frederick Douglass, an American Slave* (both in Volume 1). Focus on what constitutes a life-transforming moment for Franklin, for Douglass, and for Black Elk.

4. Compare and contrast Gertrude Simmons Bonnin's autobiographical writing and narrative voice with that of Black Elk. Both writers were Sioux; evaluate their respective roles as "holy man" and "teacher," comment on their different experiences with biculturalism, and compare the points at which they break off their autobiographical accounts.

EDGAR LEE MASTERS

1. Where does Masters seem to position himself in regard to the various voices in *Spoon River Anthology*? Does he seem to be among them? Above them? What are the problems that arise when an artist seeks to speak as or for the common man or woman and how does Masters overcome those problems?

2. Write about irony in *Spoon River Anthology*. Does it have the same effects as irony in the works of Stephen Crane? In Edward Arlington Robinson? Do the implications of the dramatic irony change from one poem to the next or over the course of several of these poems?

WILLA CATHER

1. How does *My Ántonia* reflect some of the themes and points of view of earlier regionalist writers such as Jewett and Freeman?

2. Like Garland's *Under the Lion's Paw*, *My Ántonia* is set in the West. Compare and contrast the influence of place in these stories. What mitigating vision does Cather offer, and how does it contrast with Garland's forces of economic despair?

3. Write an essay about Cather's heroine. This is a fairly long novel. Is Ántonia interesting enough to sustain it? At what points in the novel does she show growth and change?

4. Is this novel a work in the naturalistic tradition? The realist tradition? Does Cather achieve some measure of distinction from either or both of these modes? If so, where and how?

AMY LOWELL

1. Pound termed Lowell's poetry "Amygism," perhaps as a way of belittling its value, perhaps to distinguish it from "imagism." Locate early essays by the imagists in *Poetry* magazine (F. S. Flint, "Imagism," and Ezra Pound, "A Few Don'ts by an Imagist," both in the March 1913 issue), Lowell's own anthologies (referred to in the headnote to Lowell), or any other references you can find that clarify the terms *imagism* and *Amygism*. Then compare and contrast Lowell's uses of the image with that of Pound and Williams and evaluate the extent to which Lowell has been stigmatized both for writing as a "woman poet" and for writing about women's beauty.

GERTRUDE STEIN

1. In characterizing her "description of the loving of repetition" in *The Making of Americans*, Stein writes,

Then there will be realised the complete history of every one, the fundamental character of every one, the bottom nature in them, the mixtures in them, the strength and weakness of everything they have inside them, the flavor of them, the meaning in them, the being in them, and then you have a whole history then of each one. Everything then they do in living is clear to the completed understanding, their living, loving, eating, pleasing, smoking, thinking, scolding, drinking, working, dancing, walking, talking, laughing, sleeping, everything in them.

How does this purpose compare to Whitman's?

2. Discuss the linguistic transformations Stein performs on individual sentences in the excerpts from *The Making of Americans* and the experimentation in *Tender Buttons*. Locate similar sentences, identify points of transition in the prose, compile a lexicon, and note the appearance of new and startling words.

3. Sarah Orne Jewett, like Gertrude Stein, lived for many years with a woman (Annie Adams Fields, the widow of Hawthorne's publisher James T. Fields) and

wrote much about relationships between women in her fiction. Reread Jewett's *The Foreigner* and compare and contrast Jewett and Stein in terms of their treatment of relationships between women, their respective conception of mothers, and the extent to which their work expresses differences between Regionalism and Modernism.

ROBERT FROST

1. Analyze the narrator's attitude toward death in *After Apple-Picking* and in *An Old Man's Winter Night*. How does each poem serve as a buffer against mortality and meaninglessness?

2. Analyze one of the following poems to show how Frost's poetic technique itself serves as his own "momentary stay against confusion": *Once by the Pacific*, *Desert Places*, or *Design*.

3. Illustrate how Frost applies the following statement from *The Figure a Poem Makes* to his use of iambic pentameter in *Home Burial*: "The possibilities for tune from the dramatic tones of meaning struck across the rigidity of a limited meter are endless."

4. Analyze Frost's use of the sonnet form in the following poems: *Mowing*, *The Oven Bird*, *Once by the Pacific*, and *Design*.

5. One of the most striking characteristics of Frost's poetry is his creation of a speaking voice. Examine the following poems and analyze the relationship between speaker and hearer: *The Pasture*, and *The Tuft of Flowers*.

6. Examine the image of loss of Paradise, or the Fall, in *Fire and Ice*, *The Oven Bird*, and *After Apple-Picking*.

7. Analyze "*Out, Out—*" in light of the last two lines of *The Oven Bird*.

8. Choose one of the following poems not anthologized in *NAAL* for further close analysis: *A Minor Bird*, *The Investment*, *The Hill Wife*, or *The Cow in Apple-Time*.

9. In *The Gift Outright*, Frost has written a small history of American literature. In the poem, he personifies the American land as female. Trace the imagery of sexual conquest in the poem, and explore what it reveals about Frost's conception of the American poet.

10. *Directive* advises its readers to get lost to find themselves. How does this poem reflect Frost's twentieth-century worldview? What are the relative values of disorientation and reorientation? How does *Directive* offer a modern version of the American dream?

SHERWOOD ANDERSON

1. Do you see modernist concerns in *Winesburg, Ohio*? Or would it make more sense to think of Anderson as a latter-day local-colorist or realist? In answering this question, make specific reference to the selections in *NAAL*.

CARL SANDBURG

1. Sandburg may continue a poetic tradition that begins with Whitman, but does he also draw on experimentation by other poets? The imagists? Robinson? Locate

moments in the Sandburg poems where you see influences from other American poets and talk about how Sandburg blends them.

WALLACE STEVENS

1. One of the most famous lines from Stevens, and one of the most enigmatic, appears in *Sunday Morning:* "Death is the mother of beauty." Summarize the thinking process by which the speaker in this poem transforms Sunday morning from a day of Christian religious observance for the dead into a very different kind of celebration.

2. Closely analyze the sun imagery in stanza VII of *Sunday Morning.* Then write an interpretation of *Gubbinal* that builds on what you have observed.

3. Both *Anecdote of the Jar* and *Study of Two Pears* take as their central focus some inanimate object. Analyze the meaning these two poems share and the syntactic and semantic techniques Stevens uses to create that meaning.

4. Discuss the technical experiment in Stevens's *Thirteen Ways of Looking at a Blackbird.* What is the poem about?

5. *The Idea of Order at Key West* contains two poems or singers: the woman who sings and the poem's speaker. Describe the relationship that exists between them.

6. Compare poems of Robert Frost and Wallace Stevens, focusing on one of the following pairs: Frost's *Desert Places* and Stevens's *The Snow Man* or Frost's *Directive* and Stevens's *A Postcard from the Volcano.* In what ways do Frost and Stevens each contribute to the modernist's ways of knowing the world? (Alternatively, assign Richard Poirier's book on the two poets, *The Way of Knowing,* and ask students to critique his argument with reference to specific anthologized poems.)

7. Examine poems in which you see activities of (1) looking at things or (2) playing musical instruments or singing, and explore the significance of the activity for the writing of poetry in Stevens.

8. Explicate, with references to other poems by Wallace Stevens, the following statement by Professor Eucalyptus in *An Ordinary Evening in New Haven:* " 'The search / For reality is as momentous as / The search for god.' "

ANZIA YEZIERSKA

1. Read another story from Yezierska's collection *Hungry Hearts* and explore her themes of class difference and disillusionment with American promise (as she expresses them in *The Lost "Beautifulness"*).

2. Compare *The Lost "Beautifulness"* with Genevieve Taggard's poems about poor and working-class women. Evaluate their respective concerns, choice of literary genre, and effectiveness as spokes persons for their class.

3. Write an essay based on Hannah Hayyeh's statement "Democracy means that everybody in America is going to be with everybody alike." Choose other works from American literature that either explore or critique this statement.

4. Compare and contrast Hannah Hayyeh with the narrator in Charlotte Perkins Gilman's story *The Yellow Wall-paper.*

WILLIAM CARLOS WILLIAMS

1. At the end of *To Elsie* Williams writes, "No one / to witness / and adjust, no one to drive the car." Describe how he arrives at this image; then comment on how this image addresses Frost's concerns in *The Oven Bird* or *Desert Places* and Stevens's in *A High-Toned Old Christian Woman* or *Of Modern Poetry*.

2. In *A Sort of a Song*, Williams writes, "No ideas / but in things." Write an essay about the anthologized poems that appear to be about things rather than ideas: *The Red Wheelbarrow, Death, Burning the Christmas Greens*. What do these poems achieve?

3. Some of Williams's poems directly or indirectly address the writing of poetry. Discuss what the following poems tell us about his poetic theory: *Portrait of a Lady, Spring and All, The Wind Increases*.

4. Analyze the specific features of Williams's use of language in *To Elsie*.

5. Describe the form Williams invents in *The Ivy Crown*. Discuss the effects this form has on the reader. How does the form contribute to a reader's understanding of the poem?

6. Compare the two Williams poems that derive from paintings by Brueghel: *The Dance* and *Landscape with the Fall of Icarus*. Locate and study these paintings in the library. What relationship does Williams achieve between the visual and the verbal experience? Is it necessary to see the paintings to "see" the poems?

ROBINSON JEFFERS

1. Compare and contrast Jeffers's use of nature in his poems with Frost's. Choose one of the following pairs: *Once by the Pacific* and *Shine, Perishing Republic* or *Birches* and *Hurt Hawks*.

2. In several poems Jeffers takes birds as his central symbol. Closely analyze *Vulture* in the context of his other bird poems, *Hurt Hawks* and *Birds and Fishes*.

3. Unlike most of his contemporaries, Jeffers locates many of his poems in an actual place: the central California coastline. Study his references to Point Lobos, Carmel, and Monterey. Then discuss *Carmel Point*, paying particular attention to the significance of a particular place to his mood and imagination.

MARIANNE MOORE

1. Moore's work resembles that of Wallace Stevens in its interest in ideas. Choose one of the following pairs of poems, focusing on your analysis of Moore, and discuss the resemblance: *The Idea of Order at Key West* and *A Grave* or *Of Modern Poetry* and *Poetry*.

2. Moore experiments with form and line lengths in *The Mind Is an Enchanting Thing*. Analyze this poem, paying close attention to the relationship between form and meaning. How does *O to Be a Dragon* serve as a postscript to such a discussion?

3. Like Jeffers, Moore also writes poems about birds. Compare and contrast *Bird-Witted* with *Hurt Hawks*.

4. Study Moore's work for explicit statements about what poetry is and does. Analyze these statements in light of class discussion and construct a prose version of her poetic theory.

5. Analyze one of the following poems by Moore with the aim of describing the poem's form and demonstrating the relationship between form and meaning in the poem: *To a Snail, Poetry, The Paper Nautilus,* and *Nevertheless.*

EUGENE O'NEILL

1. Discuss what O'Neill's character Edmund calls "faithful realism" in *Long Day's Journey into Night.* Is this play a work of realism in the Howellsian or Jamesian sense? In what way does it extend or transform the concerns of the earlier realists to include twentieth-century concerns?

2. O'Neill suggests that modern life is more difficult for women than for men. Discuss continuities between the predicament of Edna Pontellier in Chopin's *The Awakening* and Mary Tyrone in *Long Day's Journey into Night.*

3. If you have studied early-nineteenth-century American literature, try reading *Long Day's Journey into Night* as the culmination of themes and concerns that have set a direction in American fiction from *Rip Van Winkle* on. What does the play have to say about versions of the American Dream, about individual identity, about self-reliance, about social exclusion, and about the development of consciousness?

T. S. ELIOT

1. Eliot writes, in *Tradition and the Individual Talent,* that the individual personality and emotions of the poet recede in importance and his meaning emerges from his place in cultural tradition. He writes that "no poet . . . has his complete meaning alone." Examine his use of classical allusions in *Sweeney among the Nightingales.* What does a modern reader need to know to understand the allusions and how does that understanding enhance our meaning of the poem?

2. Describe the progression and interconnection of images and themes in *The Waste Land,* locating the central image in each of the five sections of the poem.

3. Eliot himself considered *The Waste Land* to be "a poem in fragments." Explain why this is an appropriate description of the poem, how it addresses Eliot's twentieth-century worldview, and how he attempts to resolve the fragmentation at the end of the poem.

4. Analyze the persona of the speaker in *The Love Song of J. Alfred Prufrock* by examining the way he sees the world.

5. Like Williams, Eliot tried to achieve exactness and compression in creating his visual image. Find *Preludes* in the library and analyze Eliot's use of the image in that poem.

6. Eliot dedicates *The Waste Land* to Ezra Pound, who offered suggestions for revision. Read Pound's *Hugh Selwyn Mauberley,* published just before *The Waste Land,* and locate similarities between the two poems.

CLAUDE McKAY

1. Write an essay in which you discuss ways in which McKay refreshes and personalizes traditional poetic forms. Is it legitimate to call McKay a modernist poet? Why do you think so? Make reference to specific poems in preparing your answer.

KATHERINE ANNE PORTER

1. One of Porter's recurring themes is the alienation or disconnection of the self—particularly of intelligent and independent women—from the rest of the world and a lack of genuine understanding or companionship or trust. Compare the predicament of one of Porter's heroines to that of some other isolated or misunderstood women we have looked at recently: Daisy Miller, May Bartram, Edna, Mrs. Tyrone. Are there differences? Are men, or a male-dominated world, the fundamental cause of the disconnection of Porter's women?

2. Write an essay comparing Porter's prose style and rhetorical strategies to those of Kate Chopin, another southern writer who wrote of women in grim predicaments. What differences to you see in the ways they handle expository prose and begin, pace, and end a narrative?

ZORA NEALE HURSTON

1. Compare Hurston's Janie with Toomer's Fern. Consider especially the development of "conscious life" for each character.

2. When you finish reading *Their Eyes Were Watching God*, discuss Janie's full and overall development as an independent person. Comment further on the relationship between Janie and her listening friend Pheoby. Or trace Hurston's use of folklore through the novel and comment on its significance.

3. One of the commonplaces about American slavery is that slaveholders often separated members of slave families from each other. Analyze the excerpt from *Their Eyes Were Watching God* as Hurston's attempt to heal the lingering impact of separation imposed by slavery and sexism.

GENEVIEVE TAGGARD

1. Locate other poems from the 1930s in the anthology, read Taggard's poems from the 1930s, and explore to what extent this period of national economic depression provided a context for the themes and forms of its poetry.

2. Taggard, unlike Marianne Moore and even Muriel Rukeyser, seems to have no difficulty writing about women's experience. Write an essay about her representations of women's experience.

3. Compare and contrast Taggard's poem *A Middle-aged, Middle-class Woman at Midnight* with Frost's *An Old Man's Winter Night*.

JEAN TOOMER

1. What is the literary analogue in Toomer's *Cane* for Du Bois's "double-consciousness"? How does Toomer evoke "the souls of black folk" in this excerpt from *Cane*?

2. Place Fern herself in the context of other works by American male writers, such as Poe's *Ligeia* or Anderson's *Mother*. How does this tale continue or transform a conversation between American writers and the larger culture, about the valuation of women?

F. SCOTT FITZGERALD

1. In Hemingway's *The Snows of Kilimanjaro,* the narrator/protagonist recalls his friend Julian, a pseudonym for Fitzgerald, and his friend's fascination with the rich. Hemingway writes, "He thought they were a special glamorous race and when he found they weren't it wrecked him just as much as any other thing that wrecked him." Consider Hemingway's description of Fitzgerald as an interpretation of what happens in *Babylon Revisited.*

2. Fitzgerald made an often-quoted remark that "There are no second acts in American lives." Is this a theme in *Babylon Revisited?* If so, how is it developed and made interesting?

3. Compare the opening page of this story to the opening page of a Porter story or Hemingway's *The Snows of Kilimanjaro.* Describe the differences and suggest what they imply about the different ways in which these writers worked as modern artists.

WILLIAM FAULKNER

1. Keep a journal of your thoughts, frustrations, and insights as you read *As I Lay Dying.* In particular, note your use of visual reading skills. Does the novel allow you to develop visualization as a reading technique, and if so, how? Pay close attention to Faulkner's effects on your actual reading process.

2. Often the use of the journey as a plot device in a novel implies character development. Which character(s) develop in *As I Lay Dying?* Analyze the evidence of character development, or lack of it, and discuss how Faulkner's use of character affects interpretation in his novel.

3. Faulkner said that he wrote *As I Lay Dying* from start to finish in six weeks, and that he didn't change a word. While Faulkner was known to exaggerate, he conveys an essential fact about this novel: that he wrote it easily, quickly, and as if it were the product of a single action. Explore the ironies inherent in such a description of the novel's creation. Compare Faulkner's description of how he wrote *As I Lay Dying* with Addie's statement "I would think how words go straight up in a thin line, quick and harmless, and how terribly doing goes along the earth, clinging to it, so that after a while the two lines are too far apart for the same person to straddle from one to the other."

4. Throughout *As I Lay Dying,* Faulkner's characters use measurement and geometry as a way to depict the world, and Faulkner himself created a map of Jefferson County that "located" the Bundrens' journey within the larger world of his fiction. Find the map on the flyleaf of an edition of *Absalom, Absalom!* Consider Faulkner's use of spatial form and spatial relations as a unifying element in *As I Lay Dying.*

5. In class we have discussed *As I Lay Dying* as an epistemology, a set of ways of knowing the world. Explore the idea of the novelist as a carpenter and *As I Lay Dying* as one of the tools—rather than one of the products—of Faulkner's trade.

6. Critics have often commented on Faulkner's use of comedy in *As I Lay Dying*. Think about the various meanings of comedy and evaluate the extent to which *As I Lay Dying* may be considered a comic novel.

7. Examine *As I Lay Dying* from the point of view of family dynamics or social process. Is "Bundren" an identity these family members all share? What is the ontology, the way of being a Bundren? To what extent is Faulkner commenting on the American, especially the southern, family? Evaluate the perspectives with which the outsiders in the novel view the Bundrens. Which is reality? How does Faulkner demonstrate his characters constructing it?

8. Critics often associate Faulkner's portrait of the Snopeses with his perception that the "New South" following Reconstruction had lost its agrarian values. Analyze the particular "Snopesism" in *Barn Burning*.

LANGSTON HUGHES

1. Discuss what Hughes's poetry tells a reader about his theory of poetry.

2. Place Hughes's work in the context of black musical forms invented in Harlem in the early twentieth century. Is black poetry the way Hughes writes it, like jazz, a new genre? What are its characteristics? If "black poetry" is a genre, does Countee Cullen write in it?

3. Hughes's poetry is open to the experiences of women. Analyze *Mother to Son, Madam and Her Madam,* and *Madam's Calling Card* and explore the ways he transforms women's experiences into emblems of African American experience.

4. Would you describe Hughes's poetry as modernist in its themes, use of images, and style? Locate specific points at which you can see Hughes's modernism, and demonstrate it in an essay.

RICHARD WRIGHT

1. Although Wright's work appeared later than that of the poets of the Harlem Renaissance, he reflects some of their concerns. Trace the theme of manhood in poems by Sterling Brown and in Wright's *The Man Who Was Almost a Man*. What do these writers tell us about manhood as an American experience?

2. Compare Richard Wright's story with Zora Neale Hurston's prose. Are these writers exploring race or gender, or both?

AMERICAN PROSE AND DRAMA SINCE 1945

1. The teaching notes for this period include questions that can work either as a stimulus to discussion or as essay topics. You can also ask students to place a story or drama within the context of literary tradition, genre, or theme or to write an essay interpreting a short story or offering a close reading of the dialogue in a scene or a lyric poem. Whatever you decide to do, it is probably a good idea to reassure your students that diversity and vitality—rather than some particular aesthetic, moral perspective, or other hierarchy of value—characterizes the literary scene in the United States since World War II. Here are some questions meant to provoke that kind of independent response.

2. Explore the variety of themes and techniques by which late-twentieth-century writers depict their own life stories. You might include the following works in your discussion: Ralph Ellison, *Invisible Man;* Gore Vidal, *The Robin;* Annie Dillard, *Holy the Firm;* and N. Scott Momaday, *The Way to Rainy Mountain.*

3. Is heroism possible in contemporary society as it is portrayed by our fiction writers? Discuss the possibilities for heroism in the following heroes or antiheroes; Arthur Miller's Willy Loman, Philip Roth's Sheldon Grossbart, Louise Erdrich's Fleur.

4. In their efforts to record and understand the mysteries of life, many contemporary writers show special interest in the grotesque, the inexplicable, or the fantastic. Discuss this dimension of the following works: Eudora Welty's *Petrified Man,* Bernard Malamud's *The Magic Barrel,* Flannery O'Connor's *The Life You Save May Be Your Own* or *Good Country People,* Thomas Pynchon's *Entropy,* and Ursula K. Le Guin's *Schrödinger's Cat.*

5. White middle-class suburban life and marriage become a central subject for several contemporary writers. Discuss the different treatment of this subject in the following works: John Cheever's *The Swimmer,* John Updike's *Separating,* and Ann Beattie's *Weekend.*

6. While contemporary writers no longer take on themselves the responsibility for "defining" what it means to be an American, many continue to reflect on what Norman Mailer once described as "the forces now mounting in America" and "the intensely peculiar American aspect" of contemporary life. Discuss current criticisms or assessments of American life in the following works: Ralph Ellison's *Invisible Man,* Arthur Miller's *Death of a Salesman,* James Baldwin's *Going to Meet the Man,* Ishmael Reed's *The Last Days of Louisiana Red,* and Louise Erdrich's *Fleur.*

7. Betrayal by mothers—or by sisters—is one variation of the exploration of the influence of family on contemporary life. Stella, at the end of *A Streetcar Named Desire,* cries, " 'Oh God, what have I done to my sister?' " Explore relationships between women in (for example) Eudora Welty's *Petrified Man,* T. Williams's *Streetcar,* Flannery O'Connor's *The Life You Save May Be Your Own* and *Good Country People,* Toni Morrison's *Recitatif,* Alice Walker's *Everyday Use,* and Sandra Cisneros's *My Lucy Friend Who Smells Like Corn.*

8. Examine as a group the anthologized stories by these twentieth-century southern writers: Porter, Wolfe, Welty, and O'Connor. Do these writers alter the nineteenth-century concept of regionalism, and if so, how? If not, how do they extend the genre? How are twentieth-century regional writers also modernist writers?

9. Among contemporary writers, perhaps dramatists perceive most clearly the possibility for genuine tragedy in American character and American life. The heroes and antiheroes of fiction seem to disappear, or take on tragic dimensions, in the work of Tennessee Williams, Arthur Miller, Amiri Baraka, and David Mamet. Analyze one of the characters from these plays as a tragic hero, paying particular attention to the way the dramatic form enhances or frustrates such a reading.

10. Is it possible, and useful, to talk about a Native American voice in contemporary poetry and fiction? What would you say are thematic and stylistic characteristics of that voice? If you write about contemporary poets, consider especially Glancy, Harjo, and Ortiz. If you write about prose, consider Silko, Vollman, Vizenor, and Erdrich.

11. Compare and contrast the way Williams constructs Blanche DuBois's southern speech with the way Faulkner, Welty, or O'Connor do for their southern characters in the anthologized stories.

12. A number of contemporary prose writers write about the challenge of writing, of being an artist within their own group or in and for the larger culture. What do these writers have to say about that challenge? What similarities in theme do you see among them? Consider Maxine Hong Kingston, Toni Cade Bambara, Raymond Carver, Ishmael Reed.

13. Read a play by Lillian Hellman (*The Little Foxes, The Children's Hour*), Lorraine Hansberry (*A Raisin in the Sun*), Ntozake Shange (*For Colored Girls Who Have Considered Suicide*), Marsha Norman (*'Night, Mother*), or Wendy Wasserstein (*The Heidi Chronicles*) and compare it with one of the plays in *NAAL*.

14. Locate and read one of O'Neill's earlier "expressionistic" plays written during the 1920s and compare it with *Long Day's Journey into Night*.

15. Find a play, verse drama, or adaptation by a twentieth-century poet or fiction writer and compare it with one of the plays included in *NAAL* and with the poet's or novelist's other work.

16. Read anthologized selections by John Cheever, John Updike, Raymond Carver, Donald Barthelme, and Ann Beattie. Based on these stories, identify formal and thematic features of these stories by writers who have appeared often in *The New Yorker*. Then read a short story published in *The New Yorker* during the past year and evaluate its similarities to these works.

17. One of the central questions for readers of *Black Elk Speaks* involves understanding the meaning of biculturalism. Explore the concept of biculturalism for contemporary Native American writers N. Scott Momaday, Leslie Marmon Silko, Gerald Vizenor, and Louise Erdrich. Alternatively, consider the meaning of cultural assimilation for members of minority groups in America and examine the following works and their treatment of assimilation: Ralph Ellison's *Invisible Man*, Alice Walker's *Everyday Use*, Leslie Marmon Silko's *Lullaby*, and Denise Chávez's *The Last of the Menu Girls*.

18. American playwrights have often used siblings within a family to stand for divisions within the self or for two opposing forces. Consider the relationships between James Jr. and Edmund in *Long Day's Journey into Night*; Blanche and Stella in *A Streetcar Named Desire*; Biff and Happy in *Death of a Salesman*.

AMERICAN POETRY SINCE 1945

1. Test the accuracy of the following statements by and about poets based on your own careful reading of the selections in *NAAL*.

Lorine Niedecker: "Like other experimental American poets, she uses the space of the page to suggest the movement of the eye and mind across a field of experience."

Robert Penn Warren: " 'What poetry most significantly celebrates is the capacity of man to face the deep, dark inwardness of his nature and fate.' "

George Oppen: "Oppen's distinctive measure, with its hesitancies and silences, becomes itself a measure of language's capacity to say with clarity what is real."

Randall Jarrell: "He is master of the heartbreak of everyday and identifies with ordinary forms of loneliness."

Richard Wilbur: " 'The most adequate and convincing poetry is that which accommodates mixed feelings, clashing ideas, and incongruous images.' "

A. R. Ammons: "Ammons has often conducted experiments with poetic forms in
his effort to make his verse responsive to the engaging but evasive particularity
of natural process. This formal inventiveness is part of the appeal of this work."

Denise Levertov: "Her overtly political poems are not often among her best, however; their very explicitness restricts her distinctive strengths as a poet, which
include a feeling for the inexplicable, a language lyrical enough to express wish
and desire, and a capacity for playfulness."

Adrienne Rich: "Our culture, she believes, is 'split at the root' . . . ; art is separated
from politics and the poet's identity as a woman is separated from her art.
Rich's work seeks a language that will expose and integrate these divisions in
the self and in the world."

Gary Snyder: " 'I try to hold both history and wildness in my mind, that my poems
may approach the true measure of things and stand against the unbalance and
ignorance of our time.' Throughout his life Snyder has sought alternatives to
this imbalance."

Sylvia Plath: "Seizing a mythic power, the Plath of the poems transmutes the domestic and the ordinary into the hallucinatory, the utterly strange."

Michael S. Harper: "Harper writes poems to remember and to witness, but at
times the urgency of the content overpowers his form and his language cannot
sustain the urgency the poem asserts."

Simon J. Ortiz: "His sense of contemporary life, especially its absurdities, is acute.
But the America he travels conceals within it an older landscape, one animated
by spirit."

Rita Dove: "The experience of displacement, of what she has called living in 'two
different worlds, seeing things with double vision,' consistently compels this
poet's imagination."

2. Lorine Niedecker and Mary Oliver both present poetry about significant landscapes, poetry that might be called pastoral. Compare the technical or formal features of their attempts to create a spirit of place in their work.

3. Research Charles Olson's theory of poetics; read his manifesto, *Projective
Verse,* from *Human Universe.* Extend your reading of Olson's poetry beyond the
anthologized selections, and then evaluate the accuracy of the following statement: "Like certain techniques of meditation and yoga, Olson's theory seems an
effort to bring mental activity (here, writing) in touch with its instinctive physical origins."

4. Many of Elizabeth Bishop's poems concern themselves with loss and exile, yet
the tone of her poems is often one of reserve, of detached observation. Is such a tone
appropriate to Bishop's themes? Where do you see tone and theme combining (or
contrasting) most effectively in these poems?

5. Robert Hayden, Gwendolyn Brooks, and Rita Dove all wrote sequences of
poems based on life in African American communities. Compare and contrast Hayden's sequence *Elegies for Paradise Valley,* Brooks's anthologized poems from *A
Street in Bronzeville,* and Dove's poems from *Thomas and Beulah.* How do all three
poets make use of the technique of collage? What are their technical and thematic
differences?

6. Write an essay about contemporary American poetry, responding to Randall Jarrell's observation "the gods who had taken away the poet's audience had given him students."

7. What are the oppositions and tensions that energize and shape Robert Lowell's poetry? Do you see resemblances between his worldview and that of Henry Adams or other New England writers? Talk about specific poems that show these structures and conflicts.

8. Almost as if they were poetic "siblings," Denise Levertov, Robert Duncan, and Robert Creeley trace their formative influences to William Carlos Williams and H. D. Choosing representative poems by each of these three, related by their choice of literary models, explore "family" influence. You may choose to trace the influence of Williams or H. D., or you may focus instead on the "sibling" qualities of Levertov, Duncan, and Creeley.

9. A number of American poets seem to favor austerity—short lines, sparse use of metaphor, a stance of cool detachment. Others have favored long lines, lavish use of images and allusions, and overt emotional intensity. Creeley and Jarrell may seem to belong to the former group, Ginsberg, Lowell, and Roethke to the other. Write an essay about two poets who seem to have very different, or even opposite, literary voices. Describe the differences, making specific reference to poems by each writer, and then speculate on possible similarities.

10. Allen Ginsberg's use of long lines was a deliberate experiment for him, the "long clanky statement" that permits "not the way you would *say* it, a thought, but the way you would think it—i.e., we think rapidly in visual images as well as words, and if each successive thought were transcribed in its confusion . . . you get a slightly different prosody than if you were talking slowly." Read *Howl* and other anthologized poems, paying particular attention to Ginsberg's use of the long line.

11. Frank O'Hara wrote about his work, "The poem is at last between two persons instead of two pages." Explore your own sense of audience and connection with O'Hara's poems, then consider whether his statement also applies to other contemporary American poets.

12. Galway Kinnell and Philip Levine have written of Walt Whitman's influence on their work and their influence on each other. Choosing specific poems as the basis for your commentary, examine thematic and formal connections between Kinnell, Levine, and Whitman.

13. John Ashbery is often spoken of as associated with the "language" poets, including Charles Bernstein, Lyn Hejinian, and Michael Palmer. Locate the work of one of these poets and read representative poems in light of Ashbery's work.

14. Many of James Wright's poems depict in detail an actual American landscape. Close read one of Wright's poems and examine the relationship between internal and external "landscape" in his work. Would you call Wright a pastoral poet? Where are his roots and forebears in the American literary tradition?

15. In one of the poetry seminars that Robert Lowell taught at Boston University, both Sylvia Plath and Anne Sexton were students. All three of them knew Richard Wilbur, who also frequented the Boston area in the fifties and sixties. Imagine that some or all of these people have gone out for coffee one night after class and write

a conversation they might have had. What might they have had to say to each other about their work?

16. More than any other contemporary American poet, Adrienne Rich has located and explicated women's lives and their relationships to each other, to their communities, to history. Her poems also reflect her "understanding of change as the expression of will and desire." Write an essay in which you trace the continuum of women's relationships to each other that appear in Rich's poetry and in which you also locate the poems along the timeline of composition dates that Rich provides, examining evidence of what she has termed, in an essay by the same title, *When We Dead Awaken: Writing as Re-Vision.*

17. Consider the appropriateness of Audre Lorde's own phrase to describe her poetry: "a war against the tyrannies of silence."

18. Locate Simon Ortiz within the Native American tradition of literature as represented in *NAAL.* What themes, forms, and images link his work with earlier Native American writers or with contemporaries Leslie Marmon Silko or Louise Erdrich?

19. Explore the themes of Simon Ortiz's poetry: traveling, the power of storytelling, dislocations of American Indian identity, exploitation of the American land.

20. Explore the connections Rita Dove draws between individual moments of her personal history and larger historical forces. Compare and contrast her use of black history with that of other anthologized black women poets: Gwendolyn Brooks and Audre Lorde.

21. All three Latino writers included in *NAAL* intermix Spanish phrases and lines in their work. Choose one or more of the three (Alberto Ríos, Lorna Dee Cervantes, and Denise Chávez), and analyze the effects and effectiveness of the inclusion of Spanish in the work.

22. Like other contemporary American women poets (for example, Adrienne Rich and Rita Dove), Cathy Song writes about family ties and ancestors. Explore the power of family in Song's work.

23. Find examples of the use of traditional poetic or metric forms by post-1945 poets and analyze the relationship between form and meaning. Choose, for example, the following sonnets or near sonnets: Jarrell's *Well Water* or Brooks's *kitchenette building.*

24. The following poems all reflect the autobiography of the poet: Elizabeth Bishop's *In the Waiting Room,* Robert Lowell's *My Last Afternoon with Uncle Devereux Winslow,* Allen Ginsberg's *To Aunt Rose,* James Merrill's *The Broken Home,* Frank O'Hara's *In Memory of My Feelings,* and Sylvia Plath's *Lady Lazarus.* Choose one of these poems for close analysis, locating it in the context of autobiographical poems by other writers.

25. Poems that are addressed to or are about family members tell us a great deal about differences between contemporary poets as well as family relationships in the twentieth century. Explore one of the following groups of poems: (1) mothers: Gwendolyn Brooks's *the mother* and Adrienne Rich's *Snapshots of a Daughter-in-Law;* (2) fathers: Theodore Roethke's *My Papa's Waltz,* John Berryman's *Dream*

Song 384, James Merrill's *The Broken Home,* James Wright's *Autumn Begins in Martins Ferry, Ohio,* Sylvia Plath's *Daddy,* and Li-Young Lee's *The Gift* and *Persimmons;* and (c) sisters: Denise Levertov's *Olga Poems* and Cathy Song's *Lost Sister;* and brothers.

26. Poems addressed to other contemporary poets, living or dead, tell us a great deal about the poet writing the poem and the poet honored by the dedication. Choose any of the following poems for close analysis, working within the context of the anthologized work by the poet to whom the poem is dedicated or addressed: (a) Elizabeth Bishop's *The Armadillo,* for Robert Lowell; (b) Robert Lowell's *Skunk Hour,* for Elizabeth Bishop; and (c) Anne Sexton's *Sylvia's Death,* for Sylvia Plath.

27. Contemporary poets have written about nature in many different ways. Explore some of the variations: does nature become the object of perception and the reason for precision in language? does it serve as the symbolic projection of human emotions and fears? does it provide an alternative world within which the poet can locate a coherent vision? Choose several poems from the following list: Elizabeth Bishop, *The Moose;* James Dickey, *The Heaven of Animals;* A. R. Ammons, *Corsons Inlet;* James Wright, *A Blessing;* and Sylvia Plath, *Blackberrying.*

28. Locate and read statements on poetry by post-1945 poets; then analyze particular poems in light of the poets' statements. Choose, for example, Levertov, "Some Notes on Organic Form," from *Poet in the World;* Snyder, "Poetry and the Primitive," from *Earth House Hold;* Rich, "When We Dead Awaken," from *On Lies, Secrets, and Silence.*

29. Poets often first publish their poems in small books or collections. Find and read one of the following titles, study the order of poems in the collection, and then analyze the poem included in *NAAL* within the context of the other poems with which it was originally published. The titles of the anthologized poems appear in parentheses.

(a) Elizabeth Bishop, *Geography III* ("In the Waiting Room," "The Moose," or "One Art")

(b) Robert Lowell, *Life Studies* ("Memories of West Street and Lepke")

(c) Gwendolyn Brooks, *A Street in Bronzeville* ("kitchenette building" or "a song in the front yard")

(d) James Wright, *The Branch Will Not Break* ("A Blessing")

30. Read the anthologized poems from one of the following connected poem sequences and describe the intertextual connections within the sequences: Gwendolyn Brooks, *A Street in Bronzeville;* John Berryman, *Dream Songs;* Adrienne Rich, *Twenty-One Love Poems;* or Rita Dove, *Thomas and Beulah.* Or extend your reading to include all of the poems in the Brooks, Rich, or Dove sequences and consider them as a single connected work.

31. What do contemporary poets have to say about some of the traditional themes of poetry: love, death, loss, or the passing of time? Choose to analyze two or three poems from one of the following groups:

(a) Love: Lorine Niedecker, [*Well, spring overflows the land*]; Robert Lowell, *Skunk Hour;* Robert Creeley, *For Love;* Adrienne Rich, *Twenty-One Love Poems;* Gary Snyder, *Beneath My Hand and Eye the Distant Hills. Your Body*

(b) Death: Randall Jarrell, *The Death of the Ball Turret Gunner*; John Berryman, No. 384 ("The marker slants, flowerless, day's almost done"); Frank O'Hara, *The Day Lady Died*; W. S. Merwin, *For the Anniversary of My Death*; Anne Sexton, *The Truth the Dead Know* or *Sylvia's Death*; Michael S. Harper, *Deathwatch*

(c) Loss: Theodore Roethke, *The Lost Son*; Elizabeth Bishop, *One Art*; Randall Jarrell, *Thinking of the Lost World*; James Merrill, *Lost in Translation*; W. S. Merwin, *Losing a Language*; Philip Levine, *Animals Are Passing from Our Lives*; Audre Lorde, *Separation*; and Cathy Song, *Lost Sister*

(d) The passing of time: Lorine Niedecker, [*He lived—childhood summers*]; Elizabeth Bishop, *In the Waiting Room*; Robert Hayden, *Middle Passage*; Robert Lowell, *Memories of West Street and Lepke*

Part II

QUESTIONS AND TOPICS RELATED TO AMERICAN LITERARY TRADITIONS

1. In *Of Plymouth Plantation*, William Bradford writes, "But here I cannot but stay and make a pause, and stand half amazed at this poor people's present condition; and so I think will the reader, too, when he well considers the same." With this quotation in mind, examine *Narrative of the Life of Frederick Douglass*. Look for patterns in the two prose texts: How does each construct an audience? On what terms does each writer convey a sense of beginning, of "new world," both in historical and in literary terms? What specific material and ideological circumstances oppress the writers of these texts? In what way does each text establish questions that later writers will address? How do the texts differently deal with the problem of literary authority? What are the didactic purposes of the narratives?

2. Bradstreet and Wheatley were the first white and black American women to publish poetry. Examine Wheatley's poems in light of Bradstreet's *The Prologue*. Can you find any evidence of conscious encoding in Wheatley's poems? Is she aware, as Bradstreet was, that as a woman or an African American her poems might be "obnoxious" to "each carping tongue"? Compare in particular the formal elements of Wheatley's poems with some of Bradstreet's, especially stanzas from *Contemplations*, *The Flesh and the Spirit*, and *As Weary Pilgrim*.

3. Consider the extent of Bradstreet's and Wheatley's acceptance of received theology by examining one of the following pairs of poems: *Contemplations* and *Thoughts on the Works of Providence*; *The Flesh and the Spirit* and *To the University of Cambridge, in New England*; and *As Weary Pilgrim* and *On the Death of the Rev. Mr. George Whitefield, 1770*.

4. Polemical writers in each literary tradition use rhetorical language to move their audiences. Choose works from the following writers as the basis for cross-traditional analysis: Edwards, Occom, Jefferson, Apess, Fuller, Charlot, Washington, and Du Bois. Consider ideological similarities between Jonathan Edwards's "great revival" thinking in *Sinners in the Hands of an Angry God*, Apess's looking-glass in *An Indian's Looking-Glass for the White Man*, and the "Atlanta Compromise" of Booker T. Washington's *The Atlanta Exposition Address*; or discuss the radicalism (for their contemporaries) of Jefferson, Fuller or Du Bois.

5. Show how the lyric poem develops across historical periods in the works of each of the following groups of writers: Bradstreet and Taylor; Emerson, and Whitman; Wheatley, Brooks, and Lorde.

6. Demonstrate how concepts of black identity determine prose forms in works by the following writers: Douglass, Jacobs, Chesnutt, Hurston, Toomer, Ellison, and Walker.

7. The genre of autobiography reveals many differences between writers from separate literary traditions. Examine segments of some of the following autobiographical narratives, choosing figures from each tradition, and outline contrasts in social position and economic class, educational background, audience, or didactic purpose: Edwards's *Personal Narrative*, Franklin's *The Autobiography*, or Hawthorne's *The Custom-House*; Jacobs's *Incidents in the Life of a Slave Girl* or Hurston's *How It Feels to Be Colored Me*; Equiano's *The Interesting Narrative*, Douglass's *Narrative*, Eastman's *From the Deep Woods to Civilization*, or Momaday's *The Way to Rainy Mountain*.

8. Some writers, while not choosing the genre of autobiography, still include enough autobiographical allusions in their poetry or fiction to tantalize the reader or critic. Consider the use of autobiographical material in literature outside the genre of autobiography from several traditions, perhaps choosing from among the following lists: Taylor, Thoreau, Whitman, Melville, or R. Lowell; Bradstreet, Dickinson, Gilman, Porter, Levertov, or Rich; Wheatley, or Brooks; Brown, Hughes, Ellison, or Harper.

9. In an out-of-class essay, consider points of connection, useful contrasts, or central themes in each of several works that may be considered focal points for their respective literary traditions: Douglass's *Narrative*, Clemens's *Adventures of Huckleberry Finn*, Chopin's *The Awakening*, and Momaday's *The Way to Rainy Mountain*.

10. Examine a play by Susan Glaspell (such as *Trifles*) or Lorraine Hansberry (such as *A Raisin in the Sun*) in the context of class discussion of O'Neill's *Long Day's Journey into Night* or Baraka's *Dutchman*.

11. Choose an important writer in a tradition other than white male. Write an essay in which you compare the perspective a reader achieves in examining a particular text within the context of the writer's literary tradition with the perspective he or she might have in placing the text within the context of the writer's white male contemporaries. Useful writers for this assignment include Jewett, Cather, Austin, or Welty; Hurston, Brooks, or Walker; Chesnutt, Brown, Hughes, or R. Wright; or Eastman, Bonnin, Momaday, or Erdrich.

12. Analyze the following lyric poems from different literary traditions: Frost's *The Gift Outright*, Brooks's *kitchenette building*, Rich's *Diving into the* Wreck, Ortiz's *Poems from the Veterans Hospital*, Ríos's *Madre Sofía*, Cervantes's *Visions of Mexico*, Song's *Chinatown*, and Lee's *Persimmons*. Focus on the disparate voices and perspectives the poems reveal.

13. Examine characters who have been created by writers of the opposite gender. Compare a male protagonist created by a woman writer, such as Mr. Shiftlet in O'Connor's *The Life You Save May Be Your Own*, with a female protagonist in a male writer's fiction, such as Hawthorne's Beatrice Rappaccini, James's Daisy Miller, or O'Neill's Mary Tyrone.

14. Compare black characters created by white writers with black characters created by black writers, in pairings such as Melville's Babo and the autobiographical persona in Douglass's *Narrative*; Stowe's Eliza and Linda Brent in Jacob's *Incidents in the Life of a Slave Girl*; Clemens's Jim, and Chesnutt's Uncle Julius.

15. Compare women characters created by male writers, such as Irving's Dame Van Winkle, Hawthorne's Hester Prynne, James's Daisy Miller or May Bartram, O'Neill's Mary Tyrone, Toomer's Fern, Faulkner's Addie Bundren or Dewey Dell, or T. Williams's Blanche DuBois, with women characters created by female writers, such as Stowe's Eliza, Jewett's Sylvy, the narrator of Gilman's *The Yellow Wallpaper*, Chopin's Edna Pontellier, Porter's Miranda, or Walker's Mama.

16. Read works by writers outside the list of major authors in the literary traditions approach that illuminate questions of cross-gender or cross-racial interest or that increase our understanding of the development of literary traditions and explain how and why they are significant. Choose from the following list: Mary Rowlandson's *A Narrative of the Captivity and Restoration* (to examine a Euro-American woman's view of Native American men); Edgar Allan Poe's poems and stories about women, Rebecca Harding Davis's *Life in the Iron-Mills* (to raise issues of class and working conditions in pre–Civil War industrialism), W. D. Howells's *Editha* (to examine another realist's portrait of a woman character), Joel Chandler Harris (for a white man's transcription of black folk life), Henry Adams's *The Dynamo and the Virgin* from *The Education* (for a white male writer's sense of woman as a source of symbolism), Sherwood Anderson's *Mother* from *Winesburg, Ohio* (to compare a woman character by a writer who deeply influenced Faulkner with one of Faulkner's own female characters), William Carlos Williams's *Portrait of a Lady* (a poem that raises questions of literary convention), H. D.'s *Leda* or *Helen* (a woman poet's sense of woman as a source of mythology), Dorothy Parker's sketches (for an example of humor in the white women's tradition), Thomas Wolfe's *The Lost Boy* (another example of a writer using autobiographical material in a genre other than autobiography), and Hart Crane's *At Melville's Tomb*, John Berryman's *Homage to Mistress Bradstreet*, Allen Ginsberg's *On Burroughs' Work*, and Anne Sexton's *Sylvia's Death* (for questions of literary influence).

17. Examine the southern tradition as represented in *NAAL*. Focus in particular on those writers who do not figure as major authors in any literary tradition, such as John Smith, Byrd, Thorpe, Wolfe, Warren, or Dickey. What generic or thematic concerns link some of these writers? Can you describe the development of southern literature in a chronological reading of the representative figures in *NAAL*? In examining writers from the literary traditions, to what extent are their works informed by southern history or identity? Consider minority writers in the context of their chronological contemporaries. Are Douglass, Hurston, or R. Wright anomalous in their respective literary periods when we consider them as southern, rather than as black or women writers? Consider writers in different genres, such as Byrd and Jefferson, Poe and Douglass, Faulkner and Wolfe, Dickey and Warren, and Welty and Walker. Are these writers so diverse in form and theme that their southern ties become negligible or does that southern heritage link them significantly despite their differences?

18. Define a literary tradition on your own according to genre or theme. Defend your list of writers and works, and choose for class analysis a particular work that both represents your larger list and illustrates its central concerns.

19. Study the Jewish writers represented in *NAAL*: Yezierska, Rukeyser, Malamud, Miller, Bellow, Roth, and Ginsberg. Choose a representative text for close analysis and view it either within the context of other works in the tradition, with works by the writer's contemporaries from a variety of traditions, or paired with a significant work from another tradition.

20. Study the relationship between marginality and vision or social stigma and literary authority in works by white male writers: (1) The colonial period appears to be unique in American literature in that it did not produce white male writers who considered themselves marginal (with the exception of Roger Williams and John Woolman, who were not part of the Puritan community). Speculate on some of the reasons why this is the case. Might the absence of men who wrote against the established ideology have somehow made it easier for Anne Bradstreet to write at all? (None of her contemporaries chose to establish himself or herself as marginal, perhaps leaving the possibility open to a woman; and in Puritan culture, where marginality might lead a man to predict his own damnation, a woman—a flawed version of an already flawed creation—might have less to lose by embracing marginality.) (2) Many white male writers in the early nineteenth century wrote as if they were marginal. Choose representative texts (by Irving, Hawthorne, Thoreau, Whitman, or Melville) and consider what the marginal characters in these fictions have to say about the relationship between white male authors and marginality. (3) Examine Clemens's Huck Finn or James's John Marcher as representative of lonely, isolated, and marginalized characters. (4) Twentieth-century white male authors frequently explore the theme of social difference. Some created their most powerful fictions based on this theme. Examine the theme in Anderson, Jeffers, O'Neill, Faulkner, Bellow, or T. Williams and speculate on the white male writer's fascination with marginality.

Seneca Falls Woman's Rights Convention, July 19–20, 1848

In July 1848, Elizabeth Cady Stanton and Lucretia Mott gathered together a group of women to plan the first woman's rights convention, to be held in Seneca Falls, New York. They modeled their agenda on antislavery and temperance conventions, and Stanton modeled her draft of *The Declaration of Sentiments* on the 1776 *The Declaration of Independence*. After discussion and amendments, the document received a hundred signatures from both women and men. Following the convention, the proceedings were ridiculed by clergy and in the press, and many of the women who had signed the declaration subsequently removed their names and their influence. In her autobiography, *Eighty Years and More* (1898), Stanton wrote, "If I had had the slightest premonition of all that was to follow that convention, I fear I should not have had the courage to risk it." *The Declaration of Sentiments* initiated Stanton's writing career on behalf of women's lives and women's rights, a career that would extend until her death in 1902.

—M. P.

The Declaration of Sentiments

When, in the course of human events, it becomes necessary for one portion of the family of man to assume among the people of the earth a position different from that which they have hitherto occupied, but one to which the laws of nature and of nature's God entitle them, a decent respect to the opinions of mankind requires that they should declare the causes that impel them to such a course.

We hold these truths to be self-evident: that all men and women are created equal; that they are endowed by their Creator with certain inalienable rights; that among these are life, liberty, and the pursuit of happiness; that to secure these

280

rights governments are instituted, deriving their just powers from the consent of the governed. Whenever any form of government becomes destructive of these ends, it is the right of those who suffer from it to refuse allegiance to it, and to insist upon the institution of a new government, laying its foundation on such principles, and organizing its powers in such form, as to them shall seem most likely to effect their safety and happiness. Prudence, indeed, will dictate that governments long established should not be changed for light and transient causes; and accordingly all experience hath shown that mankind are more disposed to suffer, while evils are sufferable, than to right themselves by abolishing the forms to which they were accustomed. But when a long train of abuses and usurpations, pursuing invariably the same object, evinces a design to reduce them under absolute despotism, it is their duty to throw off such government, and to provide new guards for their future security. Such has been the patient sufferance of the women under this government, and such is now the necessity which constrains them to demand the equal station to which they are entitled.

The history of mankind is a history of repeated injuries and usurpations on the part of man toward woman, having in direct object the establishment of an absolute tyranny over her. To prove this, let facts be submitted to a candid world.

He has never permitted her to exercise her inalienable right to the elective franchise.

He has compelled her to submit to laws, in the formation of which she had no voice.

He has withheld from her rights which are given to the most ignorant and degraded men—both natives and foreigners.

Having deprived her of this first right of a citizen, the elective franchise, thereby leaving her without representation in the halls of legislation, he has oppressed her on all sides.

He has made her, if married, in the eye of the law, civilly dead.

He has taken from her all right in property, even to the wages she earns.

He has made her, morally, an irresponsible being, as she can commit many crimes with impunity, provided they be done in the presence of her husband. In the covenant of marriage, she is compelled to promise obedience to her husband, he becoming, to all intents and purposes, her master—the law giving him power to deprive her of her liberty, and to administer chastisement.

He has so framed the laws of divorce, as to what shall be the proper causes, and in case of separation, to whom the guardianship of the children shall be given, as to be wholly regardless of the happiness of women—the law, in all cases, going upon the false supposition of the supremacy of man, and giving all power into his hands.

After depriving her of all rights as a married woman, if single, and the owner of property, he has taxed her to support a government which recognizes her only when her property can be made profitable to it.

He has monopolized nearly all the profitable employments and from those she is permitted to follow, she receives but a scanty remuneration. He closes against her all the avenues to wealth and distinction which he considers most honorable to himself. As a teacher of theology, medicine, or law, she is not known.

He has denied her the facilities for obtaining a thorough education, all colleges being closed against her.

He allows her in Church, as well as State, but a subordinate position, claiming Apostolic authority for her exclusion from the ministry, and, with some exceptions, from any public participation in the affairs of the Church.

He has created a false public sentiment by giving to the world a different code of morals for men and women, by which moral delinquencies which exclude women from society, are not only tolerated, but deemed of little account in man.

He has usurped the prerogative of Jehovah himself, claiming it as his right to assign for her a sphere of action, when that belongs to her conscience and to her God.

He has endeavored, in every way that he could, to destroy her confidence in her own powers, to lessen her self-respect, and to make her willing to lead a dependent and abject life.

Now, in view of this entire disfranchisement of one-half the people of this country, their social and religious degradation—in view of the unjust laws above mentioned, and because women do feel themselves aggrieved, oppressed, and fraudulently deprived of their most sacred rights, we insist that they have immediate admission to all the rights and privileges which belong to them as citizens of the United States.

In entering upon the great work before us, we anticipate no small amount of misconception, misrepresentation, and ridicule; but we shall use every instrumentality within our power to effect our object. We shall employ agents, circulate tracts, petition the State and National legislatures, and endeavor to enlist the pulpit and the press in our behalf. We hope this Convention will be followed by a series of Conventions embracing every part of the country.

Resolutions: Whereas, The great precept of nature is conceded to be, that "man shall pursue his own true and substantial happiness." Blackstone in his Commentaries remarks, that this law of Nature being coeval with mankind, and dictated by God himself, is of course superior in obligation to any other. It is binding over all the globe, in all countries and at all times; no human laws are of any validity if contrary to this, and such of them as are valid, derive all their force, and all their validity, and all their authority, mediately and immediately, from this original; therefore.

Resolved, That such laws as conflict, in any way, with the true and substantial happiness of woman, are contrary to the great precept of nature and of no validity, for this is "superior in obligation to any other."

Resolved, That all laws which prevent woman from occupying such a state in society as her conscience shall dictate, or which place her in a position inferior to that of man, are contrary to the great precept of nature, and therefore of no force or authority.

Resolved, That woman is man's equal—was intended to be so by the Creator, and the highest good of the race demands that she should be recognized as such.

Resolved, That the women of this country ought to be enlightened in regard to the laws under which they live, that they may no longer publish their degradation by declaring themselves satisfied with their present position, nor their ignorance, by asserting that they have all the rights they want.

Resolved, That inasmuch as man, while claiming for himself intellectual superiority, does accord to woman moral superiority, it is pre-eminently his duty to encourage her to speak and teach, as she has an opportunity, in all religious assemblies.

Resolved, That the same amount of virtue, delicacy, and refinement of behavior that is required of woman in the social state, should also be required of man, and the same transgressions should be visited with equal severity on both man and woman.

Resolved, That the objection of indelicacy and impropriety, which is so often brought against woman when she addresses a public audience, comes with a very ill-grace from those who encourage, by their attendance, her appearance on the stage, in the concert, or in feats of the circus.

Resolved, That woman has too long rested satisfied in the circumscribed limits which corrupt customs and a perverted application of the Scriptures have marked out for her, and that it is time she should move in the enlarged sphere which her great Creator has assigned her.

Resolved, That it is the duty of the women of this country to secure to themselves their sacred right to the elective franchise.

Resolved, That the equality of human rights results necessarily from the fact of the identity of the race in capabilities and responsibilities.

Resolved, therefore, That, being invested by the Creator with the same capabilities, and the same consciousness of responsibility for their exercise, it is demonstrably the right and duty of woman, equally with man, to promote every righteous cause by every righteous means; and especially in regard to the great subjects of morals and religion, it is self-evidently her right to participate with her brother in teaching them, both in private and in public, by writing and by speaking, by any instrumentalities proper to be used, and in any assemblies proper to be held; and this being a self-evident truth growing out of the divinely implanted principles of human nature, any custom or authority adverse to it, whether modern or wearing the hoary sanction of antiquity, is to be regarded as a self-evident falsehood, and at war with mankind.

Resolved, That the speedy success of our cause depends upon the zealous and untiring efforts of both men and women, for the overthrow of the monopoly of the pulpit, and for the securing to woman an equal participation with men in the various trades, professions, and commerce.

Index